John H. Rhodes

The History of Battery B.

John H. Rhodes

The History of Battery B.

ISBN/EAN: 9783337380014

Printed in Europe, USA, Canada, Australia, Japan

Cover: Foto ©ninafisch / pixelio.de

More available books at **www.hansebooks.com**

THE
HISTORY OF BATTERY B

*FIRST REGIMENT RHODE ISLAND
LIGHT ARTILLERY*

IN THE WAR TO PRESERVE THE UNION
1861 - 1865

BY

JOHN H. RHODES
Late Sergeant in the Battery

ILLUSTRATED WITH PORTRAITS AND MAPS

PROVIDENCE
SNOW & FARNHAM, PRINTERS
1894

Entered according to Act of Congress, in the year 1893
By JOHN H. RHODES
in the office of the Librarian of Congress, at Washington, D. C.

Sergt. John H. Rhodes.

PREFACE.

THE reason for the existence of this book is an expressed desire on the part of the survivors of the battery whose history it attempts to record, that an account of their experience during the Civil War of 1861–5 should be compiled and published.

In 1875, Lieut. Gideon Spencer, Rowland L. Dodge, and Daniel C. Taylor were by the members of Battery B Veteran Association appointed Historical Committee to collect records and other material of interest.

In 1880, Daniel C. Taylor, chairman, reported for the committee that nothing of importance had been accomplished and no progress made. At their own request the committee was discharged, and John Delevan appointed Historian, who, in 1885, reported progress, and was instructed to co-operate with Col. J. Albert Monroe, Regimental Historian for the Rhode Island Light Artillery.

In 1890, Historian John Delevan reported that there was no prospect of a Regimental History of the Rhode Island Light Artillery being published, but hoped that Battery B might have one.

The publishing of the history would have been a difficult task but for the action of the General Assembly at its January session, 1891, in passing a Resolution (No. 14) to purchase 200 copies of any battery history published to the satisfaction of the Secretary of State.

At a meeting of the Executive Committee of Battery B Veteran Association, March 28, 1891, I made the following proposition: To compile and publish a history of the battery without any expense to the Association, if the records and other material that had been and should be collected by the historian or others be turned over to me.

This offer the committee accepted, and at the annual reunion of the Association, held Aug. 13, 1891, the members of Battery B Veteran Association approved the action of the Executive Committee. As author I make no claim to possess special qualifications for the work assumed, but being situated so that I could give the time which the work required, I have endeavored to bring to the front the honorable part borne by Battery B. My aim has been to avoid all appearance of egotism for the battery in the narration of its career. Every precaution has been taken to assure the trustworthiness of the work; yet some errors must be expected in this as in all histories covering the details of so many important events. If there is any matter of interest not mentioned it is because the writer was not informed of the same.

I hereby acknowledge and return thanks for assistance received from the officers and members of the battery; to Adjutant-General Elisha Dyer and his assistants for their courtesy in giving free access to the records on file, and to all others not personally mentioned thanks are tendered for valuable information furnished

The work is a plain statement of facts connected with the service of the organization, and if it proves satisfactory in a reasonable degree to the survivors and the public, I shall feel fully compensated for the labor.

JOHN H. RHODES.

PROVIDENCE, R. I., April, 1893.

CONTENTS.

CHAPTER I.

Introduction — Uniforms — The First Drill — A Bounty of Fifteen Dollars 1

CHAPTER II.

Organization, Muster and Departure—First Rations Received—Journey to Point of Rocks, Md. . 5

CHAPTER III.

Camp Sprague and Discipline—Washington, D. C., and Vicinity 14

CHAPTER IV.

To Poolesville, Md., and Battle of Ball's Bluff—Picket Duty along the Potomac River 27

CHAPTER V.

Battery Reorganized — New Guns — Winter Quarters — Thanksgiving Day and Christmas in the South . . 47

CHAPTER VI.

March to Harper's Ferry and Bolivar—To Winchester, to the Support of General Banks in the Valley—Return to Washington 65

CHAPTER VII.

Departure for the Peninsula, and Siege of Yorktown—Passing through Long Bridge—Hampton Roads and the Monitor. . . . 67

CHAPTER VIII.

March up the Peninsula, Battle of Fair Oaks, Seven Pines—York River, West Point, Cumberland Landing . 85

CHAPTER IX.

Change of Base to the James River—Seven Days of Fighting—Battles of Savage's Station, Peach Orchard, White Oak Bridge, Glendale, and Malvern Hill . 95

CHAPTER X.

Harrison Landing—Evacuation of the Peninsula—Arrival at Alexandria 106

CHAPTER XI.

Pursuit of General Lee into Maryland—Battle of Antietam—March to Harper's Ferry . . 119

CHAPTER XII.

March to Falmouth—Skirmishes by the Way—Epidemic Attack of Mutton 128

CHAPTER XIII.

Battle of Fredericksburg 137

CHAPTER XIV.

In Winter Quarters near Falmouth, Va.—The Mud March—Granting of Furlough . 146

CHAPTER XV.

Preparation and Second Battle of Fredericksburg—Marye's Heights—The Artillery Brigade 165

CHAPTER XVI.

The Campaign and Battle of Gettysburg—At Thoroughfare Gap—Peter Shevlin and the Canteens of Water 188

CHAPTER XVII.

From Gettysburg to the Rappahannock—Battery B Reorganized and New Guns 220

CHAPTER XVIII.

Advance to Culpepper—From the Rapidan to Centreville—Battle of Bristoe Station . . . 238

CHAPTER XIX.

Centerville to the Rapidan—Batttle of Mine Run—Winter Quarters—Sword Presentation . . 255

CHAPTER XX.

General Grant's Campaign—From the Wilderness to Cold Harbor—Battles of the Wilderness, Todd's Tavern, Po River, Spottsylvania, North Anna, and Cold Harbor 273

CHAPTER XXI.

General Grant's Flank Movement to South of the James—From Cold Harbor to Petersburg—Deep Bottom—Return Home of the First Three Years' Men . . 300

CHAPTER XXII.

Second Expedition of Deep Bottom—Battle of Reams's Station 323

CHAPTER XXIII.

The Winter Siege of Petersburg—The Battery Reorganized. 334

CHAPTER XXIV.

The Pursuit of the Confederate Army—General Lee's Surrender at Appomattox 343

CHAPTER XXV.

The Return to Rhode Island and Muster out of Service. 349

ROSTER.

	PAGE.
Names of Enlisted Men	351
Roll of Men Temporarily Attached	376

APPENDIX A.

The Gettysburg Gun	379

APPENDIX B.

The Gettysburg Monument and Dedication	395
INDEX	401

ILLUSTRATIONS.

The Gettysburg Gun .	Frontispiece
The Monument .	opposite page 394
Marker on Godori's field	on page 399
Portrait of Author. . . .	opposite Preface
Portrait of Capt. Thomas F. Vaughn	" page 20
Portrait of Capt. Walter O. Bartlett	" " 57
Portrait of Capt. John G. Hazard	" " 183
Portrait of Capt. T. Fred. Brown .	" " 268
Portrait of Lieut. Horace S. Bloodgood	" " 150
Portrait of Lieut. William S. Perrin	" " 137
Portrait of Lieut. Joseph S. Milne	" " 214
Portrait of Lieut Charles A. Brown	" " 289
Portrait of Lieut. Gideon Spencer .	" " 345
Portrait of First Sergt. John T. Blake .	on " 400
Portrait of First Sergt. Alanson A. Williams	" " 400
Portrait of First Sergt. John F. Hanson .	opposite " 298
Portrait of Q. M. Sergt. Charles A. Libbey	on " 375
Portrait of Sergt. Albert Straight .	" " 342
Portrait of Sergt. Pardon S. Walker	" " 59
Portrait of Sergt. Calvin L. Macomber	" " 145
Portrait of Corp. John Delevan .	" " 4
Portrait of Corp. David B. Patterson	" " 393
Portrait of Corp. Calvin W. Rathbone	" " 378
Portrait of Corp. William P. Wells .	" " 333
Portrait of Private Lorenzo D. Budlong	" " 46
Portrait of Private Levi J. Cornell .	" " 161
Portrait of Private Alfred G. Gardner	" " 272
Portrait of Private Caleb H. H. Green	" " 26
Portrait of Private George McGunnigle	" " 118
Portrait of Private William F. Reynolds	" " 66
Portrait of Private James Tillinghast	" " 13
Portrait of Private Merritt Tillinghast	" " 94
Portrait of Private Clark L. Woodmansee	" " 84

MAPS.

Union Troops represented thus ⎯⎯⎯

Confederate Troops represented thus ▬▬▬

Artillery or Batteries represented thus ıǀı ıǀı ıǀı ıǀı

Fortifications: Union, ⎯⎯⎯, Confederate ▬▬▬

Map of Northern Virginia . .		on back cover.
Map of Washington and its Defences .	on page	xi
Map of Ball's Bluff . . .	opposite page	34
Map of Fair Oaks and Seven Pines	·· ··	89
Map of Savage's Station . .	·· ··	97
Map of White Oak Bridge and Glendale	·· ··	99
Map of Malvern Hill . .	·· ··	102
Map of Antietam	·· ··	122
Map of Fredericksburg	·· ··	140
Map of Gettysburg	·· ··	204
Map of Bristoe Station .	·· ··	247
Map of Mine Run	·· ··	259
Map of Wilderness . . .	·· ··	275
Map of Todd's Tavern and Po River .	··	279
Map of the Bloody Angle at Spottsylvania	·· ··	284
Map of North Anna .	·· ··	291
Map of Cold Harbor	·· ··	296
Map of Deep Bottom	·· ··	311
Map of Reams's Station	·· ··	326
Map of Siege of Petersburg		338

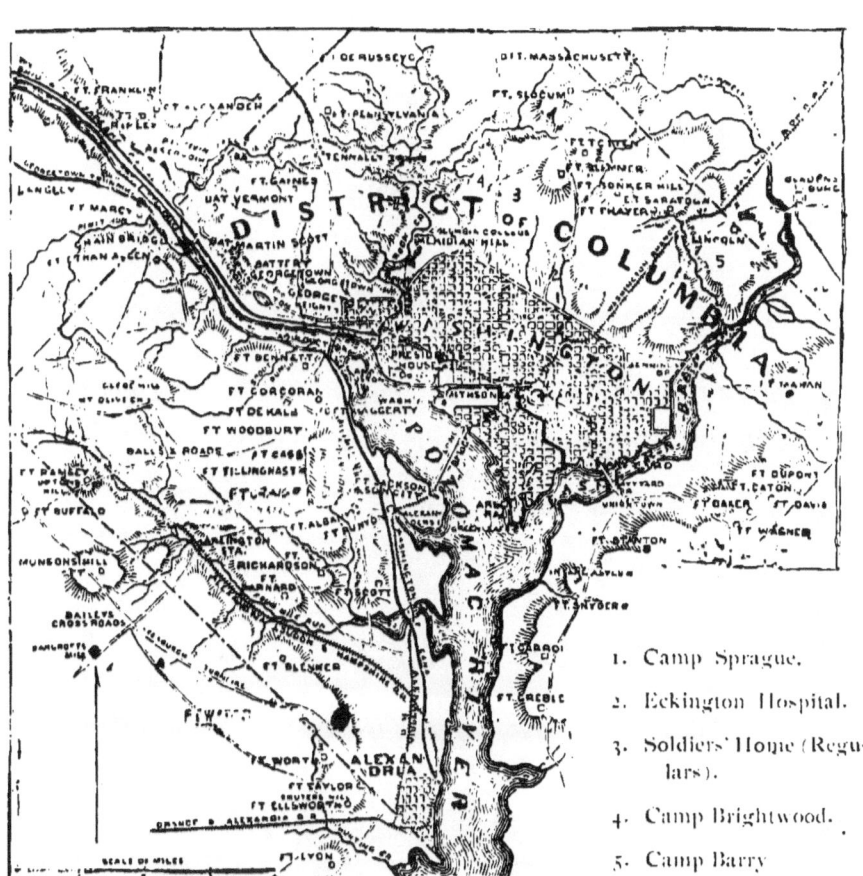

1. Camp Sprague.
2. Eckington Hospital.
3. Soldiers' Home (Regulars).
4. Camp Brightwood.
5. Camp Barry

WASHINGTON AND ITS DEFENCES.

CHAPTER I.

INTRODUCTION.

IN response to the country's call, in 1861, for defenders of her honor, integrity, and principles of liberty, there gathered together in the several armories of the State militia, young men full of patriotism, ambition and health, and offered their services. The First Regiment and Battery were formed, then the Second Regiment and Second Battery also, and left for the seat of war. The supply was greater than the demand, or more than could be equipped, for there still remained a goodly number that wished to go but could not, as the companies were full and off. Were these young men disheartened? No, not they. They were too patriotic to be discouraged, and could wait. They made their headquarters at the old armory of the Marine Corps of Artillery on Benefit Street, Providence. R. I., and those that did not live in the city boarded at a Mrs. Greene's, on North Main Street, the state paying their board; the others at their homes without pay. At the armory the men were drilled in marching, facing, and forming of detachments, and the manual of the piece pertaining to artillery drill. In a short time they became quite proficient in all the movements that could be performed in the armory. As their enthusiasm and patriotism increased so did their numbers, for at this time quite a number had enrolled their names for the Third Battery, and they were eager for the proposed field drill that had been talked of, but were waiting for uniforms. The uniforms came and were distributed to the men as far as they would go, as there were not enough for all, their number having increased since the order for them had been given. This uniform consisted of pantaloons with a piece on the inside of leg down to the knee. They were called re-enforced pants. An outside shirt or tunic, which came down to the knee, was called a blouse. A high felt hat with one side turned up, a brass eagle pinned on to hold it, with brass cross cannons in front completed the outfit. They were distributed regardless of size or fit, which gave the boys the appearance of a gang of Chinamen, rather than gallant defenders of our country. But by exchanging with one another, they soon made a very respectable appearance, and it was decided to have a field drill.

On the 10th of August, 1861, horses were procured, and the men in uniform were detailed as drivers and cannoneers and two full detachments formed. Everything being in readiness they left the armory in column for the made land northwest of the old prison and west of the Park, and were commanded by a lieutenant of the Marine Corps of Artillery, who was to drill them. They arrived on the field in fair condition, everything considered, accompanied by a large concourse of people of all sizes and condition to witness the fun. Considerable time was spent in explanation of the movements to the drivers. Then the drill commenced, and several movements were ordered. The drivers of the pieces executed them after a fashion, but the drivers of the caissons would stand fast or keep on marching, unless they received special orders, they thinking they were independent of the pieces. At last the lieutenant in very forcible language informed them that they must follow their pieces at all times, even if they went to h——.

What soon followed was convincing that the drivers were no dull scholars, and that they now fully understood the orders. The horses on the first piece were quite high spirited, and became very unmanageable by the frequent starting and stopping, so at the next movement ordered, they suddenly wheeled from the line, and started for the city on a run, in spite of all the drivers could do to stop them. They ran into Exchange Place. The drivers of the caisson who belonged to the runaway piece, with the orders of the lieutenant fresh in their minds to follow their piece if it went to h——, wheeled out of line, and with whip and spur urged their horses into a run after the piece in spite of the lieutenant, who shouted to them to halt. It now became very exciting; the piece had disappeared out of sight, the caisson making a lively good time, and the lieutenant a close third in the race. Those left behind were watching the proceedings with much perplexity and doubt, for in their ignorance of field drill were undecided whether it was a race, a runaway, or a part of the drill. The lieutenant finally succeeded in stopping the drivers of the caisson and asked them what they meant by leaving the line, and they very innocently reminded him of his instructions to them a few moments before, that they were to follow the piece, no matter where it went, and they supposed that they were only obeying orders regardless of expense. A sergeant who had been sent after the runaway piece now returned with it, and the drill was resumed, when another mishap took place, this time with the second piece. On the limber chest were seated three men, the order was given to countermarch, and in wheeling made a cramped short turn, breaking the pole short off, and the horses became entangled in their harnesses, the weight of the three men caused the limber chest to tilt forward, and the men on the ends jumped off. The chest being relieved of its weight suddenly tilted back, and the man that sat in the middle having nothing to cling to made an involuntary somersault backwards and landed astride of the trail, with his blouse turned up over his head. When asked about it he said that he was not in favor of that way for the cannoneers to dismount, and would rather be a driver. This ended the first field drill of the battery; the pole was tied together and we went back to the armory, with not quite so much enthusiasm for field drill as formerly. But this was soon forgotten, for that night we received news that another battery, the Third, was to be enrolled the next day and go to the front, and the question of the hour was, who will be the lucky ones that would be accepted, for those that were accepted had to pass a thorough examination, or they were told to wait until the next call.

On the morning of the 12th of August there was a large number of young men gathered together at the door of the armory waiting for it to be opened, all eager to be enrolled, for the news had been circulated during the day before, and they did not mean to be behind. During the forenoon all sorts of stories and speculations were being circulated, but this was soon brought to a close by an order from Capt. William H. Parkhurst to form a line. Then the excitement was great, but the line was soon formed, and, when order and attention was gained, they were informed that the legislature at the recent session had repealed the bounty law of the April session, and provided in lieu of the thirty-six dollars bounty, a bounty of fifteen dollars to all who had enlisted since the 16th day of June, or who might thereafter enlist, so that instead of thirty-six dollars as we had been told we were to receive, only fifteen dollars state bounty would be given, and all that desired to accept this offer would have to sign anew so as to be enrolled. After an address by several others on the subject of bounty and enlistment, the line was dismissed, and the boys gathered together in squads, and asking each other, "You going to enlist again? I am." Others said to their friends, "Come on, I am going to sign again, I did not enlist for the bounty." Although there were some that were quite disappointed by the order, it may be said that all but two signed again during the day, and several new names were added.

Corp. John Delevan.

CHAPTER II.

ORGANIZATION, MUSTER, AND DEPARTURE.

THE 13th of August was a busy day at the Armory, by examination of the men, for all had to pass a surgical examination by Doctors Rivers and Millar, and only those that stood the test of the surgeon's examination were accepted. There were some that looked down-hearted as they came from the examination, while others with smiling countenances would go skipping around the armory,—they had been accepted, and were going to serve their country in her hour of need. After the examination had closed, we were formed into line, and as the names were called the men would cross to the opposite side and fall into line. Those that were not uniformed had pants and blouses issued to them. About 3.30 o'clock P. M. on the 13th day of August, 1861, the following members of the Third Rhode Island Battery were mustered into the United States service, for three years, by Colonel Loomis of the United States Army:

As Organized and Mustered.

Four commissioned officers and one hundred and thirty-seven men, namely:

Captain.

First Lieutenants.

RAYMOND H. PERRY,
HORACE S. BLOODGOOD,

GEORGE W. ADAMS,
FRANCIS A. SMITH.

Quartermaster-Sergeant.
WILLIAM S. DYER.

First Sergeant.
JACOB B. LEWIS.

Sergeants.

CHARLES H. ADAMS,
SILAS G. TUCKER.

JOHN T. BLAKE,
GEORGE W. BLAIR.

JOHN McCOOMBS.

Corporals.

Darius N. Thurber, Jr.,
David B. Patterson,
Edwin A. Chace,
Luther C. Olney,
Charles A. Libby,
Napoleon B. Clark,

George N. Talbot,
David H. Phetteplace,
Edward Whipple,
Washington C. Haskins,
Calvin W. Rathbone,
Edward H. Knowles.

Artificers.

Edward M. Peckham,
Daniel B. Thurston,
Isaac W. Slack,

Daniel C. Taylor,
Welcome G. Tucker,
George O. Scott.

Guidon.
Rowland L. Dodge.

First Bugler.
Eden S. Crowningshield,

Second Bugler.
Henry Cokely.

Privates.

Adlington, Henry
Andrews, Mowry
Andrews, Albert
Aspinwall, John
Austin, Russell
Ballou, Henry H.
Bartlett, Frederick
Brickley, Arthur W.
Bromley, Henry H.
Brown, Fenner
Budlong, Lorenzo D.
Budlong, Stillman H.
Burlingame, Benjamin A.
Burt, Allen
Butts, Charles P.
Carmichael, Morris
Cassen, Charles H.
Cassen, Joseph H.
Clarance, John
Cole, Joseph A.
Collins, Stephen

Collins, Welcome A.
Cornell, Albert H.
Cornell, Charles
Cornell, Levi J.
Cornell, William H.
Cottrell, Charles
Delevan, John
Dennis, William
Dickerson, William A.
Doyle, Bernard
Duffy, Michael
Eaton, Martin V. B.
Eatock, John
England, Samuel
Fletcher, Calvin C.
Ford, Patrick
Gallup, Richard H.
Gallup, William H.
Gardner, Henry A.
Glynn, John
Goff, Joseph B.

GOFF, RUFUS
GODFREY, EDWARD L.
GREEN, CALEB H. H.
HAMILTON, WILLIAM
HANSON, JOHN F.
HART, BARTHOLOMEW
HASKELL, SOLOMON A.
HEALY, JOHN
HOWARD, EDWARD
HORTON, ANTHONY B.
HUNT, CHESTER F.
HUNT, WALTER
IDE, SYLVESTER G.
INGALLS. GEORGE
JONES, WILLIAM
JORDAN, WILLIAM T.
KELLY, JOHN
KENDRICK, JOHN
KENYON, WILLIAM J.
KING, DAVID B.
LAIRD, ROBERT
LEACH, JOSEPH
MACOMBER, CALVIN L.
MAINE, NELSON B.
MARTIN, THOMAS J.
MASON, HENRY A.
MASON, LUCIUS M.
MATTESON, BENJ. F.
MATTESON, GEORGE R.
MATTESON, WILLIAM F.
MAXCY, WILLIAM H.
MCALLEN, ARTHUR J.
MCCULLUM, WILLIAM

MCGUINNESS, EDWARD
MCGUNNIGLE, GEORGE
MCGUNNIGLE, JAMES
MCMEEKIN, JOSIAH
MORRIS, WILLIAM H.
MOWRY, JOHN B.
NILES, ROBERT A.
PAINE, CHARLES H.
PERRY, NELSON E.
PHETTEPLACE, DAVID
PHILLIPS, ALBERT A.
PHILLIPS, THOMAS W.
REMINGTON, WILLIAM F., JR.,
REYNOLDS, WILLIAM F.
RHODES, JOHN H.
RIDER, CHARLES J.
SANFORD, HERBERT D.
SISSON, JOHN J.
SLAIZER, FRANCIS
SPRAGUE, CHARLES G.
STENSON, JAMES
SWEET, JAMES A.
TANNER, WILLIAM M.
THAYER, ZIBA C.
THOMPSON, JAMES
TRESCOTT, JOHN F.
WALKER, PARDON S.
WARDLOW, JOHN E.
WELLS, WILLIAM P.
WHIPPLE, ALBERT J.
WILKINSON, ROBERT
WILLIAMS, ALANSON A.
WOOD, CHARLES W.

WOODMANSEE, CLARK L.

After the muster Capt. William H. Parkhurst addressed us, saying that he was very sorry, but he was compelled by personal considerations to decline the command tendered him, at the last moment; therefore he was not to go with us as our commander, and wished us a God-speed and safe return. The boys felt sorry to hear this, for under his active supervision we had been organized, enrolled and mustered, and learned to call him captain, and were quite disappointed in not having him for our commander. Captain Parkhurst was followed by others with remarks on the duties we had now assumed. After an address by Colonel Loomis on the duties of a soldier, we were dismissed, with orders to report at the armory the next day at ten o'clock sharp.

August 14th. Long before the appointed time the men were in attendance at the armory, and passed the time in discussing the different reports that had been circulated about their destination.

In the afternoon we were formed into line. In the meantime a guard had been placed at the entrance of the armory, with instructions that no one should be allowed to go out. We soon learned what this precaution was for. At a table sat a number of State officers, one with a small satchel, the others with books and papers, and as our names were called we proceeded to the table, and there signed our names to a paper called the " muster roll," and then received fifteen dollars, the promised State bounty. There were many smiling faces, for some of the boys had been enrolled for more than a month, and this was the first money they had received. After receiving the bounty, to each man was given a sabre and belt. At this time the non-commissioned officers were the recipients of pocket Testaments and handkerchiefs, presented by Mrs. Seth Adams, mother of Lieut. George W. Adams. The line was again formed and we marched to the Arcade on Westminster Street, and the men who had not received hats were furnished with them, like those previously described. Then we were marched to Exchange Place, and there each received a pair of shoes.

After receiving these supplies the command was marched to the railroad depot, where a large crowd of people were in attendance to see the soldier boys off. Friends bidding friends " good bye," mothers taking farewell partings of their sons, wives and sweethearts tenderly bidding the soldiers " God-speed." Before taking the cars we were drawn up in line at the west of Exchange Place, by the little triangular park, and briefly addressed by Governor Sprague, who reminded us of our obligation to the State, whose reputation was to some extent in our keeping. Bishop Clark followed by a few words of encouragement, and invoked the blessing of the Divine Ruler of the Universe upon us as we went to our work to battle for the Union.

The battery boys, under the command of First. Lieut. Raymond H. Perry, at seven o'clock P. M., boarded the Stonington Steamboat train, and left Providence, R. I., for New York city. There were twenty-three recruits for the Second Rhode Island Battery, under Captain Reynolds, who went with our party. Colonel Sanford, of the governor's staff, accompanied us to New York city, to superintend the transportation. The whole was under the command of Maj. Charles H. Tompkins.

We arrived at the Stonington steamboat landing about nine P. M., and embarked on the steamer *Commonwealth*, and left for New York city about ten P. M. We were furnished with supper on the boat, and it was three long years before some of us enjoyed another equal to it. We arrived in New York city at early dawn on the morning of August 15th. Our voyage through Long Island Sound was most pleasant, for the night was clear and starlight, and only light breezes blowing. We remained on the wharf, waiting orders. Here we received a haversack for rations, a canteen for water; also rations of hard-bread and boiled ham were issued. *And such ham!* Well, it was August, hot, muggy weather. That is enough to explain it. As I write it seems as if I can smell it now.

About one o'clock in the afternoon we embarked on a ferry-boat and steamed down the river toward New Jersey and landed at South Amboy, where we disembarked, and boarded the cars in waiting. Here the first accident happened. Fenner A. Brown was jammed between the cars as the engine was being attached to the train. He was sent to a hospital and left for medical treatment. His injury did not prove to be serious, for he was soon able to rejoin the battery.

About three o'clock P. M. we left South Amboy for Camden, passing through the following pleasant towns: Spotswood, Jamesburgh, Cranbury Station, Bordentown, Kinkora, Burlington, Beverly, and arrived at Camden at about sunset. At Jamesburgh the train made a stop. Over the door of the restaurant at the station was a sign on which was inscribed, "Twenty minutes for lunch," and a number of the men thought that they would like some lunch, and went into the restaurant and ordered it. While waiting for it they were told that they had plenty of time, but the waiters being on the alert, collected the price before it was served, and when the coffee was served it was so hot no one could drink it, and as they sat patiently eating their lunch and waiting for the coffee to cool, the engine bell rang as a signal that the train was to move, and the order "All aboard!" was shouted. Did the men hasten to leave their lunch? No, they waited until the train began to move; *then they made a move*, and as they had paid for their lunch they were not going to be cheated out of it; so one took one thing and some another in their hands and boarded the train, amid shouts from the waiters and orders from the proprietor to leave the things alone. Not they. The idea,—for them to obey orders from a civilian! Though not disciplined as yet, we had been instructed to obey orders only from our superior officers, for we were now soldiers and not civilians. And fortunately the officers knew naught of that which transpired. On the train the boys took account of stock, and found cold fowl, ham, corned beef, pie, cake, bread and pickles. Enough for quite a lunch, which the boys enjoyed eating, at the same time viewing the beautiful scenery and villages as we passed along the route.

About seven P. M. we arrived at Philadelphia, and when the train stopped we were ordered by Lieutenant Perry to leave the cars and fall into line. As soon as this was done, we marched to the "Soldiers' Retreat." This place was called by different names, such as "Cooper Union," "The Cooper Shop," and "Soldiers' Rest." Here we partook of a good and substantial supper of cold meats, pickles, white and brown bread, tea and coffee, prepared by Mrs. Cooper and other ladies of Philadelphia, expressly for the benefit of the soldiers that stopped while on their way to and from the seat of war.

Every possible attention was shown us that could add to our comfort, while we were their guests. After supper we were again ordered into line, and marched to the cars on a side-track near the depot, followed by an enthusiastic crowd of women, young ladies, and children, all anxious to shake hands with the soldier boys and defenders of the Union. We boarded the cars and started for Baltimore about nine P. M., the ladies waving their handkerchiefs, bidding us a "good bye," and invited us to call again when passing that way.

Soon after we had taken the cars, a detail was made, and a guard was stationed at the doors, with orders that no one was to be allowed to leave the car without permission from the officer of the guard. This was done to avoid accidents, as the night was quite dark and the cars swayed from side to side, and one was not sure of his footing if he tried to pass from car to car. We all unbuckled our belts and hung our accoutrements up out of the way and prepared for a rest and sleep, if possible. The cars ran very slow at first; then ran at a very fast speed at times. No stop was made until Wilmington was reached, and then only long enough to change engines, and then went on again. When within a few miles of Baltimore we were all aroused, and ordered to buckle on our side-arms and be in readiness to leave the cars at a moment's notice. The fate of the Sixth Massachusetts Regiment and their reception were fresh in our minds. There was no excitement or alarm, but we obeyed the order and waited patiently for further developments. We arrived in Baltimore about midnight. There were but few citizens stirring. We did not leave the cars, as was expected, but were drawn for two miles by horses from the Philadelphia, Wilmington and Baltimore depot to the Baltimore and Potomac Railroad depot. At one A. M. started for Harper's Ferry. We reached the Relay House, made a short stop here, and then went on again, and our next halting place was Point of Rocks, Md.

August 16th. The Second Rhode Island Battery had been ordered here from Harper's Ferry on picket duty, after the fight of Aug. 5, 1861, at Berlin, Md. We were heartily received by the men of this battery, for it was supposed we had come to relieve them, to take their pieces, horses, and equipments, and do guard duty, as they were doing, and that they were to go to Washington, D. C., and receive a battery of new pieces, horses and equipments. They were in high spirits, but it was of short duration, for General Terry on being informed that the Third Battery were raw recruits and knew nothing of field drill, had the order countermanded, and the Third instead of the Second Battery were ordered to Washington. While resting at the camp of the Second Battery the men enjoyed an object lesson of camp life, and the duties of a soldier while on picket duty. The scenery around the camp and in the distance was picturesque, magnificent and sublime. A short distance in front of the camp was the Chesapeake and Ohio canal and railroad; a few rods beyond was the Potomac River, with swift running water ever flowing onward. On the opposite side of the river was Virginia, where in the following years were enacted so many terrible and thrilling tragedies in which we were to participate. On the right in the distance were seen Loudoun Heights, which overlooked Harper's Ferry, Va. Point of Rocks is a high rocky bluff on the Maryland side of the river, where the guns of the Second Battery were stationed, and commanded the Virginia side of the river for quite a distance. While we were waiting here we received a knapsack and one woolen blanket each. We were ordered into line and marched to the cars which were in waiting, boarded the train and started for Washington, D. C., about six P. M. We arrived there the next morning, August 7th, about sunrise. On leaving the cars in the Baltimore and Ohio Railroad depot, we were again ordered into line by Lieutenant Perry and marched to Camp Sprague, and took possession of the old quarters of the First Rhode Island Battery (three months men). We were accompanied from Point of Rocks to the camp by Capt. William B. Weeden, promoted from second lieutenant of the Second Battery. At the time it was reported he was to be captain of our battery. But he only stayed with us for a week, then left for Providence, R. I., to take command of another battery, which was formed from men who had offered their services since we had left.

During the process of organizing the Army of the Potomac the commander-in-chief was reported to have said, "This is to be largely an artillery war," and it is understood that he gave more than ordinary attention to increasing this arm of defense. With what rapidity the increase progressed, few, perhaps, have an adequate idea, and it may awaken surprise, as well as indicate the strength of this department, to know that since the first battle of Bull Run the light artillery in the several armies was increased from a few batteries to upwards of two thousand guns. In this mass of power Rhode Island was nobly represented.

On the 1st of August, 1861, Hon. Simon Cameron, the then secretary of war, authorized Governor Sprague to raise and equip a battalion of artillery, to consist of three batteries, one of which, the Second Rhode Island Battery (Capt. William H. Reynolds), was then in the field. The Third, Lieut. Raymond H. Perry commanding, the Fourth, Capt. William B. Weeden commanding, were soon organized and mustered into the service under this order, and left for Washington, D. C. This battalion was under the command of Maj. Charles H. Tompkins.

Volunteering for the artillery being so brisk, Governor Sprague asked for and obtained an order to raise and equip two additional batteries to be added to the battalion, and all designated by letter instead of numerals, thus the second battery was called A, the third, B, the fourth, C, and the two additional batteries, D, Capt. J. A.

Monroe, and E, Capt. George E. Randolph. They were rapidly organized. The headquarters of this battalion was established at Camp Sprague, Washington, D. C., to which place the batteries were sent as soon as they were mustered into service.

Again, on the 13th of September, 1861, authority was granted Governor Sprague by the war department to raise three more batteries, making eight in all, to constitute a regiment, to be known and called the First Regiment Rhode Island Light Artillery. Maj. C. H. Tompkins was appointed colonel; Capt. William H. Reynolds of Battery A promoted to lieutenant-colonel; the former at Camp Sprague in disciplining and drilling the batteries, while the latter was in Rhode Island superintending the organization, and forwarding the other batteries to Washington as soon as their numbers were full. While Colonel Tompkins was with the batteries in the Army of the Potomac, Lieutenant-Colonel Reynolds had a like important agency at Hilton Head, S. C., the duties of which he successfully and satisfactorily performed.

Private James Tillinghast.

CHAPTER III.

CAMP SPRAGUE AND DISCIPLINE.

CAMP SPRAGUE was partly located in a beautiful grove near the Eckington Hospital, on the Gales farm, about two miles from the Capitol. The formation of the camp was planned and laid out by private Henry A. DeWitt, of Company C. (He was promoted to second lieutenant of engineers May 31, 1861.) The building of the barracks was superintended by First Lieut. William R. Walker, of Company E, of the First Regiment Rhode Island Detached Militia, by which troops it was first occupied. The buildings for the men were built of rough joists and boards in regular form, each company in line, and facing a street. At the head of the line was a separate hut with a porch attached overlooking the camp, this being the quarters of the company officers.

At the north of the grove, and in front of the camp, was a large level space used for company and regimental drills and parades. South of this parade ground and joining the infantry camp on the east, were the artillery barracks which previously had been occupied by the First Rhode Island Battery (three months men). The barracks for the men extended from the grove to the east in one line, all built together. At the head of the line was a separate barracks for the line sergeants, first sergeant, and quartermaster. In front of these were the officers' quarters. The first thing in order after taking possession was the cleaning of quarters and ground about the camp. It was a very busy time. Our supplies began to arrive, and woolen blankets, tin plate and a pint tin cup were issued to each. At noon the men were ordered into line by First Sergt. Jacob B. Lewis, marched to the cook-house of the infantry camp, and each man received a loaf of soft bread, a *hunk* of boiled salt beef, and a pint of coffee, after which we returned to our barracks, and there finished our dinner. As our camp cooking utensils had not been received our rations were cooked at the infantry cook-house by the cooks of Company K, Second Regiment Rhode Island Infantry. This company was stationed at Camp Sprague, and occupied the infantry quarters for the purpose of doing camp guard duty. The batterymen found it very pleasant to have friends so near, and many a social chat was enjoyed. In the afternoon two army wagons arrived at camp loaded with different supplies. These were taken care of by the quartermaster-sergeant, William S. Dyer. At four o'clock P. M. a bugle call was sounded by bugler Eben S. Crowninshield. This was followed by the well known voice of First Sergeant Lewis calling. "*Fall in! Fall in! Lively now!*" meaning that we should form into line. When the line was formed, Lieutenants Perry, Bloodgood, and Adams, came and stood about six paces in front of the line facing it. Then Lieutenant Perry explained that the men were to always form into line as they now stood whenever the assembly call was sounded. And the bugler was then ordered to blow the assembly call again that it might be understood. He then gave orders for the non-commissioned officers to step two paces to the rear, then ordered the first sergeant to form the line into detachments, and six gun detachments were formed of eighteen men each, commencing from the right of the line. To each detachment was assigned one sergeant and two corporals (who are called non-commissioned officers). The first corporal is also called the gunner, and has charge of the piece and cannoneers. The other corporal is called No. 8, and has charge of the caisson, and also does the duty of the gunner in his absence. The sergeant has charge of the whole detachment. Two detachments or more form a section, and are commanded by a commissioned officer. Battery B was formed viz.: The first (Sergeant Lewis), and third (Sergeant Blair), detachments, the right section under Lieutenant Perry; fifth (Sergeant Coombs), and sixth (Sergeant Blake), detachments, the centre section, under Lieutenant Horace S. Bloodgood; and the fourth (Sergeant Tucker), and second (Sergeant Adams), detachments, the left section, under Lieut. George W. Adams. The blacksmiths, saddlers or harness makers, wheelwrights and farriers, the drivers of the army wagons, battery wagon, and forge, and other stable men, formed the seventh or artificers' detachment, in charge of Stable Sergt. George O. Scott.

Lieut. Francis A. Smith, was chief of caissons. After this formation was made the men were dismissed. At six o'clock P. M. assembly call was sounded, and the men went again to the infantry cooks for rations for supper. At nine P. M. Bugler Cokely sounded a call. This was new and sounded something like this: "Put out your lights! Put out your lights! Go to bed! Go to bed! G-o t-o b-e-d!" This was called "taps," and after it had been sounded all lights in the men's quarters must be put out and the camp remain quiet.

Thus the first day of camp life of Battery B ended. The men seeking their bunks, turned in to sleep, and possibly to dream of friends at home. The bunks were arranged in three tiers around three sides of the barracks, their being twenty-four for each detachment. It was well that nature designed us to sleep with our eyes and mouth closed, for the dust falling from the upper bunks over the heads of those in the lower ones would have made it very annoying had it been otherwise. This falling of the dust was overcome to great extent by placing paper on the bottom of the bunks.

Sunday, August 18th. Reveille at 4.45 A. M. This call is made to awaken the men from slumber, the men to make their morning toilet and be in readiness for any duty they may be called for. At six o'clock assembly call, when the calling of the roll was made by First Sergeant Lewis. This was the first regular roll call of the men that had been made since we left Providence, R. I., and some time was spent in correcting the roll, as many of the names thereon were spelled and written incorrectly. This done, the breakfast call was sounded at seven o'clock, and we went again for rations. At eight o'clock a detail of eighteen men (three from each detachment), one sergeant and one corporal was made. This was called the guard detail. The sergeant was called sergeant of the guard, and the corporal, corporal of the guard. The men on guard were stationed at posts designated by numbers, as Post No. 1, and Post No. 2, and so on. No. 1 Post was generally at the guard house, or officers' headquarters; No. 2 at the park (that is, where the guns and caissons are stationed); No. 3 at the quartermaster's supplies. The other numbers at the stable and different parts of the camp. The guards were posted at nine o'clock, only one-third of the number being on duty at one time. Those that are posted first are called first relief, and they are on post for two hours; then they are relieved by the second relief of a like number of men, and these remain on post for two hours; they in turn are relieved by the third relief, who also remain two hours, when they are relieved by the men that were first posted, or first relief. This is designated as "two hours on and four hours off post." The whole guard is generally on duty for twenty-four hours. Also at nine o'clock the men not on duty were assembled by detachments in front of their quarters and drilled in foot movements by the chief of sections (the lieutenants) for one hour, then dismissed. At noon dinner call was sounded, and we partook of our rations. In the afternoon a supply of camp utensils arrived, and to each detachment a set of cooking utensils were issued. These consisted of a sheet-iron round stove, several mess pans, and kettles of sheet-iron; also a large round sheet-iron frying-pan as large over as the top of the stove. The next thing in order was men to do the cooking. In some of the detachments one volunteered as cook; in others it was done by detailing a man for cook for one day. By this arrangement all kinds of cooking were enjoyed. If not enjoyed they were endured, until finally each detachment had one of their number permanently detailed as cook, and cooking went along smoothly for a time. At five P. M. retreat roll call was sounded. Thus establishing two roll calls a day, one in the morning, the other late in the afternoon. The second day in camp was a very busy one, and there was so much to occupy our minds that we hardly realized that it was the Sabbath, the day for rest, prayer, and praise, to be offered up to the Supreme Ruler of the Universe. The soldier soon learns that there is no Sabbath day in the army. One day is the same as another.

August 19th. At reveille there was a smart shower, and it rained by spells during most of the morning. At six A. M. the first uncooked rations were issued to the cooks to be prepared for the men. A man was detailed as assistant to the cook, to get water, cut wood, etc. At seven o'clock breakfast call was sounded, and the men partook of a breakfast prepared by one of their own number, which consisted of fried steak, fried apples and peaches, soft bread (made of flour, so called to distinguish it from hard-tack), and hot coffee. An army ration per man is three-quarters of a pound of salt pork or bacon or salt beef, one and one-quarter pounds of fresh beef, eighteen ounces of soft bread, or twelve ounces of hard bread, or one and one-quarter pounds of flour. At the rate of one hundred rations is issued eight quarts of beans or peas, ten pounds of rice, six pounds of coffee, twelve pounds of sugar, two quarts of ground salt, four pounds of soap, one and one-quarter pounds of adamantine candles, and at times potatoes, on ions, and pressed vegetables. Soldiers cannot eat all the rations if issued to them, and for many reasons do not get their full allowance. At eight A. M. police call was sounded, and that indicated that the quarters and grounds around the barracks are to be cleaned, all litter to be swept up and carried away from the barracks. This work is generally performed by men as a punishment for some breach of discipline. At this time there were no victims, and a detail, one from each detachment, did the work. Nine A. M. guard mounting, after which we had drill call, and the men were drilled at the manual of the piece for the first time since we were mustered into service. On our arrival at Camp Sprague we found six new General James's rifled brass guns (twelve-pounders) and limbers. These were parked in front of the artillery barracks and taken possession of by Battery B, and made use of during drill hours.

August 20th. Reveille at sunrise. The officers having so well instructed the men as to their duties, and all having got into working order, we settled down into army life in earnest, performing the camp duties as regular as clock-work. At the post below the stable, yesterday afternoon, there was an incident which caused much merriment among the men at the time, but not to the participants. It was just at dusk, one of our men who had been out of camp, was trying to get in without being seen, as he had not the countersign (password). The guards (there were two) saw him skulking around, challenged him, and commanded him to halt. This he did not do, but started on a run. The guards being armed only with sabres, could only enforce obedience to their demands at close quarters. So the guards put after, and chased him quite a distance from the camp, leaving the post unguarded, and any one might have entered unobserved, or gone out if they had been in that vicinity. The guards succeeded in capturing their man, returned to camp and marched him to the guard-house—still leaving the post unguarded—feeling very elated over their success, and boasting that they were not to be trifled with. But what was their dismay and feelings when told to give up their arms (the sabres), as they were arrested for deserting their post while on duty. They were kept in the guard-house all night. Just before guard-mounting to-day the men were assembled in line, and the culprits brought out in front and reprimanded for breach of duty. Again Captain Weeden explained the duties of guards while on post, and hoped the misdemeanor would not occur again. The men were released from arrest and were the first victims for police duty. It was a long time before the men heard the last of it, and it was a lesson that was always remembered. In the afternoon, while drilling, heavy musketry was heard in the direction of Harper's Ferry, said to be skirmishing of some of our troops with the rebels in that vicinity.

August 21st. The day passed pleasantly with the regular camp duties and manual drill. At retreat roll-call the officer of the day read several orders to us, some of which were explained. Among the general orders was one in regard to profanity, which was prohibited, and for an offence a fine was to be levied. A private was to be fined fifty cents, an officer one dollar, for each and every offence. Now, while the officer was reading this order, a band which had just arrived at the infantry camp commenced to play a lively air, with heavy bass drum accompaniment, which drowned the officer's voice so that he could not be heard, and he was obliged to stop reading. Then came a lull in the music and he commenced reading again, and had proceeded as far as where the officers were to be fined one dollar, when the band struck up and let out in full blast, bass drum leading. A flash passed over the officer's face and he exclaimed, "D— that band to h—!" Then in the next breath said, "Orderly, charge me one dollar." I do not know whether that fine was ever paid, nor do I remember that a fine was ever levied on the men of Battery B for swearing.

August 22d. The Twenty-third Pennsylvania Regiment arrived and went into camp in the infantry quarters. They came here for guard duty and drill. Company K, of the Second Rhode Island Regiment, has been relieved and have gone to join their regiment at Camp Brightwood, just beyond the Soldiers' Home (of the Regulars).

August 23d. Captain Weeden, who had been in command and supervised the details of the battery since we have been in Washington, left us and went home to Rhode Island to take command of Battery C. First Lieut. Raymond H. Perry then assumed command of our battery. A detail of men under Lieutenant Adams and the quartermaster-sergeant went down to the city and returned with horses for the battery.

August 24th. Soon after reveille the assembly was sounded and the line formed; then volunteers were asked for to groom and care for the battery horses. All who desired to perform this service were told to step three paces to the front. The men that were accustomed to care for horses did so. There not being enough of volunteers, the rest were detailed, and were known as drivers, the others as cannoneers.

Sunday, August 25th. Only regular camp duty performed to-day. Capt. Thomas F. Vaughn came and took command of the battery. He was promoted from first lieutenant of Battery A, First Rhode Island Light Artillery. At retreat roll-call Lieutenant Adams introduced Captain Vaughn as our new commander. After a few remarks by both the captain and Lieutenant Adams, the men were dismissed.

With Captain Vaughn came our first recruits, three in number, viz.: Sergeant-Major Ernest Staples, to act as first sergeant, which duty had been performed by Sergeant Lewis; George A. Franklin, who takes care of the captain's horse; Hezekiah Jenks, an orderly for Major Tompkins.

August 26th. To-day the quartermaster-sergeant brought harnesses for the battery horses, and the drivers, with the assistance of the harness makers, Peckham and Taylor, were kept quite busy for some time in putting them together. The pieces were separate and packed in different boxes. To most of the drivers it was a puzzle to put a harness in complete working order.

August 27th. To-day the horses were harnessed and attached to the pieces and caissons, and a few movements were made with fair success. For better advantage in working together some changes were made in the different places the horses were to work, as lead, swing, and pole. Some horses are better adapted for leaders than others, and to that position they were changed.

August 28th was a very pleasant day. The battery was hitched up and had its first field drill as a battery. The plateau between the barracks and Eckington Hospital was well adapted for that purpose, being a level and extensive field, which the batteries made use of while quartered at Camp Sprague. Our drill was an improvement on that of yesterday, and, after two hours in executing different movements, the battery was parked and the horses stabled. From this time forth while we remained at Camp Sprague the battery was drilled at the manual of the piece in the forenoon, and mounted battery drill in the afternoon; in which the men and horses became quite proficient.

It requires considerable time to supply artillery with trained

Capt. Thomas F. Vaughn.

horses. The horse is a curious, shy, inquisitive animal, and when taken from the stable or pasture for the strategic purpose of war, demands to be handled with great care and patience. He must be gradually accustomed to the sudden and marked changes in his status,—the gleam of arms, the roll of drums, the flaunting of banners, the flash, the smoke, and the roar of the cannons, and musketry. It is remarkable, however, that when the practical war horse is thus drilled and disciplined, his proficiency in wheeling with gun or caisson at the critical moment of limbering up or unlimbering light field artillery is wonderful. At the bugle call, without a word, sign or touch from the driver, he wheels, advances and retreats with marvelous rapidity; at times compelling riders and cannoneers to spring to keep their saddles or escape his lightning-like evolutions.

August 31st. In the afternoon while the battery was out on field drill, a large fire was seen in the direction of Arlington Heights, Va. Later we learned it was the burning of the quarters and stables of some troops stationed there. No one was injured, but the damage to the men in loss of clothing and quarters was great.

After the battery had returned from drill the men were mustered for the month of August, 1861. By this is meant that the pay rolls (of which there are three, one for the company, one for the paymaster and one for the war department), had been made out, and certified to by the commanding officer with his signature. Battery B was mustered for nineteen days, from the 13th to the 31st inclusive.

Camp life so far with the men has been pleasant. We have enjoyed the privileges of passes to the city of Washington, the capital of the nation. Visited all the different places of interest and amusement, and have written to our friends at home of the sights and different places which we had visited. It seemed as if we were enjoying a visit ourselves, instead of being subjects of military authority.

Sunday, September 1st. First mounted inspection. The quarters, clothing and appearance of the men, horses, stable, pieces and caissons and all equipments were examined, after which the battery was complimented by the officers on its fine appearance, and were dismissed. A number of passes were given to the men to visit the city, and some went without them. In the evening several of the soldiers were taken with violent spasms and frothed at the mouth and nostrils, so that the men became alarmed and thought their comrades had been poisoned. There was no surgeon at the camp, so they were given hot water as soon as they revived sufficiently to take it. This made them vomit, and they soon recovered from their spasms. But it left them very weak and sick. While the men were in these spasms it would take three and four men to hold them to keep them from injuring themselves, and at times they had as much as they could do. On the arrival of the surgeon, who had been sent for from the hospital, he said their comrades had done the best thing possible in giving the sufferers hot water to drink, and that they were all out of danger except one man, who had another attack while the surgeon was there. He did not recover from it as well as the others, for he had several attacks and was very sick and under the surgeon's care for some time, and was finally discharged. From the men it was learned that they had drank beer which they had purchased of the sutler (a Dutchman), who had a shanty at the lower end of the camp, and as the weather was very warm they had drank several times there during the afternoon. The surgeon thought that there must have been some drug put into the beer which made them sick. This made the men provoked with the sutler, and they threatened to break into and clean out his shanty. But before they had succeeded in accomplishing their object they were ordered to their quarters. On being informed that the sutler was not in camp that night and that a guard would be placed at his shanty and he would be arrested in the morning when he arrived, had the effect of quieting the men.

September 2d. Early in the morning the Dutchman was seen approaching his shanty, and as it was quiet around and about the camp he went to the shanty. As he was about to enter the guard arrested him, and a more surprised Dutchman was never seen. He condemned himself at once by saying: "Why for I be arrested? I do nothing. The beer was good; that was all right. I did nothing to it!" This he kept saying as he was taken to the officers' quarters. He was ordered to the guard-house, and finally sent to the city under guard. He was found probably guilty of drugging the beer, fined, and ordered to leave the city.

The day being very pleasant the battery was ordered out on field drill in the forenoon, and while drilling were reviewed and inspected by Gen. George B. McClellan and staff, who had rode into camp as we were going out to drill.

September 7th. After the morning drill the battery was ordered to hitch up, and left camp and went down to the Arsenal for ammunition and other supplies. Left the pieces to have the vents fitted for primers, and returned to camp with caissons. While at the Arsenal a little incident happened which shows to what danger many were exposed through the ignorance of some one. Not the enlisted man, for he only obeys orders without question. Corporal Libbey, with several others, were detailed to fill a lot of shell with powder. In the ammunition room, which was quite a large room on the first floor, were several large boxes near the main or delivery door, holding between two and three bushels. These were nearly full of fine and loose powder scattered on the floor around the boxes. The shells were filled with the powder from these boxes, and, when completed, were taken out by the men to the ammunition chests and packed therein. At the time probably no thought was given to the risk that was run, but since then I have heard mentioned the danger we were exposed to by treading on the loose powder, and the liability of gravel being tracked in as we passed in and out, and the iron nails in the heels of our shoes, a spark from one of which would have ignited the powder, and there would have been a tremendous explosion which might have blown us all across the Potomac. To-day Charles Cottrell was discharged and sent home for disability, said to be caused by the drugged beer.

Sunday, September 8th. Captain Vaughn received official notice that Battery B has been assigned to General Stone's command, which was doing guard duty on the upper Potomac River.

September 10th. Governor Sprague, of Rhode Island, and General Burnside visited camp to-day. They were received with three hearty cheers from the men, who were greatly pleased to receive a visit from such distinguished personages as the war governor of Rhode Island and a hero of Bull Run. The governor and general expressed their thanks for the hearty reception received.

September 11th. Lieutenant Adams, with drivers, went to the Arsenal and returned to camp with the pieces.

September 12th. The government paymaster visited the camp to-day. The assembly call was sounded, the line formed by the first sergeant, the men marched to the captain's quarters, and, as their names were called, commencing with the non-commissioned officers first, they signed the pay-roll, the privates receiving $8.23 for nineteen days' service in the month of August. This was the first money we had received from the United States government, and paid in gold and silver.

In the afternoon Captain Vaughn received marching orders,

which was communicated to the men at retreat roll-call, by being ordered to pack up and be in readiness to move at a moment's notice. It was with regret that most of us heard this order—a move which meant to break up housekeeping just as we had become used to the surroundings and camp-life at the capital city of the Union. While on the march or in other camps, the memory of Camp Sprague will always be coupled with pleasant thoughts of the places of interest we visited while here encamped and first taught the duties of a soldier.

Among the buildings visited were the Capitol, not then finished, the White House, Patent Office, and Office of Interior, State, War, and Navy Departments, Treasury Department, Washington Monument; the Mall, with the Smithsonian Institute, the Arsenal, the Navy Yard, not forgetting a visit to the Island.

The Soldiers' Home for the Regulars was not generally visited by the volunteer soldier. It was located about three miles due north from the Capitol. The original purchase of land was 256 acres. The principal building for inmates is of white marble. It was commenced in 1852 and completed in 1891. It is of Norman gothic design, 251½ feet long by 158½ feet wide. The south part of the main building (the front) is named after Gen. Winfield Scott, the founder of the Home, and has a large clock tower. The north addition is named after Gen. W. T. Sherman. The old homestead building near to and west of the Scott building is named after Gen. Robert Anderson, of Fort Sumter renown, to commemorate the fact of his early advocacy of and great interest in the establishing of the Home, in which the first inmates were quartered. But since the renovating and repairing of the homestead in 1856, it has frequently been used as the summer residence of the presidents. President Buchanan, being the first to make use of it, occupied it in 1856–60. A visit to the above place well paid those who spent a few hours viewing and inspecting the buildings and grounds.

One other place out of the city was much visited, and that was Arlington, the residence of Gen. Robert E. Lee. The Arlington estate was originally part of the vast landed possessions of Edmond Scarburgh in the early colonial period, and consisted of 1,160 acres. Later it came into the possession of John Custis, a wealthy planter, whose only son, Daniel Parke Custis, married "the beauty and belle of Williamsburg, Va.," Martha Dandridge, and inherited the estate. After a few years of happy married life, Martha was left a

widow with two children, and in 1759 was wedded to George
Washington. She held the Arlington estate for her son, but
eventually her grandson George Washington Parke Custis became
the owner of it. He erected the fine mansion now standing on the
eastern portion of the grounds. It consists of a large centre building
with two wings, the whole having a frontage of 140 feet. It is constructed of brick covered with stucco, resembling freestone. There
is a central portico, the pediment of which is supported by eight
ponderous columns. The mansion was occupied by him until his
death, in 1857. Arlington then passed to his daughter, Mrs. Lee
(the wife of Gen. Robert E. Lee), for life, and afterwards was to
descend to her son, George Washington Custis Lee. The Lee
family lived on the estate until the beginning of the Rebellion, leaving
it forever in April, 1861, when General Lee removed to Richmond, Va.

The United States government took possession of the estate soon
after the war began, and under the tax act of 1862 a sale was
ordered, President Lincoln directing that the estate should be bid in
for the use of the government, which was accordingly done. It was
then decided to take a part of the land for a military cemetery, and
some two hundred acres or more on the heights were enclosed and is
now called, "The National Military Cemetery," at Arlington. It
is a vast field of the nation's dead. The first interment was made
in May, 1864. Here under the shade of noble oaks, are buried
16,264 soldiers of the Rebellion, their last resting place graciously
cared for by the government they died to defend.

The mansion house is occupied by the superintendent of the
cemetery, and the lower story can be inspected by visitors. The
Arlington estate was subsequently claimed by George W. C. Lee.
He brought a suit of ejectment against the United States in the
Supreme Court, and judgment was given in his favor. He then
offered the estate to the government for the sum of $150,000, which
offer was accepted by Congress, and Arlington is now in undisputed
possession of the nation.

Among other pleasant memories of Camp Sprague is that of an
old lady who used to bring milk, pies, and cakes, and other knick-
nacks, which she offered for sale at a reasonable price. She took
quite a liking to the boys of the battery, and if any of us were sick
she used to bring medicine (home made), and with a motherly way
administer to our wants; and, if without funds and the wherewithal

to purchase her dainties, she trusted us for them, knowing not whether she would be paid for her kindness. But I am pleased to say, the next day after the battery was paid off, on her visit to camp, she was paid in full. It was a precedent not generally followed towards peddlers.

Private Caleb H. H. Greene,

CHAPTER IV.

TO POOLESVILLE, MD., AND BATTLE OF BALL'S BLUFF.

SEPTEMBER 13th. Reveille at four A. M. During the morning the men were quite busy preparing for the march to the upper Potomac. Breakfast at seven o'clock, after which the cooks packed all of the cooking utensils (except the sheet-iron stove) and they were put into the army wagon to be taken with us.

Half past seven o'clock, "boots and saddles" call sounded; the horses were soon harnessed, the battery hitched up, and all in readiness to move. At eight o'clock A. M. the officers took their respective stations with their detachments, and then Captain Vaughn gave the following orders: "At-ten-tion drivers! Mount! First piece into line! Forward, march!"

Battery B then left Camp Sprague for pastures new, knowing not whether we would return again. We passed through the parade ground, by Eckington Hospital, out into the main road, turning to the left, moved toward Washington. Passed through the city by New York and Pennsylvania Avenues, passing over Rock Creek by the Aqueduct Bridge into Georgetown. Taking the Tenallytown road we passed a number of fortifications in which infantry and heavy artillery regiments were stationed. Slowly continuing our march we passed through Tenallytown and Rockville to small villages which had greatly increased in population under the squatter's act. A short distance beyond Rockville the battery halted in the road, where we remained for nearly an hour, when we were again summoned to march, and the battery was finally ordered into a field, the pieces and caissons parked, and orders given to encamp for the night. For the first time the men slept in their blankets on the ground.

September 14th. Reveille at sunrise. At eight o'clock A. M. the battery left Rockville continuing the march, passing through Darnestown (a small post town of half a dozen houses), and halted at the camp of Battery A, First Regiment Rhode Island Light Artillery. The men were well pleased with the opportunity for a chat with old friends. Continuing our march we did not stop again until we arrived at Poolesville, Md. Passing through part of the village, we turned to the left, marching about half a mile, and halted on a level tract of land, which was called Poolesville Plains (at least we called it by that name), to the southwest of the village. This was our destination, Poolesville, a small post town, about twenty-five miles northwest from Washington, D. C. The village comprised about twenty-five or thirty houses, with a hotel and a number of stores, and two blacksmith shops. It had the appearance of a thrifty little place.

Here Gen. Charles P. Stone, commanding the division to which we had been assigned, had his headquarters. The battery was accompanied on the march to this place by the Nineteenth and Twentieth Massachusetts, and other regiments, under command of Colonel (afterwards General) Gorman. Immediately on our arrival the men were given orders to form camp. The pieces and caissons were parked, horses unhitched, unharnessed, and hitched to the picket rope, which had been stretched by the cannoneers to the trees at the west of the camp. Three A tents were issued to each detachment, the six drivers occupying one, the cannoneers the other two. These were pitched in one line, east and west, about fifteen yards to the rear of the park. At the rear of the right of the line were the sergeants' tents. About ten yards from and at right angles with the line at the east were the officers' tents. In the square, in rear of officers' and privates' tents were the cooking quarters. In rear of the left of the line were parked the battery wagon and forge, beside which were the artificers' tents, and a tent for the quartermaster-sergeant. We had arrived on the plain about two o'clock P. M., by night the camp was completed, and at taps the men were tired enough to turn in, roll up in their blankets, and resign themselves to sleep, rather than explore the new country in which they found themselves.

Sunday, September 15th. The battery from this time forth on all occasions, weather permitting, established a regular routine of camp duties, as reveille at sunrise, roll-call at six o'clock P. M., followed by police call for the cannoneers, and stable call for the drivers. At seven o'clock, breakfast call; eight o'clock, sick call; nine o'clock, guard call, followed by drivers' water call (at which time the horses were taken to water). On their return, "boots and saddles," and drill call. The battery was then drilled for two hours. Then the battery was parked, horses unhitched, unharnessed, and stabled, after which followed feed call, when the horses were fed. At noon, dinner call. Rest until two o'clock P. M.; then drill call and "boots and saddles," which meant mounted drill for one and a half hours, after which the battery was parked and horses stabled. Four o'clock, stable call again, and, at five o'clock, retreat roll-call, followed by supper call; and at nine P. M., taps. On Sunday about nine o'clock A. M., instead of drill there was inspection of quarters and clothing, and once a month or when ordered, mounted inspections, at which time all battery and camp equipage was inspected. By the above it will be seen that in pleasant weather our time was pretty well occupied.

The Fifteenth Massachusetts Regiment was encamped directly south of our camp, and to the west of them was established a camp of engineers and a signal station, from which the men signaled to Sugar Loaf Mountain, and from there to Rockville, thence to Washington. During the war the code of signals by flags was brought to a remarkable state of perfection, and during different campaigns was of immense service. In many instances the firing of artillery was directed by signal officers stationed where they could overlook the fight and observe with a field-glass the effect of our gunnery. By their aid the commanding general was made seasonably acquainted with the movements of the enemy in time of battle, extending over a field of several miles. The signal service is dangerous, and men of nerve, coolness, and bravery, only are suited to it.

September 16th. Sergt. John McCoombs was sent to the hospital of the Fifteenth Massachusetts Regiment, as we had none at our camp. He was taken sick on the march from Rockville. Corp. Charles A. Libbey was appointed acting sergeant in charge of the third piece, fifth detachment.

September 18th. As the battery was getting ready for mounted drill, Captain Vaughn received orders to have the battery in light marching trim at a moment's notice. The battery was soon in readiness, the men with haversack, canteens, and blankets. About 9.30 A. M. the battery left camp and moved in the direction of the Potomac, to the southwest. We marched to Edwards' Ferry, about four miles from Poolesville, and then was sent down the river about a mile, Captain Vaughn placing the battery in position on a hill overlooking the Potomac River and commanding the Virginia shore for some distance. General Stone and staff then appeared, and the general rode up to Captain Vaughn, directing two guns to be placed near the woods at our right and front. Captain Vaughn ordered the centre section to the place designated. To reach that position the section was obliged to cross a recently ploughed field, which required considerable pulling, pushing, puffing and swearing to get the pieces across and into position. This was finally accomplished without mishap. The battery was ordered to fire shell across the river into an open field. For a few moments, judging by the way we threw shells into that field, one would have supposed that ten thousand rebels were there preparing to cross. But not a Johnnie did we see. It was subsequently learned that gatherings of men had been seen often at that place, and it was supposed that they were preparing to build a fortification; but the day that Battery B sent over their compliments in the shape of shells the rebels had not been seen in that vicinity.

At noon the battery (two sections) was ordered to return to camp at Poolesville. The right section, under Lieutenant Perry, was ordered to remain on picket duty. In the afternoon tents and rations were sent down to them. The horses were picketed in the woods, the tents pitched in a hollow at the edge of the woods, in front of which the men built fires and made themselves as comfortable as circumstances would permit.

On the 23d, a squad of men were seen on the Virginia side of the river, and by their actions it was thought they were signaling across to our side. Lieutenant Perry, taking his field-glass, went down the canal to make an observation, to see if he could make out what they were doing. While thus engaged he was shot at, but not hit. Returning to his command, he ordered, "Prepare for action!" and several shells were sent over among them. There was a scattering and a run for the woods, and no more was seen of them for some days. The section remained here until the 24th of September, when it was relieved and returned to camp at Pooleville, the center section, under Lieutenant Smith, taking its place.

September 23d. The left section, under the command of Lieutenant Adams, was ordered to Monocacy, about eight miles from Poolesville, to guard the aqueduct of the Baltimore and Ohio Canal, where it crosses the Monocacy River, a village of some three or four houses (consisting of a store and the post-office), being a short distance below the Aqueduct Bridge. The place was noted as a tie-up station for the canal boats. On a high hill southeast of the aqueduct the pieces were stationed, overlooking the river, and commanded the Virginia shore for some distance opposite the junction of the Monocacy with the Potomac. In the grove back of the hill, in a ravine the horses were picketed. On the outer edge of the grove the men built huts of rails, straw, and earth, making quite comfortable quarters. In front of the grove in the open field two A tents were pitched, one for Lieutenant Adams and the other for Sergeants Adams and Tucker. This was the headquarters of the section.

While stationed at this place the men enjoyed visits in the surrounding country, and many journeys were taken up the tow-path by the canal to the little red house near the lock at Licksville, and also the little store at the foot of Sugar Loaf Mountain. Neither were our stomachs forgotten, for Maryland rabbits (young pigs) were plenty, likewise geese and a few turkeys. The following is the way they were prepared:

Roast Pig.—It is said "necessity is the mother of invention," and "where there is a will there is a way." These sayings were fully demonstrated by the soldier in the art of cooking, or at least the way to do cooking under disadvantages, and lack of a well-arranged kitchen. About the farms on which the soldiers were encamped were young pigs roaming about; and, the thought of roast pig on once entering the mind of a soldier, he does not get rid of the desire for a feast on piggy until the fact has been accomplished. One day several of the men caught a pig, and, while one of their number was cleaning and preparing him, the others dug a hole in the ground, and, lining the sides and bottom with stones, built a fire in it. When the stones were thoroughly heated, the hole was cleaned of coals and ashes, and piggy was laid therein; the hot stones laid around him and two large flat ones laid over the top of the hole to cover it, on which was thrown earth to keep in the heat. The pig was allowed to remain in the oven thus made all night, and on taking it out in the morning it was of a beautiful seal brown color, and as juicy as could be desired, and on which we hungry mortals (soldiers) satisfied our appetites. It was a royal feast, fit for a king. In similar manner other meats or vegetables that were to be roasted or baked were cooked.

Pork and Beans.—The manner in which the army cook prepares and cooks that eatable may be novel in the culinary art of to-day. The army cook digs a hole in the ground and builds a fire therein. Two crotched stakes are driven in the ground beside the hole on which is laid a pole. On this pole he hangs a kettle over the fire, in which the beans are being parboiled, so while heating the hole, the beans are being partly cooked. When the hole is heated enough, the coals and ashes are cleaned out with a shovel, and the kettle with the parboiled beans, on top of which is placed the pork (or it may be put in the middle), the kettle nearly filled with water. This is then placed in the hole. Then a kettle large enough to go over the one containing the pork and beans is placed bottom side up over it, forming a cover. Then the live coals are placed around the kettles so as to completely cover both. It is allowed to remain in the hole all night. In the morning it is dug out, the large kettle removed, and the sight that meets your eye is the familiar dish of the Yankee as well as the soldier. The army bean when thus cooked is not to be despised. It has only one rival—that of the now famous Boston baked beans.

October 1st. The following privates were promoted to corporals, namely: Pardon S. Walker, Richard H. Gallup, Sylvester G. Ide, William H. Tanner, Charles B. Worthington.

On the 11th of October the left section was relieved and returned to camp at Poolesville, and the right section, under Lieutenant Perry, took their place, and occupied the tents and huts. In the afternoon the battery received seven recruits from Rhode Island, who were assigned to the different detachments.

Sunday, October 13th. The sentinel stationed on guard at the pieces reported that there was a large squad of men and horses surrounding a house and barn on the Virginia side. Lieutenant Perry ordered the men to their posts for duty, and after he had made observation through his field-glass, said that there was in the woods back of the house a large force of the enemy's cavalry, and ordered the pieces to be prepared for action. This was done by running them up to the top of the hill by hand, for they were kept back out of sight of field-glasses from the enemy's view. The pieces were then loaded with shell, and sent over among them, which caused consternation to both men and horses as they exploded. They did not seem to wait for orders, but turned back and put for the woods in great confusion, and a number of horses with empty saddles were seen going in all directions. Several more shells were sent into the woods as a warning that it would be dangerous to be seen at the house without an invitation and our permission. The place was kept under vigilance for some time, for it was thought and looked as if it was a rendezvous of the enemy for signaling across the river to parties at a house on our side. There were several arrests made at this house, and the men were sent to General Stone's headquarters. On the 19th Lieutenant Perry went to Washington on personal business, and Lieutenant Adams took command of the section in his absence.

Thus, on the 20th, the battery was divided, and some distance apart. The right section, two pieces, Lieutenant Adams in command, at Monocacy; the centre section, two pieces, under command of Lieutenant Bloodgood, at Edward's Ferry; the left section of two pieces and all the caissons, at the camp of the battery at Poolesville, under command of Capt. Thomas F. Vaughn. Lieutenant Perry was at Washington, and Lieut. Francis A. Smith sick in camp. Captain Vaughn received orders to prepare for light marching, and to be ready to move at a moment's notice. It was rumored that there would be an engagement soon with our troops, as the rebels had been seen lately in force at different times on the opposite side of the river.

On October 21st Captain Vaughn was ordered to Conrad's Ferry, and with the left section proceeded to the river, where Colonel Baker's brigade was crossing to the Virginia side. As the landing was crowded with infantry waiting to be taken across, Captain Vaughn left the section in charge of Sergeant-Major Staples, and went down to Edward's Ferry to bring up the centre section. While the captain was gone the landing became partly clear of troops, and Sergeant Staples moved the left section down to the landing, where great confusion reigned. There seemed to be no one to command or dispatch the troops across as they arrived. At this time Colonel Cogswell, of the (Tammany) Forty-second New York, arrived with his regiment, and, as the left section of Battery B occupied the landing, ordered it to cross. On learning that there was no commissioned officer of the battery with the section (Captain Vaughn not having returned from Edward's Ferry), he ordered Lieut. Walter M. Bramhall, of the Sixth New York Battery, to take command and cross as soon as possible so as to clear the way for his (the Forty-second New York) Regiment. The only means of crossing the river was by a large scow attached to a hawser, which had been stretched from the Maryland shore to Harrison's Island in the Potomac River. Sergt. Silas G. Tucker had his gun dismounted and placed on board of the scow. The scow was only large enough to take one gun detachment and horses, so Lieutenant Bramhall and Sergeant Tucker with the fifth piece and men crossed to the island. While they were crossing, Sergt. Charles H. Adams had his gun (the sixth) dismounted and made ready for embarkation, and, on the return of the scow, it was placed on board, and Sergeant Adams crossed to the island with his gun and detachment. As soon as the fifth piece was landed it was mounted and crossed the island. Here it was dismounted again, and the gun and carriage with the limber was placed in a small scow (or canal boat), and Lieutenant Bramhall and men crossed to the Virginia shore. Sergeant Tucker with the drivers and their horses followed in another scow. The river between the island and Virginia side was narrow, the water running very swift, and it was with great difficulty that the scows were propelled to the opposite shore. On landing the gun was mounted, when another difficulty was encountered. They were on a miry clay bank under a wooded bluff about seventy feet high, with rocks and fallen trees, making the passage for artillery very difficult. After much severe labor and with the help of the infantry, Lieutenant Bramhall succeeded in reaching the summit of the bluff with one gun and limber, seven horses, and fourteen men. The gun was placed in position in line with and to the left of the Seventy-first Pennsylvania, Colonel Baker's regiment (also called First California), where it was assailed by a sharp fire from the enemy's skirmishers and sharpshooters. They being under cover of the trees and shrubs, the service of the guns was ineffectual in checking the enemy's fire. Lieutenant Bramhall was wounded at the first fire of the enemy, and soon all the artillerymen were shot down, and the piece was worked for a time by Colonel Baker, Colonel Cogswell, Captain Harvey, and others. Colonel Lee, of the Twentieth Massachusetts, carried the last round that was fired. It was not discharged more than six or eight times. The horses were all killed, the piece and limber captured, and three men, Corp. William H. Tanner and privates Charles Cornell and William F. Matteson, taken prisoners by the enemy.

A musket ball passed through the leg of Sergeant Tucker just above the ankle joint. Corp. Luther C. Olney was severely

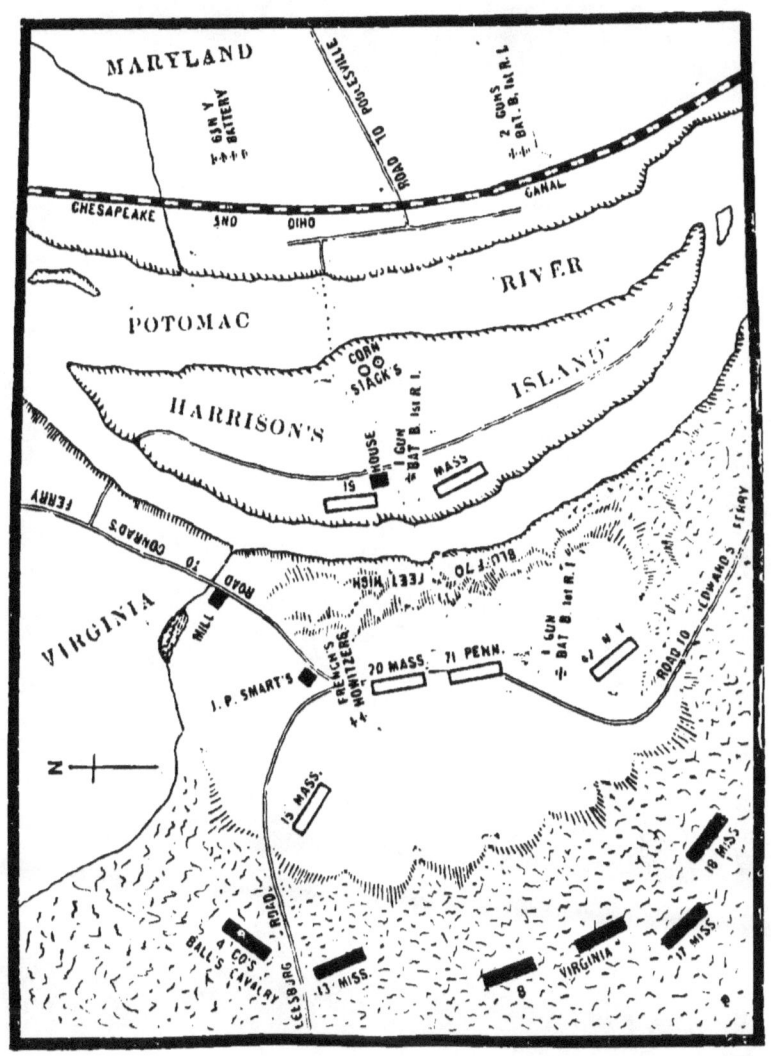

Balls Bluff, Oct. 21, 1861.

wounded, and died Oct. 22, 1862. John Aspinwall, Henry W. Bromley, Benjamin W. and George R. Matteson were also wounded. The wounded and others succeeded in getting across the river to the Island. They were then taken across to the Maryland side and sent to the hospital. Merritt Tillinghast, a driver, after the gun was abandoned, went down the bluff to recross to the island, and, being below the place of crossing with the scows, he with several others plunged into the river to swim for the island. The current running so swift, and being impeded with clothing, which they had failed to divest themselves of, they were swept past the island into the broad river. Then came a struggle to battle against the mighty running water of the Potomac. With a bold stroke for life they swam for the Maryland shore. Nearly exhausted, Tillinghast succeeded in reaching the shore, half a mile below the island, and the next day reached camp in an exhausted condition.

The sixth piece, which was to follow the fifth piece, did not succeed in crossing the river to the island until some thirty minutes after the fifth piece had landed. But as soon as it had crossed Sergeant Adams directed the cannoneers to mount, and started on the double-quick and crossed the island to the landing. Here the piece was again dismounted, and preparations made to put it on board the scow. In the meantime the drivers had unhitched the horses and taken them on board the other scow and were about to push across to the Virginia shore, when an officer came down the bluff and shouted, "For God's sake send over the infantry, we want the infantry! Can't use artillery, but send over infantry!" This officer is said to have been Colonel Baker. At the request of this officer a company of the Forty-second New York Regiment were waiting on the bank for the return of the scows as soon as Sergeant Adams should cross with his piece. By their captain's orders the infantry were loaded on the scow that was waiting for the piece, and pushed for the Virginia shore. At the same time the drivers were ordered to disembark, and gave up the second scow to the infantry. In the confusion that ensued some of the drivers and horses fell into the river instead of landing on the island. The infantry then had the scows to themselves, but the two could hardly take a company at a time, being so small.

Sergeant Adams had his piece mounted and took position on the bank of the island, about a rod from the river, overlooking the place of crossing. Soon after, Captain Vaughn came, and directed the piece to be moved back a few rods to the house, and, taking position in the front yard, prepared for action. When our men broke and made for the bluff, being hard pressed by the enemy, we did not fire our piece, as the nature of the ground was such that there was great danger of killing our own men instead of the enemy. As the bullets began to drop around us thick and fast, the men and horses were moved to the right and rear under cover of the house, where they remained until dark. While here some of our wounded of the fifth piece who had succeeded in getting to the island, were cared for, the saddle blankets were taken from the horses and given to them, and then they were sent across the river to the hospital at Poolesville. Captain Vaughn with a squad of men was sent over under a flag of truce to bury the dead left on the field. At dusk preparations were made to resume hostilities again, as it was reported that the rebels had determined to detain Captain Vaughn and his men as prisoners. About eight o'clock P. M., however, Captain Vaughn returned and ordered Sergeant Adams to take his piece back to the landing, and at nine o'clock bivouacked for the night beside two corn stacks on the bank of the river. Towards morning a cold, drizzling rain began to fall, which was anything but comfortable for the men who were without shelter. Sergeant Adams with his men and piece remained on the island until the night of the 22d, when, under the directions of Captain Vaughn, they recrossed the Potomac to the Maryland shore, and joined the centre section under Lieutenant Bloodgood, which was in position on a high bank overlooking the canal and river, covering the recrossing of the infantry. Just before midnight Captain Vaughn ordered a parting salute to be fired, and four shells were thrown in the direction of Leesburg, as the rebels were known to be there by the light of their camp-fires reflecting on the clouds. Captain Vaughn then ordered the section to limber up, and started on the return to camp at Poolesville, followed by the remnant of the left section, where they arrived on the morning of the 23d, tired and hungry. During the battle of Ball's Bluff the right section, which was stationed at Monocacy, were watching the house on the Virginia side to prevent any signaling being made to the Maryland side, but no one appeared in sight except an old negro.

The following is from a private letter written by the lieutenant in command of the section:

MONOCACY, Oct. 23, 1861.

I regret to say that owing to my being ordered to this place, my section was in the fight, but not under my command. No one can tell the agony I have suffered since then, and my orders are still so imperative that I cannot leave until I am relieved, and so I have been here, while my men were standing the brunt of the battle. One of my pieces is lost, and many of my men are killed or wounded. Although I know I should never have got out of the battle alive, still I had much rather have been there than been away. It was something that I could not help, but it has been dreadful for me to be so near and still be utterly unable to go to my right post. The lieutenant who had charge of my piece was literally riddled with bullets, but will live. As far as I can hear, some of my men were shot dead, and others drowned in the river. I had my horse saddled to go when I first heard the firing, but Major Parish told me it would be a gross act of military disobedience if I left my post here, and that it would subject me to a court-martial. So I had to stay. I wish Lieutenant Perry had not been in Washington, for if it had not been for that I should have been at the fight. Lieutenant Bloodgood was not in the battle. Captain Vaughn went over with ten men yesterday morning under a flag of truce to bury the dead. Lieutenant Bloodgood is about five miles from me and Lieutenant Perry about seven, with my remaining piece, and I still have his men and two pieces here. Everything looks as though I should have plenty to do here soon.

I have just got news from my boys.

During the battle of Ball's Bluff, on the 21st instant, Battery B, Rhode Island Artillery, lost as follows:

Missing, probably prisoners—Corp. Luther C. Olney, Corp. William N. Tanner, Private W. F. Matteson.

Probably drowned—Charles Cornell.

Wounded—Sergt. Silas G. Tucker, right leg shattered. Privates B. W. Matteson, shot through both legs; G. R. Matteson, shot through side; W. C. Haskins, shot through shoulder.

Sergeant Tucker, and indeed all the men, are spoken of as showing remarkable bravery. C. H. Greene, Morris Carmichael, John J. McAllen, and J. A. Tillinghast were perfect tigers in the fight, and escaped unhurt by swimming the river.

    (Signed,)   GEORGE W. ADAMS.

Captain Vaughn and the Flag of Truce.

In the official report of Colonel Hinks, of the Nineteenth Massachusetts Regiment, which covered the retreat across Harrison's Island, is the following passage:

On the morning of the 22d I dispatched Lieutenant Dodge of the Nineteenth Massachusetts, with a flag of truce to request of the Confederate commander permission to remove our wounded, of which numbers lay in view, uncared for, on the Virginia shore. This request was denied. Permission for my surgeon to cross and treat the wounded was also refused, except upon condition that he should remain a prisoner in their hands. Subsequently, I dispatched Captain Vaughn of the

Rhode Island battery, with another flag of truce, to obtain permission to bury the dead, which was acceded to with the stipulation that no movement of troops should be made from the island to the Maryland shore in retreat while the burying party was employed; and I dispatched Captain Vaughn with a party of ten men for that purpose, who remained till after dark, and succeeded in burying forty-seven bodies, which he reported to be about two-thirds of the number lying upon the ground; but night coming on, he was unable to bury the remainder.

During the afternoon factious complaint was made by the rebel commander that I had violated the stipulations under which the flag of truce was protected, accompanied by a threat to retain Captain Vaughn and his party as prisoners of war. I at once addressed a note to the rebel commander, denying the accusation, threw up new intrenchments, and made disposition of troops, with a view of renewing hostilities if the threat was carried into execution. Subsequently, however, Captain Vaughn returned with his party, and informed me that my explanation was deemed satisfactory by the rebel commander.

Immediately after Captain Vaughn's return, under cover of night, I commenced a retreat, in pursuance of orders previously received from General Hamilton, and transported three pieces of artillery, with caissons and ammunition, thirty-six horses, and the eleven companies of infantry under my command, numbering some seven hundred men, in good order, to the Maryland shore, without any casualties or loss whatever; and completing the retreat at twelve o'clock. I immediately passed my compliments to the rebel commander in the form of four shells from Captain Vaughn's guns, which had been placed in battery upon the high ground overlooking the canal and river.

The following is Lieutenant Adams's report:

WASHINGTON, October 28th.

GENERAL BARRY, *Chief of Artillery:*

SIR: Agreeably to your instructions, I give below a correct report of the circumstances connected with the recent battle near Ball's Bluff, October 21, 1861:

The left section of Battery B, Rhode Island Artillery, was ordered on the 20th of October to proceed to Conrad's Ferry. Captain Vaughn immediately started, camping at the New York Ninth Regiment's camp on Saturday night, and, proceeding to the Ferry the following morning, placed one of his pieces in readiness to cross the river. General Baker at that time gave Captain Vaughn orders to place the centre section of his battery, which was two miles and a half distant, in a position to shell the woods. Captain Vaughn immediately started, ordering Lieutenant Bramhall to see to the piece in the event of his not getting back in time to cross with it. Very soon after Captain Vaughn left the river, orders were given to transport one piece of artillery across the river. Lieutenant Bramhall, being at that time chief in command, crossed with the one best situated for immediate and most expeditious forwarding, which was one of Captain Vaughn's pieces. The piece was taken across the river, with the limber, seven horses, and fourteen men, including Sergeant Tucker. After dismounting the piece the men dragged it up a steep hill, and, returning for the carriage, brought it up also, mounted the piece, and commenced firing; continued to do so until all the cannoneers, with the exception of two, were shot down. Sergeant Tucker remained by the piece until his right leg was shattered by a musket ball, and then, unassisted, retired.

Lieutenant Bramhall speaks of both the sergeant and all the men, with the exception of one, who retired after the third fire, as exhibiting the greatest bravery. He was also particular to speak of the bravery shown by M. Carmichael and W. F. Matteson. His report to Captain Bunting is full of the praises of the whole detachment.

The loss sustained by the battery is as follows, namely: One James's rifled cannon, bronze, one gun carriage, one gun limber, seven horses with equipment, four men missing, six men wounded.

The following is a list of those who were in the detachment which crossed the river: Sergt. S. G. Tucker, right leg shattered; Corp. W. F. Tanner, missing, probably drowned; Corp. L. C. Olney, missing, probably drowned; privates Charles Cornell, missing, probably drowned; W. F. Matteson, missing, probably drowned; B. W. Matteson, shot through both legs; G. R. Matteson, shot through the side; W. C. Haskins, shot through the chest; John Aspinwall, shot through the arm, above the elbow; H. W. Bromley, arm grazed by musket ball; M. Carmichael, A. J. McAllen, C. L. Woodmancy and M. Tillinghast escaped without injury.

The wounded men will probably recover. Dr. Crosby informs me that he has no fears of any one wounded, but intimates that there is a possibility of its being necessary to amputate Sergeant Tucker's leg.

I feel it my duty to say that had Captain Vaughn not been prevented by illness, caused by his arduous labors in carrying the dead and wounded over the river immediately after the battle, a full and authentic report would have been forwarded to you.

Respectfully,
GEORGE W. ADAMS,
Lieutenant Battery B, R. I. A.

ADDENDA.—General Stone visited the wounded men, praised them for their bravery, and told them that no men could have worked the piece better.

G. W. ADAMS, *Lieutenant.*

[*Report of R. B. Irwin, Lieutenant-Colonel and Assistant Adjutant-General of the United States Volunteers, of the Battle of Ball's Bluff, and the Cause and Arrest of Brig.-Gen. Charles P. Stone.*]

In the autumn of 1861, General Stone's division, Army of the Potomac, comprising the brigades of Colonels Gorman, Lander and

Baker (afterwards General Sedgwick's, Second Division, Second Corps, Army of the Potomac), was guarding the ferries or fords of the Potomac River, in front of Poolesville, Md. On the 20th of October, General McCall's division being at Dranesville, Va., General McClellan telegraphed to General Stone, directing him to keep a good lookout on Leesburg, Va., to see if the operations of General McCall should have the effect of driving the enemy away, adding, " perhaps a slight demonstration on your part would have the effect to move them." This slight demonstration resulted in the battle of Ball's Bluff. Upon receiving this order General Stone ordered Col. Charles Devens, with the Fifteenth Massachusetts Regiment, to cross the Potomac at Harrison's Island to Virginia and make a reconnaissance in the direction of Leesburg. We find the opening events described as follows by Colonel (afterwards Major-General of Volunteers) Devens:

Just before twelve o'clock Saturday night, October 20th (by orders from General Stone,) I crossed the Potomac River from Harrison's Island to the Virginia shore with five companies, numbering about 300 men, of my regiment, with the intention of taking a rebel camp, reported by scouts to be situated at about a mile from the river, and of observing the country around, then to return to the river, or of waiting and reporting if I thought myself able to remain for reinforcements, or if I found a position capable of being defended and held against a largely superior force. Having only three boats, which together conveyed about thirty men, it was nearly four o'clock when all the force was transferred to the opposite shore. We passed down the shore about sixty rods by a path discovered by the scouts, and then up the bluff, known as Ball's Bluff, where we found an open field, surrounded by woods. At this point I halted until daybreak. Here I was joined by Colonel Lee, with a company of 100 men from the Twentieth Massachusetts Regiment, as rear guard, who were to protect our return. I pushed forward towards Leesburg to the distance of about a mile from the river, to the spot supposed to be the site of the rebel camp, but found on passing through the woods that the scouts had been deceived by a line of trees on the brow of the slope, the opening through which presented, in an uncertain light, somewhat the appearance of a line of tents. Leaving the detachment in the woods, I proceeded with Captain Philbrick and three scouts across the slope, and along the other side of it, observing Leesburg, which was in full view, and the country about it, as carefully as possible, and seeing but four tents of the enemy. My force being concealed by the woods, and having no reason to believe my presence was discovered, and no large number of the enemy's tents being in sight, I determined not to return at once, but to report to General Stone, at Edward's Ferry, which I did, by sending Quartermaster Howe to state these facts, and to say that in my opinion I could remain until I was reinforced. Quartermaster Howe left with his instructions at 6.30 A. M. He returned at eight A. M., and reported that I was to remain where I was, and would be reinforced, and that Lieutenant-Colonel Ward, with the remainder of the regiment, would proceed to Smart's Mill, and that communication should be kept up between us, and that by ten A. M. cavalry would report to me for the purpose of reconnoitering. For some reason they never appeared or reported to me, but came to the bluff. Colonel Baker allowed this cavalry to return without scouting. If they had reported to me, they could have rendered excellent service, as firing had begun on the outposts. I directed Quartermaster Howe to return at once and report the skirmish that had taken place, and that a force of the enemy was gathering. About ten o'clock Howe returned and stated that he had reported the skirmish of the morning, and that Colonel Baker would shortly arrive with his brigade and take command. Between ten and eleven o'clock A. M. I was joined by Lieutenant-Colonel Ward with the remainder of my regiment, a force of 625 men, with 28 officers, many of the men of the regiment being at this time on other duty.

On the morning of the 21st of October General Stone gave Col. Edward D. Baker discretionary authority to retire the small detachment then at Ball's Bluff [those that had been sent over on the night of the 20th for reconnoissance] or to send over his brigade to support it, by the following order:

> HEADQUARTERS CORPS OF OBSERVATION,
> EDWARD'S FERRY,
> October 21, 7.30 A. M.

COL. E. D. BAKER, *Commanding Brigade:*

COLONEL: In case of heavy firing in front of Harrison's Island, you will advance the California Regiment (Seventy-first) of your brigade, or retire the regiments under Colonels Devens and Lee upon the Virginia side of the river, at your discretion, assuming command on arrival.

Very respectfully, colonel, your most obedient servant,

CHARLES P. STONE,
Brigadier-General Commanding.

Colonel Baker at once, without further information, and without visiting the Virginia shore or organizing the boat service, gave the order to cross. The means of transportation consisted of a large flat-boat with the capacity of holding thirty or forty men, besides a skiff, which would carry but four or five, were used to convey the troops to the island. On the other side were two canal flat-boats which would carry about sixteen to twenty men each, were employed to transport the troops to the Virginia shore. From the Maryland shore to the island a rope was stretched. To this the boat was attached by a rope guy, and by means of pulling on the rope hand over hand, the boat would proceed from one side to the other, but it was very slow and laborious work, especially for the artillery, for the guns had to be dismounted. In support of this movement and to hold the enemy's attention, General Stone sent Colonel Gorman's brigade across at Edward's Ferry, where the principal force of the enemy had been seen and were still supposed to be. Himself remaining with Colonel Gorman, and placed Col. E. D. Baker in command of the movement by Harrison's Island and Ball's Bluff, under the following orders:

> HEADQUARTERS CORPS OF OBSERVATION,
> EDWARD'S FERRY, VA.,
> October 21st, 11.50.

Col. E. D. BAKER Commanding Brigade.

COLONEL: I am informed that the force of the enemy is about four thousand, all told. If you can push them, you may do so as far as to have a strong position near Leesburg, if you can keep them before you, avoiding their batteries. If they pass Leesburg and take the Gun Spring road you will not follow far, but seize the first good position to cover that road. Their design is to draw us on, if they are obliged to retreat, as far as Goose Creek, where they can be reinforced from Manassas and have a strong position. Report frequently, so that when they are pushed Gorman can come in on their flank.

Yours respectfully and truly,

CHAS. P. STONE,
Brigadier-General Commanding.

The Confederate commander, Brig.-Gen. W. G. Evans (Colonel Evans, who distinguished himself at the first Bull Run), early discovering both movements, and, having the advantage of a shorter line, concealed moreover by the nature of the ground, gradually withdrew all his forces save one regiment from Gorman's front, concentrated it against Colonel Baker, and about three o'clock P. M. attacked with vigor. Each side numbered about seventeen hundred men. Our troops had three light field pieces soon disabled, the enemy none; but their troops moved to the attack from commanding ground, well covered by trees and bushes, while ours, badly posted and badly arranged, were held to the bluff without room to retire or means of retreat. About twelve o'clock M. scouts reported to Colonel Devens that a force was gathering on his left; and about 12.30 o'clock a strong skirmish attack was made by a body of infantry concealed in the woods. The fire of the enemy was resolutely returned by the regiment, which maintained its ground with entire determination. Reinforcements not yet having arrived, and the enemy attempting to flank him, he withdrew his regiment into the open space in the woods, and prepared to receive any attack that might be made. When this was done he returned to the bluff, where he found that Colonel Baker had already arrived, and was posting his command as fast as they arrived from the island in the position he was going to occupy. Colonel Baker apprised Colonel Devens that he had been placed in command of this movement, and directed him to form his regiment on the right of the position he proposed to occupy, which was done by eight companies of the Fifteenth Massachusetts, two companies detached supporting one gun of Battery B, First Rhode Island Light

Artillery, on the left of the Seventy-first Regiment. In the centre two howitzers of Battery I, First United States Artillery were posted, supported by the Twentieth Massachusetts Regiment.

Capt. Francis J. Young, assistant quartermaster of Colonel Baker's staff, is reported as saying: "As soon as Colonel Baker received the last order of General Stone's at 11.30 A. M., he immediately sent for three regiments and a squadron of cavalry from his brigade, and proceeding to the crossing at Harrison's Island, crossed to the Virginia side without delay with Adjutant-General Harvey, ordering the troops to follow with the two howitzers of the United States battery, sending me back with an order for Colonel Cogswell to bring over the artillery and his, the Tammany regiment, Forty-second New York Infantry, which were on picket along the river at this place." It was now two o'clock P. M., and the troops were fast concentrating at the crossing on the Maryland side. Col. Milton Cogswell, of the Forty-second New York Regiment, says: "On arriving at the crossing I found the greatest confusion existing. No one seemed to be in charge, or any one superintending the passage of the troops, and no order was maintained in their crossing. My regiment was rapidly concentrated at the crossing, and I crossed with one company and two pieces of Battery B, First Rhode Island Light Artillery, under command of Lieut. Walter M. Bramhall* to the island, leaving verbal orders with Major Bowe, who remained in charge, to push the remainder of my regiment on as soon as possible. On landing I immediately crossed the island to make the passage of the second branch of the river, and there found still greater confusion existing than at the first landing. I pushed across and ascended the steep bluff (about seventy feet high), and reported myself to Colonel Baker. I found him near the bluff on the edge of an open field of about eight or ten acres extent, where he had formed his line with the Seventy-first Pennsylvania Regiment on the left, Twentieth Massachusetts in centre, and the Fifteenth Massachusetts Regiment on the right, with the left thrown well in front, thus forming an angle to his line. In front of the angle thus formed were posted the two howitzers.

Colonel Baker welcomed me on the field, seemed in good spirits, and very confident of a successful day. He requested me to look at his line of battle, and with him I passed along the whole front. He asked my opinion of the disposition of the troops, and I told him frankly that I deemed them very defective, as the wooded hills beyond the ravine commanded the whole so perfectly, that should they be occupied by the enemy he would be destroyed, and I advised an immediate advance of the whole force to occupy the hills, which were not then occupied by the enemy. Colonel Baker then ordered me to take charge of the artillery, but without any definite instructions as to its service, and as one gun of the Rhode Island battery had arrived upon the field it was placed on the left of the line, supported by two companies of the Fifteenth Massachusetts. About twenty minutes afterwards the hills on the left front to

* Sixth New York Battery.

which I had called his attention were occupied by the enemy's skirmishers, who immediately opened a sharp fire on our left. I immediately ordered the artillery to open fire on those skirmishers, but soon perceived that the fire was ineffectual, as the enemy was under cover of the trees, shooting down the gunners at easy musket range. Soon Lieutenant Bramhall and nearly all the artillerymen had been shot down, and the piece was worked for a time by Colonel Baker and Captains Harvey, and Stewart, of his staff, Captain Bartlett, of the Twentieth Massachusetts, and others. Leaving the gun Colonel Baker went to the right of the line. Leaving the howitzers I proceeded to the extreme left, as I saw the whole strength of the enemy was being thrown on this point, where I found Lieutenant-Colonel Wistar had been badly wounded, and that the left wing, without a commander, was becoming disorganized. I then ordered Captain Markoe, of the Seventy-first Pennsylvania Regiment, to move his company to the left, and hold on at all hazards. He moved as directed, engaged the enemy, and held his ground for some time, but could gain no advantage, for by this time the hills on our left front were fully occupied by the enemy. Two companies of my regiment, under Captain Alden, had now arrived on the field, cheering most heartily, and with this fresh force we pushed the enemy some few rods back, but they had obtained too strong possession of the hills to be dislodged. An unequal contest was maintained for about half an hour, when Captain Harvey, assistant adjutant-general, reported to me that Colonel Baker having been killed (he was going from the right of the line to the left, passed in front of the line, when he was instantly killed by the fire of the enemy's sharp-shooters), I was in command of the field, and that a council of war was being held by the remaining colonels. I repaired to the point occupied by Colonels Lee and Deveus, and found that they had decided on making a retreat. I informed them I was in command of the field, and that a retreat across the river was impossible, and the only movement to be made was to try to cut our way through to Edward's Ferry, and that a column of attack must be at once formed for that purpose. At the same time I directed Captain Harvey, assistant adjutant general, to form the whole force into column of attack, faced to the left. Having given these orders, I proceeded to the front, and, finding our lines pressed severely, I ordered an advance of the whole force on the right of the enemy's line. I was followed by the remnant of my regiment and a portion of the California regiment, but, for some reasons unknown to me, was not joined by either the Fifteenth or the Twentieth Massachusetts regiments. We were overpowered and forced back, and driven from our position to the river bank by overwhelming numbers. On the river bank I found the whole force in a state of great disorder. As I arrived two more companies (the last of my regiment), under Captains Geretz and O'Meara, had just landed. I ordered these fresh companies up the bluff, to deploy as skirmishers to cover the passage to the island, while I took a few men and moved to the left to check a heavy fire of the enemy which had opened on us from the mouth of the ravine. We were almost immediately surrounded and captured.

This took place shortly after dark. Colonel Cogswell says in conclusion: "I deem it my duty as commander of the field during the last part of the engagement to state my convictions as to the principal cause of the untoward results of the day: First. The transportation of troops across the two branches of the river was in no way guarded or organized. There were no guards at any of the landings. No boats' crews had been detailed, and each command as it arrived was obliged to organize its own. No guns were placed in position, either on the Maryland side or on the island, to protect the passage, although several pieces were disposable on the shore at the landing. Had the full capacity of the boats been employed, with boats' crews, more than twice as many men might have crossed in the time to take part in the action. Second. The disposition on the field was faulty, according to my judgment. For the hills across the ravine commanded the whole open field."

The final effect of not looking after the boat service was seen in the presence of fifteen companies of infantry (the Nineteenth Massachusetts and part of the Forty-second New York) at Harrison's Island on their way to the scene of action at the moment of defeat. This error, like the others, was the result of Colonel Baker's inexperience. No one ever sought to blame him. But with the cry of grief that went up all over the land at the untimely death of the brave and eloquent Baker, who had left the Senate to take the field, was mingled the cry of rage of a few men among his personal followers. They filled the public ear with misrepresentations, to which General Stone and his officers, restrained by discipline, were unable to reply. The whole blame was at once thrown upon General Stone, though not, indeed, by those who knew the facts and were capable of judging.

The following extract denotes the substance of such irresponsible accusations against him as reached the public at the time:

"Feb. 9, 1862. Brig.-Gen. Charles P. Stone was arrested in Washington this morning, at two o'clock, by a posse of the provost marshal's force, was sent to Fort Lafayette, New York harbor. The charges against him are: First. For misbehavior at the battle of Ball's Bluff. Second. For holding correspondence with the enemy before and since the battle of Ball's Bluff, and of receiving visits from rebel officers in his camp. Third. For treacherously suffering the enemy to build a fort or strong works since the battle of Ball's Bluff, under his guns without molestation. Fourth. For a treacherous design to expose his force to capture and destruction by the enemy, under a pretence of orders for a movement from the commanding general, which had not been given. These charges were never proven by a court-martial."

But a few days after Stone's examination by a committee on the charges, the missing link was supplied by a surprising occurrence. A negro refugee came into Gen. W. W. Burns's lines from Leesburg, with a vague and utterly groundless story of mysterious flags of truce and how much the Confederates thought of their friend Stone. When this was reported to the War Department, Secretary Stanton immediately ordered his arrest, and Stone's ruin was accomplished. He was in May,

1863, restored to duty upon the earnest request of General Banks, commanding the Department of the Gulf, and was ordered to report to him. General McClellan applied for him in vain.

General Hooker's first act on taking command of the Army of the Potomac was to ask for him as chief of staff. He reported to General Banks during the siege of Port Hudson, and rendered valuable service, though without assignment. Immediately afterwards General Banks appointed him chief of staff, and he served in this capacity until April, 1864. He was, by orders issued at Washington, deprived of his commission as brigader-general of volunteers, and ordered to "report by letter" as colonel of the Fourteenth U. S. Infantry, his old command.

In August, 1864, Lieutenant-General Grant assigned him to the command of a brigade in the Fifth Army Corps. A month later, worn out at last by the strain of the unmerited suffering he had so long endured in silence, he resigned; and thus it was that this most gallant, accomplished and faithful soldier was, upon no charges, without a hearing, upon "evidence" upon which to condemn, endured a long and rigorous imprisonment, a punishment so much worse than death that in all ages men have sought death because they lacked the courage to endure it.

Private Lorenzo D. Budlong.

CHAPTER V.

BATTERY REORGANIZED—NEW GUNS—WINTER QUARTERS.

IN the afternoon of October 23d, the cannoneers were set to work washing the gun carriages and caissons, and the drivers the harnesses. Captain Vaughn visited our wounded at the hospital and reported that they were as comfortable as could be expected, and everything that could be done for their comfort had been attended to.

October 24th. The guard stationed at the pieces of the right section at Monocacy, on the lookout watching the house across the Potomac, reported that men could be seen gathering about the place, and by Lieutenant Adams's orders two shells were fired at them, one striking the house and exploding. There was a stampede of those gathered about the place. They made for the woods in the rear, and, during the rest of the day, no one could be seen there. In the afternoon Lieutenant Perry, having returned from Washington, took command of his section, and Lieutenant Adams returned to camp at Poolesville to his disabled section.

About ten o'clock that night, lights were reported to be seen moving around and about the house and barn across the river. Lieutenant Perry ordered the men to their posts and to prepare the pieces for action, and, about eleven o'clock the house and barn were riddled with shot and shell, and the barn set on fire and burned. No more signaling was seen, nor men gathering there afterwards. The only one seen about the place was an old negro, and he was not molested.

On October 25th, Lieutenant Bloodgood with the centre section went to Monocacy, and relieved the first section, and Lieutenant Perry returned with it to camp at Poolesville.

On the 26th of October, Lieutenant Adams with a detail of men, and Quartermaster-Sergeant Dyer, started for Washington, D. C., to get a gun to replace the one lost at the Battle of Balls Bluff, Va., on the 21st instant.

On the 31st, Lieutenant Bloodgood with his section returned to Poolesville camp, the battery being relieved from guard duty at the Monocacy aqueduct. Captain Vaughn having recovered from the sickness caused by over exertion in burying the dead at Ball's Bluff, drilled the men at the manual of the piece.

One day, while the battery was doing picket duty at Monocacy, the lieutenant in command of the section was standing in front of his tent cleaning his pistol and the men were lounging about camp. The guard on the lookout across the Potomac for signals reported all quiet. A steer came running down from over the hill, and, when in front of the officers' quarters, on seeing the lieutenant, stopped and faced him. Quick as a flash the lieutenant raised his pistol and fired. The steer dropped. On hearing the report of the pistol the men rushed out towards the lieutenant's quarters to see what the firing was for, and saw the steer lying on the ground kicking. Several of the men who were first upon the scene quickly took in the situation. John Arnold rushed up to the steer and cut its throat. Others took up the tarpaulin from the limber and covered it up, and, seating themselves on the tarpaulin began to deal cards around for a game. It was not many minutes after the firing of the pistol when one of the neighboring farmers came over the hill from the direction the steer came and passed the men at card playing, entered the camp and inquired if any one had seen a steer pass that way, at the same time looking about the grounds. He was told that one had been seen going in the direction of the river. He left the camp, again passing the men at card playing, going in the direction indicated, and was soon out of sight. The men then dragged the steer to the woods where it was dressed and cut up, the offal buried, and in less than thirty minutes all traces of the steer had vanished, and there only remained what was supposed to be government beef, upon which the men feasted while it lasted, not forgetting to send some of the choice cuts to the lieutenant's table.

November 1st. In the afternoon Lieutenant Adams and men returned from Washington with a ten-pounder Parrott gun and seven horses. The battery received orders to exchange their James's guns for ten-pounder Parrotts, long range rifled cast-iron guns. It is said that the James's guns are to be withdrawn from field service. To-day the battery was mustered for the months of September and October.

On Sunday, November 3d, Lieutenant Bloodgood with the centre section left camp and started for Washington, the men in good spirits and pleased with the opportunity to visit the Capitol City again.

On the 8th, Lieutenant Bloodgood returned with two new Parrott guns and caissons. The men had a very pleasant time going and returning.

November 9th. Lieutenant Perry left for Washington with the right section, and one piece and two caissons of the left section to be exchanged. It rained when they started, which was about one o'clock P. M., and just before sunset the rain came down as if the clouds had burst; then suddenly ceased, the clouds broke away and the sun appeared, shining brightly until it passed from view behind the hills. They arrived at Rockville at eight o'clock P. M., and encamped on the Fair Grounds. Here were nice sheds for the horses, and the men slept in the building erected for exhibitions. The men appreciated these dry and comfortable quarters, rather than encamp on the cold, wet ground.

At sunrise the next morning reveille was sounded, and soon everybody was busy preparing for the march. We left Rockville at eight o'clock A. M. It was a very pleasant morning, the men in fine spirits, the roads in good condition for marching, and better than the day before. We passed through Tenallytown, Georgetown, and Washington to Camp Sprague, where we arrived about three P. M., and were surprised, but pleased to find encamped in the old artillery quarters Battery F, of Rhode Island, Captain James Belger commanding. We remained at Camp Sprague until noon of the 12th, then went to the Arsenal, exchanged the James's guns, and received two brass howitzers and one Parrott gun with caissons and ammunition, and left Washington about six P. M., arriving at Rockville about midnight and encamped there until eleven o'clock the next day, when we left for Poolesville and reached there about five P. M., November 13th. We here learned the welcome news that the paymaster was at headquarters awaiting our return. The men forgot all about the fatigue of their march, and at six P. M. were formed in line and paid for the months of September and October. The 14th and 15th were cloudy, cold, and windy days. The battery was inspected by Captain Vaughn, and the gun detachments were reorganized. The right and centre sections had the four Parrotts, and the left section the two howitzers. The men were proud of their new battery.

November 16th. Had orders to move camp; packed up and moved to a grove about one and one-half miles from the village. It was a much warmer and better place for an artillery camp, and the men were kept busy, until November 23d, in building winter quarters. The drivers made a stable for the horses by setting crotched trees cut for the purpose in two rows twelve feet apart. Long poles were laid in the crotches for stringers on which short poles were laid for the roof. For the sides, poles were placed one end on the ground the other against the poles in the crotches at an angle slanting about six feet. Then the sides and top were thatched with straw, of which there was an abundance a short distance from the camp. The stable was in the form of a square of three sides, opened to the south. A floor of small trees, and cut twelve feet long, was laid side by side, then covered with dirt, and leveled off even, so as to keep the horses' feet out of the mud. It made a warm, dry and comfortable shelter from the wintry storms. The cannoneers made the quarters for the officers and men. The officers had the square or wall tent, the men had the sixteen feet diameter, round tents, called the Sibley. These were stockaded two feet high with trees cut to lengths, split and set into the ground, and then banked with earth. The tents were then placed on the top and secured. A fire-pit was dug in the centre of the enclosure, a trench running from it ten or twelve feet outside, the pit covered with flat stones, and the trench with the limbs of the trees, all covered with dirt. For the chimney, barrels or cracker boxes two or three on end, with a pole set into the ground beside them to prevent their being blown down by the storms. In this way very comfortable, warm and dry quarters were made.

About this time a generous donation of money was received by the battery from the Hon. James Y. Smith, afterwards governor of the State; and the following acknowledgment appeared in the Providence *Journal:*

NOVEMBER 19th, 1861.

ACKNOWLEDGMENT.

The undersigned, in behalf of Battery B, First Regiment Rhode Island Light Artillery, gratefully acknowledges the receipt of *Fifty Dollars* from the Hon. James Y. Smith, for hospital stores for the wounded and sick in the hospital at Poolesville, Md.

T. F. VAUGHN, *Captain Commanding.*

Sunday, November 24th. Col. Charles H. Tompkins, of the First Regiment of Rhode Island Light Artillery, visited the camp. In the afternoon the battery was inspected by him. Then we went up to the Poolesville plains, had field drill, and fired fifty-four blank cartridges; and, after a short complimentary address by the colonel, on the manner in which we drilled, and our fine appearance, we returned to camp.

November 27th. Battery A, of the Rhode Island Light Artillery Regiment, arrived, and encamped at our right in the same grove. There was another pleasant meeting of friends and acquaintances.

November 28th. This is Thanksgiving Day in Rhode Island. The people there will attend church, to praise and thank the Lord for his blessings, and bountiful provision for their spiritual welfare. How different it is with the soldiers in the field. Their tabernacle must be under the blue canopy of heaven. But in time of war, the soldier cannot choose the house or place of worship, and so the day passed, as many others before it, in drill at the manual of the piece in the forenoon, and in the afternoon field drill. In the evening the quartermaster-sergeant arrived with turkeys, our share of those which had been sent by Governor Sprague to all Rhode Island soldiers. They arrived too late for dinner. Second Lieut. Francis A. Smith, who had been sick for a long time resigned, and was discharged to-day.

November 29th. We had our turkey dinner to-day and heartily enjoyed it, and were pleased to think that we came from a state that had a governor who was so kind and thoughtful of the soldiers' welfare.

November 30th. The extra work for the men was finished to-day, camp quarters all built, and the men are proud of their camp. Nothing more to do now, only the regular routine of camp duty and drill. During the month of November the battery, if the weather permitted, was drilled twice a day either by Captain Vaughn, or the chiefs of sections. The men and horses became quite proficient in artillery field movements, the commands being given by the bugle; which, when once learned, is far better understood than when given by the word of mouth.

The proficiency of the men did credit to their instructors. Having good physical constitutions, being young, sprightly, and supple, with that intelligence of quickly understanding the duties of the different post numbers of the gun detachment, they could at the word of command or bugle call, unlimber, stand at posts in battery, then dismount gun and gun carriage, lie prone upon the ground, then arise, mount carriage, mount gun, stand at attention, at post, then load and fire—in an almost incredible short space of time,—that of one minute and thirteen seconds. And again (the men lounging about camp and tents, the horses at picket-rope), from the time the bugler sounded "Boots and saddles" call, and the command of the orderly sergeant, "Lively, now! lively!" the horses are harnessed and hitched up, cannoneers at their posts, the men of the battery are mounted and ready to leave the park for drill in one minute and twelve seconds. It was admitted by those who witnessed these performances (and there had been a great number of officers at different times), to be remarkably quick time, and well performed.

Sunday, December 1st. Captain Vaughn having sent in his resignation, turned the command over to First Lieut. Raymond H. Perry, and left for Washington, and was discharged from the service Dec. 2, 1861.

Sunday, December 8th. The battery was inspected by First Lieutenant Perry, and a number of passes to the village were given to those that made the best appearance. In the afternoon Second Lieut. G. Lyman Dwight (promoted from first sergeant of Battery A, First Regiment Rhode Island Light Artillery), came to the battery and reported for duty.

On December 13th, reveille at three o'clock A. M., caused by having received marching orders the night before. At sunrise the battery left camp, Lieutenant Perry commanding, marched to near Conrad's Ferry, and were placed in position on a high bank overlooking the canal and river, and prepared for action. It was reported that a rebel camp was in the woods across the river on the Virginia side, and there were indications that the Confederates were building a fort or earthworks, and we were to shell their camp, which we did right merrily. Battery A, Rhode Island, was also in position on our right, shelling, but seemed to have poor luck, as many of their shells dropped into the river and some on the bank, between the canal and river, among our own pickets. This fact indicated that they were using very poor ammunition or damp powder. The few rebels that could be seen, at our first fire scattered in wild confusion, ran for the woods and were soon out of sight. We fired about thirty rounds, and, receiving no reply, we ceased firing, and, after waiting and watching (as no one could be seen in the vicinity), the battery was ordered to return to camp, leaving the centre section there on guard, under command of Lieutenant Dwight, where they remained a few days and then returned to camp. First Sergt. Jacob B. Lewis, Sergt. John McCoombs, and a number of others, who had been sick for some time, were discharged for disability, and sent home to-day. Sergt. George W. Blair was promoted to first sergeant, *vice* Lewis, discharged.

On Sunday, December 15th, the following promotions were made: Private John E. Wardlow, to first duty sergeant; Sergt. Charles H. Adams, to second duty sergeant; Corp. Sylvester G. Ide, to third duty sergeant; Corp. Richard H. Gallup, to fourth duty sergeant; Sergt. John T. Blake, to fifth duty sergeant; Corp. Charles A. Libbey, to sixth duty sergeant. The following privates were promoted to corporals: Albert Straight, Robert A. Laird, Morris Carmichael, Ziba C. Thayer, and William Jones.

December 16th. The centre section returned to camp from picket duty near Conrad's Ferry.

December 18th. As the battery was preparing for the regular afternoon field drill, Lieutenant Perry on receiving orders from headquarters, dispatched the right section under Lieutenant Adams to the river for picket duty. The rest of the battery, under Lieutenant Perry, went up to the Plains for drill. The right section went down the river to Conrad's Ferry, then moved down along the bank about a quarter of a mile below the place where the troops crossed to Harrison's Island at the time of the battle of Ball's Bluff, and took position in battery on a high bluff overlooking the Potomac, which commands the Virginia side for quite a distance, and immediately prepared for action. Quite a force of rebels could be seen at work on what looked to be, a fort or large earthworks, which they had commenced to build during the night before, and had been steadily working on the same all the morning. As soon as the section was placed in position, Lieutenant Adams gave orders to shell the works with spherical case. For fifteen minutes the rebel earthworks were rapidly shelled, and at times a solid shot was fired. After firing some forty rounds orders were given to cease firing, and when the smoke cleared away no one could be seen about the earthworks. After remaining in position for two hours and receiving no reply from the rebels, it was concluded that they had no artillery over there, and Lieutenant Adams received orders to withdraw from the river bank and move back near the camp of the infantry pickets, (the Ninth New York Regiment), bivouacked for the night, and made a rousing fire for protection from the raw, cold wintry wind. The next morning, December 19th, the guns were again placed in position on the bluff, in rear of the locality they had occupied the day before, and a guard was stationed with them as a lookout, to report any gathering of the rebels at the fort they were endeavoring to construct the day before. By Lieutenant Adams's orders the drivers built a barricade of trees, limbs and straw for the protection of the horses, as a cold, strong wind was blowing. The cannoneers constructed huts of the same material, and, by building a fire in front of them, they managed to keep quite comfortable.

On the morning of December 25th, Lieutenant Adams, with the drivers and their horses, went up to the camp at Poolesville, leaving Sergeant Wardlow in charge of the section. On Lieutenant Adams's return, there came with him two men with a mess kettle of beer, the sight of this made the men smile. When it was served to them they drank to the health of their officers, and thanked them for their Christmas treat. The men appreciated the kindness shown them, by their orderly behavior during the remainder of the day. As everything was quiet on the Potomac, Lieutenant Adams went up to Poolesville camp just before dusk.

While the right section was on picket duty at the river below Conrad's Ferry, the other two sections of the battery remained in camp, and drilled when the weather would permit, and, for a change from the monotonous camp duties and drills, the officers decided to allow the men to have a grand celebration on Christmas day. Several large loads of wood were brought into camp. A goodly supply of apples, with other vegatables, had been received from the Sanitary Commission of Rhode Island the day before. Some turkeys, geese, and a few Maryland rabbits (pigs) had been secured from the neighboring farmers. Quartermaster-sergeant Dyer, by the officers orders, procured a small barrel of beer. Just after retreat roll call the feast which had been prepared by the cooks was served, after which the barrel of beer was tapped, and the celebration began. At dusk a large bon-fire was lighted to enliven the occasion.

In the midst of the enjoyment, Lieutenant Adams went to the quarters of the left section, and, in a loud voice, called for "Reckless." This was a nick-name given to one of the men of that section, H. A. G—. First Sergeant Blair reported that he was on guard. "Have him relieved and report to headquarters with his violin," said the lieutenant. "Reckless" was relieved, and, with his violin reported to the officers' quarters, and for hours jigs, reels, hornpipes, and break-downs, were in order. James A. Sweet and others gave a fine exhibition of their skill in dancing "On the Green."

Taps were not sounded until a late hour, and it was admitted by all, that they had had a grand time, and the men, with one or two exceptions, did not abuse the privileges which had been extended them on this occasion of their first Christmas in "My Maryland."

December 31st. For the past few days our infantry under the instruction of an engineer have been very busy building a fort on a hill to the left of our station. As the fort across the river still continues to progress, the work being done by the rebels during the night, our troops also are building one to compete with it. No work is done by the rebels during the day, for if they attempt to do so we soon make it hot for them by our shells, which are sent over as a challenge to return the compliment, but they have not as yet returned our fire.

The Virginia side of the river is now picketed by the rebel infantry, and at times a squad of their cavalry can be seen. There is no firing of the infantry pickets, but at times the rebels will shout and ask, "Who's you ones over thar!" Our men would answer, "Two Hundred and Nineteenth Massachusetts" for the Nineteenth Massachusetts Regiment, and so on, not giving the right number. In answer to our pickets who would inquire where they were from, they would say, "Who's we! why, the Seventeenth Mississippi," giving their correct number, they not having caught on to the little game of the Yankees of increasing numbers.

At night the usual word was passed along our lines of "All quiet along the Potomac." And so ends the year of 1861,—All is quiet.

Christmas week in the South, is generally observed as a holiday by the colored population. During Christmas week of 1861, there was a wedding on the plantation of Mr. Smoot, near Conrad's Ferry. The happy couple were slaves that belonged to Mr. Smoot. On the day of the event, there was a general gathering of the colored people from far and near, old and young, great and small. A number of the men of Battery B who were not on duty went to witness the ceremony. Among the number was "Reckless," who, was met by others on their way to the plantation, as he was returning from camp with his violin. There was an old negro, who seemed to be master of ceremonies, having very much to say and strutted around among his people like a lord. He carried a violin, and, judging by its looks, it must have been quite aged, or very much the worse for wear. After the marriage ceremony was concluded there was a celebration, consisting of singing and dancing. It had not proceeded far, before the old negro spied "Reckless" and his violin, and would not take no for an answer to his invitation to join in the celebration. Then when "Reckless" struck up a jig, which the old negro tried to follow on his fiddle, the dancers (the negroes) acted as if they would shake themselves to pieces. The negroes had an exciting time, which they kept up all that night, and a portion of the next day.

Jan. 1, 1862. Our first New Year's day in the service of our country was made pleasant by bright and sunshiny weather. In most of the regiments of the brigade, as well as the batteries, the customary drills were omitted, and the men were permitted a holiday; passes were given to visit within the division line, and a number of the men of our battery went up to the village (Poolesville), as there were a number of sutlers located there. To-day Private Henry W. Bromley was appointed acting corporal.

On Sunday, January 5th, Col. Charles H. Tompkins, of the First Regiment Rhode Island Light Artillery, paid a visit to the officers. He also inspected the battery and camp, and, in the afternoon, with Lieutenant Perry, visited the right section near Conrad's Ferry. Isaac W. Slack was transferred and left to-day.

January 6th. James A. Sweet was promoted to wheelwright, vice Slack, transferred.

January 11th. The left section gun detachments, under Lieutenant Bloodgood, went to Conrad's Ferry and relieved the first section, which returned to Poolesville camp. Their guns were left in position, as it was too muddy to move them, and were taken in charge by the men of the left section.

Yesterday evening Battery G, First Regiment Rhode Island Light Artillery, Capt. Charles D. Owen, commanding, reached this place bringing several well-known friends, who returned our greeting. As it passed our park their twenty-pounders seemed to smile scornfully on our ten-pounders and howitzers; but they need not have done so, for were they not all in the family? indeed, it might have been naught but stately recognition, for iron faces are proverbially inexpressive. The battery bivouacked in the woods to our right at the camp lately occupied by Battery A. They subsequently occupied the fort near our picket station below Conrad's Ferry.

Capt. Walter O. Bartlett.

January 13th. The weather for the past few days has been raw and cold, the snow covering the ground to the depth of two inches. The water also has frozen an inch thick. The snow and ice have most effectually locked the wheels of our pieces and caissons, rendering field drills impossible, and even the "manual of the piece" is but a clumsy attempt at "movements most precise;" therefore drill has been suspended, and we have passed five months of military service; yet to-day, as the result of industry and laborious training, we occupy no second rank in the volunteer arm of the service; and, with the spirit that pervades the young men of the Rhode Island batteries, each month will witness greater proficiency. Comparisons are neither necessary nor always in good taste. To boast of superiority would be folly, as to depreciate the truth would be a violation of self-respect. We hear many pleasant things said of us by friends, which are received as incentives to merit their favorable opinions.

On the afternoon of January 21st, we received the welcome news that Uncle Sam's paymaster was at division headquarters, and that the battery would be paid before he returned to Washington. Just before noon on the 22d he came to our camp. The men were formed in line by First Sergeant Blair, marched to the officers' quarters, and, as each man's name was called, he signed the muster roll, and then received from the paymaster twenty-six dollars for the months of November and December, 1861. The cannoneers of the centre section were paid first, and, under command of Lieutenant Dwight, went to Cornad's Ferry, to relieve the left section, who returned to the camp, and were also paid, the paymaster waiting for that purpose.

January 31st. Late in the afternoon Capt. Walter O. Bartlett (promoted from first lieutenant of Battery E, First Regiment Rhode Island Light Artillery,) arrived. He is to have command of our battery.

February 1st. After camp and battery inspection, Captain Bartlett was introduced, by Lieutenant Perry, as our new commander, after which the captain, and Lieutenant Perry went to visit the centre section at their picket station below Conrad's Ferry.

Sunday, February 2d. Lieutenant Perry went to Washington, having a ten days' leave of absence.

February 3d. Lieutenant Adams, with the right section, relieved the centre section, and it came to camp.

February 10th. The centre section, under Lieutenant Bloodgood, relieved the right section, and returned to camp. As they left the station the rebels could be seen in force, gathered about their earthworks, and a squad of their cavalry was discovered in the edge of the woods, upon which the centre section opened fire. A few shots were also fired from our fort, the rebels dispersed, and "all was quiet again on the Potomac."

On February 13th Lieutenant Perry returned and took command of his section, the right; Lieutenant Bloodgood, the centre; Lieutenant Adams, the left; and Lieutenant Dwight as chief of caissons. Captain Bartlett commanded the battery. Thus we were now fully officered again.

On February 23d the men of the battery received new clothing, which were issued to those that were in need of any pants, shirts, drawers, socks, or hats.

February 24th the right section, under Lieutenant Perry, relieved the centre section at the river. These frequent changes were made, it was said, for the benefit, comfort, and welfare of the men; as picket duty is not always a pleasant one to perform, especially in winter weather. At noon the battery received marching orders, and Captain Bartlett at once dispatched orders for the right section to return to Poolesville with all of their equipage. Drivers with their horses were sent down for the pieces, and the section soon returned to camp. The cooks were given orders to prepare three days' cooked rations for the men. Many rumors were circulated around the camp as to the nature of these orders. One was that we were going to Washington, then to Manassas, Va. To what point an advance was to be made, could only be surmised, but the orders were obeyed with alacrity; for, however strong their admiration of Poolesville, with Camp Perry and its surroundings, the men were anxious for something more lively than camp life afforded, and welcomed a change that gave promise of a hand in putting secession *hors de combat.*

February 25th. Reveille at sunrise. Breakfast was served early, and, while the cannoneers were packing camp equipage, the drivers took the horses to the brook to water. Three days' rations of grain were packed on the caissons. Three days' rations of cooked salt beef and hard bread were issued to the men to be carried in the haversacks. The tents were struck and packed. These, with the supplies and camp equipage, that could not be carried, were placed in a barn, to be forwarded to us. They were subsequently sent to Washington and never received by the battery. At noon "boots and saddles" call sounded, the battery was soon hitched up, and a formal farewell bidden to our old encampment, as we moved out towards the village of Poolesville.

Sergt. Pardon S. Walker.

CHAPTER VI.

MARCH TO HARPER'S FERRY, BOLIVAR AND WINCHESTER. TO THE SUPPORT OF GENERAL BANKS IN THE VALLEY—RETURN TO WASHINGTON.

IN regard to the opening of the Baltimore and Ohio Railroad along the upper Potomac, General Banks's division was sent to occupy the Shenandoah Valley to Winchester, and the old division of General Stone was sent forward to coöperate with him. The combined forces were thought strong enough to resist any attack by the Confederates, then at Manassas. The division left Camp Observation on the morning of Feb. 25, 1862. Battery B, following, the troops passed through Poolesville, and Barnseville and bivouacked for the night on rising ground, at the foot of Sugar Loaf Mountain. The night being cold, raw, and windy, the men were allowed to build fires. These were kept burning all night by those who were on guard. Around the fires the men slept on the ground rolled up in their blankets. Doubtless some dreamed of their comfortable quarters and camp at Poolesville, others, of friends and loved ones at home, and as morning dawned awoke to realize the stern realities of a soldier's life with all its privations.

February 26th. About nine A. M. the battery started on a slow, hard, and tedious march to cross over the mountain, and at some places five or six pairs of horses had to be used, to a piece and caisson, before it could be moved along on account of the mud (for it had begun to rain), and the steepness of the road, with a great deal of difficulty. After severe labor we succeeded in going over the mountain, passing through Greenfield Mills, and Three Spring Mills, small villages. We continued our march onward, and arrived at Adamstown, Md., in the afternoon and halted for the night, the men quartered in a barn, a more comfortable place than some of the troops had who were compelled to encamp on the cold, wet ground.

February 27th. The roads were in such a bad condition, that the battery was ordered to the railroad depot, loaded the guns and ammunition chests aboard the cars, and, with the cannoneers, went to Sandy Hook by rail. The drivers, with the gun and caisson carriages, battery wagons and forge, went with the horses, by a country road to within three-quarters of a mile of the village and encamped for the night.

February 28th. The guns and ammunition chests were mounted again, and the battery crossed the Potomac River from Sandy Hook, Md., to Harper's Ferry, Va., on a pontoon bridge which had been built for the purpose. Everything about the place plainly showed the work of destruction and desolation. The government armory, the arsenal, and the factory for the manufactory of small arms, were in a heap of ruins.

The battery passed on through the village, up High Street, to Bolivar Heights, to the grounds and mansion lately occupied by Alfred M. Barbour, ex-civil superintendent of the United States government works at Harper's Ferry (then a brigadier-general in the Confederate army). Here we encamped. The men occupied the house, their horses the barn and out-buildings of the negroes on the place. The guns were parked on the lawn in front of the house. Here the battery remained until the advance move to Winchester. While here the battery received the following recruits from Rhode Island: Patrick Brady, John F. Craven, Daniel Capron, John Greene, Joseph Luther and William B. Wood. A number of men were also discharged for disability. While here the men enjoyed visiting the ruins and the dismantled buildings of the quaint old town, especially the old engine house, or John Brown's fort, as it is sometimes called, and in which he was captured.

March 1st. Corp. Leanord J. Whiting transfered from Battery C, First Regiment Rhode Island Light Artillery.

March 2d. Was to-day appointed sergeant, *vice* Sylvester G. Ide, reduced for breach of discipline.

March 3d. Private William A. Dickerson promoted to corporal, *vice* Whiting promoted.

March 8th. The first section under Lieutenant Perry, went up on Loudoun Heights for picket duty, while a squadron of cavalry was to make a reconnoissance in the direction of Snicker's Gap, and Leesburg.

The bridge across the Shenandoah River, had been destroyed at the same time as the one across the Potomac, when the rebels withdrew from Harper's Ferry to Winchester, June 13, 1861. The means for crossing was by a canal flat-boat. A large rope was stretched from shore to shore, with a block and running tackle at each end of the boat attached to the rope. The rapid running current of the water was the power used, and when ready to move forward the crew that worked it would draw up the forward tackle close to the rope, and let the rear tackle out until the boat was about an angle of forty-five degrees with the rope. A push was given by those on shore and away it would go, the pressure of the current against the side of the boat would cause it to move slowly at the start, but would gradually increase in speed until the opposite shore was reached. To return, the opposite end of the boat was drawn up, the other let out, and the current did the rest. In this way the section was ferried across the river. Then commenced a laborious task, the ascent up a road cut into the mountain side, which wound zigzag around to the top. The passage up was a hard one for both horses and men, twelve horses to a gun, the men ready with a large stone to block the wheels when a rest was made, which was quite often. When the top was reached it was on the opposite side from where they started. At the top a space of a few rods square, was clear of trees and bushes where a small fort had been built, but no troops in or around it. In this fort the guns were placed in position, which commanded the Loudoun valley. From this fort our guns could throw a shot five miles in any direction. From this place a magnificent view of the surrounding country could be obtained. To the south the Loudoun valley, on the west the renowned valley of the Shenandoah, to the north the valley of the upper Potomac river, to the east and below, the Maryland Heights with Frederick city in the distance. The view from these heights was magnificent beyond description, the grandest at sunrise. As the sun appeared above the Maryland Heights, its rays leaping from mountain top to mountain top, it had the appearance of a large golden flower, while the valley below lay dark and silent. The section did not stay here long, for the next afternoon, March 9th, it was ordered to return to camp at Bolivar, as the division had received orders to prepare for a move.

 Lieutenant Perry decided to attempt the descent down the mountain side, instead of the roundabout way by which they had ascended. So he ordered the wheels secured by the chain and prolonge (a rope used for dragging the gun when firing to the rear), and let them slide down, as the horses could not hold them back. even after the wheels were thus secured. The hubs were brought up against a tree, and then with a lever, the men would pry it off and it would slide to another tree; in this manner they were let down the mountain side. It was a very difficult and dangerous undertaking, but a much shorter distance to the ferry than by the road.

The only mishap that occurred was, while on the boat crossing the Shenandoah, when one of the men fell overboard and would have been lost but for the timely aid of a comrade standing near, who, by reaching over caught him by the hair as he was about to go under, and, with assistance, succeeded in pulling him on board again,—a more frightened man one never saw. The section arrived in camp at Bolivar Heights a little after dark, and found the battery prepared to move in the morning on a recounaissance towards Winchester.

March 10th. The battery left camp at nine A. M. passed through Halltown, three miles from Bolivar, and encamped at Charlestown. eight miles from Harper's Ferry, at four P. M. Pleasant and warm.

March 11th. The battery left Charlestown about eight A. M., Rickett's battery and a regiment of the United States Regulars with us. Passed through Berryville, turned to the right, and went into camp a little after four P. M. Remained here until the 13th. Left Berryville about nine A. M. for Winchester, went to within three miles of the village and halted in a field on the left of the road. Tarried here a short time, then received orders to return, arriving at Berryville about six P. M., and encamped in the same position that we had occupied on the 11th.

March 14th. Cloudy and chilly. Left for Charlestown about nine A. M. On arriving there went into camp at the same place as on the night of the 10th.

March 15th left for Bolivar about eight A. M., arrived there about two P. M., and went into camp at our old quarters, much to the gratification of the men, for all were wet through, as a cold rain-storm had set in that morning soon after we had started on the march.

We are becoming accustomed to army life now, whether in camp or on the march. Since the battery left the camp at Poolesville, there has been a great deal of rainy weather, and we have marched nearly one hundred miles, and yet, after all, are only about thirty-three miles from our late winter quarters. In the foregoing movement the brigade to which the battery was attached was in reserve as a support to the main troops in advance. As the rebels did not make a stand, there was no battle, and the battery did not become engaged.

The battery remained encamped at Bolivar Heights until March 22d, when it was ordered to Washington with other troops of the division. At noon of the 22d, broke camp and started on our return, passing through Bolivar, and Harper's Ferry taking the same route we did in February, recrossing the Potomac by the pontoon bridge to Sandy Hook. Here again the guns were dismounted, and, with the ammunition chests, were put aboard the cars, the officers and cannoneers going with them by rail to Washington, where they arrived the next day at noon, were taken to the Soldiers' Retreat, and given a good dinner, to which all did ample justice. After their repast they returned to the cars, unloaded the guns and the ammunition chests, leaving them upon the platform at the station under guard. The men were then marched to Capitol Hill, where they went into camp on the night of the 23d.

The sergeants, with the drivers and their horses, gun and caisson carriages, battery wagon, forge and baggage wagons, under the charge of Lieutenant Adams, marched from Sandy Hook to Catoctin Creek, near Berlin, and bivouacked for the night. On the morning of the 23d they resumed the march until four o'clock P. M., when they halted and encamped for the night by Ceneca Creek, a very small stream. On the morning of the 24th they again resumed the march onward, passing through Rockville and Georgetown, arriving in Washington late in the afternoon, and joined the rest of the battery at their camp on Capitol Hill. The First Rhode Island Cavalry were encamped near by, and as they had just arrived in Washington from Rhode Island, the men were asked many questions about Providence and friends.

On the morning of March 25th Lieutenant Perry, with the drivers and cannoneers, gun and caisson carriages, went to the Baltimore and Ohio Railroad station, and, mounting the guns and ammunition chests, returned to camp.

March 26th. The following privates were promoted to corporals, they having acted in that capacity for some time: William Hamilton, Anthony B. Horton, and William P. Wells. The vacancies were occasioned by a number of non-commissioned officers being in the hospital sick, who had been reduced to the ranks.

March 27th. To-day the battery received marching orders. The equipments were packed and everything got in readiness to move at a moment's notice. In the afternoon eleven recruits arrived from Rhode Island: Thomas J. Barber, Hazard W. Burton, Joseph C. Burton, Erastus D. Briggs, Aborn W. Carter, John H. Clarke, William O. Clark, Harvey Pearce, William H. Pearce, Francis T. Priestly, and Jerome Weeks.

At four o'clock P. M. the battery was hitched up and broke camp: left Capitol Hill and moved down by way of Pennsylvania avenue, marching through the city to Georgetown, down to the wharf by the Potomac, where the battery was parked, and remained all night under guard. The men were quartered in a vacant store at the head of the wharf, where we had a good night's rest. Rumor had it that we were going to the Peninsula, what one we knew not, although several places had been mentioned. But this much we did know, that to whatever place we were ordered we were going by water instead of land, as the division to which we were attached was embarking on transports from the wharf where our guns were parked.

While the commander of the Army of the Potomac was preparing his spring campaign of 1862, the soldiers were learning stern discipline, by constant drill, and frequent inspections in the art of war. These preparations conveyed to them a hint, as some of the men expressed it, that "some one higher in power was punching them to punch us." But the frequent moves and long marches had changed the routine of camp life and duties, there was not so much polishing and drill. But instead there was an unusual activity upon the Potomac, in front of the cities of Washington and Georgetown. Every description of water conveyance, from a canal flat-boat to a huge three-decked steamer, seemed to have been pressed into service, and loaded with soldiers, horses, rations, bales of hay and other munitions for the army, sailed majestically down the broad river.

When the troops received marching orders, every one was busy preparing for a move, and also conjecturing as to our destination. The private soldier is not taken into the confidence of his superiors, but is usually left in ignorance as to his fate. But rumor, with her thousand tongues, is always speaking. So what the soldier lacks in information is usually made up in surmises and conjectures; every hint is caught at, and worked out in all possible and impossible combinations. He makes some shrewd guesses (the Yankee's birthright), but he knows absolutely nothing of the part he is to perform in some great or little plan of the army to which he is attached. How the report is received or whence it comes he knows not, but it is rumored there is to be a move.

The general opinion among the troops at that time was that at last a movement was in progress, and that they were on their way to make an end of the Confederacy. They gathered in squads upon the decks of the steamers. Here and there were card parties, others slept or dozed. But the majority were smoking and discussing the probabilities of their destination, about which they really knew nothing, except that they were sailing down the Potomac River.

Private William F. Reynolds.

CHAPTER VII.

DEPARTURE FOR THE PENINSULA, AND SIEGE OF YORKTOWN.

ON the 28th of March, the battery was dismounted and put on board of the propeller *Empire*, also the battery wagon, forge, and baggage wagons, with other munitions of war. After the officers and cannoneers had embarked the propeller moved out into the stream, headed down the river, leaving the drivers with their horses on the wharf, under the command of Lieut. George W. Adams. Here they remained all night as no boat came for them.

Late in the forenoon of the next day a tug-boat with a schooner in tow, ran alongside of the wharf, and, after it had been made fast to the dock, the work of getting the horses on board commenced. It was late in the afternoon before it was accomplished as there was some delay in getting transports enough to take the horses. After all had embarked, there was another delay; when the tug-boats came to take us in tow, the captain on being informed that there was no captain on board one of the schooners, asked for the mate; we told him he was up in the village looking for the captain. After waiting over an hour the captain of the tug-boat became impatient and would wait no longer. "Well," said he, "captain or no captain, I am going to take the schooner to Alexandria, as ordered," and asked if there was anyone on board who would take the helm. He was told that one of our men was an old sailor and probably he would steer. "Where is he?" said the captain. On being questioned, our man said: "Yes, I can steer, I'll take the helm." So our ex-sergeant was placed in charge of the wheel. The tug-boat, made fast to the schooner, pulled out from the wharf, and, taking the other schooner in tow, started down the Potomac. All went well until we were nearing Long Bridge. The tug-boat had entered the draw and was passing through when the captain saw that the schooner was not following in line and headed right, so shouted to our helmsman, "Schooner, hard a port!" "Aye, aye, sir!" answered the helmsman, and around spun the wheel, the schooner swinging to the right. "Hard to port, there! Look lively!" again shouted the captain of the tugboat. Nearer, and nearer the schooner was approaching the bridge. The captain became wild, throwing up his hands and shouting "Hard a—" the rest being lost, as there came a bump and a crash, the schooner striking the abutment of the draw on the starboard bow. Our helmsman was turning the wheel, first one way and then the other, as if bewildered. The schooner, after striking, crossed the opening. On the way through it struck the abutment of the bridge on the port bow, but kept on, amid flying timbers and splinters. The captain of the tug-boat, seeing that there was to be an accident, had let his tow adrift, or the strain on the tow-line was so great that it parted. The tug-boat proceeded on its way down the river, the schooners following slowly, being kept in motion by the current, and sustaining no damage by the collision. Not so with the bridge, however, for the draw was thrown out of line, and part of one of the abutments carried away, so that the draw could not be closed to admit of passage over it. A general who was waiting, with his staff, on the Virginia side, to cross to Washington, was made wild by the accident, and imprecations loud and deep greeted us as we sailed by. The captain and mate of the schooner, who had procured a boat, now overtook us, came on board, the captain taking command, the tug-boat returned, made fast, and taking us in tow again proceeded to Alexandria. Our sailor boy was relieved of the helm. He had shown his ability to steer, with a record that not many could boast—that of carrying away two ends of a draw-bridge at one time, and he never heard the last of "Hard to port" while he remained with the battery.

While waiting at Alexandria, our hearts were gladdened by the sight of the *Canonicus* (a steamboat from Providence, R. I.) as she lay quietly on the bosom of the Potomac. It brought up pleasant visions of Rocky Point, Portsmouth Grove and Newport, only to give place, however, to the stern realities of war.

Alexandria looks dilapidated, and the objects of interest are few. The Marshall House, where Colonel Ellsworth was shot, has nothing inviting in its external appearance, while its internal parts are disappearing by piecemeal, through the industry of relic gatherers.

Many private dwellings belonging to absentee Secessionists are closed or occupied as officers' quarters. The old church, built at an early date of imported brick, and in which Washington worshiped, occupies a somewhat retired spot, and is surrounded by a high fence. It is said that his pew, prayer-book, cushions, etc., remain as they were when he last attended services. This I cannot vouch for, not being permitted to investigate for myself. The large hotels were converted into general hospitals for the sick and wounded soldiers. The buildings along the water front near the wharf were occupied by troops waiting transportation. The Potomac, in front of and above Alexandria, is full of transports, yet not in sufficient number to embark the entire force. This caused some delay, and subjected those troops, who were deprived of camping accommodations, to temporary inconvenience, a "soldier's lot."

On the morning of March 30th, about three A. M., we weighed anchor, and, with the schooners in tow, the propeller *Putnam* steamed down the Potomac. Without regret we turned our backs upon a city whose flour has a better reputation than its loyalty, and set our faces toward our future field of service. Passing Fort Washington on our left, we soon reached Mount Vernon, which is situated on the right bank of the river. The wise counsels of Washington in his farewell address were brought impressively to mind. Sadly has Virginia fallen from her first estate, and bitterly will she yet mourn the folly into which she was betrayed by unscrupulous and ambitious leaders.

The passage down the Potomac and Chesapeake Bay was not distinguished by any extraordinary occurrence. The rebel batteries on the banks of the river and bay were silent, and we passed them without any sign of recognition. They were abandoned, and navigation of the river was once more free, resulting from the fact of the possession of Manassas by the Union forces.

Just before entering Chesapeake Bay we came to anchor, the water, being rough, it caused the propeller to labor so hard, with schooners in tow, that there was fear of her swamping. A snow squall struck us as we lay at anchor, then it commenced to rain and continued until midnight, when it cleared with a cold, raw wind blowing. By one o'clock A. M., it having calmed down sufficiently to venture out, we started on our way down the bay, passing Fortress Monroe, and came to anchor in Hampton Roads, a short distance from that renowned "Yankee cheese box," the *Monitor*. Looking up the river, the wreck of the battleship *Congress* could be seen off Newport News, also some smaller vessels nearer the shore, which had been destroyed by the rebel *Merrimac.*

The writer and several others, with Lieut. George W. Adams, had the pleasure of visiting the *Monitor* and examining the indentations caused by the shells of the *Merrimac* which struck her during the engagement. None of them was of a very serious nature, except the one which struck the pilot-house. The keel of this most famous vessel of modern times (Captain Ericsson's first iron-clad), was laid in the shipyard of Thomas F. Rowland, at Greenpoint, Brooklyn, N. Y., in October, 1861; and, on the 30th of January, 1862, the novel craft was launched. On the 25th of February she was commissioned and turned over to the government, and nine days later left New York for Hampton Roads, where, on the 9th of March, 1862, occurred the memorable contest with the *Merrimac.* During her next venture on the open sea she foundered off Cape Hatteras in a gale of wind, Dec. 29, 1862.

The transports with the battery on board lay at anchor in the Roads until the 2d of April, when those who were on the propeller *Empire* were landed at the wharf at Hampton, and went into camp a short distance up in the village to wait for the arrival of the rest of the battery. Three days' rations of salt beef were issued to the cooks, to be prepared for the men.

Late in the afternoon of the 3d the schooners with the remainder of the battery were towed up to the wharf and unloaded. It was near midnight before it was all in camp, and the men, tired out, were glad to roll themselves up in their blankets to get half a night's rest. It was with wonder and amazement that we, as part of General McClellan's army, arrived at Old Point Comfort and gazed upon Fortress Monroe, huge and frowning, and saw the destruction caused by the rebel *Merrimac* in and around Hampton Roads. When we landed, and pitched our tents amid the charred and blackened ruins of the once beautiful village of Hampton, we were reminded that this town until the breaking out of the Rebellion was a fashionable summer resort, but was now a heap of ruins; and the numerous stacks of chimneys stand like so many monuments of Secesh vandalism, by whose hand the place was fired.

Here Hon. John Tyler, the "Accidental President," had a residence, to which he gave the romantic name of "Margaritta Cottage." But the place has less attractions to an eye for the picturesque than the name would imply, and a writer, with as much truth as sarcasm has said, "A summer in this site would make any man a bore." One thing we noticed as we viewed the ruins, unaccustomed as we were to southern architecture, was the fact that only three of the houses had been provided with cellars.

The only building left standing was the massive old Episcopal church. Here Washington had worshiped, and its aisles had echoed to the footsteps of armed men during the Revolution. In the churchyard tombs had been broken open, tombstones overthrown, and at the corner of the church a big hole had been dug, which showed that some one, with a greater desire for possessing curiosities than reverence for ancient landmarks, had been digging for the cornerstone and its buried mementos.

Along the shore, which trends toward Fortress Monroe were landed artillery, baggage-wagons, pontoon trains and boats, piles of boxes, barrels of rations, hay and grain. The level land in the rear was covered with the tents of the army. Here and there were groups of men frying hard-tack and bacon. Near at hand was the irrepressible army mule, hitched to and eating out of pontoon boats. Those which had eaten their rations of hay and grain were trying their teeth, with promise of success, in gnawing the woodwork of the boats. An army mule is more voracious than a soldier, and will eat anything, not excepting a pontoon or rubber blanket. The red caps, white leggins, and baggy trousers of the Zouaves mingled with the blue uniforms and dark trimmings of the infantrymen, the short jackets and yellow trimmings of the cavalry, and the red stripes of the artillery, together with the ragged and many colored costumes of the white and black teamsters, all busy in preparations for an onward move of the Army of the Potomac, made the scene an enlivening one.

The morning we broke camp and went marching up the Peninsula, the roads were very muddy and nearly impassable in consequence of recent rains, and were crowded with the indescribable material of the vast army which was slowly wending its way through the mud and wooded country. It was a bright April day— a perfect Virginia day,—the buds of the trees were just unfolding into leaves under the warm sunshine of spring; a number of peach trees were in full bloom; the green grass was shooting forth (not beneath our feet as I was about to say, for they are in the mud), but in the meadows. The march was at first orderly, but under the burden of heavy equipments and knapsacks, and warmth of the weather, the men straggled along the roads, mingling with artillery, baggage wagons, ambulances, pontoon-trains and ration wagons, in seeming confusion.

On the 4th of April, Battery B, with General Sedgwick's division of the Second Corps, left Hampton about eight A. M., marched until five o'clock, and encamped near Little Bethel. Here shelter tents were issued. Previous to this time we had used our rubber blankets for tents. Each man was provided with an oblong piece of thick, unbleached cotton cloth, about six feet long, and two-thirds as wide, bordered all around with buttons and button-holes alternately, matching respectively the button-holes and buttons of his comrade's piece. A shelter or dog tent is like a bargain, it takes two to make it. To set it up, two crotched stakes, each about four feet long, pointed at one end, are driven into the ground about six feet apart. A slender pole is then placed horizontally from one crotch to the other. Then the two pieces of tents are buttoned together, and the buttoned edges placed on the pole, drawing out the other edges tightly and pinning them down to the ground, by means of little loops fastened into them. This formed a wedge-shaped structure, simply the two slopes of an ordinary roof, about three and a half feet high and open at both ends. This accommodated two men, and in warm, pleasant weather was all that was required. In stormy weather a third man was admitted, when a piece of small rope about four feet long was tied to the top of one of the stakes and stretched out in line in the direction of the ridge-pole, the free end being brought down to the ground about eighteen or twenty inches from the stake and pinned there. The third man then buttoned his piece to one edge of the slope, carrying the other edge of his piece out over the tightened rope to the edge of the other slope, to which it was buttoned. Thus an extension to the tent was made in which knapsacks were stored, leaving the rest of the space clear for sleeping purposes. This is large enough to accommodate three men lying side by side. But will such a structure keep out rain? Certainly, just as your umbrella does, unless you rub it on the inside when it is soaked. If you do, the water will come in, drop by drop just where you rub it. To keep the water from running in along the surface of the ground, dig a small trench about three inches deep all around the tent, close up, so that the water shed from the roof will fall into it. For three-fourths of the year it is all the shelter needed, as it keeps out rain, snow, and wind, perfectly, being penetrable only by the cold.

We left camp on the morning of the 5th, at seven o'clock over the New Bridge road. I should have called it "muddy road," by its appearance, if I had not been informed differently. As we marched along we were sprinkled by the frequent showers that fell upon us, which caused our knapsacks and blankets to become no lighter. We passed lines of rebel intrenchments in front of a small hamlet of about half a dozen houses, called Little Bethel. Still advancing another line of earthworks was passed, where we encountered what the natives (the negroes) called "a right smart shower." This did not improve the roads. On we trudged passing the remains of several houses scattered over an area of a third of a mile. These constituted what was called the village of Big Bethel.

Just west of the village was an insignificant building (the only one left standing) from which the hamlet takes its name. Why the prefix "Big" was used none of us could understand, as it did not seem large enough or of sufficient consequence to be given a name. But this was a church called the "Big Bethel." Before the arrival of our troops it had evidently been occupied as officers barracks of the enemy. Here the surroundings, the roads, the village, the trees, earth works, and rifle-pits, gave evidence of the battle which was here fought on June 10, 1861, between Colonel Hill's brigade of General Magruder's rebel forces, and General Peirces's brigade of Gen. Benjamin Butler's (Union troops). In which the latter were defeated with a loss of fourteen men.

On trudged the troops through mud and water, until six P. M., when General Sedgwick's division halted and was ordered to camp at Cockletown. The battery moved to the right of the road on high ground, parked, and encamped. We were about seven miles from Yorktown. Here we remained until the 13th. As the wagons with rations and forage could not be brought up on account of the troops moving to the front and using the roads in preference to army wagons, our supplies became nearly exhausted. In order to obtain them the drivers with their horses, under command of a lieutenant, with the quartermaster-sergeant, made frequent trips to Ship Point on the Poquosin River.

On the afternoon of April 5, 1862, the advance of our column was brought to a standstill at Yorktown. Here General McClellan found the enemy in force and occupying the fortifications extending to Lee's Mills on the Warwick Creek. This forced him to halt and prepare to give battle, his right of line being at Yorktown. As fast as the troops arrived he extended his line to the left toward Lee's Mills. One of the impediments to an immediate attack on the enemy was the difficulty of using light artillery in the muddy fields in front. At that time the knowledge of the country ahead was but little understood, and had to be learned by reconnaissances in force. The siege of Yorktown was now begun by bridging the streams, constructing and improving the roads for rapid transit of supplies and for the advancement of troops. The first line of fortifications was made about a mile from and parallel with the enemy's line, which reached from the York River to Warwick Creek, a distance of about four miles in length. Fourteen batteries and three redoubts were planted, armed with heavy ordnance. Number one battery was at the right of the line, not far from the York River. While the troops of General Sedgwick's division were advancing to the front and being assigned positions in line, the battery lay at Cockletown awaiting orders; and, as the roads were almost impassable for heavy laden forage wagons, we were ordered to dismount the ammunition chests of the caissons, and the drivers, with horses and the caisson carriages, under command of Lieutenant Perry with the quartermaster-sergeant, went to Ship Point for rations and forage. The men of the battery that made these trips will always remember them. It was a journey of only four miles, but it took about eleven hours of hard tramping to go and return. No country equals a Virginia road for mud after a rain. A short distance from camp we struck it thick, from ankle to knee-deep. First the off horse would get into a hole, and as soon as he was out (and some times before) the nigh horse would be in the same predicament. Then the caisson wheels would follow, going down with a splash to the hub. Verily, this was what should have been called "heavy marching" instead of "light marching" order. The foot sank insidiously into the mud, and came out reluctantly. The noise of walking was like that of a suction-pump when the water is exhausted. We finally arrived at our journey's end, and, after a rest of an hour, loaded the carriages with forage and started on our return to camp. It seemed as if the holes were more numerous than when we came. After a hard tramp we arrived, tired, cross, and ugly. After we had scraped off enough of the mud to recognize our feet, we dried our clothes by the fire while getting suppper. And such a supper,—hard-tack and coffee,—but didn't it go good, what sauce ever equaled that of hunger? Then, how we slept! Feet wet, boots for a pillow, the mud oozing up and around our rubber blankets made a soft bed withal, and we slept the sleep of tired men.

Two such trips were made with the caisson carriages, but the road from constant travelling made such deep gullies and holes that it was almost impassable for teams. The drivers were ordered to put the valise saddles on their off horses without the rest of the harness, which was to be used as pack saddles for carrying forage, and proceeded to the Point. All went well while going. Each driver rode his nigh horse and leading the other. In this way the trip was made much quicker than with the caisson carriages. The fun commenced on the return trip. The first mile was made quite well, but the constant lurching of the loads on the saddles as the horses stumbled into the mud-holes and gullies, loosened them and some went off the saddles into the mud, which caused the driver to dismount, and invariably wade around in the mud nearly knee-deep, calling forth all manner of remarks, and resulting in the use of imprecations which were anything but mild. But that would not replace the load. Finally it was fastened on, the driver would remount, and, proceeding but a few rods, the same operation would again be repeated. There was one driver whose saddle with the load turned completely round under the horse several times during the trip, it being almost impossible to keep the saddle in the proper place upon the back of the horse, and a madder man never was seen. We wore blue pants when we started on these trips, but when we returned to camp they were terra-cotta, and something less than a hundred pounds weight.

On the 11th of April an incident occurred which for a moment excited amusement, but soon assumed too serious an aspect to be classed with jokes. A huge balloon had been making daily trips skyward from General Porter's headquarters for the purpose of obtaining knowledge of the enemy's movements. At an elevation of several hundred feet, as the occupant was preparing for the usual observation, the guys, by which the balloon was held, parted, and the gaseous vehicle sailed away before the wind towards the enemy's lines. The first impulse was to laugh, as is ordinarily the case shown an unfortunate, but the next was to shout "Open the valve." But the occupant had too little respect for the Secesh to drop himself in the midst of their encampments, which he would have done had he acted upon such advice. On reaching an upper current the wind swept the balloon back over our lines, when it was seen to descend with a velocity that nothing but the exigencies of the case would have justified, and landed near our camp. Fortunately no one was injured, and still more fortunate was it that the upper current did not carry the occupant off to the capital of Virginia rebeldom. That he obtained valuable information during his aërial voyage is probable, but it is doubtful if he cared to increase his knowledge again at a similar risk. The occupant of the balloon was General Porter. The ascensions had generally been made under the supervision of Captain Allen (a Rhode Islander). It was said that Allen was absent at the time the balloon broke away, and General Porter was alone.

April 12th. The battery received one recruit from Rhode Island, Henry J. Barber.

On the 13th, battery received marching orders, and left Cockletown and moved up to within one mile from the fortifications at Yorktown, and parked in an opening in the woods, where we made a comfortable camp, in which the headquarters of the battery remained while the siege lasted, although the gun sections were often sent to the front to assist in some movement or to perform picket duty; orders to hitch up and then unhitch were of almost daily occurrence, caused mostly by false alarms.

At sunrise on the morning of the 16th the battery received orders to hitch up double-quick, which order was duly obeyed. But it was nearly seven o'clock before we were called upon, and were then ordered to the front. The right and centre sections, under Lieutenants Perry and Bloodgood with Captain Bartlett, were ordered to the left and front. The left section (the howitzers), under Lieutenant Adams, was ordered to the right and front. The right and centre sections, going to the left about a mile to within three-quarters of a mile of the enemy's line, halted at the edge of a strip of woods. Here the centre section remained while the right proceeded through the woods to within nine hundred yards of the enemy's line. On taking position they immediately opened fire on a fort in their front. Our fire was soon answered by the rebels in the fort sending a few shells over our heads in among the tree tops, much to the discomfort of the lookouts stationed there. The centre section soon joined the right, taking position on the left. The two sections now opened a well directed fire on the fort with solid shot and some shells, which the enemy answered seemingly with wild confusion, for their shot and shells, much to our satisfaction, went over our heads into the woods.

During this engagement the gunners and cannoneers showed great skill and good judgment in handling and sighting the guns, for about every shot told, and a number of our shells exploded within the fort. At one time just as the enemy were in the act of running their gun out to fire upon us, two of our shots entered the embrasure at the same time, striking the gun; one exploded, it being a shell, the gun was dismounted, and there were no more shots fired from that embrasure during the remainder of that day. At dusk Captain Bartlett withdrew the centre section, and it returned to camp, leaving the right on picket. The proficiency of the batterymen in handling the guns was due and acquired by the long practice while on picket duty on the upper Potomac river and Monocacy aqueduct, in shelling the enemy while they were building fortifications along the river on the Virginia side in the fall and winter of 1861 and 1862.

We will now return to the left section, Lieutenant Adams with his howitzers, and an aide of Colonel Tompkins as guide, moved down to the right in front of the meadows in the low land at the left of the fort. Our lines were in the edge of the woods. The section was placed in position in the infantry intrenchments with the One Hundred and Sixth Pennsylvania Regiment. When the firing commenced on the right, the enemy's reserve line of pickets was seen advancing in our front, upon which Lieutenant Adams gave orders to direct our fire. The enemy's pickets were shelled quite lively for some moments when they were seen to retreat to the rear of the fort, and we slackened fire, which was only kept up at intervals. During this time, strange to say, we did not receive a shot from the fort. But there came several shells from far off to the left, which went to our right into the woods, crashing among the trees. At nine o'clock Lieutenant Adams received orders to withdraw from the picket line, and he returned to camp with his howitzers, none of the men nor horses were injured.

It was a current report, at the time this attack on the rebels was decided upon, that Colonel Tompkins, chief of artillery of the Second Corps, intended to send Battery A, First Regiment Rhode Island Light Artillery (Colonel Tompkins's brother was then captain of that battery), to open the engagement. But it is said that General Sedgwick, gave orders to send out Bartlett's battery (Battery B, First Regiment Rhode Island Light Artillery), and said: "We'll see if they can fight as well as clean out peddlers." At seven o'clock the battery left camp, with the two sections of ten-pounder Parrotts under command of their chief, preceded by Captain Bartlett, and an aide of Colonel Tompkins as guide, moved down on the left to a strip of woods, and leaving one section, the right, moved slowly forward through the woods by a cart-path. The men were ordered to keep as as silent as possible, and no orders to be given above a whisper. The woods being quite free of under brush and dead limbs no noise was made in reaching the position assigned them. The cannoneers marched silently beside their pieces, realizing the perilous work about to be undertaken, but appreciating, however, the honor conferred upon Battery B, in being chosen to fire the first shot. When within a dozen yards of the outer edge of the woods the section was halted and unlimbered at the outlying picket line. The guns on being placed in battery, orders were silently given to prepare for action.

Through the openings among the trees in front could be seen a clearing of considerable extent, on the far side of which loomed up the rebel fortifications. Directly in our front was a fort, in whose embrasures slumbered the frowning dogs of war. It was now a most exciting moment, for the two guns were loaded, and Battery B was about to knock at the door of the enemy. Would they be at home to receive company, and what would the reception be? Lieutenant Perry sighted the first piece. A number of officers were standing to the right and rear to see the opening shot fired. The stillness of the hour was now broken by Lieutenant Perry's order, "First piece, ready!" Number four (Stillman H. Budlong), quickly inserted the primer and attached the lanyard, and then stood waiting, and at the order "Fire," swung his right arm down behind him, at the same time swaying his body to the left; the lanyard jumped from the gun, there was a flash, a deafening roar, the gun recoiling backwards, and away flew the shell on its aërial flight, bursting over the enemy's fortifications. Down went their sentinel from the parapet. Their reply indicated that they were at home, as from one of their embrasures rose a cloud of smoke and an angry roll. Their shot went to the left in the tree-tops, and exploded in the rear of the limbers. This was quickly followed by another volley which fell short, and, landing among some fence rails, exploded, and sent them flying end over end in all directions. After observing the effect of the first shell, the second piece was fired, which hit the top of the parapet, sending up a cloud of dust. The section kept up a lively fire for some moments, then continued firing at intervals. The enemy, however, made it so warm for us that we changed our position three times to get out of range of their fire.

Our opening shot was followed by others from the batteries which were placed in the edge of the woods. They shelled the enemy's line vigorously; after which the Vermont brigade, under Gen. J. R. Brooks, of the Fourth Corps, made a splendid charge in an attempt to capture their works, but failed, not through lack of courage, but from want of support and the overwhelming number of the enemy. The intention of this assault was to gain possession, if possible, of the Warwick Court House and Williamsburg road, thus cutting off Yorktown from the support of the Confederates.

The right section, under Lieutenant Perry, remained on duty at the picket line until the evening of the 17th, when it was relieved and returned to camp; Battery G. First Regiment Rhode Island Light Artillery taking their place.

At one o'clock on the morning of the 18th the battery was hitched up and remained so until daylight, expecting to be called upon at any moment, as there was sharp musketry firing at the front all night, with some cannonading.

At seven o'clock Lieutenant Adams, with the left section of howitzers, was again ordered out to the picket line on the right and took position in the redoubts between the First Minnesota and Fifteenth Massachusetts Regiments, within 500 yards of the enemy's line. While here the men were constantly under the fire of the rebels' sharpshooters. Three nights in succession the enemy tried to stampede us, and one night three rebel regiments came out at eleven o'clock, and for ten minutes the woods were one living blaze of musketry fire, mingled with the roar of our howitzers and the angry growl of the twenty-pounder Parrott on the left. The Fifteenth Massachusetts was on our right, the First Minnesota on our left. Our orders were, not to fire until the enemy came up to within one hundred yards, and, like old soldiers, our men stood waiting, showing great nerve and determination on their part. At the word fire the enemy received a leaden welcome; the bullets fairly stripped the woods, and each time the enemy retired with considerable loss. Day and night their shot and shell fell around us, but not one of the men or horses in the battery was hit. This was miraculous, as a number of the infantry supporting our guns were killed or wounded. During the time in which the battery did picket duty every round of ammunition (except canister) had been used, making it necessary for the supply wagon to replenish us three times.

The rebels having taken quite a dislike to the twenty-pounder Parrott gun on our left, determined to gain possession of it on the night of the 19th and stop its insolence. They " plotted brave schemes," but were doomed to disappointment. War sharpens the wits, and, anticipating some such movement, General Sedgwick ordered an entire brigade of his troops to be stationed ready to receive them. Lying flat upon the ground in the form of a V, with the coveted gun in the centre (thus ⇾▷), our troops waited the arrival of their expected visitors. They had not long to wait, for, under cover of the dark night, they came just before eleven o'clock, and were allowed to approach within speaking distance of our guns, when the order was given to open fire upon them. Our men rose and gave them a leaden welcome, for which they were not grateful, and from which they retired in confusion, with " curses not loud but deep." It is not on record how the enemy liked the reception they received in endeavoring to become better acquainted with that gun.

On the 28th we were made happy by the appearance of the paymaster, and the battery was paid for the months of January and February, 1862. It was a welcome surprise, as his coming had not been anticipated.

There had been heavy rains for a week previous, rendering active operations less agreeable, though the military work had gone steadily on. Deserters were frequently coming into our lines. They were Irishmen, bringing reports of disaffection among their countrymen in the rebel army.

On the 29th, Governor Sprague visited our camp, joining the headquarters of General McClellan's army on the staff of General Barry, chief of artillery. He came to look after the Rhode Island troops, and, by the invitation and request of the secretary of war, connected himself with the movements of the army until the latter part of May. With the governor was Maj. William Monroe, the allotment commissioner from Rhode Island, an officer who was entrusted with the funds of our men that he might safely remit them to our families or friends. Quite a number of the battery availed themselves of this opportunity.

This was a red letter day in camp. In the afternoon our welcome post courier brought us a generous supply of letters and papers that had been accumulating at Washington, detained there awaiting transportation to the army in the field. How eagerly were seals broken and contents devoured? can easily be imagined by one who has long been separated from loved ones and home.

When General McClellan's army was brought to a standstill by the fortifications in front of Yorktown, which extended along the Warwick River to Lee's Mills, the approaches to the town and the passages of the river were covered by strong batteries and earthworks. General McClellan deemed it necessary to resort to siege operations before a general assault was made.

General Heintzelman, with the Third Corps, held the right of the line confronting Yorktown; General Keyes, with the Fourth Corps, held the left along the Warwick River, while the Second Division (General Sedgwick's the one present) of the Second Corps, occupied the centre, in the vicinity of Wynn's Mills.

During the siege the two sections with the two ten-pounder Parrotts of Battery B while on picket duty were stationed in what was called Battery No. 8. The howitzers were placed in the redoubts of the outlying pickets of the First Brigade, Second Corps. We expended over a thousand rounds of ammunition on the enemy's works. Although our opponents threw a shower of shot and shell at our lines when occupying the fortifications, the battery escaped unharmed. Not so the enemy, for it was known that by our shots one of their guns was disabled and dismounted.

Saturday, May 3d. The battery, for the first time since the 15th of April, was all together in camp. Three days' extra rations were cooked and issued, and it was rumored that there was soon to be a general assault on the enemy's line. In the evening very heavy cannonading was heard in the direction of Yorktown; all was quiet in our front. Early on the morning of the 4th the battery was aroused from slumber and ordered to harness and hitch up immediately. There were many speculations as to the meaning of this hurried order. The rebels had kept up a brisk fire from their heavy guns in front of Yorktown all night, which had been answered by the guns from our batteries. A bright light, which could be seen within the enemy's line, illuminated the clouds above, and the men were rejoicing in the belief that the shells had set fire to some part of the rebels' quarters or town. On our side the preparations for a general assault were about complete, and the firing yesterday was to test the siege batteries along our lines. During the early hours this morning several shots were fired from the rebel works, in our front, then all was quiet. At daylight it was reported that the rebels were about to abandon their works, and upon investigation it was quickly learned that they were not only preparing to evacuate, but had actually done so and our cavalry and horse artillery had been sent in pursuit to harass their retreat.

May 5th. The battery left the camp (which has been its headquarters since April 13th) about seven A. M. It began to rain as we started. Passing our lines, we moved into the first line of the enemy's earthworks, that we had been shelling, then through the second line and to the fort, where we dismounted one of their guns, and saw in the embrasures Quaker or dummy guns; this explained the reason of our not receiving any reply to our fire during the siege. We halted on a level plain in the rear of the fort and waited all day. As we were preparing supper (making coffee) we received orders to move immediately. The water for coffee was thrown away, everything packed, battery hitched up, and we started in just fifteen minutes after receiving the command. We went but a very short distance when we halted, and there we remained, waiting until morning. But we had our coffee just the same, notwithstanding that it rained most of the time.

It was a surprise to the entire army, as they marched through this stronghold, that the rebel commander (General Magruder) should have retreated from this line of defenses to fall back to Williamsburg. The fortifications, as to strength, were all that engineering skill and labor of a large working force could make them. The ditches were unusually broad and deep, the embankments ten to twelve feet thick, and the embrasures thoroughly constructed of sand-bags, sods or gabions.

In their haste to evacuate the rebels left large quantities of pork, flour, and other supplies, scattered about over the ground. Tents were left standing with their interior fixtures untouched, and, in private houses occupied by officers, books, papers, correspondence, and other personal effects. It is said that among some letters which were left, was one addressed to General McClellan, making a lame attempt at witticism. It read thus:

GENERAL MCCLELLAN:

You will be surprised to hear of our departure at this stage of the game, leaving you in possession of this worthless town; but the fact is, McClellan, we have other engagements to attend to, and we can't wait any longer. Our boys are getting sick of this damned place, and the hospital likewise; so, good-bye for a little while.

ADJUTANT TERRY, C. S. A.

The possession of Yorktown added fifty-one guns, and a mortar left in position, to our ordnance stores, besides a large quantity of military appliances. A number of the guns were thirty-two and forty-two pounders, and one ten-inch columbiad. In abandoning their works, it is said, the rebels left behind them abundant evidence of their vindictiveness. They buried in the ground, hid in barrels and boxes, and laid around elsewhere, a large number of infernal machines in the shape of torpedoes and bombs.

Yorktown contained between fifty and sixty houses situated along the river front. The town was well fortified,—who has not heard of the Quaker guns at Manassas? The same were found here. Logs could be seen in numbers, mounted on old wheels at the embrasures of the fortifications. But these were not the most formidable objects encountered within these fortifications, for after passing through our lines and entering those of the enemy, we encountered one of their most powerful allies — mud. It seemed in constant league with them, an efficient and defensive warfare, and took the military valor all out of a man. The soldiers declared that though Virginia was once in the Union, she was now in the mud. One would think, from reading the Northern newspapers, that we had macadamized roads over which to charge the enemy. The following well-known expression was proverbial among the stay-at-homes: "Why doesn't the army move?" It would have been most pleasing to have seen those, who supported us at so safe a distance in the rear, at the cry of "On to Richmond," plod over a five-mile course in this Virginia mud, loaded with a twenty or forty-pound knapsack, and a haversack filled with three or four days' rations. Without exaggeration, Virginia mud has never received full credit for the immense help it afforded the rebels during the war. It has never been fully comprehended, and, in order to do so, one must march in it, sleep in it, and be encompassed round-about by it. Great is mud! — Virginia mud.

On May 6th, the sun rose clear and bright. At noon the artillery trains were put in motion, and the battery moved on, passing the river line of fortifications and, entering Yorktown, proceeded to the outskirts, went into park, and awaited orders. Along the line of march we passed several places where a barrel or box was marked "Danger!" These places were shunned by the troops, as they supposed torpedoes were buried there, it having been reported that a number of the men had been killed or wounded in searching for these concealed missiles in order to mark their location or remove them. We received word to-day that the Third Corps and General Stoneman's cavalry had had a smart engagement with the rebels at Williamsburg, and the enemy is still retreating, General Sumner being in command of the Union troops. The infantry of the Second Corps was sent up in support, but was not in the fight; they were ordered to return, take transports, and advance up the York River.

Private Clark L. Woodmansee.

CHAPTER VIII.

MARCH UP THE PENINSULA — BATTLES OF FAIR OAKS AND SEVEN PINES.

ON the return of the infantry of the Second Corps from Williamsburg they were embarked on board of transports and conveyed up the York river to West Point. It was not until nine o'clock on the evening of the 6th, that the Battery received orders to pack up and move down to the wharf in front of the town, and began loading the guns, caissons, and wagons upon a steamer. It was two o'clock in the morning before all was put on board, and the men were pretty well fagged out, as this was the second night in succession they passed without sleep; and when ordered on board the steamer were glad to lie down anywhere to rest. The steamer moved out into the stream and laid at anchor all day of the 7th, while Lieutenant Adams with the drivers and horses waited near the wharf for transports. It was not until late in the afternoon of the 8th that they were embarked on board of schooners, and towed up the river a short distance, where they were anchored, and remained all that night.

At daylight on the morning of the 9th, the steamer on which the officers, men and battery had embarked, was run up alongside of the schooners, having the horses on board and taking them in tow sailed up the York river. We passed several of the enemy's fortifications situated along the river bank, now deserted. At five P. M. we dropped anchor in front of West Point, the place where the British capitulated to the American troops in 1781, and now, 1862, is occupied by the Federal army. The town lies at the junction of the Mattapony and Pamunky Rivers. These two uniting to form the York River. Vessels of every description lie here at anchor waiting to be unloaded. It was sunset before we commenced to unload the battery from the steamer and we worked until ten o'clock, when we were ordered to bivouac on the south bank of the Pamunky, to wait until the schooners with the horses were towed up to the wharf, which was not until ten o'clock A. M., of the 10th, when the unloading was completed and guns mounted, the battery was ordered to park near the bank of the river and await orders.

May 11th. The battery with the First Division marched to Eltham, about three miles from the landing, and went into camp. The men rejoiced to step on land once more after being so cramped for room on ship-board; being true landsmen and not sailors the forecastle had no attraction for them, the tents being more preferable.

On the 12th, Sergt. John E. Wardlow was promoted by Captain Bartlett, to first sergeant, *vice* George W. Blair reduced to line sergeant for breach of discipline.

May 13th. The batteries of the division were inspected and ordered to be in readiness to move the next day.

May 15th. The battery left Eltham at nine A. M., marching all day in the mud and rain, making frequent stops to let troops pass. On arriving at Austin's Meeting-house, the battery went into camp in the woods opposite.

May 16th. Lieutenant Adams, with the drivers and their horses, went back to the wagon train, and returned with grain and rations.

Sunday, May 18th, instead of attending Divine service, we were ordered on the march. Left Austin's Meeting-house about eight A. M., warm and pleasant. Passed through New Kent Court House going about two miles and then encamping in an open field. A short distance from camp was a clear running stream of water, which the men enjoyed and made use of in bathing and in washing their clothes. The horses were not forgotten, but were taken to water, soon after we encamped; eagerly they entered the stream, and it was hard work to hold them back; some did plunge in and laid down to roll with their drivers on their backs.

May 19th. Lieutenant Perry, with the drivers and their horses, and Quartermaster-sergeant Dyer with the two army wagons and drivers went to Cumberland Landing, and returned with forage and rations. Cumberland Landing is a little hamlet on the Pamunky River; by water it is nearly twenty-one miles, by land a little over ten from West Point. It now, for the first time, becomes an historic spot, as a depot of supplies for the Army of the Potomac, and the place where General McClellan temporarily established his headquarters.

May 20th. The cannoneers were set to work, cleaning the mud from gun and caisson carriages; the drivers attending to the harnesses. Once more the battery presents a respectable appearance.

May 21st. The battery broke camp at six A. M. "On to Richmond" once more. The roads were very good; the best we had traveled since landing on the Peninsula. Marched all day and halted on a knoll in a wheat field; finding for the first time a place somewhat hilly. Went into camp within two miles of Bottom Bridge, which crosses the Chickahominy River.

May 22d. Remained in camp and had an inspection of the battery. In the afternoon, a heavy thunder storm followed by hail, invaded our camp. Fortunately it was of short duration some of the hail-stones were an inch in diameter, and as they struck the horses' backs, would cause them to flinch, crouch, then shake themselves, and start to run; some did get away, and a lively time the drivers had in catching them.

May 23d. Started on the march at seven A. M., up the north bank of the Chickahominy, crossed the Richmond and York River Railroad near Dispatch Station, passing St. James's Church and Tyler's House. Marched all day with frequent halts, and went into camp at six P. M., near Cold Harbor, about six miles from the railroad, and about twelve miles from Richmond.

May 24th and 25th, battery remained in camp. Quartermaster-sergeant Dyer with the wagons went back to the railroad for forage and rations.

May 26th. The battery left Cold Harbor about seven A. M. Marched south toward the Chickahominy. The bridge not being quite ready for crossing, we were ordered back to camp. In the afternoon we received light marching orders, the battery was hitched up, but did not move.

On the morning of the 27th, the battery (guns and caissons), left camp at seven o'clock to join General Sedgwick's Division, which had been sent up to the right to the support of the Fifth Corps, it, the corps, having met the enemy in force along their line. As the battery proceeded, heavy firing was heard, and the troops were pushed forward. The infantry was drawn up in line on a wooded ridge. The batteries halted in the fields in the rear. At noon Battery B was placed in position on a small knoll to the right of the division, where it staid the remainder of the day and all that night, the men bivouacking beside the guns. This place, the scene of the recent action of the Fifth Corps, is the small post town of Hanover Court House, and is distinguished as the birthplace of Henry Clay.

On the morning of the 28th, at sunrise, the battery with General Gorman's brigade was ordered further to the right. We proceeded to a hamlet called Old Church, as a colored member of the community informed us; it consisted of several private dwellings, a tavern, and an Episcopal church. We were sent here to protect the line at this place, to prevent the enemy from turning our flank, and to support any point where our services might be required.

May 29th. General Gorman's brigade was ordered back to the corps, and the battery left Old Church, arriving at our camp (which was between Parker's Mill and the Tyler's House, on the north side of the Chickahominy River), just before noon and parked.

May 30th. Clothing and boots were issued to all who needed them. In the afternoon Quartermaster-sergeant Dyer returned with several new horses, to replace the ones that had become worn out. We had a heavy shower in the evening which lasted several hours.

May 31st. Pleasant and warm; heard heavy firing in the direction of Richmond; were ordered to pack up and be in readiness to move. Left camp at two P. M., on the march to the river; found the roads very bad on account of the rain the night before. We arrived at a place called Grapevine Bridge, and, crossing the Chickahominy River on the new corduroy bridge, built for the occasion, found the river much swoolen and overflowing the low swamp and boggy land on either side. After crossing the river we came to a stream of swift running water, formed by the overflow, which we found much difficulty in crossing. The cannoneers were in the water for an hour and a half, sometimes up to their waists. We finally succeeded in reaching what we supposed to be firm ground, but such was not the case, as only a thin crust of earth covered the swampy land, which soon became spongy by constant travel, so that the guns and caissons would descend to the hubs in the mire. The horses would sink to their knees as they struggled with their heavy loads, so, in order to relieve them, they were unhitched from the guns and caissons, and led to one side, in order to obtain a sure footing. Then the prolonges were attached to the carriages, the horses hitched on, and the cannoneers with fence rails pried the wheels up out of the mud. Then the word would be given: "A strong pull, and a pull altogether," upon which the guns and caissons would be lifted out and go on a few yards further, when car-

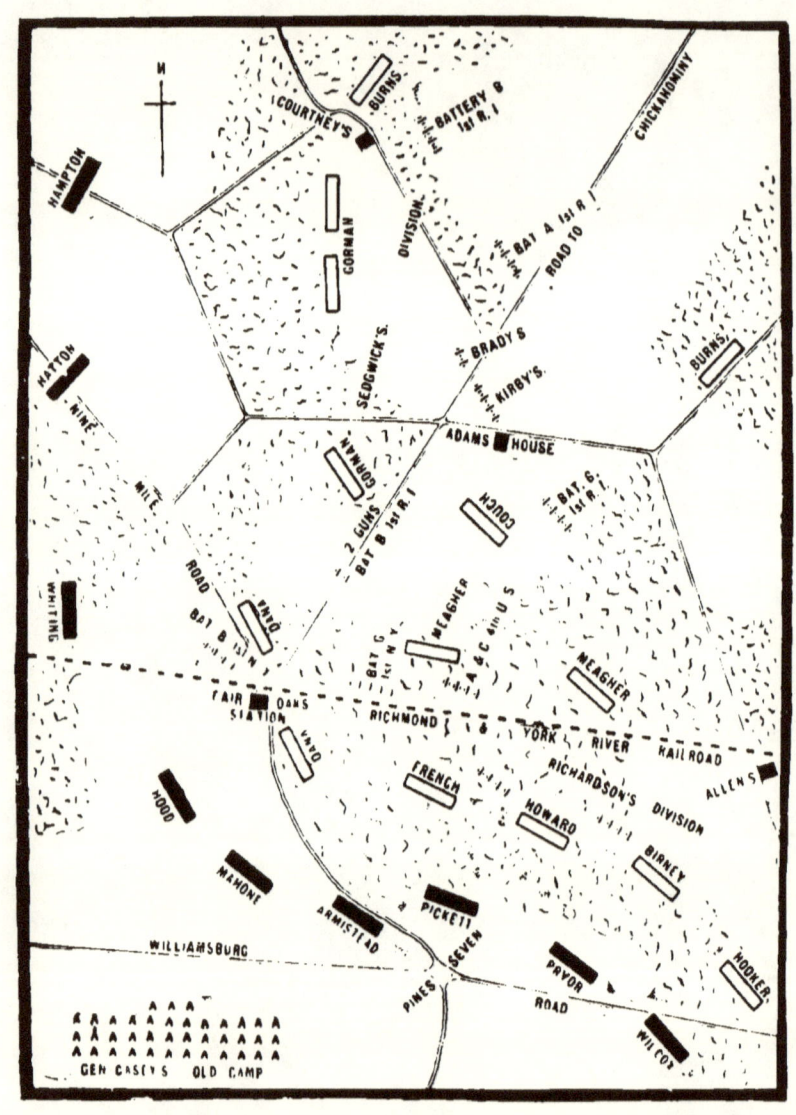

Fair Oaks, and Seven Pines, June 1, 1862.

riages, horses and men would again sink into the soft and spongy soil; at each occurrence the same manœuvres would be repeated. In this way, after six hours of toil and struggle, through mud and water, the battery finally reached firm ground and pushed forward as fast as the condition of the roads would permit, arriving on the battle-ground of Fair Oaks at nine P. M., and bivouacked for the night near the Adams's house, tired, wet and hungry. The Sixty-ninth and Seventy-first Pennsylvania Regiments of General Burns's brigade, which were with us when we started from camp, were pushed forward and sent ahead, when we became stalled in the mud caused by the recent rains.

On Sunday morning, June 1st, at sunrise, the battery was ordered further to the front. The centre and left sections, under Lieutenants Bloodgood and Adams with Captain Bartlett in command, were sent to the right of the line near the Courtney House. The Sixty-ninth and Seventy-first Pennsylvania Regiments held the line of battle in our front. Battery A, First Regiment Rhode Island Light Artillery was on the same line, to our left, nearer to the road upon which we came. The right section, under Lieutenant Perry, was sent down in the vicinity of Fair Oaks, and was halted on the road leading to the railroad station.

As the centre and left sections were being placed in position the Rebel skirmishers at our front and right opened a sharp fire upon our infantry. The left sections,—the howitzers,—were immediately turned upon them, and sent a few shells in their direction. This peppering was continued, during the forenoon, at every movement of the enemy's pickets. Our infantry in front did not become generally engaged; only the pickets of both armies occasionally firing upon each other; there was little loss on our side.

About six o'clock A. M., while we were engaged in shelling the enemy's pickets, we heard heavy musketry firing upon our left in the direction of Fair Oaks Station, which continued for half an hour; then occurred a lull with only the report of the artillery; then the firing was renewed with vigor, as though an attack was being made in force; it continued for two hours or more, when there was another lull of short duration, then cannonading commenced, again accompanied with heavy musketry. This soon ceased, and all was quiet. We subsequently learned that the troops between Fair Oaks Station and Seven Pines had had a severe engagement with the enemy, in which the right section took part just north of the station. This was called the Battle of Seven Pines, June 1, 1862.

The fighting on the 31st of May was north of the railroad, and was termed the Battle of Fair Oaks, in which Battery B took no part, not having come up from the river in consequence of the inevitable mud and water.

When the battery was ordered to the front, on the morning of June 1st, the first section under Lieutenant Perry, with an aide of Colonel Tompkin's staff, proceeded south, on the road by which the Battery came the night before, passing the position occupied by Lieutenant Kirby's battery (I, First United States), near the Adams House. Beside the rail fence, in front of the battery, a number of dead rebels could be seen, having been struck down in their vain attempt to capture the battery. The section proceeded down the road in a southeasterly direction going toward the railroad, trees lined both sides of the way. Passing through a strip of woods the road continued through a clear open field, which extended to the right and left for some distance, and in front was another strip of woods through which the road continued to Fair Oakes Station. On this road the section was halted, and the two guns placed in battery facing the west. In the strip of woods in front, which was some two or three hundred yards distant, the rebel pickets were stationed. To our left, near the road, were two regiments, the Thirty-fourth and Eighty-second New York, of General Gorman's brigade. They were not in line of battle, but had been halted, and were standing at ease, leaning on their muskets and carelessly observing a line of men which was advancing from the woods at their right across this opening; supposing they were some of our men, sent out from one of the regiments standing idly by, they made no preparation to receive them. When this section was half way across this opening we were surprised, by receiving from Lieutenant Perry, the orders "Action right! in battery!" and as soon as they were in position the order to load was given, using spherical case shell. Both pieces opened fire upon this line of skirmishers, which proved to be the enemy approaching from the woods. Our shells checked their further advance, and, after firing a volley at random, they broke and turning about ran for the woods, they had just left, as fast as their legs could carry them. After sending a few more rounds at the retreating foe, the order was given to cease firing. The infantry watched the confederates' departure, our fire and bursting shell that entered the enemy's line, with much amusement and interest, but their time of observation was of short duration, for they were immediately formed into line and sent to the woods, near the position just vacated by the rebel skirmishers.

The road where the pieces were stationed was quite firm, but the ground on the left, occupied by the limbers, was spongy and muddy. The rail fences, on each side of the road, had been pulled down the day before, in the struggle which had taken place. Among these, on the right, dead rebels could be seen, while on the left lay those of the Union soldier, and squads of our men were gathering their bodies for burial. The pieces were facing nearly west, and to our left, down the road about five or six hundred yards distant, was Fair Oaks Station on the York River and Richmond Railroad. Soon after the retreat of the enemy's pickets to the woods at the west of the opening before mentioned, a pop—pop—popping of musketry was heard in the vicinity of said station; this kept increasing and finally extended away down on the left, soon becoming terrific, as volley after volley was fired, followed by the roar of the artillery. It continued up the line to the very edge of the woods on our left, so near that the Minié balls from the enemy's rifles dropped among us as we worked our pieces, while the smoke rolled into the open space in our front. Our infantry was being forced back into this opening, and it looked as if the rebels would succeed in breaking through at this place. The Thirty-fourth and Eighty-second New York regiments were hurried to the support of our hard pressed troops, and succeeded in checking the advance of the enemy.

Lieutenant Perry, meanwhile, ordered the section to change front to the left, facing nearly south, and to open on the advancing enemy with spherical case shell. The road being narrow, and the ground on each side spongy, it was at disadvantage that the pieces were worked; nevertheless, the woods were vigorously shelled until orders were received to cease firing, the rebels having been repulsed and driven back, the ground was retaken and occupied by our troops, and a number of prisoners were captured. This engagement was called the Battle of Seven Pines. While the battle was raging, hot and fierce, a number of orderlies passed us on their way to the Adams House (which was used as a hospital), leading Gen. O. O. Howard, who had been severely wounded in the arm, having had his horse killed under him while placing his troops in position near the station.

In the afternoon, while all was quiet along the lines in our front, a mounted force of rebels was seen in the edge of the woods, at the west of the opening previously mentioned. The pieces were at once pointed in that direction, and Lieutenant Perry gave orders to shell the enemy. Soon after a few rounds had been sent into their midst, they disappeared and were seen no more in that vicinity. It was subsequently learned that it was a company of rebel cavalry reconnoitering. They had met a warm reception, and did not find General Sedgwick's men napping.

At dusk, supplies were brought up from the river, and the men were made happy by receiving rations of hard tack, salt pork, and coffee. The section remained in position all night, the men bivouacking beside the pieces, ready for any emergency.

The weather on June 2d was pleasant and warm; it was also better traveling, as the mud was fast disappearing. The infantry was kept busy burying the dead. The rebels ran a flat-car down the railroad from Richmond, on which was mounted a twenty-pounder gun, and shelled the lines in the vicinity of Fair Oaks Station, but did very little damage. The right section fired a few shots in the direction of the railroad during the day. A number of negroes came into our lines late in the afternoon, and were sent to division headquarters.

As the army approached Richmond, the slaves were found in large numbers. They visited the camp with great freedom, and didn't find the Yankees the barbarians their masters had represented them to be. All repeated substantially the same old story: "Massa told 'em dat der Yank would cut off their ears, and sell dem into Cuba." Some of them were intelligent and shrewd, and seemed to understand the difference between "de norf" and "de souf" side of Mason and Dixon's line. Subsequently a large number of the able-bodied negroes were set to work, for Uncle Sam, by Colonel Ingalls, who was in charge of the quartermaster's department at White House Landing, on the Pamunky River.

On the morning of June 3d the cannoneers were set to work building breastworks in front of the guns as a protection from the enemy's sharp-shooters. A few shells were fired during the day. All was quiet during the night, for at dusk a smart shower set in and it continued to rain until nearly morning. The battery, meanwhile, remained at the front in position, the men bivouacking behind the earthworks at night. On the 11th, they were relieved and went into camp near the tavern at Fair Oaks Station, with the other batteries of the corps. While encamped here the corps was reinforced by the addition of three full regiments of infantry, and three companies of the Sixth New York Cavalry. A corps of artillery reserve was also formed, consisting of two Rhode Island batteries, B and G, and Battery G, First New York.

While moving up the Peninsula, and encamped near the Chickahominy River, the health of the men occupied the attention of the commander-in-chief. As a preventive of fever and ague, which the miasma of this region produced, half rations of whiskey, medicated with quinine, were ordered, and issued morning and evening. This order was soon rescinded, and hot coffee substituted.

The succeeding two weeks of camp life were, in their general features, not unlike many of their predecessors. The battery's equipments were put in order and new ones received to replace those old and worn, which were unfit for further service. New clothing and boots for the men were also issued. Passes were given to the men to visit other commands to see their friends; frequent trips were also made to Savage's Station, our depot of supplies. The weather continued fitful, bestowing upon us a mingling of cloud and sunshine, hot days and cool nights (the swift precursors of chills, fever and ague). Rain caused a superabundance of mud, much to the detriment of artillery movements, the annoyance of teamsters, and the discomforture of the infantry. Corduroy road making, picket duties, reconnaissances and skirmishings, with an occasional brush of a more serious character, have occupied the time of the troops of the second corps.

June 25th. The monotonous routine of camp life was broken by the order to prepare to move, and at eight A. M. the left section, under Lieutenant Adams, was sent to the front to the breastworks, on picket duty. Heavy firing was heard on the right of the line. In the afternoon the right and centre sections, under Lieutenants Perry and Bloodgood, were ordered out to the front. A brigade of infantry was dispatched in hot haste from the corps to the support of General Hooker, who was advancing his lines. These demonstrations and movements indicated that there was soon to be a general advance in the direction of Richmond.

On the 26th, the men were made happy, notwithstanding the fact that they were in close proximity to the enemy, by the report that the paymaster was at the camp, and the battery was to be paid. At sunset the men went up to camp and received their pay for the months of April and May and then returned to the breastworks.

Early in the morning of the 27th, the right section, under Lieutenant Perry, was ordered further to the right and front near the railroad, and shelled the enemy's line at the Williamsburg and Richmond turnpike, to which the rebels made no reply. In the evening the battery withdrew from the breastworks and returned to camp, and learned that troops had been moving up to the right of the line all day.

It was reported that again the advance movement of "On to Richmond" was in order, and that General McCall's division had opened the *ball*, on the evening of the 26th, at Beaver Dam Creek, near Mechanicsville.

Private Merritt Tillinghast.

CHAPTER IX.

CHANGE OF BASE TO THE JAMES RIVER. AND SEVEN DAYS OF FIGHTING.

AT reveille on the morning of June 28th, the battery received orders to be in readiness to move at a moment's notice. The whole army was in commotion. Swiftly galloping orderlies bearing dispatches to the different commands, were moving in all directions. What was the meaning of this? why—the army was preparing to move. The gathering of such a multitude is a swarm, its march a vast migration, with long ammunition and supply trains disposed for safety along the inner roads, guarded by infantry, the artillery next in order. The cavalry were the feelers of the army, and protected its front, rear and flanks; while behind, trailing along every road for miles, are the rabble or stragglers—laggards through sickness or exhaustion, squads of recruits, convalescents from the hospitals, and special duty men going to rejoin their companies. Each command has its route laid down for it every day, the time of starting set by the watch, and its place of bivouac or camp assigned, together with the time for its arrival.

If two roads came together, the command that reached the junction first kept moving on, while the next to arrive would halt by the way-side or file into the fields, stack arms, build fires, and make their coffee. Let my reader now stand by the roadside while the troops are filing past. They march "route step," as it is called,—that is, not keeping time,—and only four abreast, as a country road seldom permits of more marching side by side, and allow space for the aides, and orderlies that gallop in either direction along the column. If the march had just begun, you would hear the sound of voices everywhere, with roars of laughter in spots, marking the place of the company's *way*. Later on, when the weight of knapsack and musket begin to tell, these sounds die out, a sense of weariness pervades the toiling masses streaming by, voiced only by the shuffle of a multitude of feet, the rubbing and straining of innumerable straps, and the flap of full canteens and haversacks, "three days' cooked rations and forty rounds" stored therein. So uniformly does the mass move on that it suggests a great machine, requiring only its directing mind.

It was not until ten o'clock at night that the battery received orders to move, and, pulling out into the road, followed the column at a slow pace. Marching all night, we arrived at Savage's Station at sunrise on the 29th, and parked. The horses were fed, and the men prepared to make coffee. Here we witnessed the great destruction of valuable munitions of war of every description. There were several stacks (as large as ordinary houses) of boxes full of hardtack burning, barrels of pork, sacks of coffee, and sugar, all making one great bon-fire. We succeeded in obtaining a generous supply of coffee, sugar, etc. Here and there were pools of whiskey, in which gunpowder and brine were mingled.

This place (Savage's Station), on the York River and Richmond railroad, had been the depot of supplies for the troops that held the advanced lines. There was also a field hospital here, composed of tents, in which were placed the sick and wounded, it occupied a clear field of several acres on the north side of the railroad, and the buildings on the south side were also used for the same purpose. When the army retreated the occupants of the hospital, with the surgeons and nurses, fell into the hands of the enemy.

About nine o'clock A. M. heavy infantry firing was heard in our rear, in the direction of the fortifications we had left the night previously. The rebels discovering that our works were vacated and our army retreating, pressed close upon our rear guard, consequently troops from the station were sent back to support our men.

Just before ten o'clock, an orderly from Colonel Tompkins came galloping up to the battery, and gave Captain Bartlett a dispatch. Then the order was given for the pieces to forward into column. Leaving the caissons, we marched back on the same road by which we came in the morning, passing General Franklin's headquarters, and turning to the left kept on down the road through a strip of woods to an open clearing. Here troops were drawn up in line of battle; the guns were placed in battery on a small ridge facing the west. In front, in the woods beyond the clearing, was the infantry of our division holding the enemy in check, and forcing them back by the help of the supporting troops that had been sent to their

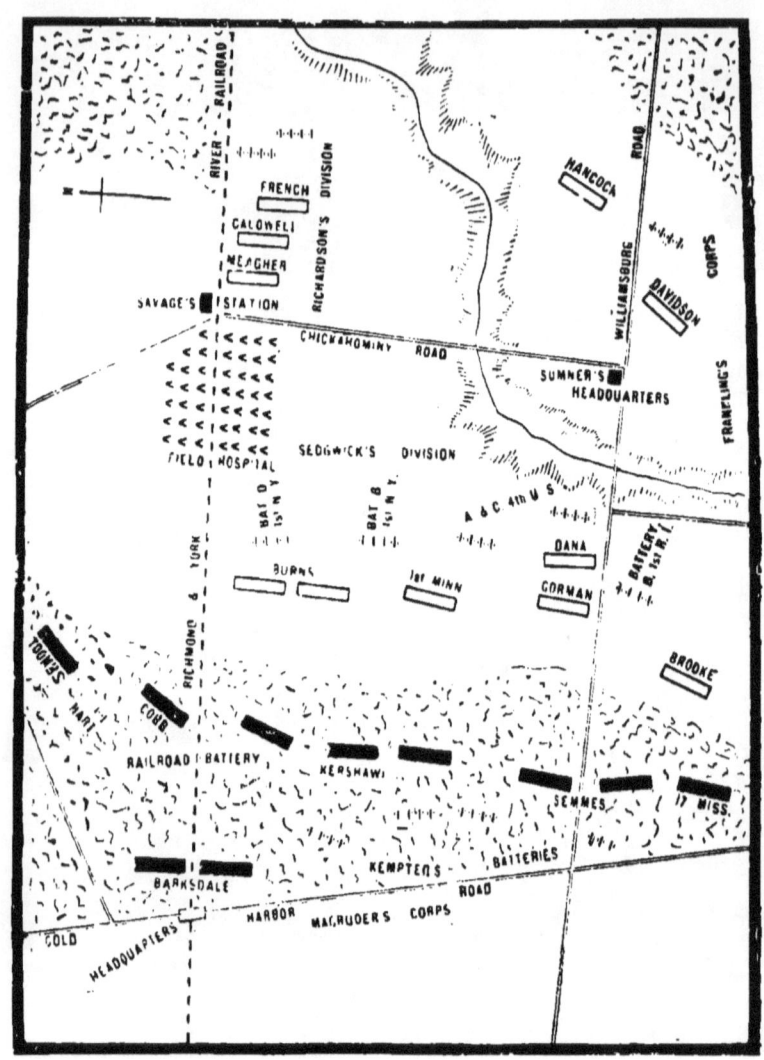

Savage's Station, June 29, 1862.

aid. A number of shells passed over our heads and to our right, one bursting over our position. No one was injured in the battery, but a number of infantrymen in our rear were not so fortunate. We were in what was called the Peach Orchard, on or near Allen's farm. The battery was not actually engaged, but remained in position on the reserve line, receiving the ricochet shots from the enemy.

The battery remained here until near noon, when orders were given to limber up, and we were marched back again to Savage's Station and parked just south of the buildings near the railroad. At our left were the other batteries of the reserve artillery corps. Our caissons were in close proximity to the woods on the east, near the ravine, where we had left them in the morning in charge of Lieutenant Dwight, when the pieces were ordered to the front. We found here the Fifteenth Massachusetts assisting in the destruction of the commissary stores, and part of General Meagher's brigade was also engaged in destroying ammunition and other artillery stores. The plains were covered with the ruins of the vast military supplies, which were destroyed in order that they should not fall into the hands of the enemy again. Upon our first arrival here in the morning we had found the fields and woods alive with troops, artillery and army wagons and to the left in the woods was the Third Corps, but upon our return at noon we found the place comparatively deserted.

The battery remained here until about six P. M., when orders were again received, and we moved by a circuitous route toward the front whence we came in the morning. Infantry firing had been going on for some time, with desultory cannonading. We were moved from point to point, finally reaching the Williamsburg road, and, turning to the left into the field, took position in battery on elevated ground which sloped to the woods in front. This was the reserve line at the battle of Savage's Station. Here we found the Sixty-ninth New York of General Meagher's Irish brigade drawn up in line near to the edge of the woods; an officer, on horseback, was riding along their line, who seemed to be addressing the men, and cheer after cheer was heard as he passed along. Then came a shout, loud and long, and the regiment disappeared into the woods on a run. Soon the pop—pop—popping of musketry was heard, which told us that they had met the enemy. A few shells from the enemy's railroad battery passed us to the right and rear, but we remained silent, obeying orders to limber up and get out as quickly as possible, and we waited for no second invitation. We moved along slowly until the road was reached, and then the order was given for the cannoneers to mount, and clambering upon the trails, axles, and pieces, or anywhere else where we could cling on (for the caissons were not with us), we started down the road on a trot. After going several miles we left the Williamsburg pike, and turned to the right, going south. This road was crowded with wagon trains, which would halt at times, then start on a gallop at breakneck speed. During one of these halts the battery pulled out to the right into the fields in order to pass the wagon trains, and started on a gallop (cannoneers mounted), to catch up with the reserve artillery train, which was a short distance ahead. We had turned into a cornfield covered with standing stubbles. As the wheel of the sixth limber suddenly sunk into a hole, after going over one of the corn hillocks, three men were thrown off the chest, one, David B. Patterson, was run over.* The other men escaped unhurt, and mounting the limber chest again, the drivers were ordered on and endeavored to overtake the battery which had preceded them, but the road and fields were so crowded with the army wagons of the different trains that it was sunset before the battery was reached. We found it halted in a wheat field awaiting its turn to cross the bridge. At nine o'clock P. M., the battery crossed the White Oak Swamp Bridge, moved on through the marsh to rising ground and turned into a field on the left of the road and parked ; here the horses were fed, having had no provender since early in the morning. The men were tired, muddy and hungry, and rolled up in their blankets bivouacked under the gun and caisson carriages over which the tarpaulins had been thrown.

We were suddenly aroused from our slumber, on the morning of the 30th, by the opening of the rebel artillery (General Jackon's) from the other side of the swamp beyond the bridge. For awhile

---

*On Sunday, June 29, 1862, on the retreat from Savage's Station, Va., I was thrown from the limber box of the sixth piece, as was also Joseph Luther and Allen Hurt, who I believe escaped unhurt. The wheel of the gun carriage passed over my left thigh and right ankle, breaking both badly. I was carried to a tree out of the way of the moving trains and left there. The rebels soon occupied the ground, and I was held a prisoner at Richmond until July 29th, just one month, when I was put on board a freight car with others and taken to City Point, on the James River. My limbs had not been set while in Richmond and my thigh, which had just begun to heal, was again broken by the jolting of the cars, subsequently my legs were set at the hospital in Chester. Penn. The doctors finding that my left leg was three inches shorter than my right, pulled and strapped it down as far as they could, but when healed it still remained one and a quarter inches shorter than the right. The knee joint also became quite stiff; but I was thankful to regain partial use of my legs instead of losing them all together.—*David B. Patterson.*

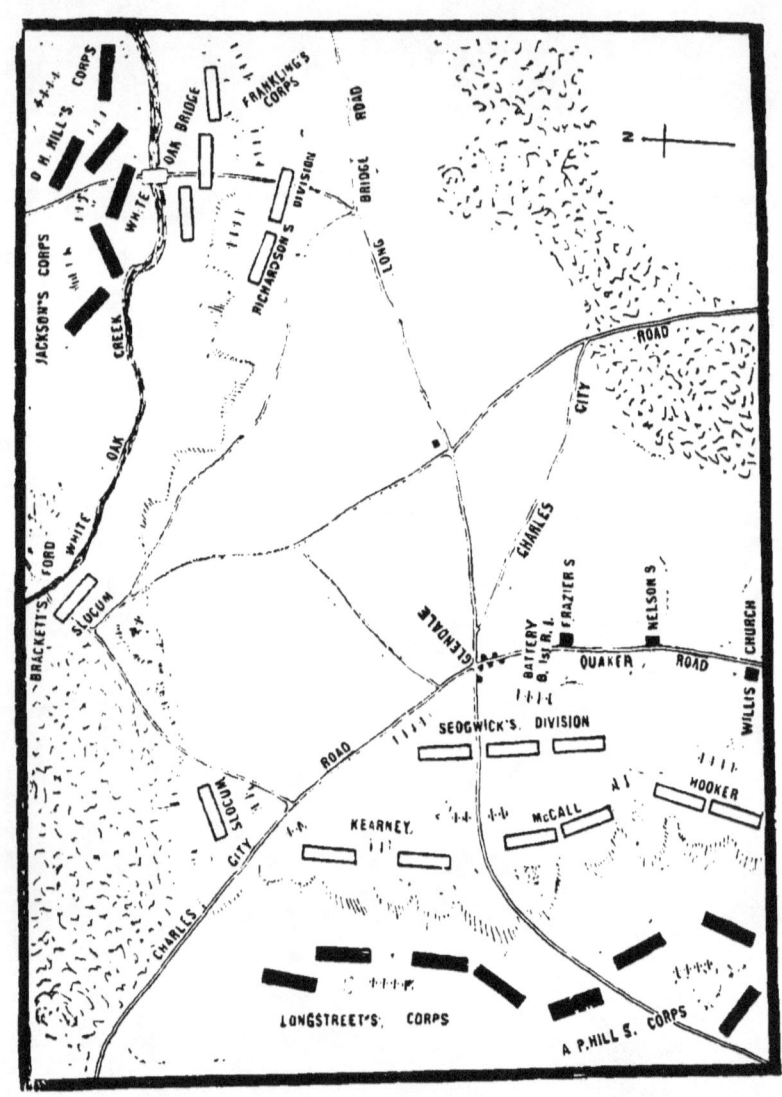

White Oak Bridge and Glendale, June 29-30, 1862.

there was dire confusion, as the shells burst in our midst. Fortunately the shelling did not last long, and order was soon restored; the dangerously crowded masses were rapidly deployed, and trains ordered to move on to a place of safety. It was remarkable that only one teamster and two mules were injured by the bursting of the shells. When the shelling began Battery B had received orders to hitch up as soon as possible. therefore, as soon as the road was cleared, it pulled out and moved along down the Long Bridge road marching in a southwesterly direction. After passing the cross roads (a point where the Charles City and Long Bridge roads form a junction with the Quaker road) the battery turned into the fields at the left and moved south along a ridge until near some small trees and bushes; here the section was ordered into position, the cannoneers to remain at post. Heavy artillery firing was heard in our rear, in the direction of White Oak Swamp bridge. The firing lasted an hour or more, after which it occured only at intervals.

About four o'clock in the afternoon skirmish firing broke out in our front, troops were rushed forward, and soon became fiercely engaged in a deadly conflict. By the repeated assaults of the rebels our line was broken, two brigades (Generals Dana's and Gorman's, under Colonel Sully,) lying in our front, having just come up from the bridge and halted while the battery was taking position, were sent forward into the gap, abandoned by General Seymour's men, when the rebels broke into our lines. The fire here was intensely hot, and, although some of the regiments which arrived in haste were thrown individually into action, and became somewhat confused by General McCall's men breaking through their forming ranks, the ground was never for an instant entirely yielded to the enemy. The brigades of Generals Burns and Dana with their supports, sustained the brunt of the action.

During this engagement (the battle of Glendale) the battery was not called into action, but remained under fire in the line of reserve. A number of shells passed over us to the rear, one bursting over our heads and wounding three men: Sylvester G. Ide, Daniel Capron, and Harry Pearce. Their wounds being slight they were not sent to the hospital, but taken into our ambulance. Soon after this accident the battery received orders to limber up, and withdrew, passing to the left through a strip of woods, toward a road running south along which three lines of wagon trains were moving.

Captain Bartlett perceiving a break in the line, ordered the battery to move down toward the road, and as soon as an opportunity offered we moved into line, then continued on the march, with the trains to the rear, down the Quaker road toward the James River, passing Frank's battery in position on the left of the road and the infantry throwing up breastworks. We moved on to where a road branched off to the left, following this (the wagons trains keeping on down to the right) and going a short distance we halted on the left of the road on the brow of a small ravine, in which was a creek. Here the battery was parked, horses unharnessed for the first time in several days, taken to water, and fed on half rations, as our supply of forage was becoming exhausted. The men built fires and soon had pots of hot coffee to wash down the pork and hard tack. The hot coffee was refreshing and went a long way toward reviving the spirits of the men, after their long, tiresome tramp.

On the morning of July 1st, the battery was moved up to the ridge, near the Binford House, the horses were then unhitched and taken back to the creek to water; after they had gone, Captain Bartlett received orders to move up to the front, and word was sent the drivers to return immediately with the horses; all had been watered by the time the order was received by Sergt. C. H. Adams, who was in charge of the drivers. The horses returned on a gallop. The battery was then hitched up and moved further to the left and front, taking position in battery in the reserve line. To our left the other batteries of the reserve artillery of the Second Corps, were in line. The infantry of the corps was lying at the foot of the slope, and hidden from the enemy's view by the rising ground in front. Between ten and eleven o'clock in the forenoon the enemy's skirmishers began firing upon the left; later it extended along the line down to our front. This was followed by artillery fire from their batteries. The enemy kept up a desultory fire until about noon, with no serious injury to our troops, who were well masked, and revealed but little of our strength or position in retaliatory firing or exposure. Up to this time our infantry was resting upon their arms in battle-line and waiting the moment, certain to come, when the enemy would make an advance charge. The rebels kept up a fire at intervals along the line until the middle of the afternoon, apparently trying to ascertain the strength of our line. Then there was a lull, an ominous silence on the part of the enemy; broken about 5.30 o'clock by the rebels. Battery after battery opened fire along the whole front, following which the infantry pressed forward in columns, covering first one point and then another selected for their attack. Regiment after regiment and brigade after brigade rushed at our batteries; but we mowed the enemy down with shrapnel shell, and cannister; while our infantry withheld its fire until the enemy was within a short range when it scattered the remnants of their columns, sometimes following them up and capturing prisoners and colors.

During this engagement at Malvern Hill, the battery was in position in the reserve line of the Second Corps, which extended along the ridge northwest of the Binford House. During the artillery fire, a rebel battery took position in our front and opened on our lines. We were not permitted to engage the battery, but compelled to stand and take their fire. Many of their shells went to our left, some over our heads; several passed through the battery between the pieces, while others struck the ground in front and burst, scattering pieces in all directions. One shell was seen to strike the ground, about one hundred and fifty yards distant in our front, then to ricochet in the air, and, striking the ground again some yards nearer, pass one of the guns, skipping along toward the horses of the gun limber, and striking one of the leaders on the ankle, breaking its leg. Lying on the ground back of, and partly under the limber chest, in the shade, were several men, among them Corp. Calvin W. Rathbone, who was lying on his side, with his head on his arm; he raised his head just as the shell came under the limber, and it struck him a glancing blow on the forehead, cutting the skin and causing the blood to flow copiously down his face. The blow stunned him instantly, and it was some time before he revived. It was thought at first that he could not survive the effects of the injury. He was taken to the hospital, where he received excellent medical treatment, and, after several weeks' absence, returned to the battery. Another remarkable incident occurred at this time. One of the recruits, John Green, a sturdy young Irishman, who came to the battery last February, was hit twice with pieces of shell, but not seriously injured. The first piece of the shell struck him a light blow on his arm, but, causing no injury, it was soon forgotten by his comrades. This happened in the forenoon, soon after the rebel battery opened fire upon us. In the afternoon, as the shelling became quite brisk, just before the charge of the enemy on General Franklin's left front, another shell exploded over the left section, and the second piece of shell hit Green on his leg, making him jump around lively. He was mad as a "march hare," using strong language profusely, and asserting "the d—n rebels has got the dead range on me sure." This, like the blow received earlier in the day, was not of a serious nature, and he soon recovered. But ever afterward it was a common by-word with the men: "Look out, John, the rebels has got a dead range on you."

Although the battery was in the reserve during these seven days of fighting, six of its horses were disabled, two of which had to be killed, and six men were wounded, but none seriously except Corporal Patterson who was left in the hands of the enemy.

During the battle of Malvern Hill, July 1st, the position of the battery was such, that, by looking to the right and front, the troops of General Franklin could be seen, and to the left of these, those of General Heintzelman; while the troops of the Second Corps lay at the foot of the slope, in front of the ridge on which the battery was in position.

Battery B was kept in position all day and evening, and, although it did not get into any engagement with the enemy, its position was such that it received the long range and ricochet shots of the rebel's artillery fire; while the battle was raging in the afternoon, and almost at its crisis, we were startled by hearing booming in our rear. Soon the cry was raised: "The gun-boats are firing." At times we could watch the shot in its flight, then it would disappear in the clouds of smoke. The gun-boats soon ceased firing, as they were unable from lack of elevation of their guns to throw their shots far enough. Our siege guns, stationed at the left of the Malvern house, General Porter's headquarters, kept up a steady fire, which was anything but pleasant to the enemy. At sunset we witnessed a charge made by the rebels, who were approaching from the woods in front of General Franklin's troops; his men were invisible to the advancing foe which had an open field to cross, consequently, when they had traversed about half the width of this field, our men seemed to rise out of the ground to receive them. They met—but the smoke of their muskets shut from our vision the deadly conflict; as soon as the air cleared, however, the rebels could be seen retreating, running for the woods, and our men in hot pursuit, firing as they advanced; they did not chase the foe very far, but retired in good order, having captured a few prisoners and colors. The havoc made by the bursting shells sent from our guns, so arranged as to sweep in any direction far and near, was fearful to behold. Pressed

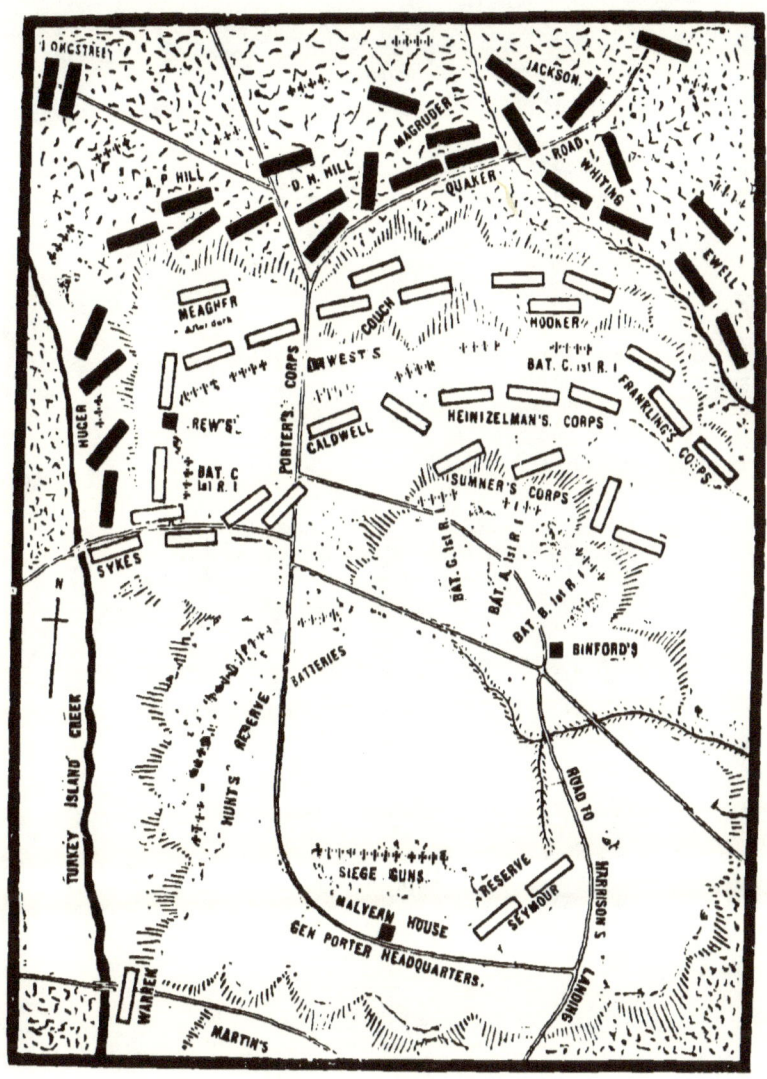

Malvern Hill, July 1, 1862.

to the extreme limit of endurance, as our troops had been during these quick marches day and night, continued without sleep and on short rations, it fully tested the courage of the soldier. The safety of our army—the life of the Union—was felt to be at stake—and our forces triumphed. It is not to be supposed that the men of the Second Corps, though concealed by the irregularities of the ground, escaped the enemy's fire. The fact is, although they were not called upon to expose themselves by pursuing the enemy, many were killed and wounded from dropping bullets and bursting shells, and bravely they bore the severe trial of remaining inactive under this heavy fire.

As night set in the firing of the infantry ceased; the artillery kept up a fire at intervals. At nine P. M. the fighting was over, the battle won. Thus ended the memorable "Seven Days Battle," which, for severity, stubborn resistance, and endurance of hardships by the contestants, was not surpassed during the war. The battle of Malvern Hill thus passes into history.

At ten o'clock on the night of July 1st, the battery with the other reserve artillery, preceded by the wagon train, withdrew from Malvern Hill by the River road, passing over Turkey Island Bridge, which spans a creek of the same name, and moved in the direction of the James River, where the lights on the gun-boats could be seen. On we marched all night, toward our destination, Harrison's Landing, which we reached about noon on the 2d, finding the fields soaked. The soil was quickly reduced to paste (new name for mud) by the tramp of men and quadrupeds. The battery was parked awaiting orders, and remained here the rest of the day and bivouacked during the night. The troops were wet and weary from their hard march over muddy roads, in the midst of a heavy rain. The infantry, artillery, and wagon trains were drawn up in an immense field of standing wheat near the Harrison mansion, also called the Berkeley House. The grain was laid down in the tents to serve as a protection from the wet ground. Neither fence rails nor wood was to be had, and the army was exceedingly uncomfortable. Fortunately the transports on the James River landed rations, which proved a great blessing, since many of the men and horses had had no food in forty-eight hours. The rain continued until shortly after midnight; the flimsy wheat floors were soon floating in pools of water, besides, the soil would not hold the tent pins and many were blown down, exposing the men to the pelting rain, their beds sinking deeper and deeper into the mud. Notwithstanding this most uncomfortable state of affairs, the men, freed from care and oblivious of danger, slept the sweet sleep of rest and awoke the next morning with a brillant sun, a happier, brighter and stronger body of men.

About seven o'clock on the morning of the 3d, while some of the men were still sleeping, and others attempting to start fires in order to get their breakfast of hot coffee, they were startled by a sudden outburst of artillery fire and shells whistling over the plains; the shots were scattering, and seemed to be directed principally at the shipping in the river. The troops were summoned to arms, but very little damage being done by the shells, the affair was soon turned to account as a joke. While the Union army was retreating, General Stuart, with his cavalry, had been operating in the centre of the Peninsula, and, learning of the exposed position of General McClellan's forces on the James, he hastened to this point and stationed his battery near Westover Church, across Herring Creek, north of the landing; a few shells from our gun-boats compelled him to speedily shift the position of his guns; and General Kimball's brigade (of General Shields's division) having just arrived from the Shenandoah, advanced, and after some lively skirmishing cleared the field of the rebels.

The army immediately took position on high ground, about Harrison's Landing, and went into camp, on an intrenched line extending several miles, the left resting on the James River, and forming a half circle toward Rawling's Mill Pond, then around to the east of Westover Church, the right resting on Herring Creek. After the departure of General Stuart and his cavalry, nothing more was seen of nor heard from the enemy for some time.

Too much praise cannot be said in favor of the officers and men who passed through these seven days of battle; enduring fatigue and hunger without a murmur, and successfully meeting and repelling every attack made upon them; from the time the Union army left Old Point Comfort it had fought the Confederates at great disadvantage. The enemy were on their own ground; they were familiar with the country; knew every nook and corner; every swamp and hiding-place; and the direction of every road and cross-road. They also had many spies, mingled with the people among whom we encamped, who gave warning of all our movements, enabling the rebels to take advantage of every circumstance that could be turned against the Union army. We, on the contrary, had everything to learn, with few reliable sources of information, and constantly liable to be misled. Nearly all trustworthy facts had to be obtained by reconnaissances. Yet, with all these unfavorable conditions, the Union arms were more than a match for the rebels; who retreated from the siege of Yorktown; were beaten at Williamsburg, West Point, Cold Harbor, Hanover Court House, and in all the battles which occurred on the Peninsula, except Gaines's Mill, which may be regarded as the solitary exception.

By the time the Union army had crossed the Chickahominy, disease had begun to make serious inroads among its ranks; still, the enemy were again beaten at Fair Oaks, Seven Pines, Savage's Station, White Oak Bridge, when the Union army was passing through White Oak Swamp, Glendale or Frazier's Farm, and finally at Malvern Hill. With the Union army it was to fight, and hold their ground; to fight again, then fall back, fighting by day, advance step by step, only to fall back at night, was all that was done. What this move accomplished, if anything, in the great struggle, more than to change from one place to another the base of supplies, time alone will tell. The army of the Potomac has now arrived safely at the James River, and established its lines at Harrison's Landing, in the form of a crescent, the right and left wings resting on the rivers, supported by gun-boats.

CHAPTER X.

HARRISON'S LANDING—EVACUATION OF THE PENINSULA.

PERHAPS the most trying experience in war is the necessity that sometimes occurs in making a retreat, of leaving the sick and wounded behind; this was sadly realized during our late movements, when our means for the removal of those in need of aid were found to be totally inadequate, and hundreds were left on contested grounds, at the mercy of the enemy. The roll-call, after a battle, tinges success with sadness. Battery B was far more fortunate than some of the other batteries of the regiment, only one of our number fell into the hands of the enemy, during those trying times of holding the foe in check. In the last chapter we left the battery safely encamped at Harrison's Landing, with other batteries of the brigade, awaiting orders.

Harrison's Landing received its name in honor of Benjamin Harrison, one of the signers of the declaration of independence and a friend of Washington; it also possesses an additional interest in being the birth-place of the late president, William Henry Harrison. During the rebellion the old mansion was still standing near the river, being used for hospital purposes. On the roof of the house the signal corps had a station and lookout, thus obtaining a commanding view of the surrounding country. The granary of the old plantation was occupied by Dr. Holmes, of Brooklyn, N. Y., as an embalming house. At this season of the year the surrounding country afforded an interesting field for the enthusiastic amateur or professional entomologist. "Every creeping thing" that Noah permitted to enter the ark, and some, perhaps, that he did not, were to be found here. Some specimens being decidedly ill-favored, and by no means desirable as companions. Talk of "rats in Brazil," or "cockroaches in Japan," they were not a circumstance to the fly tribe at Harrison's Landing. Here the most hardened and impracticable rebel would have given up, and no doubt taken the oath of allegiance, rather than endure the torture of these little pests for one week. Remember, the mercury was at 100°, and sometimes reaching 110° in the shade; you "strike the air" with a quick, irregular motion of the hand, hoping to catch your tormentors, but they only increase their zealous attacks for this attempt at self-defence. Buzz! buzz! buzz! flies on the nose; flies in the ears; flies in the food; flies in the tent; flies in the air outside; you attempt a short nap, flies take possession of you, and it is a failure; black, biting, merciless flies everywhere. Look at the poor horses at the picket-rope and those in yonder shade; you can fairly count their ribs, and despair seems depicted in their faces; how they stamp their feet, shake their heads or whisk their tails, and pull at the halter for release, but all in vain, and it is no marvel that they are often frenzied beyond recovery, and next to a miracle will it be if any escape. In a fair fight the rebels can be vanquished, but flies in fly-time—never! no, never!! Like hungry contractors, they stick till gorged, and then retire, only to return for another feast. It is said that all things have an end, and this was verified by the army making preparations to leave the Peninsula and—flies—much to the delight of the troops, who were not loth to leave their tormentors.

July 3d. In compliance with orders the position of the battery was changed twice during the forenoon, and finally was moved toward a strip of woods, where it was allowed to encamp. The picket-rope was stretched and secured to the trees, and the horses hitched to it so that they might be in the shade and protected from the hot sun. The shelter tents of the men were pitched and laid out in rows, with a street running between them. When all was finished we were allowed to settle down into camp life, and enjoy well earned rest and repose.

July 4th was a busy day in the battery, not in celebrating the national holiday, but in receiving the much needed rations and other supplies. The chests were packed with ammunition, and clothing was issued to those in need of it, as well as other supplies necessary to the comfort of the troops which cannot be had while on the march or battle-field.

On Sunday, the 6th, there was mounted inspection of the battery by Captain Bartlett.

On the 7th, President Lincoln visited the army, stopping at General McClellan's headquarters. The weather was warm and pleasant, and rumors were in circulation that as McClellan's Peninsula campaign was a failure, the president had come to see for himself the condition of the army, and what was to be done next.

On the 8th, at noon, the Army of the Potomac was ordered under arms, and turned out in grand array to receive the president, and be reviewed by him. He was welcomed with the customary official salute, and, as he rode along the lines of each division, the stentorian cheers of the men rent the air. The artillery brigade of the Second Corps was on the left of the line, and orders were given Battery B to prepare to fire a salute, but as the president and his escort did not pass us near enough for the purpose, we did not have the honor of firing. General Halleck and other high military dignitaries accompanied the president.

On the 12th, we received notice that General Halleck had been appointed commander-in-chief of all the armies. The air was full of rumors about future operations, but these soon ceased, the troops quieted down, and inactivity reigned supreme.

On Sunday, the 20th, there was a mounted inspection of the battery by Col. C. H. Tompkins and staff; after which passes were given out to the men, and many availed themselves of the privilege of visiting friends in other commands; while some went to the steamboat landing where the sutlers were located. The river at the landing displayed all the activity of a commercial life; at times more than one hundred sailing vessels and steamers could be seen lying at anchor in the stream waiting to discharge or receive cargoes. Among the steamers were the *Canonicus*, of Providence, *Commodore* and *State of Maine*, of Boston, and the *Nantasket* and *South America* of New Bedford. The ironclads *Dakota*, *Monitor* and *Galena*, moved back and forth, watchful of their defenseless proteges, and looking out for rebel demonstrations on either bank.

The bank along the shore, both above and below the landing, was lined with the officers' quarters, hospitals, ambulances, commissary stores, post-office, express office, photographic establishment, horse and mule corral, and a forest of army wagons; these with a host of contraband men, women and children, of all shades, from neutral tint to jet black, formed a picturesque scene, while their shouts, laughter and loud lingo reminded one of the confusion of tongues. The most elated, among all this multitude, were the army sutlers, whose merchandise found a ready sale, at fabulous prices, for when a soldier wanted anything that could be had, he generally obtained the article, caring naught for the expense.

On the 22d, the battery received orders to prepare for a review. The weather being fine this activity so revived the spirits of the men that the forenoon seemed to pass more quickly than usual. At noon the battery hitched up and moved out to the plain, a short distance from camp, where the Second Corps was forming into line; the First Division, General Richardson's, was on the right; the artillery in the centre, and the Second Division, General Sedgwick's on the left. The commanding officers were in front of their respective divisions and brigades. At two o'clock General Sumner, the commander of the Corps, and staff rode out and halted in front of the line. Soon General McClellan and staff rode up to General Sumner; then both generals wheeled, and followed by their staffs rode up to the right of the line; the bands meanwhile playing martial music, which was continued during the review. The enthusiasm of the troops was remarkable, and, while McClellan and Sumner, with their staffs, passed them in review, their huzzas filled the air. It was a day of compliments, and General Sumner was the recipient of many on account of the fine appearance of his corps. The entire review was most admirably conducted. The Third, Fourth, Fifth, and Sixth were reviewed in rotation, some of which Battery B's men had the pleasure of witnessing.

On the 26th the monotony of camp life was somewhat broken by the information that there was to be a grand review of the Army of the Potomac by the commander-in-chief, General Halleck. The troops proceeded to make great preparations for the event, but no review took place. General Halleck, with the president, visited General McClellan's headquarters, where an informal consultation of the corps commanders was held. General Burnside was also present, and the situation was fully discussed.

July 31st. Boots and saddle call was blown, and orders given for mounted inspection; the meaning of this was a mystery, for it was only a short time since the battery had had such an inspection. The battery was soon hitched up, and after inspection by Captain Bartlett, left camp and went down near to the landing; here the guns and caissons, with all the equipments, were turned over to the ordnance department, and in return the battery received a park of six new light twelve-pound Napoleon brass guns and caissons, with new equipments, proudly we returned to camp. One of these guns was destined to figure prominently in the annals of war, as the subsequent pages will relate.

On the morning of August 1st, between two and three o'clock. the firing of artillery was heard. The troops were ordered under arms and the battery was hitched up, remaining so for about an hour, when they were ordered to unhitch and unharness their horses, and turn in. During the day it was learned that the firing had been caused by a small force of rebels, who, with a battery, had taken position on a hill across the river and shelled our transports and supply depot at the landing, doing, however, comparatively little damage. A force of our troops, being sent across the river, soon dispersed the rebels, and at the same time seized Coggin's Point, where the elevated ground had favored the style of the enemy's night attack.

On the 2d, all was life and activity again. Part of the army was on the move—"On to Richmond." The Third Corps was advanced to Malvern Hill, and others were expected to follow. The army had become restless for want of work, and there was great rejoicing at the prospect of a forward movement.

On the 4th, we received word that General Hooker, of the Third Corps, had extended the advance line to Glendale, on the Charles City cross road; General Sedgwick, with his division, had been ordered to General Hooker's support. On the 5th these two divisions made the most important reconnaissance yet achieved; they advanced, driving the enemy from Malvern Hill and vicinity, and again taking possession of the old battle-ground. This move made the line all clear from Harrison's Landing to Glendale.

On the 7th more troops were sent out to strengthen the lines. At sunset the reserve artillery received orders to be in readiness to move to the front. At nine P. M., Battery B left camp, passed through our line of earthworks, and marched up to within a short distance of Malvern Hill, here it halted and parked for the night, the men bivouacking beside their pieces. The battery remained here, as did the rest of the reserve, until the afternoon of the 8th, when it was ordered to return to camp, which it did, none the worse for the little airing and beneficial exercise. For the last three days the general topic of discussion has been concerning the rumor floating about camp as to the future movements of the Army of the Potomac. The sick confined in camp were sent down to the hospital at the landing on the 10th; their illness being mostly light cases of fever and diarrhæa, the men having been reduced and broken down by climatic and other influences.

On the 11th the battery was placed under light marching orders, all surplus baggage, knapsacks of the men and camp equipage were sent down to the landing, and turned over to the quartermaster's department. The landing of any express matter was discontinued, much to the disappointment of the men who were expecting boxes from friends. The rumors of the past week to the effect that the army was to be withdrawn from the Peninsula, thus proved to be true, for a large portion of the troops and artillery, with the necessary transportation and forage wagons, were to be sent to Yorktown, Hampton, and Newport News, there to embark for the north, to the defence of the city of Washington. To remove the army and its entire equipage without loss, in the face of a powerful foe, was an undertaking requiring great forecast and skill. In order to conceal our future movements from the enemy, the gun-boats were kept up toward City Point, watching the enemy, and to all appearances waiting for the coming of the formidable ram from Richmond; the balloon regularly visited the upper regions, to view the surrounding country enveloped in smoke; and the tooting of bugles and beating of drums in the camps, were, if possible, more stentorian and defiant than ever, as much as to say: "Here we are, come if you dare." The usual parades, the guard-mountings and drills went on just as if nothing unusual was about to take place. Steamers coming up the river brought large companies of returning absentees, which greatly aided our plans of secrecy. Meantime, all of the sick at the landing were sent north to other hospitals. The heavy ordnance and surplus stores have been shipped on board of transports, and extra rations have been issued to all commands. We marvel at the capability of "mine host," who can daily dine his three or four thousand guests upon the abundance of the land, or clams of the sea-shore; or at the purveyor, who, under mammoth tents provides satisfactorily for from twelve to fifteen hundred hungry mortals. What, then, must be the brain-work and administrative power of the man (the quartermaster-general of the army) who, for an entire campaign, calculates and provides seasonably for an army of one or two hundred thousand men? To the unseen power, giving motion to all this complicated machinery, and producing such wonderful results, no small praise is due. But, notwithstanding all the liberal provisions made, there are times when it is needful to avail ourselves of local resources and foraging becomes an important feature as well as a necessity. Our government, however, respected the private rights of the citizens, and generously compensated those loyal to our cause who suffered from the necessary depredations of our men; these, therefore, seldom had cause for serious complaint. Occasionally, however, a professedly Union man would reveal his true colors and have to abide the pecuniary consequences.

The following incident is one of many that might be told, and was related by a colonel commanding a reconnoitering party which had encamped in a field of clover. As was natural under the circumstances, the horses, being in clover, lost no time in taking advantage of it. The owner of the field having made remonstrances without effect, demanded payment for his loss, when the following brief conversation ensued:

Proprietor of field.—" Colonel commanding, I believe?"

Colonel.—" You believe right, sir."

P.—" Well, colonel, your men and horses have trampled down my clover field and completely destroyed it. Do you intend paying for it?"

Col.—" Well, sir, are you loyal?"

P.—" Yes, sir."

Col.—" Are you willing to take the oath of allegiance to the United States?"

P.—" No, sir."

Col.—" Then get Jeff. Davis to pay you, and you get out of my tent d———d quick, you infamous traitor."

The would be unionist decamped, and so the parties separated.

The work of preparing to leave Harrison's Landing continued, to the regret of many of the commanding officers. Contrary, however, to General McClellan's expectations, the Peninsular campaign of the army of the Potomac for 1862 virtually ended on the 4th of July. From that date until the army took up the line of march from the landing, its commander was engaged in the struggle of retaining it on the James. The army was withdrawn north to the line of defences at Washington, returning to the James however in the summer of 1864.

August 13th. Capt. George O. Bartlett sent in his resignation to headquarters. In the forenoon the cannoneers were drilled at the manual of the piece by chiefs of sections, Lieutenants Perry, Adams, and Bloodgood. In the afternoon there was mounted inspection by

Captain Bartlett. Then clothing and boots were issued to all that needed or desired them. For the last time passes were given to the men to visit the landing and interview the sutlers, a few of whom still remained.

On the 15th, Captain Bartlett received his resignation, and, turning the command over to First Lieut. Raymond H. Perry, left the landing, for Washington, by way of the mail steamer. Thus for the fourth time in a year the battery was under the command of Lieutenant Perry. At five o'clock P. M. boots and saddles call was sounded, the battery was ordered to hitch up and be in readiness to move at a moment's notice. The troops of the Third Corps had been moving all day. It was not until seven o'clock, on the morning of the 16th, that the battery received the order of " Right piece forward !" and, turning our backs upon both the enemy, we had beaten at Malvern Hill, and the entomological tribe (the flies) that had shared our tents and disturbed our repose, we took up our line of march with our corps (the Second) by way of the River road. We passed through a rugged and somewhat hilly country, containing a number of splendid farms, green with fine crops of growing grain, and a great variety of fruit, to which the troops helped themselves without any invitation ; neither were the pigs nor poultry overlooked. The cornfields also received especial attention, the men indulging freely in this treat ; the horses were not forgotten, but received their share of the sweet green stalks and grain. After the troops and trains had passed through these once green fields, they looked as if a cyclone had struck them. On account of the crowded condition of the road the battery did not travel more than five or six miles the first day, bivouacking at night by the wayside. The next morning, the 17th, we made an early start, marching all day. Our course lay through Charles City Court House and several other small hamlets, we arrived at the Chickahominy late at night. A number of gun-boats were seen at anchor below the bridge, retained there in order to prevent it from being shelled by the enemy while the troops were crossing. The battery crossed on the pontoon bridge from Bartlett's Ferry to the north side, and encamped for the night a short distance from the river. This bridge was about one thousand four hundred feet in length, and built under the direction of Captains Spaulding and Duane of the Fiftieth New York Regiment ; it was a fine specimen of engineering skill, and greatly facilitated the withdrawal both of the army and the immense trains of the commissary, quartermaster's and ordnance

8

departments. All landed safely on the northern side of the river, sustaining only the loss of a single baggage wagon, which, breaking down on the way, became useless, and was burned, to prevent its falling into the hands of the enemy.

We continued our march on the 18th and 19th, and, passing near Williamsburg, encamped above Yorktown on the bank of the York River. The weather was warm and delightful, and many improved the opportunity by bathing in the river; which, though not a military, was certainly a very salutary, exercise, and greatly enjoyed. We also had lots of sport in raking (with our hands) the river bed for oysters; though there was much pleasure in catching these bivalves, there was double pleasure in eating them. During our stay here we lived on little less than oysters, a diet which was very recuperating to our overtaxed powers. At roll call, on the afternoon of the 20th, orders were read to the men, among them one from our commander, Lieutenant Perry, which restored Sergt. George W. Blair to his former rank, that of first sergeant, and reducing First Sergt. John E. Wardlow to his former rank, that of third sergeant.

It was expected that we would embark from Yorktown; but early on the morning of the 21st we were ordered to Hampton, arriving there at sunset after a hard and tedious tramp; we went into camp a short distance from the place where the battery had encamped four months previously. Here we had to remain, waiting for transports, until the 26th, when the troops of the Second Corps began to embark.

The embarking of all the troops and munitions of war gathered in the neighborhood of Yorktown, Fortress Monroe and Newport News, was an undertaking of even greater magnitude, than their removal from Harrison's Landing the previous week; in fact, taking the two together, they are without parallel in the military history of our country. It more particularly deserves attention because such work, in connection with the active operations of an army, is seldom appreciated; upon the promptness and care with which it is executed may depend, in no small degree, the success of an enterprise involving momentous consequences. In the present instance the embarkation was commenced and industriously pursued, until every transport had received its full complement of men, horses or munitions of war; great credit is due to those under whose immediate supervision the whole was effected.

It was late in the afternoon of the 27th before the battery received orders to move down to the wharf where it was to embark. Owing to the crowded condition of the landing, it was nearly midnight before the work of loading was accomplished. The officers, with the cannoneers, guns, caissons, wagons, and a number of horses embarked on the propeller *Putnam*, which drew out into Hampton Roads and anchored for the night; the drivers with their horses, under command of Lieut. George W. Adams, remained on the wharf, where they bivouacked for the night.

At eight o'clock on the morning of the 28th, the *Putnam* steamed up the Chesapeake Bay, and stopped at Acquia Creek landing, on the Potomac. Here the captain of the propeller received orders to proceed to Alexandria, arriving there at sunset of the 29th; the propeller run alongside of the wharf and the battery unloaded, mounted, and parked beside the landing; the officers and men were quartered in shanties and tents along the river bank, to await the arrival of Lieutenant Adams with the remainder of the battery.

About seven miles below Washington on the Potomac lies the ancient city of Alexandria, it was settled in 1748, and called Bellhaven; in its early days it was a thriving sea port, having a large foreign trade, but the bright prospects of its youth were never fulfilled, and to-day it is chiefly noted for what " it might have been." To us the city looked sadly dilapidated, and the objects of interest were few; the Marshall House, where Colonel Ellsworth was murdered, had nothing inviting as to its external appearance, while its inside was disappearing piece by piece, through the industry of relic gatherers. The public buildings, and many private dwellings belonging to absentee secessionists, were occupied as officers' quarters or as hospitals for the sick and wounded. There was one object of interest, however, the old Christ Episcopal church, erected in 1765, and built of imported brick; in this edifice General Washington once worshiped, and was a member of its vestry; his pew, prayer book, cushions, etc., still remained as they were at the time he last attended service. The church was accessible to visitors, though it occupied a somewhat retired spot and was surrounded by a high fence.

Among the numerous vessels lying at anchor in the stream was a small sloop loaded with watermelons. One of our boys decided that he would like to sample the luscious fruit, and formed a plan, which he was not slow in attempting at night, when all was quiet, and having posted the guard (being corporal of the guard that night), he went up along the shore to where an old dory was moored, this he untied, and, getting in, pushed off, paddling out to the sloop by means of a piece of board. On climbing on board he was surprised to find that all the melons had been placed in the hold, and the hatch down, under which was one end of a rope; this led up to and over the boom, to which a large stone had been attached, hence, if he raised the hatch the stone would drop to the deck and awaken the one in charge of the sloop, who was supposed to be asleep in the cabin. Corporal W—— took in the situation at once, and taking hold of the stone cut the rope and placed it quietly upon the deck, he then noiselessly raised the hatch, and selecting some of the largest melons he could find, put them into the dory, and reached the shore in safety. In a short time the melons were transferred to his quarters, and the dory sent adrift down the stream; and as it passed the gun-boats the "bang, bang" of the sentries could be heard, they having received no reply to their challenge, as it passed. The corporal little thought who were to eat those melons, for as the men were making their morning pots of coffee, in rolled a train heavily laden with wounded from the battle-field of the second Bull Run. The train stopped by the camp of Battery B, and, to the request of the wounded who asked for water or a swallow of coffee it was freely given. No one ever left Battery B hungry, as long as they had any rations to give. The corporal distributed thirteen melons among these sufferers, and their gratitude fully paid him for the trouble he had had in procuring them.

Peddlers would flock to the train to sell their eatables, and one poor drummer boy, minus an arm, which had been left on the battle-field, begged for an apple; but the peddler with a basket of tempting red apples, said, "I sell my apples, I don't give them away." One of the battery men, Ned G——, said, "Oh, give the poor boy one." "Not by a d——n sight," was the reply. Just then something happened, and the peddler sat down in a most unexpected manner: the basket of apples changed hands, and the drummer boy had more than one apple.

We will now return to Hampton, where we left Lieutenant Adams with the horses and drivers waiting for transports. To while away the tedious hours the men began fishing for crabs, the water was fairly alive with them around the dock. Strings were procured, to which a piece of pork, or even a piece of rag, was attached; the crabs would cling to this bait, and by a quick steady pull be dexterously landed on the wharf; when enough had been caught two large mess kettles were borrowed from the infantry (who were in waiting), a fire was soon made, and when the water was hot the crabs were thrown in; twenty minutes were allowed for boiling; then they were taken out. What a treat they were to us soldiers! soft shell crabs upon—I was going to say toast—but no! on hard tack, with hot coffee, was the bill of fare that night for supper.

It was late in the afternoon of the 29th, when a tug-boat, with two schooners in tow, came up to the wharf, and Lieutenant Adams gave orders to get the horses on board, which was finally accomplished about nine P. M. Then the tug-boat with the schooners in tow started out into Hampton Roads. We passed the new gun-boat *Ironsides*, near Fortress Monroe, whose lights soon faded from view as we sailed up the Chesapeake Bay. About ten o'clock it began to rain, and by midnight it was blowing a gale and raining in torrents. The sea was so rough that those in charge of the tug-boat had to cut the tow-line and let the schooners adrift in order to keep the tug from swamping, while those in charge of the schooners had to manage as best they could. For a short time all was in confusion on the schooners, no sails had been set, and the two vessels were in danger of colliding or of being driven by the wind in shore; but this, however, was avoided by the sailors, who, with the help of the battery men, succeeded in setting the jib, and then the foresail under reef. The schooners were then headed for Hampton Roads, and sailing back at a lively rate of speed, reached our destination about eight A. M., August 30th, and anchored off Fortress Monroe; it was still blowing quite hard, but the rain had ceased. About ten A. M. Lieutenant Adams and two sailors with a dory went ashore to report and obtain orders; returning about noon.

September 1st. The men and horses were still quartered on board of the schooners at anchor, and Lieutenant Adams again went ashore and, upon his return, brought rations of soft bread for the men; this was a rarity and a treat which was greatly appreciated.

September 2d, still found us aboard the schooners off Fortress Monroe awaiting orders; Lieutenant Adams having been on shore every day. At noon a water-boat came alongside and filled the water casks of the schooners with fresh water, and just before sunset a propeller took the two schooners in tow and started once more for the Potomac River. We sailed all night and the succeeding day and night, reaching the mouth of the Potomac early on the morning of the 4th, having enjoyed a pleasant sail up the river. It was just sunset when we anchored off Alexandria.

At sunrise, on the 5th, Lieutenant Adams with the drivers and horses disembarked, much to the gratification of the men, who were anxious to step on *terra firma* once more. Lieutenant Perry met us at the wharf, and, under his directions, were soon with the battery; the forenoon was spent in obtaining and issuing rations and forage; and in preparing the battery for a march.

In the afternoon the battery was hitched up and the men ordered to their stations. Then Capt. John G. Hazard (promoted from first lieutenant of Battery A, First Regiment Rhode Island Light Artillery, to the command of Battery B) was introduced by Lieutenant Perry. The captain with the other officers inspected the battery, and for the third time Battery B had its full complement of officers, viz.: Capt. John G. Hazard commanding; Lieutenants Perry, Adams, and Bloodgood, chiefs of sections; and Lieutenant Dwight, chief of caissons. A number of recruits came with Captain Hazard, viz.: George O. Bartlett, Samuel J. Goldsmith, William W. Pearce, Joseph B. Place, John H. Richards, and Lewis W. Scott.

Private George McGunnigle.

CHAPTER XI.

PURSUIT OF GENERAL LEE INTO MARYLAND—BATTLE OF ANTIETAM.

WHEN it had become clearly manifest that General Lee's intention was to cross the Upper Potomac, the Second, and General Williams's (the Twelfth) Corps, both under the command of General Sumner, and forming the centre of the army in its new dispositions, were ordered to Rockville, Md. It was not known for a certainty whether the enemy intended to move down the Potomac toward Washington, or to invade Pennsylvania; the subsequent progress of affairs pointed to the latter move, and for that reason the Second Corps was successively advanced to meet the situation.

At two o'clock P. M., on the 5th, the battery, having received marching orders, left Alexandria and moved up to Fort Corcoran, opposite Washington, and bivouacked.

At nine o'clock on the morning of the 6th, the battery took up the line of march with the Reserve Artillery Brigade of the Second Corps, which was moving along the road extending parallel with the Chesapeake and Ohio canal; we crossed the Potomac River by the Aqueduct Bridge to Georgetown, and, passing on through Tennallytown, bivouacked for the night. About midnight we were routed out; hitched up, and marched until sunrise of the 7th, and, after passing through Rockville, we encamped two miles beyond the village. During our stay here we received two more recruits. Alfred G. Gardner and Ezekiel W. Seamans. Clothing and boots were issued to those in need of them. Privates George R. Matteson and William W. Pearce were promoted to corporals *vice* Napoleon B. Clarke and George H. Talbot, reduced to the ranks for breach of discipline. On the 9th, the battery continued marching until near Middleburg where we remained for two days.

On the 11th, we went to Clarksburg and encamped. On the 12th, broke camp at eight A. M. and resumed our march; after passing through the hamlets of Hayattstown and Urbana we bivouacked for the night. Early on the morning of the 13th, we received orders to be in readiness to move at a moment's notice. Tents were struck, battery parked and hitched up; at sunrise we broke camp, and for several hours moved at a lively pace. We marched through Monocacy Mills, a thriving little village, situated on the Monocacy River, in the midst of a fine agricultural country, and doing a flourishing business in grain and whiskey. The battery made a halt of two hours at this village, in order that the horses might be watered and fed, as they had had nothing since the night before.

At noon we resumed our onward march, and crossing the Monocacy River, soon struck a broad, smooth road, which made marching much easier; the road was macadamized and wide enough for three columns to move without interference. As we proceeded up this road and entered Frederick we noticed that nearly every house had the American flag displayed from house top, window or porch, and a word of welcome to the troops as they passed by. What could be the meaning of such strong Union demonstration? The battery passed on through the town about a mile and bivouacked.

Probably no soldier who entered Frederick on the morning of the 13th of September, 1862, will ever forget the cordial welcome the rescuing army received from the loyal inhabitants. During the five months in which the battery, with the Second Corps, had been upon Virginia soil, every native white face encountered had borne an expression of intense hatred as " the invaders " marched through or encamped in a region, which, to a northern eye, was inconceivably desolate and forlorn, barren fields affording the only relief to the dreary continuity of tangled thickets and swampy bottom land. Here, in this rich valley of the Monocacy, shut in by low mountains of surpassing grace of outline, all nature was in bloom; signs of comfort and opulence met the eye on every side; and now, as the full ranks of Sumner's brigades, in perfect order and with all the pomp of war, passed through the quaint and beautiful town, their proud commanders and glittering staffs, and General Sumner at the head, the inhabitants responded with applause, and, from balcony and windows fair faces smiled, and handkerchiefs and scarfs waved to greet the army of the Union, as they passed along the streets from which, only the day before, the Confederates had been driven, after a brisk skirmish.

Amid all the desolate scenes of war; amid all that was harsh and terrible, in the struggle of these brave soldiers to maintain the Union, that bright day of Sept. 13, 1862, with its charming natural beauty, the quaint southern city, and that friendly greeting, formed a picture which can never pass from the memory of any one whose fortune it was to enter Frederick upon that day.

On the morning of the 14th, the battery had time to prepare to march without hurrying, and moved out of camp about eight A. M. We passed on up into the mountain regions of Maryland, from whose heights, looking to the front (west), we could see the flashing lights of our guns, while on the other mountain range, at Turner's and Fox's Gaps, could be seen the battle of South Mountain, which was being fought by the First Corps, General Hooker, and the Ninth Corps, General Reno, under command of General Burnside.

The Second Corps, though not engaged, was in support of the attacking force on South Mountain at Turner's Gap, and passed to the front only at nightfall, to relieve the Ninth Corps, which had suffered severely in its victorious engagement of the afternoon.

At dusk on the evening of the 14th, while the battery was waiting beside the National road, (the Frederick and Hagerstown turnpike), near the old toll gate, an ambulance passed us containing the body of General Reno, who had been shot by the enemy's sharpshooters while reconnoiterimg on the skirmish line in the vicinity of Fox's Gap At nine P. M. the battery was ordered to bivouac in the field south of the village of Bolivar.

On the 15th, about eight A. M., we marched up the mountain road to the heights, passed over the battle-ground, and, turning to the right, proceeded through Turner's Gap, by the Mountain House, and through Boonsboro, and Keedysville to within one mile of the main battle line, where we halted and bivouacked for the night.

On the 16th, the battery was ordered up on the left, and at three A. M. went back through Keedysville, turned to the left, and, passing through a meadow, halted by the woods and parked the guns, but the horses were kept harnessed and ready to move at a moment's notice; heavy firing was heard on our right.

On the 17th, we moved to the front about eight A. M., passed through a strip of woods and halted in a field, the infantry meanwhile going forward; in about an hour we started on again, crossing the Antietam Creek, near H. F. Neikirk's house, and, going north, halted in a field with woods in front. The enemy's shells flew around us quite lively, making it necessary to change our position several times; we finally moved to a field with woods on each side and in front, and although this position was frequently shelled, we were fortunate in not having any casualties. Between twelve and one P. M. there was heavy musketry firing in our front, which lasted for some time, then there was a lull, followed by renewed firing further down on the left, then all was quiet again, with occasional picket firing. Quite a number of prisoners had been taken, and were under guard in the woods near us. In the afternoon the battery was ordered to the front to relieve Battery G, First New York, Capt. J. D. Frank. We proceeded to the battle-field of Antietam, taking position in battery, a little to the left and rear of D. R. Miller's house, on the Hagerstown turnpike. This situation was anything but desirable, as the odor from the dead horses lying around was nearly suffocating.

A few of the remaining hours of the afternoon were spent in straightening and strengthening the line, and gathering those who had become scattered; in issuing ammunition to the troops in line, and, in some instances, bringing forward fresh batteries to replace those which had become partially disabled in the recent engagements. The men bivouacked on the field, guns in position, in readiness to move forward at any moment; while all around lay the slain Unionists and Confederates.

The crash and roar of battle from Burnside's position, away down on the left, raised our highest expectations. At intervals the artillery broke out into a furious cannonading, while here and there some ambitious battery commanders tested the range of their guns and the skill of their cannoneers, in a duel across the crouching lines of infantry. Among the galloping staffs, which crossed that bloody field in the early afternoon, was one whose notable bearing held the gaze of the men as it passed down the line from right to left. At its head rode a general whose magnificent physique, commanding air and splendid horsemanship were well calculated to impress the beholder; while behind him rode as dashing a group of aids-de-camp as ever graced a battle-field. The leader is the noble Hancock, sent in haste from his brigade of the Sixth Corps, to take command of the First Division of the Second Corps, at whose head the gallant Richardson

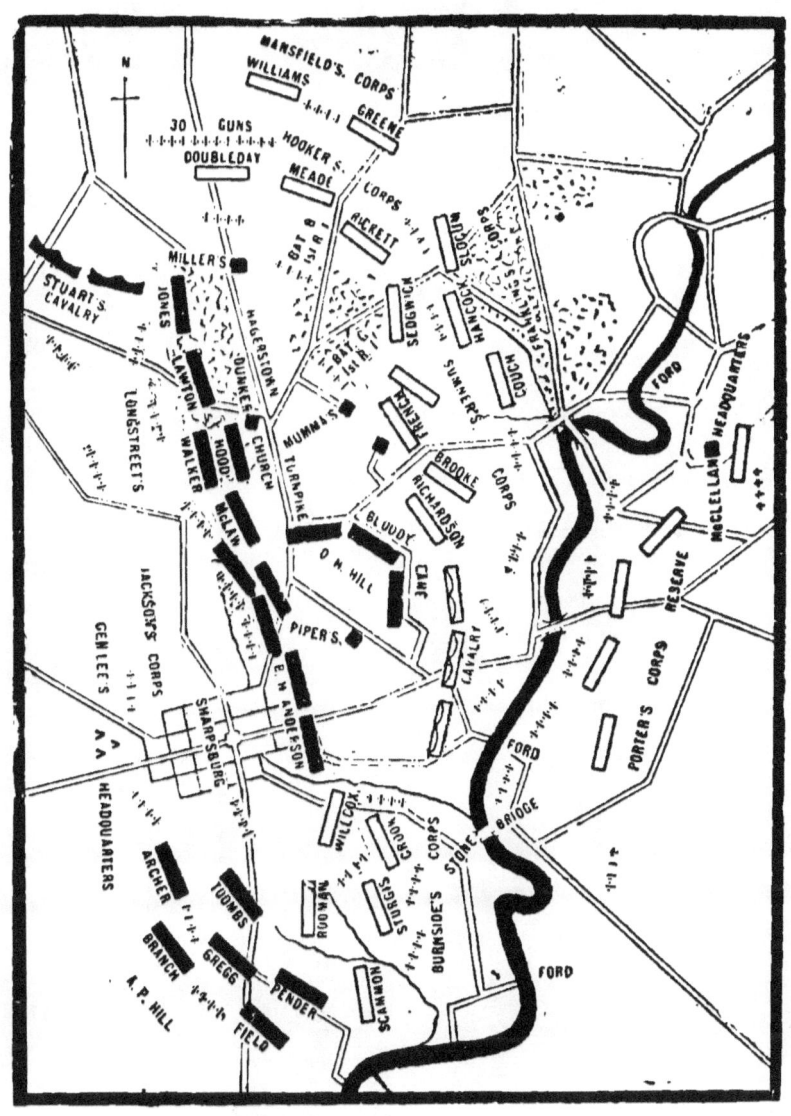

Antietam, Sept. 17, 1862.

had fallen, never again to mount horse or draw sword in the defense of his country.

It is not amid the pomp of a review, with playing bands and well ordered lines; but on the trampled battle-field, strewn with bloody stretchers, amid the dead and dying, and the wounded limping or crawling to the rear; and with shells shrieking through the air, that Hancock comes to meet and greet the brave regiments he is to lead in a score of battles. While Hancock drew his sword for the first time in the Second Corps, another brave general was being carried bleeding from the field, mourning a personal loss in his gallant relative and staff-officer, who was killed at his side; and suffering even a deeper and dearer loss in the broken battalions that had been the pride of his heart.

It is Sedgwick leaving the Second Corps, to become, upon his recovery, the beloved leader of the Sixth; often in the crisis of some hard fought battle he would bring his new command to the succor and support of his old corps; always greeting them with a hearty kindness, whether in camp or on the march. Gen. O. O. Howard succeeded General Sedgwick to the command of the Second Division.

During the engagements of the battle of Antietam, it was the fortune of Battery B to be in the reserve of the Second Corps, on the field, ready for service, but not called into action; several of the men improving the opportunity went through a woods to the ridge, and witnessed a portion of the engagement. The battle array, with flying banners, gleaming bayonets, and countless hosts moving in every direction, was a grand spectacle, while the steady roar of musketry and the loud pealing of the artillery, spoke in unmistakable language of the determined spirit in which assaults were being made and resisted. The ablest generals of both sides led the flower of the Union and rebel armies to almost hand-to hand encounter, and by the setting of the sun the fate of one would be decided. Henceforth Antietam will be known as the scene of indomitable courage and triumph of the Union arms.

However magnificent a battle may appear to a spectator, posted at a safe distance, when over, an inspection of the field dissipates the illusion, and the shocking details of carnage speak more emphatically than words can express of its sanguinary fruits. Let us take a closer survey, now that the flag of truce is flying. Here are the mangled remains of a noble fellow who was in the front rank during the charge; a cannon ball has carried away the upper part of his head.

he doubtless never knew what hurt him. There lies one pierced through the heart by a bullet, he fell face downward, still holding his musket in the strong grasp of death. These heaps of dead bodies tell of the fatal effect of our artillery, as it poured an enfilading fire upon an advancing column of the rebels. This ditch, used as a rifle-pit, and strewn with men sunk in the sleep that knows no waking, shows with what certain aim the leaden messengers were sent among them.

Near that solitary house, shaded by a neighboring wood, stands a caisson, and around it lay, as they have fallen, the bodies of six Confederate artillerymen; a faithful horse shot in the traces mingles his blood with theirs; and forms a group not easily to be forgotten. Close beside yonder fence where they fell, lie a number of men belonging to a Louisiana regiment which had been sorely pressed; their spirits have fled, gone where the cannon's roar is never heard, " and gory sabres rise and fall" no more. Here is a barn, now used as a temporary hospital, and crowded with the victims of the day; while lying upon the ground outside are many of the wounded, imperfectly protected from the elements, waiting to receive the surgeon's attention. Their shelter is now of the rudest kind; but later those who chance to survive will fare better.

The question is occasionally asked, how does one feel in battle? The testimony of the bravest is, that at the commencement of a fight a certain trepidation is experienced, which soon wears off; but to stand unconcernedly before an imposing force in the face of death and abide the calm that precedes the first flash of artillery or the first volley of musketry, thinking of home and the possibilities of the hour, requires *some* nerve. The man who trembles when he first hears "the death-shot hissing from afar," is not to be branded a coward; for though he may be as brave as Cæsar, his blood will quicken, his heart throb faster, and through his whole frame "some sense of shuddering" be perceptible. But soon after the opening of an engagement the spell is broken, that strange and indescribable sensation, passes away; and as the clamor and wild excitement of the battle increases he becomes oblivious of danger, and even finds in the last exploding shell or the patter of Minies a subject for jest.

The battery remained in position on the line of battle near Miller's house all day of the 18th. While a flag of truce belonging to the enemy was seen floating in the breeze down on the right near a cornfield; the privilege had been granted them to succor their wounded and bury their dead. All is quiet on our front, but firing was heard some distance off on the right. In the afternoon quite a smart shower of rain passed over us, cooling the air a little, and lessened the stench arising from the dead horses. Fatigue parties of both armies are out between the two lines of skirmishers. There was not much work for our party, as about all the dead or wounded which lay between the lines belonged to the rebels.

Thus the day closes, and night shuts in the scene of carnage, leaving many thousand men, helpless and bathed in blood upon the field, to watch for the return of light, and wait for removal and the dressing of their wounds. Who can imagine the suffering of that night, and the work for the surgeons on the morrow?

On the morning of the 19th, at sunrise, there was a general bustle of activity among the troops in our front, caused by orders received for a general advance of our lines. Skirmishers were thrown well out to the front followed by the main line; then it was discovered that the enemy had retreated and there was no one to oppose our advance. Under cover of a flag of truce, the rebel commander had withdrawn his troops from Antietam to the Potomac River; and General Lee's intended invasion of Pennsylvania was abandoned in consequence of the terrible losses sustained at South Mountain and Antietam.

At noon the battery was withdrawn from the main line of battle, and, passing through a strip of woods reached a clearing where it encamped on a ridge beside a small ravine, through which ran a small stream of clear sparkling water; this was gladly and freely used by the men for laundry purposes, hoping to enjoy the luxury of a clean shirt.

Broke camp on the morning of the 22d, after an encampment of three days, and started for Virginia. Marching along the Hagerstown turnpike, we soon reached Sharpsburg. This town, not long since, was a charming settlement of some 1,500 inhabitants, but now presented a dirty, dilapidated appearance; scarcely a house or barn having escaped the effects of shell and musketry. Here and there a dwelling had been pierced by a ten-pound Parrott shot, or a chimney-top unceremoniously knocked into the street, and many other evidences of destruction, anticipating the waste of all-devouring years. Such is war. Passing on we crossed the Antietam Creek at the Old Furnace, and proceeded to Maryland Heights, where we went into camp.

On the 25th, left the Heights and marched to Sandy Hook, forded the Potomac River to Harper's Ferry and proceeded to Bolivar Heights, where we went into camp just beyond our old camping ground of last March. The troops of the Second Corps occupied Bolivar Heights, while the Twelfth Corps, General Williams's, encamped at Sandy Hook and Harper's Ferry. Both corps were under the command of General Sumner.

The President's "Proclamation of Emancipation" was issued September 22d, three days after the withdrawal of General Lee's army to Virginia; and officially communicated to the Union army on September 24th; the battery received the news while at Bolivar Heights, on the afternoon of September 25th.

October 1st. The monotony of camp life was broken by orders to prepare for inspection. There was unusual activity and commotion among the troops upon hearing that President Lincoln was at headquarters. In the afternoon, during a mounted inspection by our captain, John G. Hazard, the President, General McClellan and General Sumner with their full staffs, rode through our camp and passed the battery on a tour of inspection, after which we were dismissed, and passes given to visit old familiar places. It was freely rumored at the time that the President visited the Army of the Potomac for the purpose of seeing for himself, if, as General McClellan represented, the army was in no condition to pursue General Lee's forces into Virginia.

On the 6th, broke camp, and moving to the government grounds at Bolivar, encamped, and resumed the usual routine of drill and discipline, cleaning equipments, inspection, and visiting friends in other commands. We were encamped upon these same grounds during the previous March.

On the evening of the 8th a change was made by the signing of the muster-rolls, every one was happy and smiling; the paymaster was coming, and we were expecting to receive our four months' pay.

On the 9th the paymaster arrived, and each received the full amount due him for the months of May, June, July and August. This was harvest time for the sutlers, for though the men grumbled at the exorbitant prices demanded, they nevertheless indulged in such luxuries as molasses cookies, ten for a quarter, butter and cheese sixty to eighty cents a pound, and invariably a very small pound, while condensed milk was fifty cents per pound can.

In the afternoon we were notified of General Sumner's leave of absence, and that General Couch was to take command of the Second Corps, to which the battery was attached.

On the 12th of October, First Lieut. Raymond H. Perry's resignation was accepted, and he left the battery, going home to Rhode Island. In the afternoon the battery had a mounted inspection by Captain Hazard. First Lieut. G. W. Adams took command of the right section, First Lieut. H. S. Bloodgood of the left section, and Second Lieut. G. L. Dwight the centre section. After the inspection the captain complimented the men on their fine appearance.

On the 16th, the battery receiving orders, was hitched up, to be ready to move at a moment's notice; remained so for two hours, when we were ordered to unhitch and sent to quarters, our services not being required.

The only episode which interrupted the pleasant monotony of rest and recruiting of the Second Corps after the fatigues of the Manassas and Antietam campaigns, was a reconnaisance conducted by General Hancock with the First Division up the Valley of the Shenandoah to Charlestown, with the view of discovering whether the enemy were there in force. This reconnaissance developed nothing; they found only cavalry supporting a battery, which was handled by a captain of remarkable merit, who defended his position with great daring and tenacity against a superior weight of fire, only yielding ground to an actual advance of our infantry. The brave fellow was afterward found minus a foot, in a house near Charlestown, when our troops occupied that place. This officer was Capt. B. H. Smith, Jr., of the Richmond Howitzer Battalion.

On the 29th, renewed life and activity was manifested by the troops upon receiving orders to prepare and cook three days' extra rations to be carried in the haversacks. Prospects of a move at last.

CHAPTER XII.

MARCH TO FALMOUTH — SKIRMISHES BY THE WAY.

IN pursuance with repeated and urgent requests from the War Department, General McClellan, after a halt of five weeks, set the Army of the Potomac in motion, the Second Corps taking the lead, followed by the rest of the army. On the morning of October 30th, the infantry of the Second Corps crossed the Shenandoah River, and, marching around the base of Loudon Heights, entered the valley in the vicinity of Hill's Grove; then continuing the advance it moved along the Blue Ridge Mountains, and occupied successively the several passes over the mountains westward to the line of march, in pursuance with general orders and under favorable weather, this was remarkable from the fact, that, during the summer and early autumn. there was almost a daily contest between sunshine and rain. Midday warmth would be followed at night by a sudden downward slide of the mercury, chilling the blood to the marrow, and preparing many an incautious one for an attack of typhoid delirium, or for the Society of Shakers. Successive changes of drizzle, rain and piercing winds from the mountains would be followed by a day of soft, genial atmosphere and as beautiful moonlight night as ever illuminated our own Christian Hill, or scattered sparkling gems upon the ruffled bosom of Narragansett Bay.

On the morning of October 30th, Captain Hazard received orders to have his battery ready to move at noon; although anticipated, this order made us realize more fully the pleasant life this camp had afforded us. We had tarried at no place, since leaving our winter quarters at Poolesville, Md., better adapted to the enjoyment of army life. It was in close proximity to railroads connected with the north, and luxuries could be obtained in abundance, while its mail facilities were another source of pleasure, which we knew must be sacrificed when we moved. The magnificent mountain scenery at sunrise added much to its grandeur and attractiveness as an abode for man, weary and in want of rest.

Leaving Bolivar at one P. M., we bade farewell to our old camp, and, moving down through Harper's Ferry turned to the right, passing along the bank of the Shenandoah to the Old Foundry, then crossing the river on a pontoon bridge, we wound along the base of Loudon Heights through the valley to the Leesburg road, and halted at Vestal's Gap, where we encamped near the little hamlet of Neersville, remaining here nearly two days.

On the afternoon of the 31st, the muster rolls were made out for September and October.

On the morning of November 1st, the troops were again active, and at noon the battery broke camp, moving along the mountain road, which being hilly and somewhat stony, made many of our horses footsore. After passing Hillsborough (a small post town), the battery was placed in position on the edge of a level open field facing southwest, and bivouacked. All was quiet during the night, and the battery remained in position until nine o'clock A. M. of the 2d, when the march was resumed at a slow pace along the mountain roads of the Blue Ridge. At noon a halt of an hour was made, that we might make some coffee, after which we again marched onward until six P. M., when we halted on a thrifty looking farm; its flourishing condition indicated that thus far it had escaped the ravages of the army; and the order to park the battery and encamp here for the night was hailed with delight by the men; the officers' mess was not the only one that boasted chicken and potatoes for breakfast the next morning.

At an early hour, on the morning of the 3d, the battery was ordered to prepare for a move, but it was eight o'clock before we left our camping ground to follow the van. Having a good road we did not halt until noon to make our coffee, after which we continued our march until a halt was ordered at seven o'clock, just as we were getting ready to encamp, the pieces and caissons were ordered to the front on a trot; the firing of our advance guard was heard as we drew near to where our division was drawn up in line of battle. The battery was ordered to take position in the open fields on rising ground, and, placing the guns in battery prepared for action, but did not open fire. From our position we could distinctly see our skirmishers advance, then halt, fire, load, and advance again, while little clouds of smoke from their muskets would arise, circling in the air. To those that were watching and saw their manœuvering (at least to us battery men), it was a novel sight. It was not a drill with an imaginary enemy, but one with the real foe as adversaries, and our men's skill showed the result of their training. The enemy retreated as our skirmishers entered the wood in pursuit and were soon lost to view.

The enemy thus encountered was a battalion of cavalry, Colonel Ashby's men, who were out raiding and trying to get at our wagon trains. They had been cut off from the mountain gap by the unexpected arrival of our advance; they exchanged a few shots with our skirmishers and then retreated, trying to gain Snicker's Gap. Fortunately, however, the raiders were intercepted by General Pleasanton's cavalry, which was guarding the passage to the gap, and the men at the muzzle of their carbines ordered the raiders as they rode up to halt and become their guests and take a trip north as prisoners of war.

At sunset the battery limbered up and advanced to Snicker's Gap, bivouacking near the little hamlet of Snickersville, we remained here until noon of the 3d, when we broke camp and marched through Bloomfield and Upperville, where the advancing column had an artillery duel with Stuart's mounted cavalry battery, which was moving towards the mountains to escape through Ashby's Gap.

The battery, with General Howard's division, proceeded to Ashby's Gap and encamped at Paris, where we remained for two days, and heard the following episode relating to our chief of artillery:

The night of November 4th was cold and gloomy. General Couch had an inveterate aversion to making his headquarters in a house, greatly preferring the benignant shelter of a Virginia rail fence. On this occasion, however, it being very probable that frequent dispatches would be sent and received, General Couch gave Capt. C. H. Morgan, his chief of artillery, permission to select a house for headquarters. Delighted at this concession to the bodily infirmities of the staff, Morgan galloped gayly into the yard of a spacious mansion on the outskirts of the village. Here was an old man, evidently the proprietor, who appeared somewhat shaken by the recent artillery fire and pistol shots of the cavalry. "Good evening," said Morgan. "Good evening," responded the owner. "General Couch proposes to make his headquarters at your house to-night—that is, if you have no objection." Now, the old man had a great many *objections*, but did not dare to state them; he, however, began at once to make excuses, saying, "Of course he should be delighted to have the general with him, but was afraid he could not make him comfortable: perhaps the general had better go where he could be better accommodated." "But," said Morgan, "you have a large house." This fact could not be denied, and the luckless proprietor had to admit that the house was commodious. "But," he added eagerly, "I have a large family." "Well, now," asked Morgan, "what family have you got?" "In the first place," said the old gentleman, "I have three nieces." "Say not another word; we'll take the house," Morgan replied. The general and his staff did establish themselves in the house, and three saucier vixens could hardly be found in all rebeldom than those three maidens, was the verdict from our chief of artillery.

On the 6th, the battery left Paris, and after moving in a southeasterly course turned to the west, passing through a small village of four or five houses and as many barns. At the corner of the roads was a blacksmith shop, if such it might be called, consisting of a forge covered by a shed of three sides. This hamlet had the romantic name of Kerfoot. Here the battery halted and bivouacked. The left section, under Lieutenant Bloodgood, was sent out to the right on picket, guarding the road which led to Manassas Gap.

On the 7th, upon the return of the left section from picket, the battery moved near to Rectortown and bivouacked. The right section, under Lieutenant Adams, was sent back on picket to guard the road by which we came. While halted at Rectortown, General Sumner returned and rejoined the army, but did not assume command of his old corps (the Second), for the scheme of forming "grand divisions," consisting of two corps each, having been determined upon, the veteran (Sumner) was selected for one of these higher commands.

It was while the troops were here encamped, on the night of the 7th, that the order from Washington was received at the headquarters of the army, which permanently relieved General McClellan from the command of the Army of the Potomac, and Gen. A. E. Burnside was placed in command.

While the battery lay at Rectortown we had a mounted inspection; forty-five horses were condemned and turned in to the quartermaster's department as unserviceable. During the day it snowed enough to cover the ground; it was very cold and disagreeable.

On the 8th, leaving the right section on picket, the battery resumed the march and passed a short distance beyond Rectortown, where it halted until sunset, to allow the wagon trains to pass and get out of the way, then we continued our march until midnight, when we encamped at the little village of Vernon Mills. Early on the morning of the 9th, the right section rejoined the battery and we started on again. The very bad condition of the roads necessitated slow traveling, and we were obliged to borrow horses from Battery A, First Rhode Island Light Artillery, to help us along, as our number was limited. In this way we passed through Warrentown, and encamped about a mile beyond the village.

On the 10th, the weather was warm and pleasant, and the battery, with the Second Division of the Second Corps, was ordered to turn out to bid farewell to Gen. George B. McClellan.

The three divisions of the Second Corps, were drawn up on the left side of the Centreville Pike, at Warrenton, in columns of regiments at intervals, affording sufficient space for the artillery. On the right of the pike stood the Fifth Corps in a similar formation. Between those two gallant corps, so long his comrades, slowly and sadly rode their beloved chief, taking a last farewell; every heart of the thirty thousand was filled with love and grief; every voice raised in shouts expressive of devotion and loyalty to one whose presence had ever inspired them with courage and confidence.

In general, the battery was in good condition during the march from Harper's Ferry along the east slope of the Blue Ridge Mountains to Rectortown, only one exception need be mentioned.

A distressing hoof disease caused much trouble among the horses, and grew more and more serious as the army advanced, until at Rectortown and Warrenton both cavalry and artillery were to a great extent disabled. The quartermaster's service was not proportionally so disturbed, the tough mules resisting the conditions, whatever they might be, that favored the extension of the pest. From one battery alone in the corps sixty horses out of 119 had to be turned in as useless, and in Battery B forty-five out of 114. So prevalent did this become, that many guns were sent back to Washington by rail, being returned when enough serviceable animals were obtained to draw them. During this march an epidemic attacked, not the horses this time, but the men; its name was mutton.

On the Peninsula no mutton had been discovered, and, during the march to Antietam, our men had scrupulously respected the loyalty of the Western Marylanders. But upon the appearance of some fat fleecy sheep upon Virginia soil, discipline for the moment gave way, at least in a degree, to tempting mutton. At first forays were made only at night, but soon the raids went beyond bounds. In vain did officers storm and swear, and in vain even did the provost guard of one division (the Second), turn about and fire ball-cartridges at the fellows who deliberately left the ranks to go after mutton.

The commanding general was enraged; he instructed each division commander to assemble a court-martial for the trial of these offenders; consequently every evening, after going into camp, three courts were in session in the Second Corps, with sheep-killing subjects. Sharp and summary were the punishments inflicted; but all to no purpose,—the killing went on just the same. Of the three division commanders, General Hancock, of the First, was peculiarly sensitive to the slightest imputation of indiscipline. One day as the head of the column was feeling its way on the advance, and was nearing one of the gaps in the mountain range, infantry skirmishers were sent out, as the rebels were thought to be in the vicinity. Soon the men were seen running to and fro along a fence; then they appeared to be running to the rear. Their manœuvres amazed and perplexed the commanding general who had just rode up to the head of the troops, and turning to the colonel in command said, "Colonel, what is the meaning of this, your men are running to the rear, have they struck the enemy? Your skirmishers are being driven in by the rebs." The colonel answered, "Sir, my men never run from a rebel." Making a closer observation through his glass, the colonel saw his men running this way and that, and instantly muttered, "Enemy! the rebs be d——d! it is a d——d flock of sheep they are after!" There was a well attended court-martial that evening.

Upon another occasion some men of the same brigade, having fallen out of ranks, upon some pretense, were observed by General Hancock to steal around a bit of woods, manifestly bound on plunder: determining to make an example of them, he left the column, accompanied by his staff, and, galloping rapidly around the woods from the opposite side, surprised the group gathered around an unfortunate victim about to be sacrificed.

Some of those whose attention was less closely engaged in the prospective slaughter, caught a glimpse of the coming doom in time to climb over a high fence and escape; but upon the principal offender the general pounced with drawn sword and eyes flashing fire. Down on his knees went the thoroughly frightened transgressor. "Arrah, dear gineral, don't be the death of me; I didn't do it, indade I didn't," cried the soldier. "You infernal liar!" shouted the general, "what do you mean by telling me that?. I saw you, you scoundrel! I'll teach you to disobey orders! I'll teach you to kill sheep!" At the close of this tirade the general flourished his sword as if about to begin execution; when, in the most opportune moment, up jumped the innocent subject of this controversy, and giving vent to its feeling in a quavering ba-a-a, ran off; while, amid the shouts of the staff, the general put up his sword and rode away. We may firmly believe that the Irishman was hardly less pleased than the sheep. Let us hope that the scare he got destroyed his appetite for mutton, and that he returned forevermore to his native pork.

In the afternoon of the 10th, Captain Hazard sent a detail of men, under the command of Lieutenant Adams, with the quartermaster, to the railroad station; they returned with forty-five new horses for the battery, by whose addition it was again fully equipped and in marching trim. The army has again been reorganized, this time into grand divisions. The battery is still with the Second Division of the Second Corps, Right Grand Division. We remained encamped near Warrenton until the 14th of November, when marching orders were received.

On the 15th of November, the battery again broke camp and took up the line of march, moving with the division back through Warrenton, and, turning in a southeasterly direction crossed the Owl Run and Virginia Midland Railroad, above Midland Station, and halted at Elk Run, where we bivouacked for the night.

On the 16th, the battery made an early start leaving camp just before six A. M., the morning was cloudy and air raw and chilly. Passing through several small villages, we finally halted on an open plain and encamped for the night. Left camp at eight A. M. on the morning of the 17th, and continued our march in a southeasterly direction until the middle of the afternoon when we halted. All long range gun batteries were then ordered to the front. Heavy cannonading had been heard for some time in the direction of the Rappahannock River, to which place the batteries had been ordered.

On the 19th, the Ninth Corps marched by the battery's encampment going in an easterly direction toward the river. The battery broke camp on the morning of the 20th, and moving eastward about two or three miles halted in a deep ravine and went into camp. The troops were moving in all directions, changing their camping grounds, locating picket stations along the river bank, and building earthworks. This bustling scene indicated that the army was going into winter quarters.

On November 5th, Second Lieut. Joseph S. Milne, promoted from sergeant of Battery E, First Regiment Rhode Island Light Artillery, reported to our battery for duty, and was assigned chief of caissons.

On the 26th, we had a battery inspection by Captain Hazard, and everything was found to be in fighting trim.

November 27th was Thanksgiving Day in Rhode Island. To a soldier in the field one day was the same as another, Sundays not excepted, for when not fighting we had drill and inspection of equipments and quarters; and after the regular camp duties were over we found no Thanksgiving dinner of roast turkey and accompaniments, mince pie, plum-pudding, etc., awaiting *our* inspection. No! the soldier knocking at the enemy's door may be thankful if, after a hard fight, or a long and fatiguing march, he secures a pot of coffee and a few hard-tack to satisfy his empty stomach. A piece of salt pork or salt junk in addition was considered a great treat.

To-day, Second Lieut. G. L. Dwight received a commission as first lieutenant, and was transferred to Battery A, First Regiment Rhode Island Light Artillery.

On the 20th, the drivers were drilled in harnessing and hitching up the horses and battery in readiness to move; they accomplished the feat in ten minutes and thirty-seven seconds from the time the bugler blew "Boots and saddles" call; this was considered very quick time.

On December 1st, Quartermaster Sergt. William S. Dyer, who had been ill a long time, received his discharge for disability and left for Rhode Island. Sergt. Charles A. Libbey, who had been acting as quartermaster sergeant *pro tem.*, was promoted to that position. Corp. Anthony B. Horton was promoted to sergeant, and Private John Delevan to corporal.

On the 2d, the battery broke camp and, leaving the ravine, moved toward the river to a hill covered with woods in the rear of Falmouth, Va., which was opposite the north part of the city of Fredericksburg. The men were now kept quite busy building huts for winter quarters, and a stockade to shelter the horses; in cutting down trees, digging out stumps, and clearing a place in which to park the guns and caissons.

On the 9th, Second Lieut. William S. Perrin, having been promoted from sergeant in Battery C, First Regiment Rhode Island Light Artillery, reported to our battery for duty and was assigned chief of centre section.

On the 10th, Captain Hazard inspected the battery; the men were in good spirits, and the equipments in excellent condition. In the afternoon three days' rations were issued to be kept in the haversacks, which meant that a movement might be expected at any time; and, later in the day, at retreat roll call, the following circular from headquarters was read to the men:

HEADQUARTERS SECOND DIVISION, SECOND CORPS,
Dec. 10, 1862.

Officers and Soldiers of the Second Division:

I am expecting to command you in another battle very soon, and I am exceedingly anxious for you to do well. If we succeed in the coming battle, and I believe we shall succeed, our work will be well nigh over, and we may soon return to our coveted homes.

With what joy, with what pride, will be our welcome among those friends who are so eagerly watching our course, provided we shall have faithfully performed our part. I earnestly entreat every officer and man to do his best to make this the decisive battle of the war.

At Antietam it is said we gave way. I have endeavored to shield you from blame. On the Rappahannock our conduct must be above reproach.

Stand by your country, stand by your colors with unflinching constancy. and by the blessing of God a complete victory will be your reward.

[Official.]   (Signed,)
O. O. HOWARD,
Brig. Gen. Commanding.

H. M. STINSON, *Lieut. and A. D. C.*

Lieut. William S. Perrin.

CHAPTER XIII.

BATTLE OF FREDERICKSBURG.

IN anticipation of the pending engagement, the Second Corps, on December 9th, was reinforced by five large, new regiments of infantry. Four being of the nine months' class lacked experience, but were composed of excellent material and good officers. On the evening of the 10th, General Hunt, chief of artillery of the Army of the Potomac, began to occupy the left bank of the Rappahannock with batteries in order to cover the crossing of the two columns. The whole river side thus became one vast battery; one hundred and forty-seven pieces having been put into position. Though the troops, generally, had gone to rest with no premonition of the coming battle, headquarters were alive with the work of preparation, and before daybreak the troops were called to arms. In silence and in darkness the several divisions were concentrated around the different places whence they were to cross the river.

On December 11th, reveille was sounded an hour before sunrise with orders to prepare breakfast as soon as possible. The battery was hitched up, and left camp under light marching orders just after sunrise in the following order, Capt. John G. Hazard in command; First Lieut. George W. Adams, in command of right section; First Lieut. Horace S. Bloodgood, in command of left section; Second Lieut. William S. Perrin, in command of centre section; Second Lieut. Joseph S. Milne, in command of caissons. Moving south toward the river, we halted under cover of the hills, near the Lacy House. Here was massed all of the Second Division of the Second Corps, while other troops were still moving further south, and some batteries going east. Infantry firing could be heard apparently from in front of the Lacy House, and was at times quite heavy; we learned that it came from the enemy's sharpshooters, who were opposing the laying of the pontoon bridge.

About 9.30 A. M., we moved to the east and front, and were placed in position in battery on a bluff to the right of the Lacy House, overlooking the city of Fredericksburg, Va., and in line with the other batteries of the corps. As soon as the light fog hanging over the river began to rise, men could be seen moving about the town and on the river bank. The Engineer Corps (men of the Fifteenth and Fiftieth New York Regiments) were still trying to put down the pontoon bridge by which the troops were to cross. They had been at work since early morning, but so far had made very little progress on account of the enemy's sharpshooters. At noon, however, the order was given for all the batteries to shell and burn the city in order to dislodge the enemy, the shelling of the morning having failed to do so.

About 12.30 P. M., Battery B opened a rapid fire which was continued for about an hour then slackened, and sighting more carefully would send a shot through the gable of a house, the steeple of a church, or the top of a tree, in fact, at any objective point where a shot would prove effective. It is impossible to fitly describe the effects of this iron hailstorm hurled into the town. The roar of the cannon, the bursting of shells, the falling of walls and chimneys; added to the fire of the infantry on both sides, the smoke from the guns and burning houses, made a scene of the wildest confusion, terrific enough to appall the stoutest hearts. Under cover of this bombardment, the engineers made another unsuccessful attempt to finish the bridge, the enemy again interfering. Finally, the Seventh Michigan and Nineteenth Massachusetts Regiments crossed the river in pontoon boats, and drove the enemy's sharpshooters from the rifle-pits and cellars along the bank, and advanced up into the town thus gaining the lower streets. Then, and not until then, were the engineers successful, completing the bridge about sunset.

The battery remained in position on the bluff all day, but at dark withdrew under cover of the hill, here we parked and the men bivouacked for the night. The ammunition chests were refilled, as we had used about one-half of our supply of 786 rounds.

On the morning of the 12th, about six A. M., the battery left its camping ground and moved circuitously to the river side in front of the Lacy House, and at seven A. M. crossed the pontoon bridge into Fredericksburg, and turning to the left halted on the bank near the river in column of sections, where we remained all day and bivouacked at night. Battery B was the first battery of the Right Grand

Division to cross the pontoon bridge. We found the buildings had been badly shattered by our shot and shell, which had shown no respect for stone, brick or wood, but had left their marks wherever they chanced to strike. In one instance a shell took a musical course; entering a house it struck the back right hand corner of a piano, and, passing through it diagonally over the sounding-board cut about every string; it then passed out at the left hand front corner, and, entering the next room, exploded, shattering the furniture into kindlings. Beautiful and costly paintings with rich mouldings shared the same fate.

On the morning of the 13th, we busied ourselves in making coffee by fires which we tried to conceal from the enemy's view, so as not to draw their fire on us. About ten o'clock A. M. Captain Hazard received orders to move up into the city. We left the river bank in column of pieces, the caisson at the rear, and marched up into the town and halted on Caroline Street awaiting further orders. The carelessness with which the enemy threw shot and shell into the city compelled us to change our position several times to escape the range of their fire. During the forenoon there was heard, at a distance down on the left, heavy musketry firing, and at intervals some cannonading; while in the afternoon it commenced pretty sharp in our front.

About 3.45 P. M. an officer was seen in earnest conversation with our captain; then we received the order of "At-ten-tion! drivers and cannoneers! mount, forward, trot, march!" and away we went down Caroline Street, turning to the right into Hanover Street; passed Battery A in position on our left, at the outskirts of the city, who saluted us with "There goes Battery B to h——ll!" Taking no notice of their salute we proceeded on the double quick, going toward the Heights; the troops of General Gorman's old brigade gave us hearty cheers as we passed.

By orders, Lieutenant Milne led the caissons into a field at the left of the road and parked in the rear of the canal. The pieces, led by Captain Hazard, continued up the road to within a short range of the enemy's line; the left and centre sections were ordered into position on rising ground, to the left of the road, while the right section, under Lieut. G. W. Adams, was advanced about thirty yards and took position in the road, right piece a little ahead of the other, and opened fire upon the enemy's rifle-pits at the foot of the hills, sending shot and shell in quick succession.

The sixth piece was the first to open fire after taking position, and Joseph Luther received a bad wound in the hip; next Corp. W. P. Wells was hit in the foot, then Lewis W. Scott was knocked over, and Michael Duffy's wheel horses were shot dead. William T. Jordan's horses met the same fate, as also did John Richards's and Clark Woodmansee's. M. Carmichael was hit by a spent ball in the groin, which laid him up, and one knocked William H. Cornell over. Corp. C. W. Rathbone received a bad wound in the ankle, and Bartholemew Hart one in the wrist and neck; several others followed in quick succession. But the cannoneers did not shirk their duty, they kept the guns blazing forth an angry roar sending shot and shell against that *famous stone wall*. The drivers of the caisson limbers came up with chests full of ammunition and relieved the piece limbers which were empty, and going to the rear, where the caissons were stationed, refilled the chests and brought them again to the front; in this way the guns of the battery were kept supplied with ammunition during the engagement.

Our position was a perfect hornet's nest, with the hornets all stirred up. Minie balls were flying and singing about us, with a zip and a u-u-u, or a thud as they struck; though they flew thick and fast we were too busy to dodge them, but kept our guns blazing away much to the consternation of those in front of us.

We continued this cannonading for about three-quarters of an hour, when the battery was ordered to cease firing, and permit the infantry (General Humphrey's troops) to pass through the battery to charge on the enemy's line at the *stone wall*, left and rear of the *Brick House*. After the infantry had passed, the battery, being ordered to limber up, withdrew in good order from the field, in the face of the enemy, taking all our guns and caissons, but for lack of horses we were forced to leave one limber on the field. The battery went back into the city and parked in an open lot on Caroline Street near the old position we occupied before going into action. Captain Hazard asked for volunteers who would go back to the field for the limber; Sergeant Horton was the first to reply, being the first to understand the nature of the request, as the men were all more or less busy in preparing the camp for the night. However, Sergt. Anthony B. Horton with three drivers, Levi J. Cornell, Clark L. Woodmansee, and Benjamin A. Burlingame with their horses, under command of Lieut. Joseph S. Milne, went back to the field, and returned safely to camp with the desired limber.

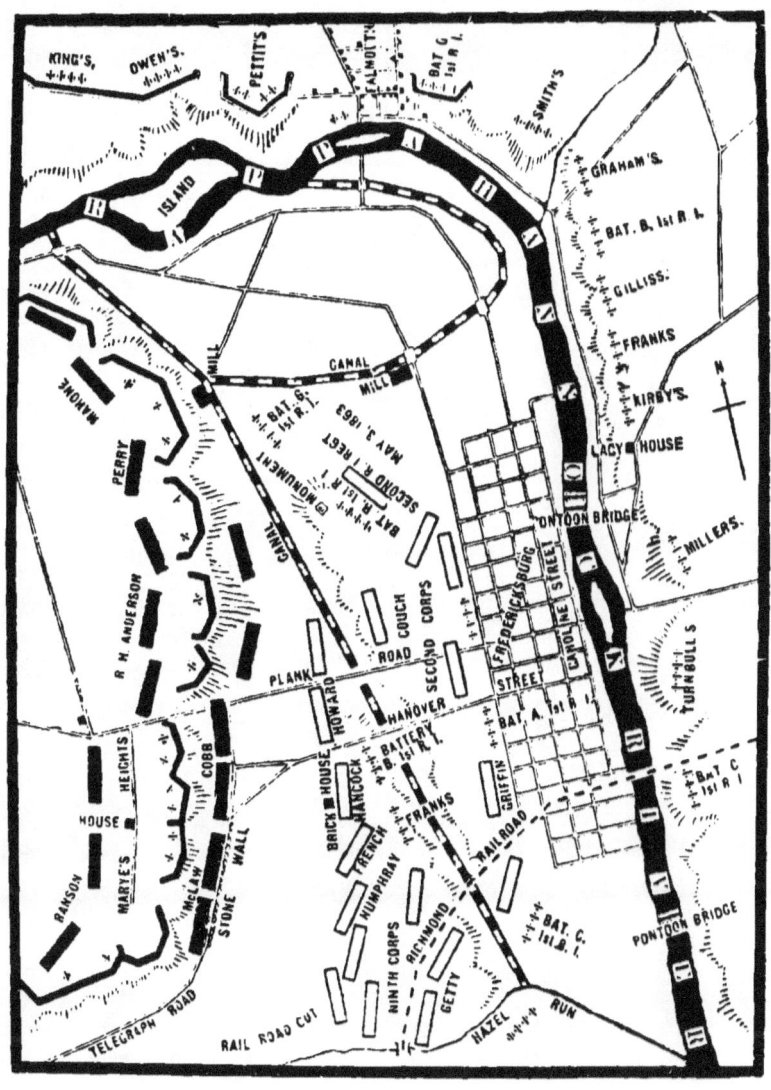

Fredericksburg, Dec. 13, 1862, and May 3, 1863.

The casualties of the battery in this battle of Fredricksburg December 13th, were sixteen men wounded, namely: Corporals Calvin W. Rathbone, William P. Wells, Alanson A. Williams; Privates Lorenzo D. Budlong, Morris Carmichael, William H. Cornell, Henry A. Gardner, Caleb H. H. Greene, John F. Hanson, Bartholomew Hart, Albert E. Hendrick, Edwin F. Knowles, Joseph Luther (died of wounds in hospital), William F. Reynolds, Lewis W. Scott, John J. Sisson.

Three of the above remained with the battery, their wounds being slight; while the others were sent to different hospitals.

It was very remarkable, considering our close action with the enemy, that none of the batterymen were killed. Fifteen horses were killed, and Captain Hazard's, Lieutenant Bloodgood's and Lieutenant Milne's were shot under them. The officers and men were very thankful that they had passed through the ordeal so fortunately, for the battery had been ordered to the front, to be sacrificed if need be, in order to give inspiration to the infantry in the last and great struggle of our troops to carry the works of the enemy at the *stone wall*. It was in vain that the men rushed forward into the midst of a shower of musket balls, for in spite of their bravery they were forced to succumb, and the goal (*the stone wall*) could not be reached. *

---

* WHAT MAJ.-GEN. D. N. COUCH SAYS OF THE ASSAULTS OF OUR TROOPS ON THE STONE WALL.

To the left, on line of the Brick House, a slight basin in the ground afforded protection to men lying down, against the musketry of the enemy behind the stone wall, but not against the converging fire of the artillery on the heights.

My headquarters were in the field on the edge of the town, overlooking the plain. Without a clear idea of the state of affairs at the front, since the smoke and light fog veiled everything, I sent word to Generals French and Hancock to carry the enemy's works by storm. Then I climbed the steeple of the court-house, and from above the haze and smoke, got a clear view of the field. General Howard, who was with me, says I exclaimed: "Oh, great God! see how our men, our poor fellows, are falling." I remember that the whole plain could be seen covered with men, prostrate and dropping; the line men running here and there, and in front closing upon each other and the wounded coming back. The commands seemed to be mixed up. I had never before seen fighting like that; there was no cheering on the part of the men, but a stubborn determination to obey orders and do their duty. I was in the steeple hardly ten seconds, for I saw, at a glance, how they were being cut down, and was convinced that we could not be successful in front, and that our only chance lay by the right. I immediately ordered General Howard to work in on the right, with the brigades of Owen and Hall, and attack the enemy behind the stone wall in flank, which he did. About two P. M. General Hooker, who was in command of the Centre Grand Division, came upon the field. Whipple's division of Hooker's troops had crossed and gone to the right to relieve General Howard, so that he might join in the attack in the centre. Generals Humphreys and Sykes, of Hooker's troops, came to my support. Towards three P. M. I received the following dispatch:

An opinion of the enemy in regard to Battery B, as learned by our captain, John G. Hazard, who says: "The day after the battle I went over the river with Capt. C. H. Morgan, Chief of Artillery of the Second Corps, and another officer of his staff, under a flag of truce conveying messages to General Lee in relation to the burying of our dead. As usual our senior officer, Captain Morgan, advanced and met the senior officer of the enemy, and after introducing themselves they in turn introduced the others, and then the interchange of documents was made. After the official business was ended, some

> "HEADQUARTERS RIGHT GRAND DIVISION, ARMY OF THE POTOMAC,
> Dec. 13, 1862—2.40 P. M.
>
> GENERAL COUCH: Hooker has been ordered to put in everything. You must hold on until he comes in.
>
> By command of BREV. MAJ-GEN. SUMNER.
> W. G. JONES, *Lieutenant, Aide-de-Camp, etc.*
>
> Hooker was the ranking general, and as I understood that he was to take command of the whole fighting line, and the putting in of his fresh men beside mine might make a success. His very coming was to me, therefore, like the breaking out of the sun in a storm. I rode back to meet him, told him what had been done, and said: "I can't carry that hill by the front assault; the only chance we have is to try to get in on the right." Hooker replied: "I will talk with Hancock." He talked with him, and, after a few minutes, said: "Well, Couch, things are in such a state I must go over and tell Burnside, it is of no use trying to carry this line here," or words to that effect, and then went off. His going away still left me in command. It was a little after two P. M. when he went away, and it was nearly four o'clock when he returned, which was after General Humphreys had made his last charge, and we were holding our lines.
>
> While Humphreys was at work, Getty's division of Wilcox's corps was ordered about three o'clock to the charge on our left by the unfinished railroad. I could see the men were being dreadfully cut up, although they had not advanced as far as my men. I determined to send a battery upon the plain to shell the line that was doing them so much harm, so I ordered an aide to tell Captain Morgan to send a battery across the canal and plant it near the Brick House. Morgan came to me and said: "My God! General, you will lose your guns, a battery cannot live there!" My reply was: "Then it can die there! I would rather lose my guns than so many of my men; put them in." Hazard's Battery B, First Regiment, Rhode Island Light Artillery, was the one to be sacrificed.
>
> Without a murmur, Captain Hazard dashed, with his six twelve-pounders, into the street, over the bridge, and, getting into action on the left of the road, opened fire with a rapidity which well served my purpose, to hearten our men lying down in front, and create in the mind of the enemy the expectation of a new assault, which would draw their fire and relieve the pressure on the Ninth Corps.
>
> The right section of Hazard's battery, under Lieut. G. W. Adams, a cool and capable officer, is still further advanced in the road in line of the Brick House. Three number ones are struck down in quick succession, at the muzzle of the guns, but still the pieces were served in that perilous place as steadily as if at a review.
>
> Men never fought more gallantly. When General Hooker returned to the field he ordered Frank's battery (G, First New York) to the ridge on Hazard's left in support. But this last effort did not last long. Never before, I believe, was artillery so far advanced in plain sight without cover against an intrenched enemy. The object of the daring enterprise was accomplished, and the guns were ultimately withdrawn without the loss of a single piece; and Battery B, First Regiment Rhode Island Light Artillery, Capt. John G. Hazard commanding, was placed upon record.
>
> [Signed] D. N. COUCH,
> *Major-General commanding.*

thirty minutes were spent in a social way. During the time, the senior officer of the enemy said to Captain Morgan, 'I saw yesterday one of the most gallant deeds, performed by a battery of your artillery, coming out between the lines and getting into action under a fearful fire from our artillery and infantry, that I ever saw.' Captain Morgan replied, ' Colonel, allow me to introduce to you again Captain Hazard, who commanded and led that battery into action. The colonel at once stepped up to me, offering his hand, saying, ' Captain, I congratulate you and your men on their deed of gallantry.' I replied that we did not desire any congratulation from a military point of view—the battery was sent merely as a morale support to our infantry, rather than for any effectual work we could possibly do. The colonel replied, ' All the same, it was a most daring deed.' "

Following is a copy of Capt. John G. Hazard's report of the battery sent to Division Headquarters:

HEADQUARTERS BATTERY B, FIRST REG'T R. I. LIGHT ART.
NEAR FALMOUTH, VA., Dec. 17, 1862.

CAPTAIN: I have the honor to report that on Wednesday, 10th instant, I received orders to put my battery in light marching order, preparatory to removing early on the following day. At the break of day on the morning of the 11th instant, received orders from Capt. C. H. Morgan, Chief of Artillery of the Second Corps, to move my command to near the Rappahannock River. Halted in rear of the Lacy House under cover of the hill. At 9.30 A. M. was ordered to report to Col. C. H. Tompkins, and placed my battery in position on the bluff, to the right of the Lacy House, overlooking the city of Fredericksburg.

During the day I expended 384 rounds of solid shot and shell upon the enemy's sharpshooters' rifle-pits that lined the opposite bank of the river. At dark I withdrew my battery, by orders of Captain Morgan, about 1,000 yards to the rear and parked.

On the morning of the 12th, at six o'clock, I received orders from Captain Morgan to cross the river with my battery and report to General Howard, commanding Second Division Second Corps.

Crossed the river at seven A. M. and formed in column of sections on the bank near the river. I remained in this position until ten A. M. of the 13th, when I moved out, by orders of General Howard, in columns of pieces on Caroline Street.

At 3.45 P. M., I received orders from Captain Morgan to take my battery to the front on the double-quick, and placed them in position on an eminence some 150 or 200 yards in front of the enemy's rifle-pits. I placed the centre and left sections on the brow of the field to the left of the road, and the right section in the road about thirty yards in advance of the other sections, and opened on the enemy with solid shot from the left and centre sections and shell from the right. I continued firing with rapidity for forty-five minutes, when General Humphreys requested me to cease firing that he might charge through my battery with his brigade on the enemy's works. After the infantry passed I withdrew my battery by orders of Captain Morgan to my old position in the city.

Before getting into battery and during the engagement, I sustained a loss of sixteen men and twelve battery horses, also the horses of Lieutenants Bloodgood's, Milne's, and my own were shot. Owing to the loss of my horses I was forced to leave one limber on the field, and withdrew the left piece of the left section by hand. After arriving in my old position I asked if any sergeant would volunteer to go back and bring the limber from the field. Sergeant Anthony B. Horton was the first to reply, and said, "I am your man," and succeeded in bringing it into camp.

The list of casualties on the 13th were: Henry A. Gardner, Albert E. Hendrick, Joseph Luther, Caleb H. H. Greene, Bartholomew Hart, Lewis W. Scott, and Corp. Calvin W. Rathbone were badly wounded. Corp. William P. Wells, in foot; Edwin H. Knowles, in thigh; Lorenzo D. Budlong, in arm; Morris Carmichael, in groin; William F. Reynolds, lungs; slightly wounded, Corp. Alanson A. Williams, William H. Cornell, John F. Hanson, John J. Sisson.

On the morning of the 14th, by order of Captain Morgan, I recrossed the river and reported to General Hunt; went into park in rear of the Lacy House. I remained in this position until 12 M. of the 15th, when I returned to my old camp near Falmouth, by orders of Captain Morgan, and reported to General Howard.

In conclusion I would respectfully beg leave to allude to the bravery and endurance of my men, *not a man quitting his post on the field*.

As to the conduct of my officers, Lieutenants Adams, Bloodgood, Perrin and Milne, I can only say I am proud to have associated with me such gallant and self-possessed officers.

JOHN G. HAZARD, Capt. 1st Reg. R. I. Lt. Art.,
Commanding Battery B.

On the morning of the 14th, Captain Hazard received orders to recross the river, and at nine o'clock the battery was again parked in the rear of the Lacy House. While here our ammunition chests were refilled, and our supply wagon having been ordered up, rations were issued, and the spare horses from camp were brought down to take the places of those killed. All the equipments and harnesses were examined. At noon we received eighteen infantry recruits, detailed from the Fifteenth Massachusetts and Nineteenth Maine regiments, to take the places of our wounded. Thus the battery was again ready for action.

All day of the 15th, the battery bivouacked near the Lacy House awaiting orders. The morning of the 16th was cold and rainy, and continued so throughout the day. Last night our troops evacuated Fredericksburg, and recrossing the river in safety bivouacked along the east bank of the Rappahannock. The rebels again occupied the city, and during the morning their pickets could be seen skirmishing through the streets as if they expected to meet with further opposition from our troops.

Upon orders received by Captain Hazard at noon, the infantry recruits were returned to their regiments, and the battery proceeded to its camp near Falmouth; the remainder of the day was devoted to rest. Being in camp again the men began to revive from the demoralizing effects of the retreat after a hard fought battle.

Sergt. Calvin L. Macomber.

CHAPTER XIV.

IN WINTER QUARTERS NEAR FALMOUTH, VA.

THE 17th, found us in our old camp trying to finish our winter quarters, which were laid out in an oblong square with the park in the centre. The officers' and first sergeant's quarters were on the east side, and along the north side were those of the men; on the west side were the quarters of the quartermaster-sergeant, the artificers, blacksmith, and stable sergeant, also those of the cooks and kitchen; on the south side, extending half way up the square, was the stable, a stockade of poles and frame-work covered on the top and north side with pine boughs and straw; the south side was open, and the ground descending in this direction made the stable dry and comfortable for the animals. The quarters of the men were log huts with canvas tops, each containing a fireplace or pit. The chimneys of the fireplaces usually did good service, but if the wind chanced to blow very hard the smoke would sometimes be carried in the wrong direction. Notwithstanding many little inconveniences, our quarters were quite comfortable considering the existing circumstances.

In the afternoon, at retreat roll call, the following was read to the command:

HEADQUARTERS 2D DIV., 2D CORPS,
Dec. 17, 1862.

General Orders, }
No. 173. }

The general commanding the division now takes occasion officially to tender his hearty thanks to the commissioned officers of every grade, and to the enlisted men, for their gallant conduct during Thursday, Saturday, Sunday and Monday in the battle of Fredericksburg. He realizes that his interest is identified with theirs, and purposes to care for them with the same untiring energy that they have displayed since his connection with them. Through you, their comrades, he tenders his strong feelings of sympathy to the wounded, and to the afflicted at home. We will cherish the names of the fallen, and emulate their example.

Our lives are still spared for some good end, and we can use them (or sacrifice them if need be) in no nobler cause than that in which we are now engaged, in the preservation of what our fathers purchased for us. Our cause is just, and with troops like Sedgwick's Old Division and the Divine blessing will not falter.

[Official.]   (Signed,)   O. O. HOWARD,
Brig. Gen. Commanding.

H. M. STINSON, *Lieut. and A. D. C.*

December 18th. The weather was pleasant but cold. The officers' and men's quarters were finished, as was also the stockade for the horses. In consequence of our having no drills, camp duties were very light and we had quite an easy time.

December 23d, was pleasant and warm. Just after noon, as the cannoneers were drilling at the manual of the piece, there marched into camp a squad of infantry; all had their knapsacks but were without arms. They were halted in front of the park at parade rest, and remained in line, watching the cannoneers drill, while their lieutenant in command went to battery headquarters. They were not all strangers, as many of them were the volunteer recruits who had been detailed to the battery after the battle of the 13th instant, and had been returned to their regiments only a few days before; recruits not having been received from Rhode Island as was expected, this squad of infantry had now returned to serve in our battery. At the conclusion of the drill, the recruits were assigned to the different detachments, and there was much hand shaking and renewal of acquaintances formed a short time before, and such remarks as : " I told you that I would come back again, and here I am."

On December 24th, it was pleasant and warm, and the battery was ordered to turn out in full force for mounted inspection. General Sumner and Col. C. H. Tompkins, with their staffs, witnessed the manœuvres. Colonel Tompkins complimented us upon our fine appearance and the excellent condition of our guns and equipments.

The following letter was then read to the command :

EXECUTIVE MANSION,
WASHINGTON, D. C., Dec. 22, 1862.

To the Army of the Potomac:

I have just received your commanding general's preliminary report of the battle of Fredericksburg. Although you were not successful the attempt was not an error, nor the failure other than an accident. The courage with which you, in an open field, maintained the contest against an entrenched foe, and the consummate skill and success with which you crossed and recrossed the river in face of the enemy, show that you possess all the qualities of a great army, which will yet give victory to the cause of the country and of popular government.

Condoling with the mourners for the dead, and sympathizing with the severely wounded, I congratulate you that the number of both is comparatively small.

I tender to you, officers and soldiers, the thanks of the nation.

                      (Signed,)   ABRAHAM LINCOLN.
[Official.]
E. WHITTLESEY, A. A. Gen.

Maj. Gen. Sumner, then addressing us said:

"It is with pride and pleasure that I look upon you brave men, who were given as a sacrifice for their country. You have safely passed the ordeal as men worthy of your calling. You were tried and not found wanting. I shall never forget you. And I heartily congratulate you on the worthy record you have made."

Captain Hazard then dismissed his command, and passes were given to those who wished to go to the village or visit other commands. Every one seemed in good spirits, and those who did not have enough went in search of more.

December 25th. The weather was fine, and, it being Christmas day, Captain Hazard gave orders that no work was to be done only the necessary camp duties. So Christmas came and passed as pleasantly as could be expected in the midst of civil war, on rebel soil, and in front of a rebel army. The Christmas dinners displayed a great variety of skill. In some messes the capture of a case-back (wild hog), whose nimble bound was overmatched by swifter running feet, supplied a savory feast, while a chicken graced some other festive board. The less fortunate, however, had an opportunity to test their skill in manufacturing a treat from pork or salt-junk and hardtack. A lean larder developed in the soldier much ingenuity in the culinary art.

On the 26th, at retreat roll call, the following order was read to the command:

                HEADQUARTERS 2D ARMY CORPS,
                    NEAR FALMOUTH, VA., Dec. 26, 1862.
General Orders,
No. 34.

In compliance with special orders No. 92, from Headquarters Right Grand Division, the undersigned hereby assumes command of the 2d Corps. All existing orders will remain in force.

                  (Signed,)   JOHN SEDGWICK,
[Official.]   *Maj. Gen.*
E. WHITTLESEY, A. A. G.

General Sedgwick had returned, and, having no command, was assigned to the Second until the return of General Couch, who had been granted a leave of absence.

On the 28th, after battery inspection, the men were ordered into line and the officer of the day (Lieutenant Bloodgood) read the following complimentary circular :

Circular :
HEADQUARTERS 1ST. REGT. R. I. LT. ART.,
FALMOUTH, VA., Dec. 28, 1862.

The Colonel Commanding hereby communicates to the regiment, with mingled feelings of pride and pleasure, the following order of His Excellency the Governor of Rhode Island.

STATE OF RHODE ISLAND, ETC.
ADJUTANT GENERAL'S OFFICE,
General Orders, } PROVIDENCE, Dec. 23d, 1862.
No. 60.

The Commander-in-Chief presents his thanks to Colonel Tompkins, officers and men of the First Regt. of Rhode Island Lt. Artillery, who took part in the battle of Fredericksburg, on the 13th instant. The officers and men of this favorite corps must know with what pride he receives the report of their honorable and efficient conduct.

The report of Colonel Tompkins is added as a part of this order:

"The six batteries, of this regiment, with this army were all engaged in the recent battle, and sustained a loss of six killed, twenty wounded, and one missing.

"Battery B was more hotly engaged than either of the others, having sixteen men killed and wounded.

"The battery was ordered up to the front line, to give confidence to the infantry who were wavering. As they came into battery an entire regiment broke and ran to the rear, passing through the battery.

"To their credit, be it said, *not a single cannoneer* left his post but all stood by their guns, and, as soon as the infantry got out of the way, opened fire upon the enemy.

"The conduct of Captain Hazard, his officers and men was creditable in the highest degree; the others all behaved well with the exception of some of the men of Battery D, who did not keep up with their guns when they went into the fight.

"Captain Arnold of Battery A, took command of his battery that morning, and proved himself a good officer under fire."

(Signed,) By order of the *Commander-in-Chief.*
EDWARD C. MAURAN, *Adjutant General.*

Battery commanders will, upon the receipt of this, have the above read to their respective commands.

(Signed.) By orders of COL. C. H. TOMPKINS,
Commanding Regiment.

G. L. DWIGHT, 1st *Lieut. R. I. Lt. Art., Adjutant.*

Dec. 29th. The weather had continued warm and pleasant for nearly two weeks, there had been little frost and the men found it very comfortable for that time of the year.

On the 31st, the weather turned quite cold, with high winds and threatening clouds; in the afternoon it snowed enough to cover the ground. The muster-in rolls were signed for the months of November and December, there was four months' pay due the men. The changes that had occurred during the past two months were, one officer left, being promoted, and two officers reported for duty. There were sixteen men in the hospitals for disability on account of wounds or sickness. Five have died, two were discharged, and one taken prisoner on the march from Warrenton (was with the broken down horses), one deserted on the march. There were present for duty 128 men, and nine on detached or extra duty.

Jan. 1, 1863. The weather was pleasant and growing warmer. The infantrymen had become quite proficient in the artillery drill, so as to be called artillerymen. To-day was established a new feature, and that was a school for instruction of the non-commission officers, by Captain Hazard. Each lieutenant is to teach those of his section.

On the 5th, First Lieut. Horace S. Bloodgood bid adieu to Battery B, having been commissioned captain and appointed to Battery G, First Regiment Rhode Island Light Artillery, and Lieutenant Adams and First Sergt. George W. Blair are mentioned for promotion.

On the 11th, Chaplain Perry visited the battery and with him came fifteen recruits from Rhode Island. There was only one a native of Rhode Island, of the others, ten were of Massachusetts, one of New York, and three of Pennsylvania. They had enrolled at Providence, R. I., for the artillery service and were sent to Battery B, namely:

John T. Boyle, David Brown, Charles Clarke, Samuel H. Collington, Martin Cummings, Daniel N. Felt, Charles Fried, Joseph Hammond, Daniel Hare, John Kane, Frederic Mahre, Peter Ryan, Carl Skifer, A. R. Stone, Charles Warren.

The Rhode Islander, David Brown, and the New Yorker, Charles Warren, did not remain with the battery but a short time, when both deserted.

On the 13th, the battery had mounted inspection and were complimented by the inspector, Lieut.-Col. C. H. Morgan, now assistant inspector-general and chief of staff of the Second Army Corps.

Lieut. Horace S. Bloodgood.

Jan. 17th. For the past week there have been grand reviews of the Army Corps, and the Second Corps was reviewed to-day by Gen. A. E. Burnside, accompanied by his staff and other officers. There was not much enthusiasm shown on this occasion, for there was discontent among the troops, caused by the disaster on the 13th of December. Had the losses been sustained in an equal fight it would have been borne by the troops with a very different feeling. The privates in the ranks knew just as well as their officers that they had not had a fair chance at Fredericksburg. The open-eyed intelligence and quick insight into mechanical relations, which characterize the American volunteer, and which make him, when properly led, the most formidable soldier of the world, render him also a very poor subject to " fool with."

Another cause, which aggravated the discontent, was the failure of " Major Cash " to make his appearance at headquarters, for some of the troops had not been paid in several months ; this occasioned dissatisfaction among the soldiers and their friends at home, and many letters were sent through the mail from the army with this inscription written thereon :

> " Soldier's letter and na-ray a red,
> Hard-tack in place of bread ;
> Postmaster, please pass it through,
> Na-ray a red, but four months due."

And others with the following inscription : " Please pass free, dead broke and 1,000 miles from home, and no pay from Uncle Sam in six months." The failure of the pay department caused the number of desertions to increase to a fearful extent.

January 20th. Cloudy and cold. There was a battery inspection held to-day, and we were put under light marching orders and expected a move ; all equipments in good order, horses in good condition, but the men were not in very good spirits, as their pocket-books were empty and no money to get anything with. Troops began to move to the right, which indicated that the contemplated movement against the enemy's left was about to take place at the fords above Falmouth. At noon it commenced to rain, this made very hard traveling for the troops and artillery ; struggling on, the men bivouacked at night, lying upon the soaked ground in an unrelenting, down-pouring rain, that continued throughout the night and all the next day.

On the morning of the 21st, the battery was ordered to hitch up; the horses remained in harness all day. We were expecting to move, but did not, for in the afternoon the battery was ordered to unhitch and unharness, and the men were sent to their quarters, much to their satisfaction that for once they had been favored, and not been obliged to tramp through mud and rain to no purpose.

On the 23d, the troops returned from the right in a disorderly condition wet, tired and muddy from their fruitless and unprofitable " Mud March," and from toiling at pontoons and cannons that would not budge for all the pushing and hauling of men and beasts. Verily did we, and the men of the Second Corps, sympathize with our comrades in arms and at the same time congratulate ourselves that for once we had escaped a like ordeal.

January 24th. The sun rose clear and bright throwing a warm ray of light over the camps of those yet weary from fatigue, as if trying to make amends for the unpleasant and dreary weather of the past. This beautiful morning was welcomed by all, the men attending to camp duties more cheerfully, and it was not long before the effects of the " Mud Campaign " began to disappear.

January 25th and 26th. The general routine of camp duty marked the events of the battery, while with that of the Army and Corps there was a change

General Burnside, who had been in command of the Army of the Potomac since the 7th of November last, was relieved and Maj. Gen. Joseph Hooker appointed its commander.

The other change was the retirement of General Sumner from the army. Borne down by increasing infirmities, he retired from active field service where he had borne himself with a courage, simplicity and fortitude rarely seen in men. In bidding farewell to the troops he had so long commanded General Sumner said : " I have only to recall to you the memory of the past in which you have fought so many battles always with credit and honor ; in which you have captured so many colors without losing a single gun or standard, and to urge that keeping this recollection in your hearts you prove yourselves worthy of it. It is only in so doing that you can retain for yourselves a reputation well won, and which I feel will be preserved under the gallant and able commander, Maj. Gen. D. N. Couch, to whom I confide you." No one of his comrades had ever imagined that the brave old man would die in his bed ; but so it was, and within the brief space of three months his life of stirring endeavor, of heroic devotion to duty, of daring enterprise and unshrinking exposure to danger, was to end peacefully at his home in Syracuse, N. Y., from mere exhaustion of vital principle powers.

January 27th. Cold and rainy. But if one, in a comfortable shanty listening to the patter of rain or the music of the wind, were inclined to be cynical and to engage in special fault-finding it would be at the irregularity of the time at which the paymaster makes his appearance with the cash; but it is wiser to regard disappointment "an accident of the day," and take refuge in the pleasure of hope. But hark! what is it that is borne by the gentle breeze from camp to camp? That little bird (rumor) is around, what news does it bring? Why, Major Cash is at headquarters with piles of greenbacks for the boys. This fact stimulates an activity of new life among the men, and, as Bugler Crowningshield sounds the assembly call, and upon the sharp loud voice of First Sergeant Blair commanding to "fall in," the men seemed to vie with each other to get into line first as if this was an occasion when delays might be dangerous and the greenbacks take wings and disappear. The line is formed and the men were paid for the months of September and October only. This was a disappointment and caused dissatisfaction in not getting paid for the other two months, November and December that were due.

On the 28th, there was a severe snow storm with high winds blowing; the snow fell to the depth of about four inches. It rained the next day and froze as fast as it fell; very disagreeable weather to be about.

On the 30th, the weather changed to pleasant and warm, and the snow disappeared as fast as it came.

On the 31st, it was pleasant and warm and the army had settled down in winter quarters and re-organized, which it was supposed would give it greater efficiency. The grand divisions were superseded by army corps again, and the artillery was brigaded as a unit under the command of a chief of artillery attached to each corps, and all of the cavalry with the Army of the Potomac was consolidated and formed a corps under one commander.

February 1st, was very cold and cloudy. The news, however, that furloughs were to be granted stimulated the men to renewed life and activity, and there was much speculating as to who might be the lucky ones. The excitement of the march, the inspiration of the battle, or the quietude of an agreeable camp life failed to make the soldier forgetful of home; consequently after an absence of a year or more he greets with no ordinary pleasure the furlough that grants him the privilege of visiting scenes familiar and dear.

February 6th. The weather had been very cold and last night was the coldest we had yet experienced. It snowed nearly all day; toward night it turned to rain and hail and then to a chilly drizzle. Virginia was very extreme in her weather, and when the shower-king suddenly put Old Sol under a cloud an outpouring, that would have been creditable to antediluvian times, was quite sure to follow. Then succeeded warm mid-day and chilly evenings.

On the 7th, First Lieut. George W. Adams was commissioned captain to the command of Battery I, First Regiment Rhode Island Light Artillery. First Sergt. George W. Blair received a commission as first lieutenant in the same battery; and on the eighth both left Battery B, and started for Rhode Island.

First Duty Sergt. John T. Blake was promoted to first sergeant; Third Duty Sergt. John E. Wardlow to first duty sergeant; and Corp. Alanson Williams to sixth duty sergeant. General Couch, having returned, resumed command of his corps (the Second), and General Sedgwick went to take command of the Sixth Corps.

On the 13th, it was pleasant although a chilly north wind was blowing. There was nothing of exciting interest occurring at this time and consequently no incidents worthy of note. The battery stood parked in grim silence ready to report when called upon, and the encampments of the army generally were in quietude. The rebels, on the contrary, were reported busy on the other side of the Rappahannock along our entire front. Earthworks had been thrown up opposite Falmouth and rifle-pits dug near the margin of the river. Possibly these additional preparations, on their part, were based upon the supposition that we were intending to revisit our old battle-field, but it was evident that our apparent quietness alarmed them and they intended to be in readiness for whatever might transpire. On our side, however, greater attention was paid to picket duties and to the strengthening of our lines and proper connections on the right and left of each command. This was a wise and judicious measure as it tended to prevent any sudden surprises by rebel raiders.

February 14th. The weather was very changeable. The rain of the previous night seemed to have dampened the ardor of the rebels for they had stopped work and all was quiet on the Rappahannock. In the afternoon First Lieut. T. Fred. Brown reported for duty. He was promoted from second lieutenant of Battery C, First Regiment Rhode Island Light Artillery.

On the 16th, the weather was fine, and, it being the first suitable day we had had for some time, the battery held camp inspection and drill at the manual of the piece, Lieutenant Brown in command. Captain Hazard left last evening for Rhode Island on a furlough.

February 22d. The birthday of Washington was ushered in by one of the severest snow storms of the winter; grand in itself, as a natural phenomenon, it was shorn of its poetic sublimity when viewed from the long lines of tents scantily provided with fuel or deficient in extra blankets.

A national salute of thirty-four guns was fired at noon by the artillery of the different divisions, and, had the weather permitted, the troops would have paraded to hear read extracts from Washington's "Farewell Address." To the loyal states, and to loyal men in the rebel states, the wise counsels of that address were never so full of expression as now. The angry whirl of the snow and the hoarse voice of the storm were appropriate demonstrations of the spirit in which, if living, the founder of the republic would have rebuked those seeking to destroy it. Under canvas the hours of discomfort were whiled away by ingenious attempts to keep out the sky dust (snow), or in an imaginary comparison between a winter in front of Fredericksburg and a Revolutionary winter at Valley Forge.

February 28th. Though cloudy and warm the weather for the past few days had been exceedingly variable changing from snow and sleet to warm April rains, and the mercury in a few hours would fall from seventy down to twenty degrees. The sanitary condition of the men was favorably reported and the number on the sick list, in the camp hospitals, did not exceed the usual average and was less than might have been expected, after the fatigue and exposures of the earlier part of the winter. Our camp hospitals were not intended for patients requiring serious attention, being usually occupied by those whose cases called for only the simpliest treatments; as soon as it was evident that some weeks or months would elapse before recovery the patients were removed to some general hospital. Battery B was to be congratulated in regard to the health of its men. There was a hospital tent and hospital steward but of patients there were none, all seemed to give the hospital a wide berth.

In the beginning of the war no one foresaw or imagined that in less than two years nearly one hundred and fifty thousand sick and wounded men would require medical and surgical treatment; according to the most reliable sources of information this number was in the various hospitals in the beginning of the year of 1863. For the improvement visible in general and camp hospitals much was due to the labors of the sanitary commission. By the inspections and suggestions of its medical agents many evils, resulting from inexperience and other causes, were removed, and, by the seasonable supplies of hospital stores it furnished, the sick and wounded were greatly relieved. The services rendered in the camps on the Peninsula, on the fields of Antietam, Fredericksburg, and elsewhere, were among the gratifying evidences of its usefulness as an auxiliary to the medical bureau. The agents came laden with blankets so much needed by the wounded exposed to the rain or a chilly night; and most welcome were the changes of raiment they brought to those whose garments were stiff with dirt and gore. The value of such work could not be overestimated, and the commission that carried it on so vigorously deserved the hearty and liberal support of the patriotic and humane whose spirit it so faithfully represented. The relation it held to the army was vital. To the voluntary service of women, as nurses who constantly visited local and camp hospitals, great praise was also due; their presence and sympathetic words even more than their gifts cheered thousands of wounded men, far from home, whose sufferings were making them victims of despondency, and left an impression on grateful memories that could never be obliterated.

March 1st. Rained in the morning but was warm. Mud is king. Since the army returned to its winter quarters from its late attempt to cross the Rappahannock, snow, rain, frost, and drizzle had preserved the monarch's domain, and all attempts of sunshine and wind had failed to diminish its extent. Let one undertake a pleasure jaunt of ten or a dozen miles and they would be convinced that the story of a battery gun being sunk, on the late expedition, until nothing remained visible but the rims of the wheels, gun and carriage being covered with mud, was anything but a slightly exaggerated form of speech. One had only to tramp a few miles and then bivouac surrounded by mud to appreciate the situation. The provost marshal vigorously exercised his functions against sutlers of feeble conscience. At Belle Plain, a few days ago, a cargo of forbidden goods (*whiskey*) was seized and confiscated, so that what was one's loss was another's gain.

March 2d. As Lieut. T. Fred. Brown was inspecting the battery Col. C. H. Morgan, inspector-general of the corps, rode into camp and also made an inspection of the battery, the camp, and quarters; after which he made a short address complimentary to our fine appearance, neatness of camp and equipments. The men were then dismissed and Lieutenant Brown accompanied the colonel to corps headquarters.

March 3d. Warm and showery. It was a gala day with the men, especially with those that had received boxes from friends at home. The long looked-for vessel, the *Helen and Elizabeth*, arrived the first of the month at her destination (Acquia Creek Landing), after a long and boisterous voyage, full freighted with vegetables for the Rhode Island troops, and boxes for individuals from thoughtful friends. The cargo of vegetables was in good condition and made a welcome addition to camp fare. Battery B received eight barrels of potatoes, onions, and apples and quite a number of boxes for the men; they appreciated the many tokens of remembrance and shared with those tent-mates who were not so fortunate as themselves.

On the 4th, Captain Hazard returned from his furlough and assumed command of the battery. Orders were received and great preparations made for the grand review of the artillery brigade which was to take place the next day.

March 5th. Cloudy and cold with high winds. At nine A. M. the battery was hitched up, and, under light marching orders, left camp for the plains near corps headquarters. We were unfortunate in having several nervous and vicious horses, and, as they passed the bands, being frightened at the music, would lunge, prance, then suddenly turn and as to high kicking they had no equals. With such horses it was difficult and tedious work getting along, and, to cap the climax, one team succeeded in turning a gun carriage upside down, and another in breaking a limber pole. To avoid any further trouble they were sent back to camp. Battery B finally reached the place of review, with four guns and caissons, on time and taking its place in line the men put on their best behavior and dignity. The headquarter batteries, Battery I, First United States and Battery A, Fourth United States, had the right of line; next, those of the First Division, Battery B, First New York, and Battery C, Fourth United States; then Second Division, Battery A, First Rhode Island, and Battery B, First Rhode Island; last the Third Division, Battery G, First New York, and Battery G, First Rhode Island.

The review was conducted by Col. Charles H. Morgan, chief of staff, to whom credit is due for the promptness with which the line was formed. The review was witnessed by a great number of officers of the infantry. To many one of the most interesting features of the day was the martial music played by the bands of the corps, drawn up in line in the rear of the artillery.

About eleven A. M. General Hooker with invited guests and attended by all his staff officers, preceded by a band of 120 pieces consolidated for the occasion, started down the line. When near and opposite Battery B they halted, then continuing on they passed around to the rear of the line and returned to headquarters. The review then being at an end the line was dismissed, and the commanders of the different batteries marched their commands back to their camps, where we arrived without any further mishaps though much fatigued. We were well satisfied with the work of the day, it was one of compliments, and none received more than Battery B, First Regiment of Rhode Island Light Artillery, on their fine appearance and discipline. But more interesting to the men was the remark that there would be four furloughs instead of three granted Battery B as their reward on this occasion.

March 11th. The weather had been variable as usual during the past few days; first warm and pleasant, then cold and raw with a disagreeable wind followed by snow and then rain. Rowland L. Dodge, guidon, was discharged to accept commission as second lieutenant Company L, Third Regiment Rhode Island Heavy Artillery. He started for Rhode Island in the evening after bidding his comrades adieu.

March 17th. Cloudy and warm. The Irish brigade celebrated St. Patrick's day with horse racing near General Meagher's headquarters. In the afternoon heavy firing was heard upon the right. Our cavalry had been sent to Kelly's Ford, on the Rapidan, on a reconnoissance. The Rhode Island cavalry was the first to cross and being attacked by a force of the enemy got somewhat cut up.

March 20th. Snowed again last night and continued doing so all the morning, this put a stop to field or any other drills. Received news of the cavalry reconnoissance of the seventeenth instant. General Averill had a sharp engagement of four hours' duration with the rebel cavalry under General Stuart. The enemy was routed with the loss of one hundred men and fifty prisoners; our loss was reported to be about forty. The fight was considered a most brilliant cavalry affair and reflected great credit on the spirit and ability of General Averill, considering that the enemy had received word of the intended reconnoissance. The First Rhode Island Cavalry were in the hottest of the fight and displayed great bravery. They lost Lieutenant Nichols and two men and had eighteen wounded.

The rebel General Stuart apparently had an exalted opinion of female influence and consequently turned it to account, in the rebel cause, by appointing a Miss Antonia J. Ford an honorary aide-de-camp; as such he required her to be "obeyed, respected, and admired by all the lovers of noble feminine nature." Miss Ford has been styled "a modern Delilah." Through her much information reached the rebel lines, but she was finally arrested at her home, near Fairfax Court House, by the military authorities, which act may have saved the Union Samsons of that outpost from betrayal into the hands of the Philistines (General Stuart's men).

On the 21st, it was still snowing but had gained the depth of only two inches; it cleared off at noon causing the snow to fast disappear but rendering traveling in the mud very fatiguing. To-day another new feature was introduced, that of "corps badges," which became very dear to the troops, a source of much emulation on the part of the several commands, and a great convenience to the staff in enabling them to quickly identify corps, divisions, or brigades upon the march or along the line of battle. At retreat roll call the following order was read:

HEADQUARTERS OF THE ARMY OF THE POTOMAC,
March 21, 1863.

Circular Order.

For the purpose of ready recognition of corps and divisions of the Army; to prevent injustice by reports of straggling and misconduct, through mistakes as to their organization, the chief quartermaster will furnish without delay, the following badges, to be worn by the officers and mustered men of all the regiments of the various corps mentioned. They will be securely fastened upon the centre of the top of the cap.

The inspecting officers will at all inspections see that the badges are worn as designated.

First Corps, sphere; Second Corps, trefoil; Third Corps, lozenge; Fifth Corps, Maltese cross; Sixth Corps, cross, four points; Eleventh Corps, crescent, points up; Twelfth Corps, star, five points. Color to designate divisions, red for first division; white for second division; blue for third division; light green for fourth division.

The sizes to be according to pattern.

By command of
Major-General HOOKER.
(Signed,) S. WILLIAMS, *A. A. G.*
[Official,]
Lieut. C. H. HOWARD, *A. D. C. and A. A. G.*

This idea originated with General Butterfield, chief of staff of the Army of the Potomac, who not only instituted the badges but devised them in detail.

March 27th. Governor Curtin, of Pennsylvania, while visiting the troops from that state was entertained with an exhibition of skill in various athletic sports enlivened by the music of several bands. A stand, some two hundred feet in length, was made from pontoons and other bridge material, near at hand, in the rear of the encampment of the Second Corps, occupied by the governor and suite, corps, division, and brigade officers, also invited guests, which included quite a number of ladies whose temporary presence had of late graced the camps.

The amusements comprised a steeple chase, scrub, foot, and sack races, greased pole climbing, and other like gymnastics. If less classic in order and execution than those of Isthmian fame, they were quite as amusing and satisfactory to the large assembly of spectators who witnessed the performances. For several weeks past occasional episodes of this kind have received the sanction and presence of the commander-in-chief, giving healthful excitement to the soldier amid the graver duties of military routine. Human nature is the same in the army as out of it.

The men crave provocations to mirth, and Mars does wisely by now and then yielding a point to Momus. Under the judicious arrangements and organization of General Hooker the morale of the army had been constantly improving for the last two months. Its present condition was in agreeable contrast with its jaded spirit immediately after what had been facetiously called the "Mud Expedition." The rest, brief leaves of absence, a good supply of vegetables and soft bread, and other special attentions to the comfort of the soldiers had infused, as it were, new life among the men. Cheerfulness prevailed, the jocund laugh rang out with hearty sound, discipline improved, confidence increased, only one thing more was needed and that was "Major Cash," the paymaster; all hoped that he would soon make his appearance and square up the old account of last year.

The experiences of ten days' leave of absence were not without interest, especially to those who enjoyed the privilege for the first time in eighteen months. The anticipation, during the somewhat tedious preliminaries of obtaining the necessary papers duly signed, being over and the coveted document safely stowed in the lucky recipient's "inside pocket," fancy plumes her wings for speedy flight to distant waiting joys. Turning his back on camp and comrades he eagerly sets out on the tramp to Acquia Creek Landing; he heeds not the distance, his mind is occupied with thoughts of home. At last he safely embarks on board the government mail steamer, the lines are thrown off and the vessel headed for Washington. But fancy and facts are in conflict. Imagination succumbs to stern reality. Expectation drinks from the cup of disappointment. The tide is low and the channel tortuous with its many windings; suddenly the steamer strikes a sand bar where she lies puffing and floundering like a stranded cetaceous monster, affording the meditative mind ample opportunity, amid noise and confusion, to philosophize upon the uncertainties of this world and to exercise patience while reflecting that the delay is using up the hours at the wrong end of the route. But another trial is in store. Night comes, but "sleep is no servant of the will" and is courted in vain. There comes no "rosy dreams and slumbers light," rest is as impossible as peace to a troubled mind, and, tossing from side to side, while waiting the coming day, the mind reverts to blankets, tent, or bivouac where sleep was both deep and sweet. Morning comes at last, and the capital city is finally reached. A much needed bath, enjoyed at Wiliard's, makes partial atonement by its refreshing effects for the vexatious delays. The time of departure at last arrives, and turning his back on steamer and city the traveler takes the cars at six P. M. Puff, puff goes the iron horse rushing over the road with lightning speed, and, at the end of thirty-six hours, the traveler finds himself at his destination giving unexpected friends an agreeable surprise. The hearty greetings, the multiplied seals of affection and social divertisements, that awaken memories of more peaceful days, beguile the hours and bring too soon the moment of departure so that one is disposed to think old Father Time has been rejuvenated, and, for the purpose of hastening matters, has borrowed the famed "seven league boots."

In Washington and Baltimore the evidences of existing war were abundant, but in Philadelphia and New York they had nearly disappeared. The Soldiers' Rest in the former city, which has refreshed so many thousands of our weary men, indeed reminded us that sympathy for the defenders of the Union was still warm. Chestnut Street, however, was as gay as in the palmiest days of peace. In New York Broadway teemed with busy life, and its merchants were making princely fortunes. Fashion had never been arrayed more extravagantly, promenades never more brilliant, and places of amusement never more crowded. Except the old barracks on the Park and the few soldiers who found a temporary home at the Rest, little was to be seen indicative of the civil conflict. The same was true of Providence. Westminster Street was as lively as before the first gun was fired on Sumter; familiar faces were met at every corner; the cars were, as usual, bringing and carrying their living freight; the ships at the wharves were loading and unloading with unabated activity; smoke was going up from the numerous factories, foundries and machine shops, and scarcely noticeable was the depletion in population made by the thousands sent to sustain the government in suppressing the Rebellion. Thus it was throughout the North; with the exception of a recruiting station here and there nothing looked like war.

April 1st. Warm and pleasant. At two o'clock A. M. Lieutenant Potter, General Howard's aide, came galloping into camp and requested the guard to awaken the officer in command. Lieut. T. Fred. Brown received orders to have the battery hitched up as soon as possible as it was expected the rebels were going to try and cross the river above Falmouth. In a short time the camp was aroused, the horses were harnessed and the battery remained in readiness to move, under light marching orders, until sunrise when it received orders to unhitch, unharness and picket the horses and return to its quarters, for it was only an "April fool." The enemy had no intention of paying us a visit just now.

April 4th. Pleasant in the morning, but at noon the weather changed becoming cloudy and windy, then it commenced to snow and by night a fierce storm had set in and the snow was three inches deep and drifting. It snowed all night and until nearly noon on the 5th when it ceased, and the weather again became warmer; by the seventh the snow was all gone and mud held possession of the fields and roads.

On the 8th, the battery received orders to prepare for a grand review of the Second Corps before the Presidential party. For some reason Battery B did not go to the review but remained in camp in readiness to move at a moment's notice. In the afternoon the battery was unhitched and unharnessed and the men returned to quarters. It was said that the whole army was to be reviewed by the President. Rumors of a move on foot.

April 12th. Pleasant and warm. For the past few days there

had been quite a lively time going on in the different corps enlivened by the granting of furloughs. Civic amusements, inaugurated on the 17th of March under the auspices of General Meagher, and culminating in an athletic entertainment given in honor of Governor Curtin under the sanction of General Hooker, had been succeeded by military galas honored by the presence of the President, Mrs. Lincoln, Master Lincoln, the Attorney-General, and others. These distinguished guests reached Acquia Creek Landing in a fierce snow storm on the evening of the 4th instant, remaining on the steamer until noon of the 5th, when they proceeded to Falmouth, where they were received by General Butterfield, chief of staff, and were then escorted by a squadron of cavalry to General Hooker's headquarters.

The storm and the snow-drifts piled up about the camps; the sharp winds and the mud which followed the receding snow; the examination of encampments and hospitals, gave the Presidential party a much better idea of the vicissitudes of a soldier's life than could have been derived from official reports.

During the President's visit every corps of the army, the infantry, artillery, and cavalry passed in review before him. Ladies were always welcome visitors to the camp and never failed to be received with due courtesy. The presence of Mrs. Lincoln was honored with every respect; a tent was fitted up for her use which, though less sumptuous than the White House, was neat and comfortable. At reviews she occupied a carriage, apparently taking a warm interest in the passing scenes. Of the President a characteristic anecdote is related. After the review of the 8th instant an ardent admirer of the regulars, in disparagement of the volunteers, called his attention to the more exact discipline of the former as they stood statue-like without moving their heads when he passed, while the latter almost universally dressed to the left that they might keep him in view along the entire line. He did not, however, take the impression intended to be given and simply replied: "I don't care how much my soldiers turn their heads if they don't turn their backs." The Presidential party returned to Washington, and all was again quiet along the Rappahannock.

April 13th. Pleasant and warm. Every command was active in view of a move though as yet we had received no orders. Our cavalry, however, moved to the right taking a large amount of forage and it was rumored that they were going on a raiding expedition.

No mails were to be sent from the camps until further notice. Clothing which had been ordered the first of last month was received. On the 14th, new clothing was issued to those men who wished it. In the afternoon there was battery inspection by Lieut. T. Fred. Brown. Everything in tiptop condition.

April 19th. Pleasant and warm. Captain Hazard returned from his furlough, but, as he did not feel well and was still on the sick list, he did not assume command but applied for a sick leave of absence. To-day Second Lieut. Charles A. Brown, promoted from quartermaster-sergeant of Battery E, First Regiment Rhode Island Light Artillery, reported for duty and was assigned chief of caissons.

Private Levi J. Cornell.

CHAPTER XV.

PREPARATIONS AND SECOND BATTLE OF FREDERICKSBURG OR MARYE'S HEIGHTS, VA.

ON the 20th of April the cavalry supply train returned from Kelly's Ford. The train guard had quite a number of rebel prisoners who were sent on to Washington. The sick from the different division hospitals had been sent north; this fact and other preparations indicated that a movement of some kind was soon to take place.

On the 21st, part of the cavalry corps returned from the right and went down to the left of the line having been ordered to Port Conway. The First, Third, and Sixth Corps were ordered to be massed at General Franklin's old crossing below Fredericksburg. The feint of our cavalry at Port Conway caused a large body of the rebel troops to move down the river. Our cavalry reported that the rebels had been apprised of the activity in our camps pending a move, and that they had immediately sent reinforcements to guard the different fords along the river. A week of fair weather put the roads in a more passable condition, and large bodies could move with greater certainty in carrying out general orders.

On the 22d, signed the muster rolls. The men were in better spirits afterward for it was reported that we were soon to be paid.

April 24th. Chilly and raining; the battery received marching orders. To our delight "Major Cash" appeared among us and most welcome he was.

The paymaster and Rhode Island allotment commissioner, Henry M. Amesbury, visited the battery and we were paid for the months of November, December, January, and February. The receiving of this four months' pay and the settling up brightened a multitude of faces with smiles. The allotment arrangement by which the men sent money home was an admirable one for safety and many improved the opportunity by sending remittances to their families or parents.

April 26th. Pleasant and warm with high winds. The battery did not go to a review as first ordered but had mounted inspection instead. A Swiss military celebrity, General Fogliardi, accompanied by Colonel Repetti and Lieutenant Lubin, the latter as interpreter, had been enjoying for a short time the hospitality of General Hooker. The object of their visit was to obtain a knowledge of the character and efficiency of our army. To this end they were favored with reviews and inspections. These, it was said, elicited much praise complimentary to the artillery.

Amid the forty-eight guns which formed the battery of the Second Army Corps, of the Army of the Potomac in April, 1863, a skilled eye could not discern which belonged to the regulars or which to the volunteer batteries, even though the former included such as I of the First, and A of the Fourth United States Artillery, with Kirby and Cushing in command. For the first time, since the beginning of the war, the difference between regulars and volunteers ceased to exist as far as this arm of the service was concerned. Up to this time, notwithstanding the rare excellence of certain batteries like Hazard's B, and Arnold's A, of the First Rhode Island, and Pettit's B, First New York, with their peerless gunners, there had been a perceptible difference distinctly observable at the beginning of a campaign, but more so at the close of one. Good officers with well disciplined men had caused it to disappear entirely.

The artillery was carried to a point of perfection in all its exercises never before thought of. Our volunteer gunners had from the first been wonderfully expert, though it was not merely the straight shooting on certain occasions which made a battery useful. There must be care of guns, horses, equipments, and ammunition both in camp and when on the march, and a thorough discipline of men and horses was necessary to enable a battery to endure a long and arduous campaign, amid discomforts and privations, without loss of strength or spirits, never becoming demoralized at critical moments. There are a hundred exigencies with artillery, beyond those known to infantry, which render first-class training and discipline enormously profitable in a campaign. In the spring of 1863 the volunteer batteries of the Second Corps stood side by side with the regulars as *par excellence*.

April 27th. The troops had been moving up to the left since early morning indicating that the long anticipated flank movement of General Hooker was to take place. The battery received orders to be in readiness to move early the next morning.

April 28th. Pleasant and warm. Reveille sounded at three A. M., broke camp and packed all surplus baggage and forage in the wagons; the sick were sent to the hospital. Three days' rations were issued. At sunrise the battery hitched up and left camp, moving in the direction of Falmouth, Lieut. T. Fred. Brown in command, Captain Hazard being on sick leave of absence. Large bodies of infantry were in motion giving an animated appearance to the scene in every direction.

We left our old encampment with pleasant recollections of the comforts it had afforded us; but while we missed our commodious huts and the conveniences ingenuity had contrived, we were content to dispense with them in looking forward to future victory.

The battery moved to a high hill, north of the town of Falmouth, relieving Pettit's New York Battery at the fortification overlooking the north part of Fredericksburg. The First and Third Divisions of the Second Corps had left their position in front of the city. They had been ordered up to Banks's and United States Fords leaving the Second Division, under General Gibbon, to guard the fords at Falmouth. Battery G, First Regiment Rhode Island Light Artillery, had also been left with the Second Division as Battery A, First Rhode Island, had been ordered to go with the Third Division instead. The Fifth Corps, General Meade's, the Eleventh, General Slocum's, and the Twelfth, General Howard's, were ordered up to Kelly's Ford. The advance of our cavalry, under General Stoneman, on the 13th instant, had been the signal for a general movement of the army; but after the return of the President and his party to Washington the elements had been unpropitious. With the down-pouring of floods the Rappahannock increased its proportions; the little streams filled to repletion, and the roads rivaled their condition in the memorable " mud expedition " of January; so that little more could be done than patient waiting, leaving to Sol and Boreas full power to repair damages. By their joint industry the roads and by-ways had been so far improved that, under the inspiration of a balmy atmosphere and smiling skies, the army had commenced to move. First by cavalry reconnaissance to the right at Kelly's Ford, then down to the left at Port Conway where the troops, under General Doubleday, made a show of building bridges and actually crossed in boats to the opposite side. While these feints were made troops were being massed at the old crossings at Fredericksburg and others sent to the right at Kelly's Ford.

April 29th. The pieces of Battery B were placed in position in the fortification, which had been occupied by Pettit's New York Battery through the winter, from here a good view of the northern part of Fredericksburg could be had. The camp quarters were pleasantly situated, more so than the winter quarters of Battery B. Cannonading was heard down on the left this morning; the rebels doubled their picket line along our front; this information was gained from a lieutenant who deserted from the enemy and came across to our lines. He was taken to General Hooker's headquarters.

April 30th. Warm light showers. The music had changed this morning, and cannonading was heard up to the right, this was from the two divisions of the Second Corps which met the enemy's pickets as they approached the river at United States Ford. As the corps advanced, the pickets retired to the opposite side. The corps crossed at about three P. M. Meanwhile General Sedgwick had caused to be built four pontoon bridges near the scene of General Franklin's crossing in December. Below the city two divisions were ordered over, and everything was done to create the belief that the real attack against General Lee's right flank was again to be made at this point. From the battery's position the men had a good view of the advance of these divisions and the skirmish fighting as the rebels retreated from the plains to the woods on the hills. It could no longer be kept from General Lee's knowledge that the Army of the Potomac was in motion. Though it was now impossible to make a feint of crossing up to the right, General Hooker manœuvered the left wing, consisting of the First, Third and Sixth Corps, with General Gibbon's division (the Second) of the Second Corps, all under command of General Sedgwick, in such a manner that it kept General Lee gravely perplexed as to his real intentions. The concentration of the right wing in the vicinity of Chancellorsville had been not only brilliant but audacious and accomplished without loss. The Third Corps was also ordered up from the left, as soon as the occupation of Chancellorsville was assured, which indicated that the coming battle would take place at that point.

May 1st. Pleasant and warm, making very fine weather. Reveille at three o'clock this morning; had orders to hitch up and stood in harness all day. Heavy skirmishing was heard on the right; it was reported that all our troops were beyond the Rapidan and in the enemy's rear. A general order was read to the men that the enemy would now have to come out and fight us on ground of our own selection.

May 2d. Early this morning the right section was ordered to hitch up, and the battery remained hitched up by sections all day under light marching orders. The First Corps recrossed the river below Fredericksburg and was ordered up to the right, which left only the Sixth Corps and the Second Division of the Second Corps in front of Fredericksburg.

On the 3d, the battery was aroused at 12.30 A. M. and ordered to hitch up as soon as possible. At 1.30 A. M. we pulled out from the fortification and moving down to the left took position on the right of the Lacy House thus covering the laying of the pontoon bridge. While this work was going on one shot came screeching from a rebel battery on the opposite hills and landed in the bank in front of the house, which was all the opposition the rebel artillery gave to our division in crossing. This was answered by a battery of Parrott guns on the left of the Lacy House. By seven A. M. the pontoon bridge was finished and the infantry of General Gibbon's division began to cross going to the right in front of the town, but his advance to the right was stopped by the canal over which it was impossible to lay bridges in face of the fire from the enemy's artillery and infantry on the hills. Battery B soon followed, the infantry being the first battery to cross. It happened in this way: Batteries B and G, First Rhode Island Light Artillery, stood in park to the right of the Lacy House on the north bank of the river where the batteries were hitched up awaiting orders. A staff officer came with orders to the battery commanders and meeting first Captain Adams, of Battery G, delivered an order to him. Captain Adams immediately commenced to move his battery, going toward the road leading to the pontoon bridge. As he passed in front of Battery B he saluted the officers and said "Good-bye" with an air which indicated his pleasure at the honor of leading the way. The staff officer, upon leaving Captain Adams, rode up to Lieut. T. Fred. Brown, in command of Battery B, and ordered him to report, with his battery, to General Gibbon (in Fredericksburg). He was not ordered to follow Captain Adams.

At the battle of Fredericksburg, in the December previous, Lieutenant Brown was with Battery C, First Rhode Island Light Artillery, and consequently was familiar with the roads leading down to the pontoons. There were two, one was long and easy while the other was steep and difficult. To the delight of Lieutenant Brown, Captain Adams took the easier though longer road, and immediately after the last caisson of Battery G had passed the front of Battery B, Lieutenant Brown ordered Battery B into column, pulled out and headed for the bluff nearly above the pontoon bridge. Upon arriving at the steep and difficult road, orders were given to lock the wheels, which was instantly executed by the cannoneers who quickly comprehended the situation. The descent from the bluff was made in safety, and Battery B began to cross the bridge just as Battery G came around the bend in the longer road. Captain Adams was forced to halt until Battery B had passed on to the bridge. As Lieutenant Brown passed Captain Adams he returned his salute and said "Good bye" with the same air and manner that Captain Adams had bestowed upon him on the bluff. (The battery commanders were jealous of each other and anxious to excel, considering it an honor to lead the way or to be first on the field at an engagement.) Thus for the second time Battery B was the first battery to cross the pontoons and enter the town of Fredericksburg from and in front of the Lacy House. On reaching the bank the battery turned to the right following the street which ran alongside of the river. After going a short distance we turned to the left and passed through the town to an open field in front, then Lieutenant Brown gave the command "In battery." As this order was being executed, Battery G, First Rhode Island, came galloping up on our right and took position. Battery B immediately received orders to limber to the rear and moved to the left under fire, again taking position near the cemetery and the monument of Mary Washington (George Washington's mother).

We commenced firing at a rebel battery in the fortifications on the hill. In this engagement (the storming of Marye's Heights May 3d) the battery did some very good work, for our shot and shell landed right in the embrasures of their fortifications silencing one of their guns for a time, while two of them they could not work at all on account of our fire. Though we had a good range upon them we were fortunate enough not to receive any of their fire. We were within too short a range of their works and they could not depress the muzzles of their guns enough to bear upon us without coming out from behind their forts. Battery G, however, was not so fortunate, it had one officer and several men killed or wounded and was badly cut up. Battery B was supported through this engagement by the Second Rhode Island Regiment (under Col. Horatio Rogers), which lay at the rear of the battery ready for a charge if the enemy had come out from their works.

While the Second Division of the Second Corps was preparing to lay their pontoon the Sixth had not been idle while coming up from the plains below the town. General Sedgwick's troops had been opposed by the pickets of the enemy whose skirmishers he soon brushed away and the town was again occupied by our troops.

It was in the gray of the morning that the advance of the Sixth Corps reached the rear and left of Fredericksburg. An old negro came into our lines and reported that the heights were occupied in force and the enemy was cutting the canal to flood the roads. To ascertain the truth of this report caused some delay. Those in command were not acquainted with the topography of the surrounding country, and consequently the advance was compelled to move with great caution through the streets and outskirts of the town. As morning dawned Marye's Heights, the scene of the fierce attack of our troops last December, was presented to view.

The troops were speedily moved into position along the open ground between the town and heights, this movement discovered the enemy in force behind the famous *stone wall* at the base of the hill. (General Lee had left General Early with his division and Barksdale's brigade, a force of about 10,000 men, to hold Fredericksburg Heights.) They were protected by strong works and supported by artillery. It was at once felt that a desperate encounter was inevitable and the recollection of our previous disaster was by no means inspiriting.

It was a beautiful Sunday morning the 3d of May. The town was perfectly quiet, most of the inhabitants having fled not a person could be seen on the streets, while the numerous windows and blinds of the houses were closed. The marks of the previous fierce siege were everywhere distinctly visible.

As soon as practicable General Sedgwick prepared to attack the Heights. The right of the line by the canal was assigned to General Gibbon's Second Division, of the Second Corps, which went into position while under fire of the enemy's artillery on the hills, which was answered by Batteries B and G, of Rhode Island, with good effect. The direct attack was made on Marye's Heights by the centre troops, consisting of the Third Division, Sixth Corps, under

General Newton. Two columns, each marching by fours, were formed on the Plank and Telegraph roads, supported on the left by four regiments of the Sixth Corps. The right column, under Colonel Spear and composed of the Sixty-first Pennsylvania and the Forty-third New York, of the Light Division, was supported by the Sixty-seventh New York and Eighty-second Pennsylvania, under Colonel Shaler. The left column, under Colonel Johns, including the Seventh Massachusetts and the Thirty-sixth New York, was supported by the Light Division and the Twenty-third New York in line of battle, the Fifth Wisconsin acting as skirmishers.

An order to advance was given about eleven A. M., and, as the columns emerged from the town, the movements of the enemy showed that they were preparing to receive the attack. Both columns and line advanced on the double-quick without firing a shot until the ridge above the dry canal was passed. The enemy meanwhile kept up an incessant artillery fire, reserving their musketry fire until our men were within easy range. Then came a murderous storm of bullets from the *stone wall*, while shot and shell from the hill above burst upon the assaulting troops. For a moment the head of the columns was checked and broken. The battle line of blue on the green field paused and slightly wavered as if to recover breath. Generals Sedgwick and Newton looked on with unconcealed anxiety. The suspense was intense. Was it to be victory or defeat? Was this place for the second time to be a "slaughter-pen?" Was the Sixth Corps to be driven into the river? Staff-officers and aides, waving their swords and hurrahing to the men, dashed down the Plank and Telegraph roads. A blinding rain of shot pierced the air. It was more than human nature could face. The head of the column as it reached the lowest part of the decline, near a fork in the road, seemed to melt away. Many fell; others bending low to the earth hurriedly sought shelter in the undulation of the ground, the fences, and the wooden structures along the road. Then, as if moved by a sudden impulse and nerved for a supreme effort, both columns and line in the field simultaneously sprang forward. The *stone wall* was gained and the men were quickly over it.

The Seventh Massachusetts was leading the left column in the assault on the *stone wall* and were within thirty or forty yards of the enemy's line when they received a murderous volley. There was an exclamation of horror and a momentary wavering amid cries of "Retreat! Retreat!" Others yelled "Forward! don't go back!

we shan't get so close up again!" In front of the *stone wall* facing down the road was a house standing in a V-shaped plat and enclosed by a high board fence. To this goal the men rushed for shelter, this gave them a breathing spell. On looking through the board fence the enemy's unprotected flank was seen. The word was given and in a moment the men rushed to the fence and went through pell-mell right upon the rebels' flank, at the same time giving them the contents of their muskets point blank without aiming. The whole thing was a surprise as the enemy were not prepared for anything from this quarter, our men having been hidden from them by the house and fence.

This brilliant and successful charge occupied perhaps ten or fifteen minutes, and immediately after the *stone wall* was carried the enemy became panic-stricken. In their flight they threw away guns, canteens, and haversacks, everything that might retard their flight. The *stone wall* gained, the heights were also carried at eleven A. M. by the advance of the whole line.

As soon as our infantry had gained the heights Battery B was ordered to limber up, the cannoneers mounted and went on a trot up the Plank road in pursuit. On gaining the hill the battery was ordered into position and sent a few shot at the fleeing enemy, after which we limbered up again and advanced with our division to the plain beyond the hill. The battery halted at the right of the road just beyond a large barn. The right section, however, under command of Lieut. T. Fred. Brown, kept on for a mile or more when it halted and again unlimbering sent shot and shell after the retreating foe. As the battery reached the summit of the hill an exciting scene met the eye. The broad plateau was alive with fleeing Confederates, riderless horses were galloping here and there, and others hitched to army wagons running hither and thither, while last but not least in point of interest could be seen far to the left the Marye's Mansion now surrounded by our men advancing in force.

As Marye's Heights were now in our possession and the enemy on the retreat, the Second Division, of the Second Corps, was halted at the enemy's second line of defense, while the Sixth Corps continued to advance following up the advantage gained. General Gibbon was ordered to return in order to hold the town and guard the pontoon bridges and fords. Lieutenant Brown, with the first section, returned when the Second Division of the corps came back and ordered the battery to countermarch; following orders we went through the town to the pontoon bridge and recrossed the river going up on the bluff to the right of the Lacy House, while the guns were placed in position to guard the crossing. Here the battery bivouacked for the night.

The storming of Marye's Heights was one of the most prominent and bloody events in the second battle of Fredericksburg and was accomplished with heavy loss. While our batteries along the lines were thundering at the enemy, a plan of assault was determined upon which was to attack simultaneously from the right, centre, and left. But inasmuch as General Newton's men were successful, being the first to penetrate the enemy's line, the advantage thus gained was quickly followed by the troops of the right and left attacking columns pouring in upon the enemy in such numbers as to throw them into utter confusion. Many of the foe were slain in their places, in the pits where they firmly stood until the last moment, and even then resisted as our men clambered over the walls. Meanwhile, on the left, matters were somewhat the same, the enemy's line having been gained. The right went up along the Plank road taking hill after hill, while the Confederates fled at sight hotly pursued. The rebels turned at bay several times but continued retreating until they arrived at Salem Church where they received reinforcements and made a formidable stand, and in turn drove our troops in confusion (the Sixth Corps).

The fierceness with which these engagements raged may be judged from the fact that the entire loss of General Sedgwick's command was about six thousand. He held on until assailed by a superior force, and then retired across the river at Banks's Ford in good order.

May 4th. Things had a different aspect this morning. The enemy made their appearance on the top of the hills to the right of the town and showed themselves in a large force in the afternoon. The right section, under Lieutenant Perrin, was ordered up to Falmouth to guard the ford. Heavy firing was heard up on the right. Our troops still hold the town. The pontoon bridges have been made ready to swing so as to be taken up at a moment's notice.

May 5th. Cloudy and warm, began to rain in the afternoon. The Second Division, of the Second Corps, which had held and guarded the town, recrossed to the north side of the river and the pontoon bridges were taken up, the enemy was again in possession of the place. In the afternoon the battery was ordered up to Falmouth and went into park in the church-yard, the right section came up from the river and joined the battery. The guns remained in position and commanded the ford. The men quartered in the church. At dusk a thunder shower came up which turned into a cold storm. It rained nearly all night making it very disagreeable for the troops, especially for those who had lost their blankets during the engagements.

May 6th. Still very cold with some rain. General Hooker's whole army, the Army of the Potomac, has recrossed to the north side of the Rappahannock River. The enemy, General Lee, is in possession south of the river. The troops are returning from the right in anything but a pleasant mood.

May 7th. Cold with frequent showers. The enemy's ally "General Mud" in command; the rain has again converted the whole country, under the tread of men and horses, into a vast morass, which rendered traveling and the movements of artillery and trains almost next to an impossibility.

May 8th. The weather still very chilly. The troops were slowly returning to their old camps, or else taking up new camping grounds. The Second Rhode Island Regiment looked tired, jaded, and forlorn as they passed by, and it was not to be wondered at for they had endured many trials since parting from us on the noon of the 3d instant, after the capture of Marye's Heights; but, nevertheless, many pleasant words were exchanged as they passed.

May 10th. The weather changed and it was so pleasant and warm that quite a number of the men of the Nineteenth Maine Regiment went in bathing, and some went almost across the river to the enemy's side. On their return they were placed under arrest and confined in the guard-house. A balloon went up to-day from near General Hooker's headquarters, to take an observation of the enemy's doings.

May 12th. Had official notice of General Jackson's (Confederate) death. Had camp inspection and still keep three days' rations on hand. The weather was very fine and the rebel pickets did a large business in fishing, on their side of the river, using both boats and seines.

The pickets on both banks of the river had lately kept up lively conversations, bandying jokes like old acquaintances (as indeed many were). From one of the Confederate posts in our front came the cry: "Where is Joe Hooker now?" "Gone to the funeral of Old Stonewall Jackson" was the quick response from our side. The answer was deemed sufficient, consequently no further questions were asked on that point. The troops settled down in their camps and things were again quiet on the Rappahannock.

For some time after the return of the troops, from their nine days' campaign, changes were made in the location of many encampments prompted by sanitary considerations and comfort. Again the management of the artillery of the army was changed which was considered a still greater improvement.

Previous to the fall of 1861 the field artillery was in an unsatisfactory condition. The high reputation which it had gained in Mexico was lost by the active and persistent hostility of the war department, which almost immediately dismounted three-fourths of its authorized batteries. Congress in 1853 made special provision for remounting them as schools of instruction for the army, a duty which the war department on shallow pretexts evaded.

Again in 1861 Congress amply provided for the proper organization and command of the artillery in the field, but as there was no chief nor special administration for that arm, and no regulation for its government, its organization, control and direction were left to the fancies of the various army commanders. General officers were practically denied it, and in 1862 the war department announced in orders that field officers of artillery were an unnecessary expense and their muster into service was forbidden.

Promotion necessarily ceased, and the able artillerists could only receive promotion by transfer to the infantry or cavalry. No adequate measures were taken for the supply of recruits, and the batteries were frequently dependent on the infantry of the divisions to which they were attached for men enough to work their guns in battle. For battery-draft they were often glad to get the refuse horses after the ambulance and quartermasters' trains were supplied. Still many of the batteries attained a high degree of excellence, due mainly to the self-sacrifice, courage and intelligence of their officers and men.

On taking command of the army General Hooker had transferred the military command of the artillery to his own headquarters, to be resumed by the chief of artillery only under specific orders and for special occasions, which resulted in such mismanagement and confusion at Chancellorsville that he consented to organize the artillery into brigades. This was a decided improvement and would have been greater if the brigade commanders had held adequate rank.

Of the fourteen brigades organized four were commanded by field officers, nine by captains, and one by a lieutenant taken from their batteries for the purpose. The number of field batteries was sixty-five of 370 guns, 212 with the infantry, fifty with the cavalry, and 108 in the reserve.

May 13th. Pleasant and warm. The battery still lay bivouacked near the church. At roll call in the afternoon the following order was read, viz. :

HEADQUARTERS ARMY OF THE POTOMAC,
CAMP NEAR FALMOUTH, VA.,

Special Orders, } May 12, 1863.
No. 120.

In consequence of the reduction of the strength of the infantry, of the divisions, a consolidation and reduction of the artillery, attached to the Army Corps, will be effected.

The artillery assigned to each corps will constitute a brigade under the command of the chief of artillery of the corps, who will be responsible to the commander of the corps and to the chief of artillery of the army for the command and administration.

The following named batteries, now serving with divisions of the Second Corps, will report without delay to Brig.-Gen. R. O. Tyler, commanding artillery reserve: Battery C, Fourth United States Artillery, Lieutenant Thomas commanding; Battery B, First New York Artillery, Captain Pettit commanding; Battery G, First New York Artillery, Lieutenant Ames commanding; Battery G, First Rhode Island Artillery, Captain Adams commanding.

The batteries remaining with the corps will be completed to a thorough state of efficiency with the number of guns they now have by the transfer of sufficient of such men, of the remaining batteries of the corps, as are attached from the infantry.

The artillery ammunition train of the batteries attached to corps will be reorganized and placed under the direction of the commandant of artillery of the corps. The supplies will be transferred to the artillery reserve.

By command of   Major General HOOKER.

(Signed,)
S. WILLIAMS, *A. A. G.*

The artillery brigade of the Second Corps consisted of Battery A, Fourth United States Artillery, Lieut. A. H. Cushing commanding; Battery I, First United States Artillery, Lieut. C. Kirby commanding; Battery A, First Rhode Island Artillery, Capt. W. A. Arnold commanding; Battery B., First Rhode Island Artillery, Capt. J. G. Hazard commanding; under the command of Lieut.-Col. C. H. Morgan, assistant inspector general of Second Corps, G. L. Dwight, first lieutenant Rhode Island Light Artillery, acting adjutant.

On May 15th, after mounted battery inspection in the morning, Lieut. T. Fred. Brown received orders to move down to the left on the bluff in the fortification which has been occupied by Battery G, First Rhode Island, that battery now being placed in the reserve, Battery B takes its place in the breastworks. The men were kept quite busy in cleaning and fixing up the quarters, the guns were placed in position in the earthworks, which had a commanding point above the ford and quite an extending range of the north part of Fredericksburg.

On the 16th, Sergt. John E. Wardlow was detached to acting sergeant-major of the artillery brigade, and left the battery and reported to headquarters for duty.

For the past few days the weather had been pleasant and warm, and only the regular routine of camp duty was performed.

The camp life of a battery is diversified with a variety of calls, sounded by the bugle. First comes reveille, announcing what is not always the fact, that " tired nature's sweet restorer " has done all the night work craved. But the voice of the bugle is inexorable, and the half wakened sleeper tumbles out, wondering at the hasty departure of the sable goddess, and breathing a wish that " sweet forgetfulness of life " could have been protracted another hour. Then follow stable and feed calls for the drivers to feed, groom and care for the animals; and next police call for the cannoneers to clean the camp. Breakfast call follows when the men are formed into line and march, headed by the sergeant of the day, to the cook department (if fortunate to have one), and there receive a pint of *hot coffee* and a rasher of salt (horse) beef or salt pork. Sick call next for those who wish to be excused from manual labor during the next twenty-four hours. They form in line and are escorted by the first sergeant to the surgeon's quarters, where they receive a potion of salts or pills to be taken on the premises. Now comes the call for guard mounting, after which the water call for the drivers and those taking care of the animals to go with them to some creek or river to drink of that sparkling southern water which looks, after a rain, like so much milk spoiled with treacle. Drill call comes next, weather permitting. Stable call again, and then dinner call. Drill call again, and late in the afternoon water call again, which is followed by stable call, and as night approaches the retreat call is sounded at which the men assemble and form in line and the roll of detachments is called. The next is supper call. At nine o'clock P. M. tattoo is sounded and the men retire to their quarters. Taps soon follow when lights are extinguished, mirthful voices are silent, and sleepers go off to dreamland, while others spend a wakeful hour in speculation as to what the morrow may bring forth. To these calls should be added that of boots and saddles which is sounded when the battery is to be hitched up for any purpose. The assembly call is sounded at any time the command is wanted to be called together.

For some time after the return of the army from its nine days' headquarters in the saddle campaign, changes were made in the location of many of the encampments of the troops prompted by sanitary considerations. Many of the camps had been tastefully arranged with an eye to comfort, but war assures " no constancy in earthly things," and, judging from the past as well as present signs, we looked upon our abode as only temporary. At this season of the year the valley of the Rappahannock was clad in picturesque garments, though it showed many unseemly rents. From Acquia Creek Landing to Falmouth the woodman's axe had spared but little of the forests with which it had been heavily covered; excepting a clump of trees here and there or an occasional large grove, countless stumps alone told of the deep shades that, during the heat of summer, had been the pleasant retreat of the numerous feathered and animal tribes.

On the 17th, the weather was fine. The balloon was sent up again, and there was a little more activity among the troops. Lieut. Col. C. H. Morgan, who had had command of the artillery brigade since its organization, turned over the brigade to the senior artillery officer, Capt. William A. Arnold, of Battery A, First Rhode Island Light Artillery, who was present for duty; this was in accordance with order No. 114 from Second Corps headquarters, May 16, 1863.

May 18th. It was a busy day with the men in preparing equipments, pieces, caissons, horses and themselves ready for a move of some kind. The activity inspired the men with new life, while "Dame Rumor" circulated all sorts of reports; as for the men they could do nothing but impatiently await the issue.

On the 19th, at reveille, there was no loitering in the quarters, for the men were up and stirring around betimes. Their night's repose had not made them forgetful of the excitement and speculations of the previous day.

During the duties of the morning the question, "What does this activity mean?" still remained unanswered. About nine A. M. an aide from the artillery headquarters galloped into camp, and, going to the officers' quarters delivered papers, saluted, and was off again. Would those papers settle the question? They did.

HEADQUARTERS ARTILLERY BRIGADE 2D ARMY CORPS,
May 15, 1863.

Special Orders, }
No. 3.   }

(Extract.)

Battery B, First Rhode Island Light Artillery, will report to General Owen on the plain near the Lacy House this day as near two P. M. as practicable, for the purpose of a drill in co-operation with his command.

By order of
Capt. W. A. ARNOLD,
1st R. I. Lt. Art., com'dg Brigade.

After our surprise at the contents of the papers speculation dropped 100 per cent. "Dame Rumor" immediately took wings and flitted away. After all, our active and extensive preparations were simply for a division drill, and the men had to abide by the decision. At half-past one Battery B, Lieut. T. Fred. Brown commanding, left its camp at the fortification and going down to the plain took their place in line with Owen's brigade. At the commencement of the drill the battery executed, with the infantry, a number of field movements which were very easy to perform, on an open plain, with no enemy to object; these manœuvres were very instructive both to the infantry and artillery, as well as to those who witnessed it. At four P. M. the battery returned to its camp well pleased with the drill and the part it had performed; having been highly complimented on the fine appearance of its men, and the manner and ease with which the movements were executed.

The 20th was very quiet in camp until after dinner, when orders were given to prepare for mounted inspection. At half-past one the battery was hitched up and pulled out from the breastworks to a level field to the right and rear of our camp, where it went into park and then into battery with the cannoneers at their posts. About two o'clock P. M. Captain Arnold, of Battery A, First Rhode Island Light Artillery, commanding artillery brigade, accompanied by his staff and First Lieut. T. F. Brown, passed around and through the battery on an inspection, asking questions of both drivers and cannoneers. At the conclusion of the inspection the battery was dismissed and ordered back to quarters, upon reaching which the men could no longer restrain their mirth, but burst out with a hearty laugh at what had transpired in one of the detachments during the inspection. To explain the cause we will start from the beginning: When the order to prepare for inspection was given we knew there were to be no field movements nor drill at the manual of the piece, only to take position in battery and cannoneers at posts fully equipped as for action. Upon the issuing of these orders to a battery there commenced a scene of great activity about camp; uniforms were brushed and cleaned, boots blacked, sabres and scabbards brightened, gun and caisson equipments put into their proper places, harnesses overhauled, and everything put into as good shape as circumstances would allow. The battery, at this time, happened to be short of cannoneers, required to fill all the posts of the gun detachments, on account of many being detailed for extra work; those on guard were not required to attend the inspections nor the supernumeraries, which included the cooks, those caring for extra horses, drivers of the battery wagons and forge, and officers' servants. There were two or three men in the battery who, unfortunately, must have been born under an "awkward star." They had been drilled and drilled, but all to no purpose, for, after months of training and service, the only occasion upon which they equaled their comrades was when they drew their pay and rations. They were, however, kept in the battery with the supernumeraries because they had to be somewhere. A first class cannoneer had to be cool, intelligent, keen, and quick to understand, also being able to perform the duties of two or more posts at the gun, as was often necessary when in action. A slow, awkward person should hold no place in a gun detachment of light artillery; he could better find his level in the infantry where in action they worked more individually, and, after a manner, each was a power in himself and any awkwardness would not materially interfere with the working of his comrades. On the contrary a gun detachment of artillery was like a machine, no one worked individually but all in unison and with the precision of clock-work, every man on time and in time; one mistake or awkward movement would cause confusion and tend to dire results. An observer unacquainted with the fine points of artillery drill, but aware of the unity of action required, would naturally suppose that, when in action, if one or two men were suddenly disabled it would cause confusion and retard its working; but such was not the case, provision was made for casualties but none for mistakes or blunders. In drilling the men were taught to work at "reduced numbers." Each man in position was known by a number when on drill or in action, and not by name, as: No. 1, who rams home the cartridge; No. 2, who inserts the cartridge, and so on; each number had a certain part to perform.

When cannoneers were killed or disabled their duties were immediately assumed by the survivors; and by their increased activity the gun was served with apparently the same regularity and precision as before. Considering that there were to be no drill or field movements during this inspection, the awkward men were assigned to gun detachments for the occasion as before stated. When ready the inspector, a smart appearing artillery officer "dressed in his Sunday best," started on the round of inspection examining critically every man, gun, carriage, horse, and all equipments, etc. At times the inspector would stop suddenly at a gun and, placing his hand on some part, would inquire of a cannoneer, calling by number, "What is this?" Every part of a gun or carriage has a name, for instance: the gun has the bore, muzzle, face of muzzle, muzzle band, swell at muzzle, neck, chace, trunions, reënforce, vent, breach, cascable, neck of cascable, knob of cascable, etc. The men were supposed to answer promptly any questions asked. The inspector passed slowly along when suddenly he stopped, and, placing his hand on the face of the gun, said: "No. 2, what is this?" No. 2 looked at the officer and then at the gun but did not reply. (He was one of the supernumeraries.) The inspector sharply repeated the question. No. 2, now realizing that he must answer, hesitatingly replied: "The end of the gun, sir." This answer staggered the officer, who, giving one glance at No. 2, appeared to take in the situation; he then passed quickly to the rear of the gun where stood No. 4, a sharp, quick-witted, rollicking Irishman, who was well posted and could answer correctly any question pertaining to his duty. The inspector placed his hand on the knob of the cascable, the extreme rear end of the gun, and said: "No. 4, what is this?" Quick as a flash came the reply, "The other end, sir!" This answer paralyzed the inspector, who, followed by the other officers, quickly left the gun as if in fear it, as well as themselves, would explode. A few moments later the battery was dismissed and the men returned to their quarters to give vent to their pent up laughter.

May 25th. The past two weeks, in general, had not been unlike their predecessors since the return of the troops from Chancellorsville.

Capt. John G. Hazard.
BREVET BRIG. GEN.

The weather had continued to bestow upon us a mingling of sunshine and cloud, hot days and cool nights (the sure precursors of typhoid and "chills"), and the warm pleasant weather of the past few days had caused the effects of rain and mud to disappear leaving the fields and roads very passable. There had been more activity, however, than may have appeared to those at a distance. Road-building, picket duties, reconnaissances of the cavalry, with an occasional brush of a more serious character (in all of which Battery B took no part), had filled up the time, and, though our entire line occupied mainly the north bank of the Rappahannock River, in preparation and renewed energy our troops possessed advantages that promised well for the future.

Capt. John G. Hazard returned to the battery from sick leave, looking hearty and well and reported for duty. By virtue of being the senior officer in rank of the artillery officers, he assumed command of the artillery brigade of the Second Army Corps, in accordance with special order, No. 114, May 16, 1863, from headquarters of the Second Corps. Captain Hazard being on detached service Battery B was still under the command of First Lieut. T. Fred. Brown.

May 29th. Pleasant and warm. Little could be known of military affairs outside of our own encampment. All that came to us from headquarters (except by orders) was borne on the wings of rumor and was received with liberal deduction; facts and many fictions reached us by this lightning messenger so instantly, that by the time orders reached their destination their contents were "stale and flat." "Dame Rumor," however, to-day brought news which we hoped would not be so stale, it was the paymaster's appearance at brigade headquarters, and, of all visitors, to the army, the paymaster received the warmest welcome. Happily, we were not doomed to disappointment, for at four P. M. assembly call sounded, and the men were quickly ordered into line and marched to the tent occupied by the paymaster and his clerk. The officers were paid first, then the non-commissioned officers, next the privates in alphabetical order. If any one was out of camp, on detail, and not able to be present, the officer in command generally signed for the absent one and received the money, handing it to the owner upon his return to camp. The men of Battery B were paid for the months of March and April 1863.

May 30th. For a month past the weather and the Rappahannock

River had afforded piscatory attractions, and, for a time, both rebel and Union pickets had improved the opportunity of varying their ration to a fish diet. Suddenly, sundry citizens of Falmouth were smitten with a desire for the scaly luxury, and repaired with suspicious frequency to the river, ostensibly to fish or make purchases, but really, it was believed, to communicate intelligence to the rebels. This led to an order prohibiting angling on the part of our pickets, and a notice to the enemy that if they persisted in the practice they would be fired upon. "So ended all display of Waltonian skill," and no longer, except by stealth, did the ichthyous family "greedily suck in the twining bait" of Unionist or secesh.

May 31st. Reveille at five o'clock A. M. Pleasant and warm. Last night, about midnight, the left section, under the command of Lieutenant Milne, was ordered to hitch up on the double-quick and left camp going down to the river, by the old church in Falmouth, to do picket duty and command the fishing ground. This was in consequence of the enemy still persisting to fish after being notified by the commanding general to desist.

The general commanding the division at Falmouth by the following order was authorized to render such assistance to the pickets as might be needed:

HEADQUARTERS 2D ARMY CORPS,
May 30, 1863.

Circular Order.

The major-general commanding the Army of the Potomac having notified the commander of the enemy's troops opposite to us that seine fishing must cease on the Rappahannock between the armies, you will give such orders to the officer of the day of the division pickets as will cause such practices to cease.

The officer of the day will give such verbal notifications to persons apparently intending to violate this order as may be convenient, in order that innocent persons may not suffer. Such notifications will not be repeated after the first attempt at violation of the same, and all offenders will be fired on.

If assistance is required in the matter it will be furnished by Brigadier-General Gibbon commanding Second Division.

By command of
Major-General HANCOCK.

(Signed,)
JNO. S. SCHULTZE,
Captain and A. A. A. G.

[Official.]

H'd. Qrt's Art'y Brig. 2d A. Corps, May 31st.
L. G. DWIGHT, *1st Lieut., Act. Adj't.*

At early dawn, when the fog began to rise and the opposite side of the river was clearly discernible, the rebels could be seen preparing their boats and seines for the usual morning's occupation. There was also more activity among the Union pickets; their force had been doubled during the morning. The cannoneers of the left section of Battery B were at their posts watching events. We saw an officer of the enemy approach the fishermen, and, by his gesticulations and attitude, appeared to be holding a spirited conversation with those in the boats, which, in the meantime, were drifting from the shore and down the river. A squad of rebel infantry was seen to approach the officer and halt. Their appearance seemed to bring the rebs in the boats to the sense of the situation; returning to the shore they disembarked and hauled the boats up on the bank going off towards Fredericksburg with the seines and other trappings on their shoulders. Thus the fishing expeditions were brought to a close, and all chance of exchanging or sending information to the enemy from our lines was stopped.

The battery did not have the usual Sunday inspection after the regular duties of the morning were over, but passes were given to those who wished to visit friends at other camps, or visit the village sutler to exchange government greenbacks for such luxuries as tobacco, butter, cheese, molasses cookies, peaches in brandy, and many other articles which were not issued to the soldiers from the quartermaster's department. The battery received another lot of clothing to-day.

June 1st. The weather for the past few days had been so dry that clouds of dust filled the air, which was anything but pleasant; let one take a drive of a few miles and their clothes would look as if they had been at work in a flour mill. Our quartermaster-sergeant took our new pants and jackets back to Acquia Creek, and exchanged them for those worn by artillerymen, as those sent us were for infantry.

On the 2d, Lieut. T. Fred. Brown entertained a number of visiting officers by a drill of the cannoneers at the manual of the piece. In the afternoon clothing was issued.

On the 3d, there were indications of a general movement. There was more activity among the troops than there had been for some time, while the Sixth Corps received marching orders and packed up.

June 4th. The activity increased and it was rumored that General Hooker was going to try General Lee again, this time by the left flank below Fredericksburg. Which way the army would move was all speculation on the part of the troops.

June 5th. Reveille at half-past four, but there was no unusual activity in our division, everything was quiet on the Rappahannock; at noon we received orders to have three days' cooked rations on hand and to prepare for light marching. In the afternoon heavy firing was heard down on the left of the line.

June 6th. Pleasant and warm. Reveille at sunrise. There was continued activity going on among the different commands, and, for a few days, it was evident that, whatever the enemy was about, something of importance on our side was soon to take place. Yesterday speculations were brought to a focus. A reconnaissance in force on the left was ordered, and a division of the Sixth Corps crossed at the lower ford (General Franklin's old crossing) by throwing a pontoon bridge across, and held position on the south side of the river having, as reported, taken about two hundred prisoners. There was smart cannonading last night. Our battery was under orders to be in readiness to move at a moment's notice, with three days' rations in haversacks, in what direction we knew not.

June 7th. Last night, just after midnight, our wagon, with a detail to load, was ordered to the supply depot at Acquia Creek for three days' extra rations of grain. At noon the left section returned to camp from picket duty at the ford in front of Falmouth. The knapsacks and all surplus baggage were turned over to the quartermaster's department. This reduced the cannoneers' clothing kit to one blanket, one square of shelter tent, one blouse, one jacket, two pair of drawers, three pair of socks, one pair of boots or shoes, and a cap. The drivers had the same, except in place of a blanket they had a great-coat. This was called light marching order. The detached men serving with the battery were paid to-day. In accordance with special order No. 134, from headquarters of Second Corps, the men of the Thirty-fourth New York Regiment, serving with the battery, were relieved and returned to their regiment to be mustered out of the service.

June 8th. Pleasant and very warm. Reveille at sunrise. No camp duty except that of guard and taking care of the horses; in the cool of the evening the cannoneers greased the axles of the gun and caisson carriages, and the spare men did the same to the battery wagon and forge. The granting of furloughs and leaves of absence had been stopped for the present.

On the 9th, there was only the general routine of camp duty performed. All the batterymen that were absent on furloughs returned to-day. Every one was busy getting their kits and equipments in readiness to move, for every one realized, just as well if the order had been issued and read, that our stay in this place was short. Second Lieut. Joseph. S. Milne, who had had command of the left section of the battery, was detached and ordered to duty in Cushing's Battery A, Fourth United States Artillery, of the artillery brigade of the corps.

On the 10th, Major General Couch left, on a leave of absence, for Washington, and Major General Hancock was temporarily placed in command of the Second Corps.

On the 11th, there was no special change in the battery. It was still encamped, at the breastworks, with the pieces in position overlooking the northern part of Fredericksburg and guarding the ford at Falmouth. All was quiet with the rebels, but it was evident that something was going on over there, as well as on this side of the river.

By a circular order from army headquarters, under date of June 11th, all ladies (of whom there were quite a number) and visiting friends, as well as citizens, not having official business relations with the government and army, were notified to depart at once.

To-day the Army of the Potomac was again put in motion, the First, Third and Eleventh Corps were on the move in pursuit of the enemy. General Lee, with a part of his army, had left our front and was moving north toward the mountains.

CHAPTER XVI.

THE CAMPAIGN AND BATTLE OF GETTYSBURG.

WHEN it became certain that Lee's army was in motion (he commenced to move June 8, 1863,) it only remained for the Army of the Potomac to follow his example, ascertain his designs and thwart his purposes, or, what was better, compel him to surrender. Preparatory to our leaving the base of supplies and the withdrawal of the army from Falmouth, the sick and wounded were transferred to the hospitals of Washington and vicinity, and the army stores, not needed for immediate use, secured on board transports. Materials not worth removing were destroyed, so that the village of government buildings, at Acquia Creek Landing, so lately teeming with busy life and gleaming with weapons of war, suddenly became as desolate as " the wide waste of all devouring years."

For the past two weeks the eyes of the whole country had been fixed with anxious gaze upon the two opposing armies, separated by the Rappahannock, watching each other with the mutual consciousness of having an able foe to deal with. Movements and countermovements had been made without materially changing their relations. What the outcome was to be could only be anticipated.

June 12th was a day of rest, the men were not called upon to do any duty but to care for the horses. Received official notice of General Pleasanton's cavalry engagement with the enemy's cavalry, near Brandy Station on the 9th instant, capturing 200 men and one battle flag.

On the 13th, the weather was fine being pleasant and warm. At noon the following order was received:

HEADQUARTERS SECOND ARMY CORPS,
June 13, 1863.

Special Orders,
No. 140.

"Extract."

In case of a movement the following directions will be observed by commanders: All calls may be sounded as usual except such as indicate a move. No property will be burnt or fires lighted that will attract unusual attention. The tents will not be struck until a movement is ordered. Three days' cooked rations are to be issued to the men, to be carried in their haversacks, and five days' cooked rations to be carried in the wagons including the supply of forage. The order of march will be First Division, Third Division, and Second Division, as rear guard. The artillery will move as hereafter indicated.

[Official.]
By order of Major General HANCOCK,
 Com'dg Second Corps.
G. L. DWIGHT,
First Lieut. First R. I. L. Art., Adjt. of Art. Brig.

June 14th. Reveille at sunrise, cloudy and cool. All was quiet on the opposite side of the river, there were not many rebels to be seen stirring about. The sick call was sounded an hour earlier than usual, and for a wonder no one responded.

About three P. M. orders were received at battery headquarters, and, at four P. M. three days' rations of pork, hard-tack, coffee, and sugar were issued to the men. Next, stable call, at five o'clock, when the horses were watered, fed and groomed. Supper call was sounded at six o'clock, and about seven P. M. the assembly call sounded when orders were given to quietly pack up, and to harness the horses and hitch up the battery. As soon as this was done the battery pulled out from the breastworks, and parked beside the Telegraph road headed north.

The battery was under the command of First Lieut. T. Fred. Brown; the right section under First Lieut. W. S. Perrin; the left section under Second Lieut. C. A. Brown; while the battery wagon, forge, forage wagons, spare horses, and supernumeraries were under the charge of First Sergt. John T. Blake. Here the battery waited until about eight P. M., when the following orders were given: " Battery at-ten-tion! drivers prepare to mount—mount—first piece forward into line—march!" The battery then moved, leaving Falmouth and Fredericksburg behind, marching in a northerly direction our destination unknown.

We marched all night and arrived at Stafford Court House about 4.30 A. M., June 15th. Here we bivouacked, first placing the pieces in position in battery facing the direction from which we came. The men then prepared breakfast; hot coffee, toasted pork, and fried hardtack comprising the bill of fare.

The reason the battery faced to the rear was, that the Second Corps was rear guard to the army and Battery B was with the Second Division, General Gibbon's, which was to bring up the rear. On entering the village we found most of the buildings in flames, having been fired by stragglers from the preceding column. The place consisted of a court-house, jail, and perhaps half a dozen rusty looking dwellings, with a few outbuildings, and presented an appearance neither interesting nor attractive.

We halted here until about ten A. M. when the battery was ordered to hitch up, and we were soon on the move again leaving the right section, Lieutenant Perrin in command, on a knoll by the side of the road as guard. The rest of the battery, after going on for about half a mile, took position in battery on a high hill commanding the road for some distance back. The right section arrived about eleven A. M.; the rest of the battery limbered up, and pulled out into the road resuming the onward march, and, about one P. M., reached Acquia Creek which we forded without any accident, and halted a short distance from the ford. After a short rest we were ordered to proceed about half a mile further to rising ground, where we took position in battery, in an open field, and bivouacked for the night. The day had been intensely hot, and the march, through the dusty roads, proved most fatiguing to the men, hundreds of whom fell out of the infantry columns. There were numerous cases of sunstroke and all the ambulances of the corps were brought into service, at the rear of the column, to bring forward those who could not keep up with their commands.

About midnight the bivouac of the Second Division of the Second Corps was rudely disturbed by hideous outcries, and men rushed hither and thither among frightened mules and horses. Headquarters turned out in dire alarm, and the soldiers, awakened suddenly from the deep slumber which followed a painful march, seized their arms. The coolest believed that a band of guerillas, hanging upon the flank of the column, had taken advantage of the darkness and dashed in among the sleeping troops. The battery was aroused and cannoneers ordered to their posts ready for action, while the drivers commenced to harness the horses. It was finally discovered that all the fright was caused by a soldier being seized with nightmare, and his frightful screams had alarmed the guards.

June 16th. Reveille at 2.30 A. M. We were ordered to hitch up and at three A. M. the battery resumed the march, and, arriving at Dumfries about seven A. M., passed through the village and halted. A century ago this town was of some importance in a business point of view; but now it was a dirty looking place inhabited by "poor white trash" (the F. F. V's. point of view). So far our march had been through a thinly populated region. The battery stopped at Dumfries two hours, allowing the men time to get breakfast and feed and water the horses; three days' rations were also issued.

At nine A. M. we were on the march again, which, like that of the previous day, was one of great fatigue; it was not so hot, but many of the men were sunstruck, falling by the way. The battery crossed the Occoquan Creek, by the ford at Wolf Run Shoals, and, going a short distance, halted on the left of the Telegraph road, and bivouacked for the night at eight P. M.; the tired men were soon in the arms of sweet repose dreaming perhaps of home and friends.

On the 17th, reveille was not sounded until long after sunrise. After the usual morning duties, the jaded troops and horses had an opportunity to refresh themselves by bathing in the clear running water of the Occoquan, a luxury not always obtainable. The country through which we had passed was very hilly, making the march most fatiguing, and the welcome rest, which the battery had, was greatly appreciated by both man and beast. It was one P. M. before the battery packed up and resumed the march, traveling very slowly, until about six P. M. when we reached Sangster's Station, on the Virginia Midland and Alexandria Railroad, and bivouacked.

On the 18th, the battery remained in camp until near night, when, as ordered, it hitched up and went back across the railroad, to the First Division, and took position in battery on picket to guard against a surprise, remaining on duty all night. All was quiet. There were light showers, during the night, which cooled the air and made it very comfortable for sleeping.

On the 19th, the corps resumed the march at early morning, the Second Division and Battery B as rear guard. Yesterday the Sixth Corps went to Fairfax Court House, which is twenty-one miles west of Washington city, and, until the Rebellion broke out, was a quiet little village of two hundred or three hundred inhabitants. Now it was a dirty looking place and bore all the marks of having been under the curse of secession. In a military point of view its importance, at this time, arose from the fact that it commanded the Warrenton turnpike leading to Centreville, seven miles beyond, and thence across Bull Run, at Stone Bridge, to Little River turnpike and the road leading to Vienna.

At one P. M. the battery resumed the march again with caissons in front. The weather was cool with frequent light showers. In accordance with circular order from headquarters of the army, under date of June 18th, the officers of batteries were placed under light marching orders, and the light wagon, which was used to carry their baggage and battery headquarters supplies, had been sent to the chief of ambulance brigade of the corps, together with the battery ambulance.

The battery reached Centreville about seven P. M., halted, then moved to the left and placed the guns in position in the fortifications, which had been built in 1862, and bivouacked for the night.

On the 20th, reveille at five A. M., but it was noon before the battery resumed the march, and, going in a southwesterly direction, passed over the old Bull Run battle-ground of July 21, 1861. Here could be seen bones of every part of the human body protruding out of the ground, the ravages of time and the rain having washed away the earth with which the dead were covered, in their hasty burial, after that eventful meeting of the Union and Confederate forces. The battery crossed Bull Run Creek, by the Stone Bridge, then left the turnpike road going southerly, and, leaving Groveton to the north, passed through Gainesville and Haymarket to Thoroughfare Gap. Here we halted about nine P. M. and bivouacked for the night.

Early on the morning of the 21st, the battery was ordered to move to the left of the road, on a hill near General Hancock's headquarters, where we placed the guns in battery and bivouacked awaiting orders.

From the 21st to the 24th, the battery remained encamped near headquarters as a guard. Close by was a small stream of cool, clear water which received prompt attention. During the hot, dusty march from the Rappahannock, over the old corduroy roads, the men's clothing became very dirty, and, now that there was a chance to improve their looks and appearance, they made use of time and water. The men consequently were very busy washing shirts and socks, brushing the dust from their clothing, until finally they did not look like the same troops that stopped there two days previous.

On the 23d, the supply wagons, from the train, came up to camp and the battery received a fresh supply of forage and rations. The visitor who, at this moment, would meet the warmest welcome was the post-courier. No mail had been received for the past two weeks and tidings from loved ones at home were greatly missed.

Life in camp and life on the march had some features in common, yet in prominent characteristics they differed. In the former monotony soon rules, and when off duty weariness of spirit generally pervades. In the latter there is a constant shifting of scene to refresh the eye, a prospect of adventure that feeds the imagination, and an amount of fatigue that gives sweetness to the slumbers of the bivouac. Then again if, as it sometimes happened, rations were scarce, foraging by the way became an agreeably exciting episode in matters gustatory. On the route salt beef and hard-tack were often diversified with poultry, eggs, milk, fresh meat, and vegetables purchased, of course, with governmental scrip, or Secesh shinplasters, but oftener with an "I promise to pay" order on the quartermaster. A very proper order against pillaging existed, which I fear a man of unbounded stomach, stimulated by the incentive of savory meat, may have less scrupulously observed than conformed with due reverence to the law. If any such exceptional cases did occur, and, in some unexplained way, a barn-yard representative found its way into camp, charity remembered how hard it must have been for men, under the potent sway of appetite and the tempting presence of dainties, to " defy that which they love most tenderly," and, therefore, spread her mantle over the deed.

June 25th. Reveille at sunrise, pleasant and warm. While the men were preparing their morning meal the pickets, in the vicinity of Thoroughfare Gap, were heard firing quite lively. The battery was ordered to hitch up double-quick, and, moving toward the Gap, some five hundred yards, came into battery and remained there for about an hour, when, the firing having ceased and all being quiet, the battery was ordered back to their camp at headquarters. About eight A. M. the right section, under command of Lieutenant Perrin, was ordered up near the Gap. The troops had commenced leaving the vicinity early in the morning, the trains in advance, while the battery, with the Second Division, was again rear guard to the corps. At about ten A. M., everything being in readiness to leave, the battery pulled out into the road headed for Haymarket, the caissons were sent on in advance. The enemy's cavalry were hanging around the rear of our army, and, from their position, had a view of our line of march as it turned north from Haymarket; here they had posted a battery and commenced to shell our troops and trains as they passed.

With cannoneers mounted, Battery B proceeded on a walk while the woods hid it from the enemy, but just before the opening was reached the order was given to trot, the flash and bursting of the shell, upon gaining the clearing, started the frightened horses into a gallop. Led by Lieut. T. Fred. Brown the battery turned to the right, into an open field, and, forming into battery, opened fire on the enemy's battery. The right section, which was in the rear of the column, after advancing a few rods further also turned to the right into the field and got into battery, the caissons kept on with the main column. While this was going on, Battery A, Fourth United States Artillery, had taken position further to the left and obtained a raking fire on the enemy's battery, which in a short time was silenced. Our infantry was advancing upon it, when it limbered up and withdrew. The battery casualties were two missing, James Bean and John T. Gardiner, both detached men; whether wounded or taken prisoners by the enemy's cavalry was not then known. Later they were returned to the battery from the hospital. They had been picked up by the ambulance corps having fallen exhausted during the run in passing the enemy's battery. Several horses were slightly wounded by flying fragments of shell. On the sixth caisson one was killed and two wounded causing us to halt in the road. The fifth caisson in turning out to pass the sixth was upset, turning completely bottom side up, caused by the narrow road and the ditch beside it, the stock and pole were broken rendering it useless, consequently it was destroyed.

After the enemy's battery was silenced Battery B limbered up and repaired damages as best the time and circumstances would permit; changing the wounded horses for those of the lost caisson, we were soon in readiness and resumed the march until late in the evening.

It chanced that, on the morning of the 25th of June, as the Second Corps was moving from Thoroughfare Gap to resume the march north, the Confederate cavalry, under General Stuart, was passing through New Baltimore, toward Gainesville, upon that raid which was destined to cause General Lee the loss of nearly his whole cavalay force. At the little town of Haymarket, where General Hancock's line of march turned to the north, Stuart opened fire, with a battery, upon the rear division, wounding several men, also killing and wounding many horses. Still further annoyance was caused by this unexpected appearance of the enemy's cavalry. General Zook's brigade of the First Division, which was at Gainesville, was temporarily cut off from communication with the rest of the corps, and several aides, passing between Generals Hancock and Zook, were captured, thus causing some delay. The enemy's cavalry, however, were soon dispersed and the corps resumed its march. The battery continued to move until ten P. M., when it reached Gum Springs, in the midst of a drenching rain, and, halting in an open field, bivouacked for the night. We had marched nineteen miles to overtake the corps, which got some distance in advance on account of the delay to the rear guard at Haymarket.

On the morning of the 26th, reveille was not sounded until after five A. M. Warm and showery. After breakfast, "a pot of hot coffee, fried or broiled pork and hard-tack," there was an inspection of the battery and it was found that our loss, on the day before, was two men missing, James Bean, of the Nineteenth Maine, and John T. Gardiner, of the One Hundred and Fortieth Pennsylvania, and three men slightly wounded. Two horses were killed and six wounded, two being unfit for further use in the battery, and one caisson was destroyed so as to render it useless to the enemy. All the equipments were saved and placed in the battery wagon for future use.

At ten A. M. the battery left Gum Springs, and, resuming the march, arrived in the vicinity of the Potomac River; at four P. M. halted. Here the men improved the opportunity by making coffee. At seven P. M. we again started on the march, but it was eleven o'clock before we reached the river, on account of the road being blocked by the wagon trains. We finally crossed on a pontoon bridge to Edward's Ferry, and going a short distance halted. It was two o'clock in the morning before we bivouacked, but the men, rolling themselves up in their blankets, were soon asleep.

No reveille was sounded on the morning of the 27th, we were given a chance to sleep and rest. At ten A. M. the following order was read:

U. S. MIL. TELEGRAPH OFFICE,
FROM WASHINGTON D. C.,
June 25, 1863.

GENERAL HOOKER:

The President has assigned General Hancock to the command of the Second Army Corps.

(Signed,) E. D. TOWNSEND, *A. A. G.*

At his own request General Couch had been relieved from command in the Army of the Potomac, having gone to Washington, on the 10th of June, for that purpose. A few days later, in recognition of his distinguished service, he was assigned to the command of the new Department of the Susquehanna, which was formed to resist the threatening invasion of Pennsylvania, the troops being at Harrisburg and Columbia, Penn.

It was noon before the battery was ordered to hitch up, and, after breaking camp, resumed the march. After leaving Edward's Ferry we passed through a country which was familiar to most of the men in the battery. Arriving at Poolesville we passed through a part of the village to the road leading to Barnesville, and at seven P. M. halted and bivouacked. Sixteen months had made but few changes in the features of the spot, or of its surroundings. The old fields, the scenes of many thorough drills, the adjacent hills and those near the river (the Potomac), from whose summit skillful gunnery was occasionally displayed, the prostrated forest, exposing an uninterrupted view of the "Sugar Loaf" lifting its head to the skies in the wild pomp of mountain majesty, all remained essentially as they appeared when we first pitched our tents in Secessia. Though memory recalled amusing episodes in camp life spent there, the roll call casts a shadow upon mirthful thoughts by reminding us that some who marched with us from this camping ground in the spring of '62 were still in death, a noble sacrifice to their country's cause.

On the 28th, reveille was sounded at sunrise, it was pleasant and warm. After hasty preparations the battery was ordered to hitch up and resume the forward march at seven A. M. We passed through Barnesville and Urbana, small but flourishing towns in producing "*corn juice.*" About sunset the battery halted at the little hamlet of Monocacy Junction and bivouacked. This is a thriving little town. From this place a branch road of the Baltimore and Ohio Railroad leads to Frederick; the main road crosses the Monocacy River at Point of Rocks. On our march up the Monocacy Valley we passed through a number of pleasant villages, indicating, in their appearance, a higher refinement than that we had been accustomed to witness in Virginia. The country was diversified with hills and valleys, fertile fields and dense woods, imparting to the scenery a highly picturesque character. The people along the route appeared loyal, and hailed the presence of the Union army with marked evidences of satisfaction.

The ovations to the troops and their commanders, on entering the towns along the route of march, were inspired with intense enthusiasm, such as might be expected from a rescued people toward their deliverers. If any of the throng sympathized with Lee, in his invasion of Maryland and Pennsylvania, they were prudent enough to conceal it.

When the battery halted at Monocacy Junction the first section, under command of Lieutenant Perrin, was ordered up to the left on the Baltimore turnpike to guard the bridges crossing the river. All was quiet during the night.

Early on the morning of the 29th, the first section rejoined the battery, and, about eight o'clock A. M., we resumed the march onward passing Frederick to Liberty. We passed through several small, but pleasant and picturesque villages, and then through Johnsville to Uniontown. It was ten P. M. when the battery halted and bivouacked, having marched thirty-three miles. It was a hard and tedious march, and very fatiguing to both men and horses; the long and continuous tramp, up hill and down, caused many men to drop by the wayside. It was remarkable that, during the march, the corps had moved upon a single road with its troops, artillery and trains. At Uniontown the reception of the troops, by the inhabitants, was cordial and inspiriting. Liquid refreshments were freely offered at the gates and porches, while kind words and good cheer lightened the hearts of the weary soldiers, crowding onward to battle for the Union.

On the morning of the 30th, reveille was not sounded until six o'clock, affording the men extra time to rest from their march of the previous day. When reveille sounded, however, the camp commenced to show signs of life; the men were up and attending to the duties of the day. At morning roll call the following was read:

HEADQUARTERS SECOND ARMY CORPS,
June 29, 1863.

Circular.

The major-general commanding the corps thanks the troops under his command for the great exertion they have made this day in achieving a march of full thirty-three miles.

This severe labor would have only been exacted of them from urgent necessity.

It was required by the Major-General commanding the Army, who has

expressed his appreciation of the manner in which the duty has been performed.
(Signed,)
By order of Major-General HANCOCK,
W. G. MITCHELL,
A. D. C., A. A. A. G.

The rumor which had been circulated about camp and on the line of march, to the effect that the army was to have another commander, was fully vindicated by the following order, which was also read:

HEADQUARTERS ARMY OF THE POTOMAC,
FREDERICK, MD., June 28, 1863.

General Orders,
No. 65.

In conformity with the orders of the War Department, dated June 27, 1863, I relinquish the command of the Army of the Potomac. It is transferred to Maj.-Gen. George G. Meade, a brave and accomplished officer, who has nobly earned the confidence and esteem of the army, on many a well-fought field. Impressed with the belief that my usefulness as the commander of the Army of the Potomac is impaired, I part from it, yet not without the deepest emotion. The sorrow of parting with the comrades of so many battles is relieved by the conviction that the courage and devotion of this army will never cease or fail; that it will yield to my successor, as it has to me, a willing and hearty support. With the earnest prayer that the triumph of its arms may bring successes worthy of it and the nation, I bid it farewell.
(Signed),
JOSEPH HOOKER, *Major-General.*
[Official.]
S. WILLIAMS, *Assis't Adj't General.*

HEADQUARTERS ARTILLERY BRIGADE, SECOND ARMY CORPS,
UNIONTOWN, MD., June 30, 1863.

[Official.] G. L. DWIGHT,
First Lieut. First R. I. Lt. Art'y, Adjt of Art. Brig.

General Meade, on taking command of the Army of the Potomac, issued the following order:

HEADQUARTERS ARMY OF THE POTOMAC,
June 28, 1863.

General Orders,
No. 66.

By direction of the President of the United States, I here assume command of the Army of the Potomac. As a soldier, in obeying this order, an order totally unexpected and unsolicited, I have no promises or pledges to make. The country looks to this army to relieve it from devastation and disgrace of a hostile invasion. Whatever fatigues and sacrifices we may be called upon to undergo, let us have in view constantly the magnitude of the interests involved, and let each man determine to do his duty, leaving to an all-controlling Providence the decision of the contest. It is with just diffidence, that I relieve, in the command of this army, an eminent and accomplished soldier, whose name must ever appear conspicuous in the history of its achievements; but I trust that the generous support of my companions-in-arms will assist me efficaciously in the discharge of the duties of the great responsibility which has been placed upon me.

   (Signed),   GEORGE G. MEADE,
             Maj. Gen. Comd'g.

[Official.]
S. WILLIAMS, *Ass't Adj't-Gen.*

It was a serious matter to change the commander of an army on the eve of battle, or, as President Lincoln expressed it, to "swap horses while swimming a stream." The Army of the Potomac, however, was fortunate in the selection of its new commander; he had served in it from the beginning, was thoroughly acquainted with its history and many of its officers, while the army had learned to know and trust him in return.

While the battery remained at Uniontown Lieut. T. Fred. Brown ordered a battery inspection of guns, caissons, ammunition, and equipments; and the gunners to see that the equipments were in their proper places. The drivers inspected the harness, and everything was found to be in excellent condition and ready for business.

The battery, at this time, had two of its officers on detach service. Capt. John G. Hazard was chief of artillery of the Second Corps, and our Second Lieut. Joseph S. Milne was with Lieutenant Cushing's battery (A, Fourth United States). First Lieut. T. Fred. Brown was in command of the battery; First Lieut. William S. Perrin, of the right half; Second Lieut. Charles A. Brown, the left half; and First Sergt. John T. Blake was in charge of the caissons.

On the morning of July 1st, reveille was sounded at sunrise, and, after the usual duties were performed, three days' rations of salt pork, hard-tack, sugar, and coffee were issued to each man to be carried in his haversack. At seven o'clock orders were given for the battery to pack and hitch up. At eight o'clock we left Uniontown, and, at noon, after passing through Taneytown, we halted for a couple of hours to make coffee. At two P. M. we resumed our march north on the Taneytown pike, tramping along until seven o'clock when we halted and bivouacked, beside the road, within three miles of Gettysburg. We heard that our cavalry, under General Buford, had met the enemy beyond the town of Gettysburg; that the First Corps had gone to their support, and that General Reynolds was killed, by a rebel sharpshooter, while forming his line. There was some hard fighting, and, as the enemy outnumbered our troops they were forced to fall back to the town, and there form a line with those sent up to their support.

At two o'clock on the morning of July 2d, the battery received marching orders, and the men on being suddenly aroused from slumber, tumbled out of their blankets, wondering if there was to be a night attack from the enemy. Soon everything was in readiness, all packed and hitched up, awaiting orders to move, but at sunrise we were still waiting while the infantry was moving forward. While waiting we improved the time, small fires were built and a pot of hot coffee soon made to refresh the inner man for the work that was before us.

At five A. M. orders were received to move up to the front, and the battery was soon in motion on the Taneytown pike moving towards Gettysburg, which place we reached about ten o'clock, and were assigned position on the left of the Second Corps' line, with General Harrow's Brigade (the first of the Second Division), on Cemetery Ridge, our left being joined by the Third Corps. Our pieces were placed in battery on slightly elevated ground, while the caissons were parked a few rods in our rear, in a hollow, the rolling nature of the ground making a slight protection for them.

General Sickles advanced the Third Corps to the front, about two o'clock P. M., thus making a gap, and leaving the Second Corps exposed on its extreme left flank with only Battery B to fill the space. While the Third Corps was engaged, at Devil's Den and Peach Orchard, in a struggle with the rebels for possession of Little Round Top, the guns of Battery B, at four o'clock, were advanced to the right and front, a few hundred rods, to a ridge in front of the main battle line at General Gibbon's (Second Division of Second Corps) left front, known as the "Godori's field." On reaching the position Lieutenant Brown ordered us "in battery" at once, and we opened fire upon a rebel battery which had obtained a good range upon General Meade's headquarters. After a well directed fire, of a few moments, the rebel battery could hold out no longer and withdrew, our fire made it so hot for them that they did not even send us a parting salute.

The following will explain Battery B's position more clearly: General Gibbon's line at this place, ran nearly parallel with the Emmitsburg road; we were on General Gibbon's left flank, on a slight ridge in Godori's field, between his line and the road at an angle of about 45°. The battery's left was nearest the road with the right extending back to within one hundred yards of the main line, at the stone wall, facing nearly northwest, our line of fire, therefore, was diagonally across the Emmitsburg road toward and to the left of the Lutheran Theological Seminary. The battery had been thrown forward toward the Godori house, by orders from General Gibbon, in order to get it out of the way for a time while he was trying to cover his left flank, which had become exposed by the abrupt advance of the Third Corps which caused a gap in the main line. The Fifteenth Massachusetts and the Eighty-second New York regiments lay along the road beside the fences.

Shortly after we had ceased firing on the rebel battery a large force of the enemy was seen coming out of the woods, on our left flank, moving to the road in the direction of the gap. At first we mistook them for our own men, supposing that the Third Corps was falling back to its old position; but when we commenced to receive their fire and heard that well known "rebel yell," as they charged for our battery, we were in doubt no longer, but sprang to the posts at the guns ready to receive them. This force of the enemy proved to be General Wright's brigade, of General Anderson's division, making for the gap between the Second and Third Corps.

The enemy were in solid front of two lines of battle. As our artillery fire cut down their men they would waver for a second, only to soon close up and continue their advance, with their battle flags flying in the breeze, and the barrels of their muskets reflecting the sun's dazzling rays. The violent forcing back of General Humphrey's division, of the Third Corps, brought destruction upon the force under Col. George H. Ward, consisting of his own regiment, the Fifteenth Massachusetts, the Eighty-second New York, Lieutenant-Colonel Huston, and Battery B under Lieut. T. Fred. Brown. As the enemy (Wright's brigade) advanced a desperate resistance was made by this little band, which was far overlapped on their flanks, and at last compelled to retreat.

While the enemy were forcing General Humphrey's right toward the line they first occupied, to the left of the first position occupied by Battery B in the morning, General Hancock came galloping up (going north) towards the right of his line, he saw a portion of the enemy (Wilcox's brigade) coming out into the opening from a clump of bushes. He looked right and left for troops, and turning round saw a regiment coming up from the rear. Dashing up to the colonel, and pointing to the enemy's column, he exclaimed : "Do you see those colors? Take them!" And the gallant First Minnesota (Colonel Colville) sprang forward and precipitating themselves upon the advancing foe, lost three-fourths of their regiment in the impetuous onset. Thus was the gap partially closed, but on came the advancing foe.

Lieutenant Brown ordered the battery to change front left oblique and to then begin firing four second spherical case shell.*

By the change of fronts, only the left and centre sections (four guns) of the battery could be brought to bear effectually on the advancing enemy, while the right section shelled the woods. By their exposed position the battery received the concentrated fire of the enemy, which was advancing so rapidly that our fuses were cut at three, two, and one second, and then canister at point blank range, and, finally, double charges were used. Then came the order "Limber to the rear," and shouts from our infantry, "Get out of that, you will all be killed." From the batterymen it was "Don't give up the guns."

During this time the enemy were advancing and firing by volleys. Having failed in their attempt to secure the gap, their objective point now seemed to be the capture of the battery, but, as we were well supported by the Sixty-ninth and One Hundred and Sixth Pennsylvania boys, we succeeded in retiring with four pieces leaving two on the field, the horses having been killed.

In retiring the battery came under a heavy enfilading fire from the wing of the flanking foe, which had overlapped us, and many of our men and horses were wounded before we could retire behind our line of support, for only one piece at a time could go through the narrow gap in the stone wall which afforded breastworks for our infantry.

The drivers of the sixth piece were forced to halt as they were approaching the gap, it being partially blocked by two pieces, the third and fifth, trying to get through at the same time. As a conse-

---

*These are shell filled with leaden or iron bullets and sulphur with powder enough to burst them. Ours contained seventy in number.

quence one of the horses, on the sixth piece, was killed and another wounded causing such confusion that the drivers were forced to abandon their horses and the cannoneers their gun. The enemy were right upon them, and they sought safety by lying down, or making for the gap, from each side of which streamed a vivid flame sending forth messengers of death to the foe.

When the order was given, by Lieutenant Brown, to limber to the rear, Sergt. Albert Straight waited and had his piece, the fourth which was loaded, fired before he repeated the order, and, in consequence two of his horses were shot and fell making it impossible to execute the order. He then ordered the men to look out for themselves, leaving his gun in position on the field. In the diary of Sergeant Straight, under date of July 2, 1863, is written:

"We were ordered to limber to the rear when they (the rebs) had got very near to us, two of my horses got shot just as the order was given, and I could not get my piece off, and the boys had to look out for themselves, as the Johnnies were all around us, and the bullets flew very lively, with some shot and shell, all my horses were killed. David B. King was hit and lived but a few minutes, and one man was taken prisoner. I got my piece again after the charge was over."

The other pieces, which reached the rear of our battle line, got in battery at once and opened fire again upon the advancing foe, but soon stopped to enable our infantry to charge them. Then came a struggle for the possession of those two guns. The gallant Sixty-ninth Pennsylvania, backed by the One Hundred and Sixth, held their ground, and advancing, with the brigade on the charge, drove the foe back and held the guns. When the rebels were finally driven back across the Emmitsburg road, we withdrew our two pieces from the field to the third position occupied by the battery. After the charge the brigade fell back at the wall, its old position on the ridge.

Owing to the loss of men and horses the fifth and sixth pieces were sent to the rear, where the reserve artillery was parked, while the serviceable horses and men were put into the other four detachments making them complete.

Our casualties of July 2d were one officer wounded, three men killed, seventeen wounded and one taken prisoner, viz.: First Lieut. T. Fred. Brown, commanding battery, wounded; Corp. Henry H. Ballou, acting sergeant, mortally wounded; died July 4th. Killed, privates Ira Bennett, of the Nineteenth Maine; Michael Flynn, of the Fifteenth Massachusetts (both on detached service); and David B. King. The wounded were: First Sergt. John T. Blake. Sergt. Edwin A. Chase, Corp. Charles D. Worthington, Bugler Eben L. Crowningshield, and privates Mowry L. Andrews, Russel Austin, James Baird, Dyer Cady, Michael Duffy, William Maxcy, George McGunnigle, Lewis Moulton, Charles H. Paine, Peleg Staples, Herbert Sanford, and Albert J. Whipple. Taken prisoner, Joseph Cassen. Making a total of 22.

During the engagement our caissons, with a full compliment of men and horses, were parked in the rear of the reserve line of infantry of the corps, and remained undisturbed. It was owing to this circumstance that the battery was enabled to take part in the battle of July 3d with four guns fully equipped. Lieut. T. Fred. Brown was wounded while withdrawing the battery from the Godori field, and the command was turned over to First Lieut. William S. Perrin, by orders of Capt. John G. Hazard, chief of artillery of the Second Corps.

The following incident, connected with the above engagement, is worthy of note. To men in line, on a battle-field, water was a precious article, and no exception in our case, while in position on Godori's field, waiting under the hot rays of the afternoon's sun. In the sixth gun detachment was a short, thickset "detached man" from the One Hundred and Fortieth Pennsylvania Regiment. Not a drop of cowardly blood flowed through his veins, he was good natured, clever, and obliging, but so awkward and blundering that, many times, he was in the way and more of a hindrance than help. But this occasion was an exceptional one. The water in our canteens was getting low, and there was little prospect of refilling them as we could not leave our posts. "Coplar, I will take the boys' canteens and go to the house beyant there, shure, there must be a well, and I'll fill them and be back in a jiffy." Thus spoke little Peter Shevlin to his corporal, John Delevan. Glancing at the house (Godori's) the corporal said, "Yes, there might be a well there, and the enemy beyond in the woods, and they might make it red-hot for you, and make you turn up your toes." "Divil a bit of it," said Peter, "for shure, our skirmishers are beyant the house, and as long as they stay I'll be safe. When they run, shure, I can run too." Corporal Delevan said, "Well, Peter, if you go, you will go at your own risk." However, Peter was willing to take the risk, and was soon loaded with a dozen or more canteens (each would

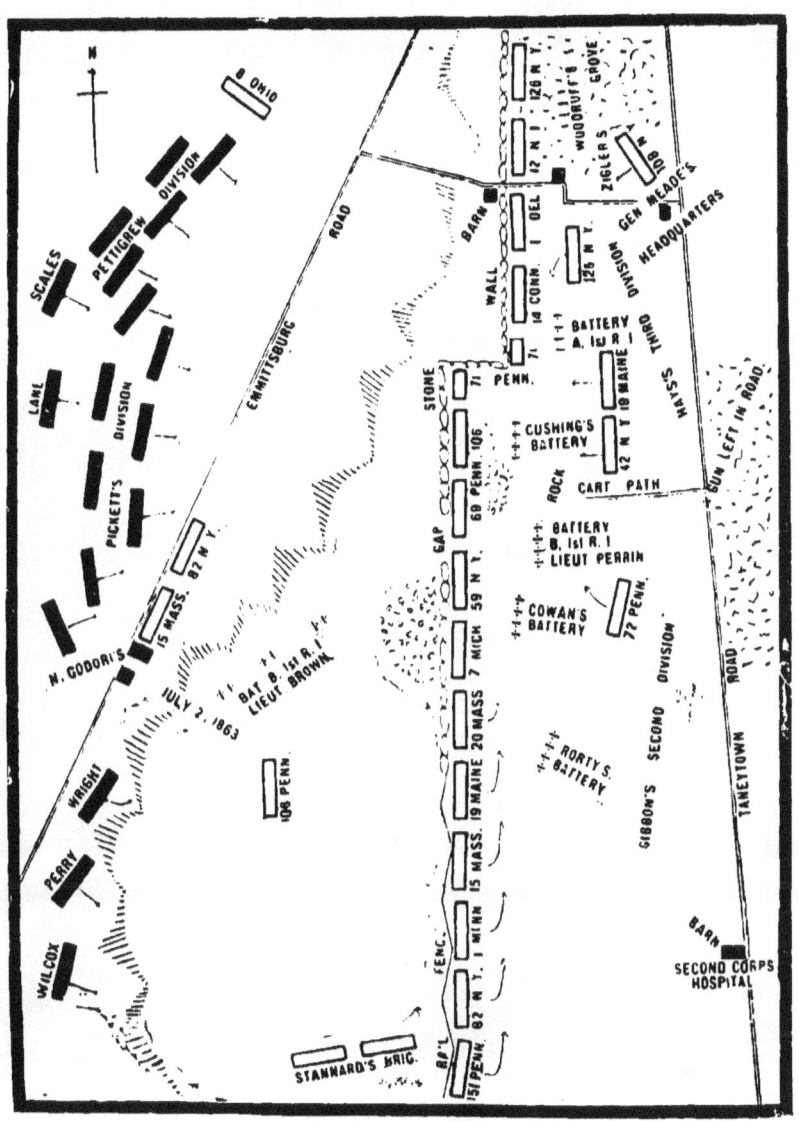

Gettysburg, July 3, 1863.

hold three pints when full) going off in the direction of the house "beyant."

In the engagement of the battery, which soon followed, Peter with the canteens was forgotten. After the charge was over, and we were congratulating one another on our escape, a familiar voice was heard saying, "Ah, ah! boys, here's yer wather!" For a moment the men seemed paralyzed. There stood Peter with a grin on his face, and the canteens, filled with water, attached to his shoulders.

The grimy cannoneers gathered about him in surprise, exclaiming: "For God's sake, Peter, how did you escape not being gobbled up by the Johnnies?" Although our mouths were parched we listened to Peter's story. He said: "When I came to the house beyant, I found a well and bucket, but the bucket was so big, and the muzzle of the canteens so small that it took a long while to fill them. I got them filled, after a bit, and got them on me shoulders, and had jest started to return, when pop! pop! I heard behind me. I looked and our skirmishers were firing and running, and the rebs were coming. I tried to run, but the canteens would trip me up. At first I thought I would fling them away, but no, I said to meself, I won't, for the boys wants the wather. Soon the rebs came up to me and one of them, a long lank divil, ran to me with his baynet and asked me, if I would surrender; I told him, of course I would. I had no gun; and said I, to him, 'see me condition, I can't fight.' Then said he, 'Get to the rear.' Then another one seed me, and came at me with his baynet asking if I would surrender. I told him to see me condition, I had no gun and could not fight; and he told me to go to the rear. Four or five of these divils took me prisoner and asked me to surrender, and I told them all to see me condition. I had no gun, and could not fight. Then there came a big roar up at the battery. I looked and seed the battery had opened on them, and the shot came tearing up the ground, and the shells bursting among them from our guns. At this they left me and went for our battery. There was a big rock convenient to me so I went behint it with the canteens and squat down, like a hen with her chickens, and stayed there while the fight was going on. Bye-and-bye the Johnnies came back in such a hurry, that divil a man of them stopped to ask me would I surrender. Then I got up and come in. So here is your wather, boys." As we raised those canteens to our parched lips, we drank to the health of little Peter.

Night closed the scene. White robed peace flung her mantle, for a brief interval, o'er the victor and the vanquished, the dying and the dead. Hushed was the fearful strife, and welcome sleep closed the eyelids of men weary and worn with battle. How many were sleeping their last sleep on this earth, dreaming of the loved ones at home, of their childhood days, or, perhaps, of the last sad parting. Morning came all too soon, and ere the golden orb had tinted the east with his splendor the call to arms was heard. Again we looked death calmly in the face while patiently awaiting the summons to battle. Stern duty lay before us, an enemy to conquer, a government to honor and uphold.

The dawn of July 3d broke in splendor, but before the calm beauty of that magnificent landscape was revealed, by the first rays of the sun, the clamor of human strife broke forth; it rose and swelled to fury, along the rocky slopes of Culp's Hill, on our right. The Twelfth Corps, returning from the left, had found their old position occupied by the rebels (Johnson's division), and only waited for daylight to advance and drive the intruders out. The contest was sharp, but the nature of the position did not permit of rapid and decisive work. Little by little the enemy was forced back (though reinforced by three brigades) until finally they were compelled to give up the ground and abandon the position to the Twelfth Corps.

The position now occupied by the two armies had each their advantages and disadvantages. On the Union side, General Meade's shorter, convex line gave him the important advantage of being able to transmit orders and transfer troops with great celerity; on the Confederate side, the long range of hills afforded space for a greater number of batteries, than could be brought into action by the Union commander. Of this fact General Lee was preparing to take advantage, having in view a grand assault. Where? He had tried the right, also the left, and the next would naturally be the Union centre along Cemetery Ridge.

The Union troops were more systematically arranged, in regard to the unity of army corps, than was possible on the two previous days. General Slocum with his Twelfth Corps and the First Division; General Wadsworth, of the First Corps, held Culp's Hill; General Howard with his Eleventh Corps and the Second Division, General Robinson, of the First Corps, held Cemetery Hill; General Hancock with his Second Corps and the Third Division; General Doubleday, of the First Corps, held Cemetery Ridge; then the Third Corps, under General Birney, extended General Hancock's lines. The Fifth Corps, General Sykes, still extended the line to the summit of Round Top. The Sixth Corps, General Sedgwick, was held mainly in reserve.

In his survey of the Union line, for his third assault, General Lee hit upon the ground occupied by the Second and Third Divisions of the Second Corps. It is desirable, therefore, to describe the nature of this position more explicitly. Between Cemetery Hill and Cemetery Ridge was a small strip of woods known as Ziegler's Grove, in which was posted Battery I, First United States, under Lieutenant Woodruff, holding the right of the Second Corps; then came the Third Division, General Hays, on whose line was posted Battery A, First Rhode Island, Captain Arnold; the Second Division, General Gibbon's, extended the line. First on the right, connecting with Hays's Division, was the Second Brigade, General Webb, on his line was posted Battery A, Fourth United States, First Lieutenant Cushing; next came the Third Brigade, Colonel Hall, on his line was posted Battery B, First Rhode Island, under the command of First Lieut. William S. Perrin; next the First Brigade, General Harrow; on his line was posted Battery B, First New York, Captain Rorty. The line was continued by the Third Division, of the First Corps, General Doubleday; then next to the First Division, General Caldwell, of the Second Corps. In front of General Hays's and part of General Gibbon's troops, of the Second Corps, was a low stone wall surmounted by a post and rail-fence. On General Hall's left, in front of General Harrow, instead of a wall was an ordinary rail-fence. The ground and troops thus described and posted will afford some idea of the scene previous to the engagement, which, however, was known only to the rebel commander.

The four pieces of Battery B, on the morning of July 3d, were so posted that its two centre pieces were a little in advance of its right and left pieces, thus enabling them to bear upon and command a given point. The third piece, Sergt. A. B. Horton and Corp. Samuel J. Goldsmith, gunner, was on the right of the battery; next to the left was the fourth piece, Sergt. A. Straight and Corp. J. M. Dye gunner; then the second piece, Sergt. A. A. Williams and Corp. John F. Hanson gunner; the first piece, Sergt. R. H. Gallup and Corp. Pardon S. Walker, was on the left of the battery. Several rods further to the left, on line with our battery, was Captain Rorty's Battery B, First New York, in position, while several rods to our right, and a little further to the front, was Lieutenant Cushing's Battery A, Fourth United States. Of the infantry, the Fifty-ninth Pennsylvania regiment held position, in the main battle line, to the left of the gap at the stone wall, and the Sixty-ninth Pennsylvania regiment was in position at the right of the gap. These two regiments were in front of Battery's B's position. In reserve, several rods to the right and rear, lay the Forty-second New York and the Nineteenth Maine regiments; while the Seventy-second Pennsylvania regiment was at the left and rear of the battery.

In the morning a desultory fire of artillery was kept up, during which the rebels succeeded in exploding one of our ammunition wagons and several of the limber chests along our line, in retaliation we performed the same service for them, which was acknowledged by both parties with continued shouts and cheers. As the forenoon wore on there came a lull, a stillness even unto death. A feeling of oppression weighed upon all hearts, the silence was ominous and portentous of coming evil. It was the calm which precedes the storm.

Early this morning, as we lay in line of battle waiting, word had been sent to the rear for rations, as most of the men were out, not being able to procure them the previous day on account of the engagement. It was past noon and still no rations. What was the trouble? What had befallen Bob Niles, the veteran driver of our ration wagon? We were watching for him, with almost a wolf's hunger. But as we looked anxiously across the plain, to our rear, we saw him coming with four head-strong mules, well in hand, on the full jump.

Robert A. Niles, but to us better known as Bob Niles, whether in camp, on the march or on the battle-field, would try to overcome all obstacles to reach us, if sent for. He was one of the reckless artillerymen of Battery B, shrewd and quick to grasp the situation, surmounting all difficulties without complaint. Here he was, on this fearful field, mid shot and shell to feed us. But, he arrived too late, for we were suddenly called to our posts of duty by a quick flash and the report of the enemy's gun. It proved to be their signal gun followed by gun after gun along their line; we could not leave our posts, so, amid a shower of shot and exploding shell, Bob was forced to return to the rear, and we to continue our fast.

About one o'clock in the afternoon a cannon shot, from the enemy's Washington Artillery, was fired on our right soon followed by another, thus breaking the silence brooding over the scorched battle-field. This signal was well understood, and the smoke from those guns had not dispersed before the whole rebel line was ablaze. From the throats of over one hundred cannon, which obeyed the signal, burst forth a concerted roar rivaling the angriest thunder. Our cannoneers jumped to their places and the drivers to their horses waiting for the order to commence firing.

It was ten or fifteen minutes before we received orders to fire. Then the shrieking shot and shell were sent upon their work of destruction, proving it to be one of the most terrible artillery duels ever witnessed. Then came Pickett's grand charge to break the Union centre, sweep the Second Corps from their path, and on to Washington. How Lee succeeded history tells. Through this ordeal Battery B still sustained its well earned reputation of stability and resistance, and though suffering heavily in both men and horses, did not leave its position nor slacken fire until relieved by orders of chief of artillery of the corps Captain Hazard.

During this fierce cannonade one of the guns of Battery B was struck by a rebel shell, which exploded killing two cannoneers who were in the act of loading. No. 1, William Jones, had stepped to his place in front, between the muzzle of the piece and wheel on the right side, and, having swabbed the gun, stood with sponge staff reversed (which is also the rammer) waiting for the charge to be inserted by No. 2. Alfred G. Gardner, No. 2, had stepped to his place, between the muzzle of the piece and wheel on the left side, and, taking the ammunition from No. 5, was in the act of inserting the charge when a shell struck the face of the muzzle, left side of the bore, and exploded. No. 1 was killed instantly by a fragment of the shell, which cut the top of the left side of his head completely off. He fell with his head toward the enemy, while the sponge staff was thrown two or three yards beyond him.

Alfred G. Gardner was struck in the left shoulder, almost tearing his arm off. He lived a few minutes, and died shouting: "Glory to God! I am happy! Hallelujah!" His sergeant and friend bent over him to receive his dying message; which was, to tell his wife that he died happy, and to send her his Bible.

Sergt. Albert Straight, and the remaining cannoneers, tried to load the piece, but, in placing a charge in the muzzle of the gun, they found it impossible to ram it home. Again and again, with rammer and an axe, they endeavored to drive in the shot, but their efforts were futile, as the depression on the muzzle was too great, and the attempt had to be abandoned. As the piece cooled off the shot became firmly fixed in the bore of the gun.

This piece was the so called "Gettysburg Gun" of Battery B, First Regiment Rhode Island Light Artillery.*

Lieut. Charles A. Brown, who was then in command of the section of the third and fourth pieces, informed the writer that, when he saw the sergeant trying to drive the shot in with the rammer, he ordered one of the cannoneers to get the axe, from the limber, and use it.

These letters, and others, received by the writer, proved that the

[*Extract from a letter by the sergeant of this piece, to his brother John, July 7, 1863.*]

* "We arrived near Gettysburg, Penn., on the night of July 1st, and on the 2d, we had a fight. I had one man killed, David B. King, of my detachment, six horses killed and one wounded.

"The rebels charged our battery, and we had to retire a short distance to the rear of our second line of infantry; our support in front gave way. But the rebels fared badly, for but few of them got back to tell the story; they were repulsed with so terrible a loss. I also had one man missing; probably he was taken prisoner, as the rebels were within a few paces of us when we left. Lieutenant Brown, commanding the battery, was badly wounded, also Sergeant Chase, and many others. But this was nothing to the next day's fight. The rebels collected all their artillery and opened a concentrated fire upon us. It was terrible beyond description; the air was full of shell hissing and bursting. They came so thick and fast, there was no dodging them. Three shot or shell, before they exploded, struck my piece, one of them killing my No. 1 and No. 2, tearing the head off of No. 1, William Jones, and the shoulder and arm off of No. 2, Alfred G. Gardner. He lived a few minutes, and died shouting, 'Glory to God!' and saying he was happy. He requested me to send his Bible to his wife, and tell her he died happy. He was a pious man, and he and I have been tenting together on this march.

"Your brother,

[Signed,] ALBERT STRAIGHT."

[*Extract from letters, written July 3d, 1863, by the Gunner of the Fourth Piece, Corp. J. M. Dye, a detached man from the One Hundred and Fortieth Pennsylvania regiment.*]

"Billy Jones and old Mr. Gardner were killed, and my No. 3 wounded, and went to the rear; my No. 4 was played out and lay on the ground, I tried to get him up to thumb vent, while the sergeant and myself tried to load the gun. But he wouldn't budge, so I got a stone and tearing off a piece of my shirt laid it on the vent. I then went and held the shot in place, which the sergeant had placed in the gun, while he swung on the rammer. I had to hold the shot in on account of a dent in the muzzle, made by the rebs' shell which killed Jones and Gardner, and we could not get it in. Some one came with an axe, and as they were going to make a strike with it, a rebel shell struck the cheek and exploded knocking out a spoke; this raised the gun up on one wheel, but did not dismount it, but it settled back. This put a stop in trying to load it; the gun, in cooling, had clamped on to the shot, so that we could not get it out again, and the gun went to the rear with the shot in the muzzle."

piece and carriage were struck three times, first the axle of the carriage, then the piece on face of the muzzle, and lastly the cheek. The sergeant says his piece was struck three times before the shell exploded. If these missiles had been solid shot they would have dismounted the piece, and there would have been no explosion. The writer distinctly remembers seeing the explosion when the two men were killed, but thought the piece had been fired until told that it was struck by a rebel shell. The shot, which was placed in the gun after the explosion, still remains firmly fixed in the bore, and is not a *rebel shot* as some have claimed it to be. Sergeant Straight finding that the piece could not be loaded, reported it disabled, and was ordered by Lieutenant Perrin to have it taken to the rear, to where our battery wagons were parked.

About half-past two o'clock P. M. Battery B's fire began to slacken from want of men and ammunition, and, at quarter of three P. M., a battery (Cowen's First New York Artillery) came up to the ridge on a trot, wheeled into battery, on the left and front of Battery B's position, and opened fire, with spherical case shell, on the enemy's line of infantry moving then from the woods toward the Emmitsburg road. Battery B had been ordered to cease firing, and, being relieved by Cowen's Battery, withdrew from the field by orders of Capt. John G. Hazard, chief of artillery of Second Corps.

As the battery was limbering up and retiring, the enemy's line of battle could be seen advancing from the woods on Seminary Ridge, three-fourths of a mile away. A line of their skirmishers sprang forward into the open field, closely followed first by one line of battle, then by a second, and then by a third line.

General Gibbon's division, which was to stand the brunt of the assault, looked with eager gaze upon their foe marching forward with easy swinging step, and along the Union line the men were heard to exclaim: "Here they come! Here comes the Johnnies!" Soon little puffs of smoke issued from the skirmish line, as it came dashing forward, firing in reply to our own skirmishers; it never hesitated for an instant but drove our men before it or knocked them over, by a biting fire, as they rose up to run in.

This was Pickett's advance, which carried a front of five hundred yards or more on that memorable charge of the Confederates against the Union centre. The repulse was one of the turning points against the Confederates, and helped to break the backbone of the Rebellion.

As Battery B was leaving the line of battle, the field in rear of its position was being swept by the enemy's shot and bursting shell. The gun detachments and drivers, in order to avoid this field, went with three pieces to the right (as they were facing to the rear) diagonally toward the Taneytown road. The other piece, of which the writer was lead driver at that time, instead of following the first three went to the left, down a cart-path, toward the same road.

We had not proceeded far when a rebel shell exploded on our right, and a piece of it struck the wheel driver, Charles G. Sprague, on the forehead, cutting a gash from which the blood flowed copiously down his face, blinding him so that he could not manage his horses. He got off his horse, saying, " I cannot ride but will try to lead them."

I asked the swing driver, Clark L. Woodmansee, to take the wheel horses and let his swing horses go alone. He did so, thus relieving Sprague. Then we started down the path again. The flash of the bursting shell, and the screeching of solid shot, which were flying thick and fast around us, caused the swing horses, now that they had no driver, to plunge frantically from one side to the other and then backward, entangling themselves in their traces and interfering greatly with our progress. Looking to my left I saw one of our cannoneers, a detached man from the One Hundred and Fortieth Pennsylvania Regiment, Joseph Brackell, lying beside a large boulder rock. I called to him to come and drive the swing horses as we could not get along. He came, and, after clearing the horses from their traces, mounted. This somewhat calmed the horses, and we started for the road again. When within a few rods of the road, where the path descended, a shell at our right exploded, and a piece cut through the bowels of the off wheel horse, another piece struck the nigh swing horse, which Brackell was riding, on the gambrel joint breaking the off leg. Still another piece swept across the saddle of my off horse cutting the feed-bags loose, whereby I lost my cooking utensils and extra rations. Whipping up my horses I shouted to the other drivers, " Let's get into the road!" We continued and finally swung around into the road, which was three feet lower than the field. Here the wheel horse dropped dead, and we could go no further. Having cleared the horses from the piece, we were about changing the harnesses, from the dead and wounded horses to the uninjured swing horse, when a shot struck the gun-wheel taking out a spoke, and then went screeching into the woods. This was followed by a shell exploding in the woods in our rear. The horses were frightened, and Woodmansee's ran down the road, he after him. Brackell, who had changed the saddles from his crippled horse to a sound one, now mounted and followed Woodmansee. The poor crippled horse, seeing his mate going off, hobbled on trying hard to keep up. Being thus left alone I could do nothing, so mounted and, leaving the piece where it was, went down the road hoping to find the battery. I found the road anything but pleasant to travel, for shot and shell were flying about quite lively.

On reaching a barn, on the west side of the road, used as the headquarters of the Artillery Brigade of the Second Corps, and also as a hospital, I found behind it several staff officers, aides, and some cavalry, and asked them for Battery B. They pointed down the road. Meeting Woodmansee we kept on together. We had not gone far before we heard a crash and report, and, on looking back, saw men and horses, which were back of the above mentioned barn, scattering in all directions. A shell had struck a corner of the barn and exploded. Not far from the barn, in an opening among the woods on the east side of the Taneytown road, and about a mile from our position on the battle-field, we found Battery B parked and the men in bivouac, some already having the shelter tents up. I reported that one of our pieces was left up in the road near General Meade's headquarters.

Late in the afternoon, after the firing had subsided and all was quiet along the lines, Lieutenant Perrin with a detail of men, the writer being one of the number, went back to the battle-field. Our troops had advanced from the position they occupied when the battery left. and the ground was strewn with torn haversacks, battered canteens, broken wheels of gun carriages, and piles of knapsacks and blankets overturned, silently telling of the destruction which had visited the place.

Our men, under Sergt. Albert Straight and Corp. Calvin L. Macomber, dug graves, near a clump of bushes at the left of the gap in the wall, and our dead, Alfred G. Gardner, William Jones, David B. King, Ira L. Bennett, and Michael Flynn, were buried, and a rough marker placed at the head of each dead comrade.

The men gathered such accoutrements as belonged to the battery, and which had been left on the field when it withdrew. In returning to camp, by way of the cart-path, we reached the place where the third piece had been left. The dead horse lay beside the road, but the piece and harnesses were gone. We could get no information from any one near by as to who carried it off, or in what direction it went. We knew it could not have fallen into the hands of the enemy, being within our own lines, therefore it was evident that some battery, ordnance or supply wagon had taken it to the rear, where all condemned ordnance was parked. As the number of the gun was unknown to the officers of the battery, it was not returned nor any information concerning it as far as the writer could learn.

Battery B's casualties, on the 3d of July, were: Killed, Alfred G. Gardner and William Jones; wounded, John Green, mortally (and died July 16th), John T. Boyle, Amos Broard, Bernard Doyle, Daniel L. Felt, Ezra L. Fowles, Jacob Frizee, John Gray, Joseph Hammond, Michael Kelly, George R. Matteson, Peter Phillips, Thomas W. Phillips, Charles G. Sprague, John D. Wishart; missing and said to have deserted, William H. Gallup, and was so reported on the company rolls. The battery's loss, during the two days' engagement, was seven killed, thirty-one wounded, one taken prisoner on the field, and one deserted, making a total of forty men. Official records credit Battery B with only a total of thirty-two. Eighteen of the wounded were taken to the hospital from the field; thirteen were cared for in the battery and attended the sick call daily, but seven were subsequently sent to the hospital, where one (Herbert Sanford) died, and only two others returned to the battery for duty. There were twenty-nine horses killed and thirty-six wounded, seventeen of which were unfit for further service, making a loss of forty-six horses disabled in action.

Our captain, John G. Hazard, chief of artillery of the Second Corps, had his horse shot under him during the fierce cannonading, and his adjutant, Lieut. G. Lyman Dwight, met the same casualty. Lieut. William S. Perrin's horse was disembowelled, soon after he had dismounted, at the commencement of the cannonading.

The only Rhode Island officer killed at the battle of Gettysburg was Second Lieut. Joseph H. Milne, of Battery B, who was on detached service with Lieutenant Cushing's Battery A, Fourth United States Artillery. He was mortally wounded during Pickett's charge on the third, but is not credited to the battery's loss by reason of being on detached service.

July 4th. Cloudy and showery. The momentarily expected order to advance had not been given. The Union commander was evidently content with the victory won, and willing that the troops

Lieut. Joseph S. Milne.

should rest on their arms, bivouacked on the field. Toward morning there arose a terrible storm, one of those instances which seems to establish a connection between a battle of nations and one of the elements. In this instance, at any rate, the downfall was equal to the violence of the preceding cannonade. The troops were drenched, in an instant, by the sudden torrent which swept over hill and plain, as if to wash out the stains of the great battle. The fact, however, that the Army of the Potomac had at last won a great victory could not be obliterated, nor the fact that the backbone of the Confederacy was broken on the field of Gettysburg, from which time the southern cause went steadily backward.

Fourth of July, the birthday of our National Independence. One year ago the Army of the Potomac, exhausted by the fatigue and excitement of its "Seven Days'" battles, was reposing at Harrison's Landing on the James River. The brightness of the national anniversary was then shadowed by disappointment, in view of being withdrawn from the Peninsula, without gaining the prize almost within our grasp. This year, however, it was enlivened by brilliant deeds, and the victory long delayed. In a spirit becoming the event, General Meade issued the following order to the troops:

HEADQUARTERS ARMY OF THE POTOMAC,
NEAR GETTYSBURG,
July 4, 1863.

General Orders, }
No. 68. }

The commanding general, in behalf of the country, thanks the Army of the Potomac for the glorious result of the recent operations. Our enemy, superior in numbers, and flushed with pride of successful invasion, attempted to overcome or destroy this army. Baffled and defeated, he has now withdrawn from the contest. The privations and fatigue the army has endured, and the heroic courage and gallantry it displayed, will be matters of history to be ever remembered.

Our task is not yet accomplished, and the commanding general looks to the army for greater efforts to drive from our soil every vestige of the presence of the invader.

It is right and proper that we should, on suitable occasions, return our grateful thanks to the Almighty Disposer of events, that in the goodness of His providence, He has thought fit to give victory to the cause of the just.

By command of   GEORGE B. MEADE,
Maj. Gen. Commanding.

S. WILLIAMS, *A. A. Gen.*

During the forenoon the men were kept quite busy taking account of equipments on hand, and of those lost in action, or on the recent march. But that which gave the most satisfaction, and was most heartily received, was the appearance of Robert A. Niles with the ration wagon. The rations were soon issued, and all were made happy by being well fed on salt pork, hard-tack and coffee.

There was another interesting event during the forenoon, and that was the arrival of the drivers, Charles Fried, lead, and Levi J. Cornell, wheel, with the disabled fourth piece having the shot still in the muzzle. When they were ordered from the field to the rear with the gun, they went north toward the town instead of south, not knowing where the reserve artillery was encamped. Not finding the battery before night, they bivouacked in the woods, south of Culp's Hill on the east side of the Taneytown road, and in the morning again started to find the battery. When they came into camp they were asked: "Where did you come from?" and if they had been to Baltimore since the fight. The men gathered around the gun, and many questions were asked by those who had not witnessed the explosion. Upon examination the gun and gun carriage showed that they had been struck three times with shell. Thirty-nine bullet marks were also plainly visible, serving to remind those who may chance to look upon it of the ordeal through which it passed during that fearful struggle. This gun (the fourth piece of Battery B, First Regiment Rhode Island Light Artillery, now called "the Gettysburg gun"), with other condemned ordnance, was sent to the Arsenal, at Washington, D. C., and placed on exhibition where it remained until May, 1874.

About four o'clock in the afternoon, having received orders from artillery headquarters, the battery was hitched up, and the drivers, with a detail of cannoneers, took the guns, caissons, battery wagon and forge, under command of Lieutenant Perrin, nearly to Gettysburg, and parked where the ordnance department was encamped. The battery was condemned on account of its condition. Subsequently our remaining serviceable horses (sixty-five) were turned over to Battery A, Rhode Island, to take the place of those it had lost.

On returning to camp we passed along the ridge, in rear of our battle line, where so many brave defenders of the Union fell yesterday. The description of this carnage would be but a stronger repetition of the ghastly scenes presented at Malvern Hill and Fredericksburg. The field after the battle exhibited all the terrible features of Antietam intensified. In no previous battle had the number of killed and wounded been so great. Over an area of miles lay, thickly strewn, the dead and wounded men, also horses, broken caissons, disabled attillery guns, muskets, haversacks, canteens, and other appurtenances of war.

The destruction visible on Cemetery Hill, of shattered monuments and broken gravestones, silently told of the fierce struggle for its possession on the night of the 2d. Looking to the west, along and beyond Seminary Ridge, the Confederate army could be seen, still in position within easy cannon range. General Lee maintained a firm front, and stood at bay behind earthworks which, though hastily thrown up, were none the less formidable.

Looking to the north the town of Gettysburg could be seen and the beautiful Cumberland Valley, " Pennsylvania's land of promise."

Gettysburg, Pa., is situated at the head of a beautiful valley, lying between Catoctin and South Mountain, from which issues roads to nearly every point of the compass. Two streams pass near the town, the Rock Creek on the east, and Willoughby Run on the west; the former, the most important of the two, runs nearly due south. Between these two streams run three ridges, almost due north and south and nearly parallel to each other. One of these ridges, the shortest in length and lowest in altitude, forms the eastern border of Willoughby Run, where the battle commenced early on the morning of July 1st. The second ridge runs just through the western outskirts of the town, and derives its name "Seminary Ridge" from the Lutheran Theological Seminary* situated thereon. On this ridge General Lee, with the Confederate army, had taken position with reference to the then coming battle. The third ridge, which was occupied by the Union forces, would, if prolonged northward, run through the eastern border of Gettysburg; but, just before reaching the town, it bends sharply around and curves backward until it reaches the banks of Rock Creek upon the east. The elevation of this ridge varies greatly throughout its course, which is briefly defined from south to north. At the south, about three miles from the town, is a sharp, rocky, and densely wooded peak known as Round Top. From this the ground slopes toward the north to again rise in a similar peak, though not so high, known as Little Round

---

* The observatory of this college General Lee occupied during the battle as a place of observation.

Top. At the foot of this, and to the west, is a rocky gorge called
"Devil's Den." From here the ground declines toward the north
to a small plain which rises again to a ridge known as "Cemetery
Ridge," the ground then continues to ascend, as Gettysburg is approached, when it curves around and is bent backward, forming an
uncommonly strong defensive position. At this curve the ridge is
known as Cemetery Hill, because of the village cemetery there enclosed. Ths ridge still continues to curve around to the southeast,
falling off sharply, for a little distance, to again rise into a rocky,
woody eminence known as Culp's Hill, having an abrupt eastward
face, along the foot of which flows Rock Creek. The highways
which traverse the surrounding country and enter the village of
Gettysburg, are: The Baltimore turnpike crosses Rock Creek and
enters the town from the southeast; the Hanover road, from the
east, and the York pike, from the northeast, both enter the town at
the same point. The Harrisburg road, from east of north, and the
Mummasburg road, from west of north, both enter the town by
the Carlisle road. Chambersburg road enters from the northwest,
and Fairfield road from the west (General Lee's line of retreat).
The Emmitsburg road, from the southwest, crossing the south
road, intersects and enters the town with the Baltimore pike. The
Taneytown road comes directly from the south, and enters the town,
after crossing the Emmitsburg road, at the foot of Cemetery Ridge.
By the Taneytown road the greater part of the Union army arrived
on the field of battle. There was nothing in the place, nor in the
surrounding country of Gettysburg, to invite the presence of war.
Its seat of learning, its school of the prophets, its beautiful cemetery, and the calm of its rural scenery, all suggested quiet and
peaceful pursuits. As has already been stated, it was not, apparently, General Lee's original intention to deliver battle here, but the
engagement was forced upon him by his inability to proceed directly
to Harrisburg.

The preliminary manœuvres, in the morning, on both sides having
been made, the battle was opened on the 1st of July, by General
Reynolds, continuing throughout the day. It was severely fought
and terminated, with a heavy loss on both sides. General Reynolds,
while examining the field for an advantageous disposition of his
men, was mortally wounded and soon expired; in consequence, the
command of the troops devolved upon General Howard. By orders
from General Meade, General Howard was superseded in command
by General Hancock.

Early on the morning of the 2d, the battle line was continued to the vicinity of Little Round Top, and by additional troops soon extended nearly three miles to Culp's Hill. On the arrival of General Meade the headquarters of the army were established at a small house on the west side of the Taneytown road directly in the rear of this centre. It was a dangerous but convenient spot for observing operations, and sending orders to the right or left.

The battles of the first and second day determined nothing. If, the first day, the Unionists gained anything, they lost equally as much. The second day's fight was more death-dealing than the first, for the rebels hurled a heavy force against our left, only to be beaten back with immense slaughter. The centre was similarly assailed, but with no better success. A like experiment was tried on the right, and, after a short, doubtful state of things, was repulsed with heavy loss. The battle continued until half-past eight o'clock in the evening, terminating with a bad record for the rebels.

Friday, July 3d, was the great battle day, and developed the full power and skill of the opposing armies. Which, now, was to be master of the situation—the Union or Confederate army—Meade or Lee? A few hours would and did decide. The stake with General Lee was the Confederacy—with General Meade, the salvation of Pennsylvania, and the preservation of Baltimore and Washington. No wonder that both commanders braced themselves, like mighty giants, for the struggle of the day. And when they met—what a concussion! Language is feeble to describe it. The charge and the repulse; the rally and the charge repeated; the surging of heavy rebel columns against the impenetrable walls of Union artillery and infantry; the rush of cavalry, and the shouts of the moving masses; formed a succession of pictures intensely exciting.

The Confederate army struggled as if hanging between life and death. The generals fought their men with that fierce recklessness displayed at Malvern Hill one year ago. But victory now as then refused them her laurels, and, abandoning all hope, their wagon trains were put in motion, toward the Potomac River, while the battle continued, in order to gain time for their safe departure. Just as General Lee had stood at bay behind Antietam Creek, all through the 18th of September, 1862, that he might make his retreat orderly and save his trains, so, now on the 4th of July, 1863, he maintained a firm front, upon Seminary Ridge, though withdrawing his left wing which had menaced Culp's and Cemetery Hills.

CHAPTER XVII.

FROM GETTYSBURG TO THE RAPPAHANNOCK—BATTERY B REORGANIZED.

JULY 4th was again freshly consecrated by a Union victory at Vicksburg, as well as at Gettysburg. The recent battle-field was still red with the blood of noble heroes slain for their country's cause.

The work of interring nine thousand dead, and of removing about twenty thousand wounded to comfortable quarters, was a herculean task. The Confederates had left a large number of their badly wounded lying on the field, and most of their dead remained unburied. It was necessary to make interments everywhere, and often ten to fifty bodies were buried in one trench. It was only after the rebel prisoners had been pressed into this work, especially in covering up the bodies of their fallen comrades, that the sad duty was finally completed.

This battle so murderous in effect was particularly disastrous for those commanding officers, on both sides, who had most gallantly exposed themselves while leading their troops to combat. The Confederates were: Major-Generals Heth, Hood and Trimble wounded, and Pender mortally; Brigadier-Generals Armistead, Barksdale and Garnett killed, and Semmes mortally wounded; Brigadier-Generals Anderson, Hampton, Jones, Kemper, Pettigrew and Scales were wounded, while Archer was taken prisoner. The Army of the Potomac had lost Major-General Reynolds, and Brigadier-Generals Vincent, Weed and Zook; Major-Generals Butterfield, Barlow, Doubleday, Hancock, Gibbon, Sickles and Warren, and Brigadier-Generals Brooks, Barnes, Graham, Paul and Stone were wounded. The triumph of the victors had been costly, for " mid the thundering of artillery and the shouting of infantry" was heard the wail of the dying thousands.

On the 5th, Lieutenant Perrin received orders to report to Battery A with his command, and at noon the men of Battery B, with their blankets and tents packed and slung upon their shoulders, tramped over to the camp of the former, and were assigned to the left section, with First Lieut. William S. Perrin in command of the section. The batteries (A and B of Rhode Island) having lost heavily, were, by orders of the chief of artillery of the corps (Capt. John G. Hazard), temporarily consolidated and known as Battery A, First Regiment Rhode Island Light Artillery, Captain Arnold commanding. Remaining together they followed the Confederate army back into Virginia to the Rapidan.

The writer, however, will continue to speak of the left section as Battery B. Our reports were made out, and sent to artillery brigade quarters separately, and signed by Lieutenant Perrin as commander.

At five o'clock in the afternoon the battery was ordered to pack and hitch up, and left camp moving down to Two Taverns, a small hamlet on the Baltimore pike about two miles south of Gettysburg, where we went into camp.

The 6th was cloudy with showers. A detail of twenty men of Battery B (some with horses), under command of Lieut. A. Brown, were ordered and went to draw the condemned pieces of Battery A, Fourth United States Artillery, up to Gettysburg where the condemned ordnance was parked. When we arrived, at the battery's camp, our services were not required, as mule teams from the ordnance train had performed the task, and we returned to our camp. The battery, meanwhile, had received orders to prepare for a move.

On the 7th it was still cloudy with light showers. Reveille at sunrise. After breakfast (hot coffee, hard-tack and pork) the battery was ordered, by Captain Arnold, to pack and hitch up; about eight A. M. it left Two Taverns, and, going in a southerly direction, halted at Taneytown and encamped for the night. Just before going into camp we passed a grove wherein were collected from eight hundred to one thousand rebel prisoners, who had been taken in the morning, at the front, and sent to the rear under guard. The Second Corps, on account of its heavy loss in the engagement of July 3d, was the rear guard to the army in this movement. The Fifth and Sixth Corps were in advance, with cavalry on their flanks. Thus the Union army was following up that of General Lee, which had fallen back to the Potomac River.

July 8th. Reveille at five A. M. Nearly all were up long before it was sounded, trying to light fires; some met with poor success, while others succeeded by holding up a rubber blanket for their comrades to start a fire under. The difficulty arose from the fact that it rained very hard, and the fires were put out as fast as they were started; however, " where there's a will there's a way," and it must be a second flood to cheat an old veteran out of his hot coffee for breakfast, providing he is allowed sufficient time. It rained quite hard until about ten A. M., when it cleared off warm and pleasant, inspiring the men with renewed activity and animation. Blankets and other clothing, which had become drenched, were spread to catch the warm rays of the sun and gentle southern breeze. Just before noon the order was given, and the clothing, blankets, tents, and other equipments were soon packed, the battery was hitched up and resumed its march.

We left Taneytown about twelve o'clock, and, after passing through several small but thriving villages, crossed Big and Small Pipe Creeks, continuing on through Woodboro to within a few miles of Frederick, at which place we halted and camped for the night. The Monocacy Valley, through which the corps had passed, was one of the vintage grounds of Maryland; the picturesque villages, fertile fields, sturdy farmers, portly women, and buxom maidens, all betokened prosperity, good living and happiness.

The 9th was pleasant and warm. At the close of the morning's routine of duty, the camp was thrown into joyous excitement by the cry of "Letters, letters!" It was a "red letter day" for Battery B. The welcome post courier, Charles H. Adams, brought a generous mail, which had accumulated at Washington while awaiting convenient transportation to its destination. The mails were looked for with eager interest. Nothing tended so strongly to keep up the spirits of the men, as the privilege of frequent correspondence with cherished friends at home. The eagerness with which seals were broken and contents devoured, can only be imagined by one who has long been separated from loved ones at home. These letters, filled with local gossip and words of cheer, from loving mothers, sisters, and sweethearts, were "like glow-worms amid buds of flowers," casting a pleasant light upon the beautiful treasures of memory, and inspiring courage that nerves the arm for deadly strife.

At ten o'clock A. M. boots and saddles call was sounded. The battery was soon on the march again, and, leaving camp, passed through Frederick and over the Catoctin Mountains to Jefferson situated on the western slope. Passing through the town we turned north and crossed the Catoctin Creek going to Burkittsville, where we halted for about an hour to let the troops get ahead. Again resuming the march, we went over the South Mountain range of the Blue Ridge Mountains, by way of Crompton's Gap, and passed over part of the battle-field of Sept. 14, 1862. The engagement fought here was between the Sixth Corps, under General Franklin, and the Confederates, under General Anderson, two days before the battle of Antietam, Lee's first invasion of northern soil. The battery encamped near Rohrersville for the night.

On the 10th, reveille sounded at four A. M., and, after hasty preparations, the corps was again on the move. The battery, however, did not leave camp until eight o'clock, when it pulled out into line resuming the onward march. We passed through the village of Rohrersville, to the small hamlet of Buena Vista, and then to familiar ground, over which the battery had previously passed, in September, 1862, to Keedysville. Still moving north, we crossed the creek and battle-field of Antietam, and went into camp near the village of Tighlmantown. In this section of the country the villages are adorned with some quaint and odd names, such as Rohrersville, Keedysville, Buena Vista, Tighlmantou, and Funkstown. The etymology of these rather uneuphonic names rests in obscurity. For aught that appears to the contrary, it may have been the hunting ground of the original Peter, whose numerous progeny have obtained an unenviable notoriety. However this may be, the last named is one of the principal villages, washed by the Antietam Creek, and boasts a population of seven or eight hundred, while many of the other villages do not exceed a hundred inhabitants.

The 11th was pleasant and warm, a most glorious day. The Confederate army was still at bay on the banks of the Potomac at Williamsport. The swollen river prevented Lee's army crossing, hence there were strong indications that a battle would occur in this vicinity. At nine A. M. the battery advanced a short distance to the front and halted, the corps going into position in line of battle on the left of the Fifth Corps.

This place where the roads cross was called Lapham's Corner, said to be about six miles from Sharpsburg, Boonsborough, and Hagerstown, and about five miles from Williamsport. Some sharp skirmishing was heard upon the right, and the battery was placed in position in rear of the First Division. Here the men bivouacked for the night, and, as it was ordered that no large fires be made for fear of attracting the attention of the enemy, small squads of men could be seen hovering around a smouldering fire of twigs, preparing their supper of coffee, toasted pork, and fried hard-tack.

On the morning of the 12th no reveille was sounded, as we were too near the enemy, but the men were up betimes, and busy preparing something hot for the inner man, hoping to sustain both body and spirits for the work before them. All was quiet along the lines in our front. In the afternoon the battery advanced (changing its position twice) and placed the pieces in position in battery with the First Division. The caissons and wagons were parked about a quarter of a mile to the rear of our position. Here the battery bivouacked all night.

July 13th. Last evening there was a very heavy shower, and this morning it still continued to rain by spells, making it anything but comfortable for both man and beast; such, however, was a soldier's life, and the old veterans had become hardened to hardships of the march, battle, and camp life. In the afternoon the pieces were advanced to a small line of breastworks in their front, which had been thrown up by the infantry during the night. At five P. M. we were advanced still further to the front to a second line of breastworks. On taking position the battery prepared for action. The enemy could plainly be seen actively throwing up breastworks, and squads of men moving about indicated that they were preparing either for action or a retreat.

Darkness fell while the troops were momentarily expecting the order to advance, and the men bivouacked on the field, under arms, ready for action at a moment's notice. Our Second Lieutenant, Charles A. Brown, went to Battery I, First United States Artillery, on detached service.

On the 14th the troops were aroused at daybreak, and a reconnoissance in force being made, from the front of each corps, it was discovered that the enemy had retreated during the night and escaped across the river into Virginia. About six o'clock A. M. Captain Arnold received orders to withdraw from the breastworks, and, going to the rear where the caissons were in park, we prepared for light marching. The grain and surplus equipments were taken from the gun limbers the caissons were unlimbered, the pieces and the caisson limbers, by a roundabout way, advanced to the right and gained a high hill, taking position overlooking the enemy's works without opposition, as there were no enemy there to dispute our advance. Limbering up the battery again advanced to within a mile of Williamsport, when, turning to the left, it moved down the road toward Falling Waters, passing two abandoned rebel caissons, also played out horses, broken harnesses, muskets, and ammunition strewn along the road, all indicating a hasty retreat. Our cavalry, which was in advance of the battery and infantry, coming upon the rear guard of the enemy, found it with stacked arms indicative of surrender, but seeing only a small squad of cavalry advancing, the rebels jumped for their guns, and fired a volley into the advancing cavalry, killing and wounding about forty. The battery immediately went into position, and fired a few shell at the enemy who had retreated into the woods. Our cavalry, having been reënforced by another squad, charged, and, being well supported by our infantry, captured about six hundred prisoners. The number of Confederates killed and wounded was not known, but it must have been great, as the cavalry showed the enemy no mercy after the cowardly ruse they had played. The battery remained here all night, bivouacked in line of battle.

On the morning of the 15th, the battery was aroused at daybreak, and, after a dry wash, and a hasty breakfast of hard-tack and coffee, returned to where the caissons and the rest of the battery had been left encamped. We reached our destination about ten A. M., weary and exhausted from the tramp through the mud. Though the roads were in a very bad condition there was no time for rest, and, therefore, as soon as the caissons were limbered up, battery packed, and horses cared for, as well as circumstances would permit, we hitched up again, about one o'clock P. M., and resumed the march. Leaving Lapham's Corner we passed through Tighlmanton, and over part of the battle-field of Antietam, to Sharpsburg. The latter town still showed visible signs of the struggle enacted here on the 17th of September, 1862. Passing through the town, we crossed Antietam Creek, at the Old Iron Works, and moved up into the mountains, and at dark halted on the northern part of Maryland Heights, and we went into camp near the Twelfth Corps.

On the 16th, at six o'clock A. M., the battery was again in motion. Passing down through Sandy Hook and on to the hills at the northeast we went into camp near Weverton, a picturesque village in

Pleasant Valley, situated on the southwest slope of South Mountain, about three miles north of the Potomac River. Here the men pitched their tents with some prospect of a rest, which, although short, was most welcome to the men after their hard and tedious tramp through the mud, up hill and down.

When the Union army commenced the pursuit of General Lee, it was generally believed that he would be compelled to give battle at Hagerstown or Williamsport, and that nothing would be more gratifying to the Army of the Potomac than to finish the work begun at Gettysburg. These opinions may have been entertained by those at a safe distance from the smell of gunpowder, or, possibly, by those troops not engaged, but not by the soldiers confronting General Lee's army, as he stood at bay around Williamsport on the morning of July 14th; they were greatly relieved to find the enemy gone. Why? Not for lack of courage, but because of the fearful strain they had undergone since the beginning of this campaign, their forced marches to reach and protect their national capital, the three days' continuous fighting, and the final forced circuitous tramp through a mountainous country in pursuit of the retreating foe. And, I repeat, the men were thankful for a respite from the long strain and menace of "Lee's Northern Invasion." The latter was safely back in Virginia, with only two-thirds of his army, many rebel prisoners having been left in the hands of the victors. Henceforward any future moves against the Confederate army must constitute a new campaign.

July 17th. Reveille at five A. M. Only regular camp duty was performed. It being a rainy day the men remained under cover of their tents. By orders Lieutenant Perrin sent to general headquarters a requisition for new pieces for Battery B. It cleared off in the afternoon, and the sun's bright rays seemed to reanimate the weary troops. At retreat roll call the following resolutions were read:

STATE OF RHODE ISLAND AND PROVIDENCE PLANTATIONS.

RESOLUTION IN REGARD TO THE VOLUNTEER SOLDIERS OF THE STATE OF RHODE ISLAND.

RESOLVED, That the General Assembly hereby declares its high appreciation of the distinguished service of the volunteer soldier, of the State of Rhode Island, on numerous fields of perilous duty, in bravely maintaining her honor, enhancing her reputation, and illustrating her history anew by their courage, loyalty, patriotism, and valor.

The General Assembly proudly and gratefully recognizes their claims to the approval and regard of their fellow citizens, and renewedly pledge to them its cordial good will and unfaltering support.

Resolved, That the General Assembly tenders expression of sympathy to the many hearts and homes that have been bereaved and. saddened by the casualties of the present conflict, and assures them that the State will ever cherish the memory of the brave men who have fallen in the defence of Union, liberty, and law.

Resolved, That His Excellency the Governor be directed to transmit copies of the above resolutions to the commanding officer of the regiments belonging to Rhode Island now in the field.

I certify the above to be a true copy. In testimony whereof I have hereto set my hand and affixed the seal of the State.
This the sixteenth day of July, A. D. 1863.

[Seal.]   JOHN R. BARTLETT,
Secretary of State.
[Official.]
CRAWFORD ALLEN, JR.,
First Lieutenant and Adjutant 1st Regt R. I. Light Artillery.

July 18th. Reveille at sunrise. The army again in motion. The battery, after a hasty preparation, broke camp early in the morning, and resumed the march back through Sandy Hook to the Potomac River, crossing on the pontoon bridge to Harper's Ferry. This was the third time that Battery B had crossed at this place. The ruins, the roads, and the hills were all quite familiar; and passing through the town to the left we continued moving up along the bank of the Shenandoah to the Old Foundry; here we again crossed the river to the foot of Loudon Heights, and, moving along up the mountain to the pike road, passed Vestal Gap, and encamped for the night at Hillsboro.

We were now, after an absence of some three weeks, treading again the soil of Secessia. In our temporary absence time had failed to clothe it with new beauties, or to inspire reverence for its presiding spirit. Treason was as hideous as when its brazen trumpet first sounded defiance to constitutional law, and sent a thrill of horror through the land.

Yesterday John Healy, with a companion, who had crossed ahead of the troops, and were foraging for the artillery headquarter officers' mess, were made prisoners by a squad of Mosby's men, and taken across the river to Charlestown, and then to Richmond.

On the 19th, the weather was quite warm and the army was proceeding slowly. The battery did not break camp until noon, and then marched about five miles to Woodgrove, where it parked in a field of blackberry bushes, from one to two feet high, laden with large, ripe berries. We were encamped in a field of plenty. That night the inner man was refreshed by hot coffee, broiled pork, hardtack, and for dessert—why—blackberries and sugar on toasted pilot bread.

The 20th was still pleasant and warm. Resuming the march at eight A. M., we passed through Broomfield, and went into camp for the night.

On the 21st, the battery remained quietly encamped all day. The horses were allowed to graze in a field of nice green grass. Some of the horses were, at first, a little wild at gaining such freedom, and commenced running and jumping, but failing to induce their companions to join them, quieted down and went to eating grass. They were allowed to feed for about an hour, when each driver caught his horse and returned to camp.

At noon on the 22d, Captain Arnold received marching orders, and at two P. M. the battery broke camp to resume its march, following nearly the same route that the army did last fall, under General McClellan, when following the Confederate army back into Virginia after the battle of Antietam. The battery passed through Upperville and turning westerly passed through Paris and moved up into Ashby's Gap, where it went into park and bivouacked on the old camping ground occupied during our visit to this place on the 4th of last November.

On the morning of the 23d reveille was sounded at three A. M., and, after a hasty preparation, the battery left camp about sunrise and resuming the march in the cool of the morning, passed through a small village situated among the hills of the Blue Ridge, about midway between Ashby's and Manassas Gaps, and having the appropriate name of Kerfoot (foot of the mountains). At two P. M. the battery halted at Markham (to allow the Third and Fifth Corps to pass) and went into park in front of a large white house, occupied by a family named Ashby, cousins of the rebel General Ashby, of White Horse cavalry fame. After waiting two hours for the corps to pass the battery resumed the march up into Manassas Gap, passing through several small mountain hamlets of a few houses each. On arriving at Linden the battery went into park and bivouacked for the night.

In a military point of view this place was of importance, as it commanded the approaches from the west, and all roads entering the Gap. Front Royal on the Shenandoah Valley Railroad was about five miles distance.

On the 24th, the battery remained quiet in camp until about noon, when boots and saddles call was suddenly sounded, and hasty preparations were made to leave the place, and, at one P. M. broke camp and marched back to Markham, and went into park near the Ashby mansion, encamping for the night. The officers of the battery were entertained during the evening with music and songs by two pretty young rebel ladies, who were stopping at the Ashby mansion.

July 25th. Reveille at daybreak, and at half-past five A. M. the battery was on the road moving in an easterly direction, passing through Rectortown to near White Plains, and went into park and bivouacked for the night. At this place a very cool and audacious piece of work was accomplished by a squad of rebel cavalry. At a spring a few hundred rods to our rear where our men were getting water, the rebels rushed out from the wood and surrounded the men, driving them towards and into the woods. They succeeded in making off with five infantrymen prisoners. This was just at dusk, and by the time it was known what had been done, and word sent to headquarters, and before a squad of our cavalry was sent in pursuit, the rebels with their prisoners were beyond danger of being overtaken.

On the 26th, at seven A. M., the battery was again in motion, broke camp, passed through White Plains to Broad Run Station (on the Manassas Gap Railroad west of Thoroughfare Gap), then turned to the right marching due south, passing Bethel Academy to Warrenton, where a halt was made for an hour, to water and feed the horses. The men here improved the opportunity and made coffee. At two P. M. continued the march to Germantown; then moved up to within a few miles of Warrenton Junction, where we halted and encamped for the night. It had been a very hot day, and very fatiguing to both man and beast, so much so that five of the horses, that had been worn out on the march and could not be made to travel any further, were condemned and shot. The roads were very dry and dusty, and the clouds of dust which rose covered the men and horses; it could well have been said that we were now the army of the gray instead of the blue. But, after a few hours in camp, this gray robe was shaken from our garments and we appeared in our true colors, Union blue.

July 27th. Cloudy with frequent showers, the battery lay in camp all day. Sergeant Straight, with a detail of men and the quartermaster-sergeant, went up to the station at Warrenton Junction for horses. As there were none there, they returned as they went.

On the 28th, the battery moved to Elk Run, and the quartermaster-sergeant again went back to the Junction for horses. As they had not arrived, he returned without any.

July 29th was cloudy and quite cool for summer weather. At noon the battery moved to near Morrisville and parked; it remained here all day and night, but was under orders to be in readiness to move at a moment's notice.

On the morning of the 30th Sergeant Straight, with a detail of eighteen men, was again sent up to Warrenton Junction for horses. At five P. M. the battery moved through Morrisville and bivouacked near division headquarters, remaining there all night, and at an early hour on the morning of July 31st, the battery, with the Third Division of the Second Corps, moved down to within a few miles of Kelly's Ford, on the Rappahannock. Here Sergeant Straight and the men arrived with a few horses for the battery. They did not get as many as expected, and one died on the march to the camp. Horses were scarce for the artillery. The hot weather and marching had worn out many of the animals, and several of the men dropped by the wayside.

August 1st. Pleasant and very warm. The battery with the division was ordered back to Elkton to guard the roads which centred here. This hamlet boasted of five houses, seven barns, and one blacksmith shed. Five roads centred there, and a house on each road. "Right smart town" the negroes called it. The opinion of the whites could not be obtained. There were none at home on the occasion of our visit. The battery took position on a hill overlooking the roads. Placing the guns in battery we bivouacked for the night.

On the 2d, after the morning duties were over, orders were issued for the men to pitch tents and make camp quarters as comfortable as possible as the troops were to remain here for a short time. This news was gladly welcomed, and the men went to work with a will.

August 3d. Pleasant and hot. No camp duty to be done, only the care of the horses and guards on the lookout watching the roads. At ten P. M. the assembly call sounded. What was it for? Everything was quiet all about us. The infantry was not out; their camps were quiet. For once Dame Rumor was asleep, or had gone making morning calls elsewhere, for surely she was not in camp, for no one seemed to know why the call was sounded. However, the men were soon in line, and, under the command of the first sergeant, the order was given, "Right face, forward march!" and the column moved towards the officers' quarters. The column halted as the tent was reached, and, as the names of the non-commissioned officers were called, they marched into the tent. It then became known that the men were to sign the muster rolls and the word was passed along the line, "The paymaster is here, the paymaster is here!" and so it proved, and the men were paid for the months of May and June. Also the detached men, who were not carried on the battery's muster rolls, were sent under command of a sergeant to their regiments, where they were made happy by receiving the few greenbacks due them from Uncle Sam.

On the 4th, Major Monroe, allotment commissioner of Rhode Island, visited our camp for the purpose of taking such money as the comrades desired to send home. The allotment arrangement was an admirable one for safety, and many of the men improved the opportunity by making remittances to their families, parents or friends. Not a dollar thus sent since the system was organized, failed to reach its destination.

On the 5th, Lieut. Charles A. Brown, who had been on detached duty with Battery I, First United States Artillery, returned to Battery B.

On the 7th, Sergeants Straight and Williams, with twenty men, were sent up to Catlett's Station, and at dusk they returned with seventy-two horses and one mule for the baggage wagon to replace the one that had died on the march. Nothing of exciting interest had occurred during the past three days, and few incidents of any sort worth noting. Our pieces stood parked in battery, and in grim silence, ready to report if called upon, and the encampments of the troops in general were quiet.

On the 8th, the monotonous duty of camp life was broken, when the men of Battery B were ordered to pack up and be in readiness to move. Lieutenant Perrin had received orders to report to the Second Division headquarters with his command. The old drivers were detailed to care for the horses received yesterday, and at three P. M. we bade adieu to the members of Battery A, and left their camp, and, going to headquarters near Morrisville, encamped on the plain. A jolly set of men, full of enthusiasm, life and activity. Now there seemed to be good reasons to hope we would have guns again, and not be attached to another command.

August 9th was a busy day in Battery B, the receiving and issuing of new supplies, under the direction of Lieut. C. A. Brown, while the horses were mated, and gun detachments formed. Elliott Collins, Morrison Heal, and Sumner Merrill, detached men from the Nineteenth Maine regiment, returned to the battery for duty. These three men with others had volunteered and came to the battery on the evening of the 2d of last July on the battle-field of Gettysburg. On account of being reduced to a four-gun battery their services were not required and they were returned to their regiment. Second Lieut. Willard B. Pierce, promoted from first sergeant of Battery A, First Regiment Rhode Island Light Artillery, reported to Battery B for duty.

On the 15th, the battery received a new army wagon and six mules, for carrying supplies. The weather was fine. Nothing of note had taken place with us for the past few days; having only light camp duties to perform while waiting for our new guns we were growing too fat for business. Late in the afternoon Lieutenant Perrin received orders to be in readiness to move, with three days' rations in the haversacks of the men. This infused new life and activity among the men.

Early on the morning of the 16th, Lieutenant Perrin with his command went up to Bealton Station and there received a park of four new Napoleon brass field guns, light twelve-pounders, with new equipments, four caissons, battery wagon, and forge complete, also harnesses for the horses and equipments for the sergeants' horses. In the afternoon we returned to camp near Morrisville in good spirits, well pleased with our new battery. At retreat call the following order was read, Major-General Hancock being on a leave of absence:

       HEADQUARTERS SECOND ARMY CORPS,
           August 16, 1863.

General Orders, }
 No. 27. }

In pursuance of special orders No. 216 from headquarters Army of the Potomac of the 12th instant, Major-General G. R. Warren hereby assumes the temporary command of the Second Army Corps.

No changes are made in the previous positions of staff officers at these headquarters.

By command of

Major-General WARREN.

(Signed,)

FRANCIS A. WALKER,
Lt. Col. U. S. A., A. A. Gen.

On the 17th, the battery was supplied with ammunition, and the chests were packed with 192 solid shot, 192 spherical case, 64 shell, 64 canister, and 800 primers. This was fixed ammunition of a charge of one and one-quarter pound of powder. Battery B was now fully reorganized as a four-gun battery complete, Lieut. William S. Perrin in command; Lieut. Charles A. Brown commander of right section, and Lieut. Willard B. Pierce commander of left section. There were present for duty three officers, seventy-two enlisted men and thirty-seven detached infantrymen; total enlisted men, 109. There were absent on detached service and sick in hospital forty-six men, and Captain Hazard on detached service at artillery brigade headquarters; First Lieut. T. Fred Brown was on sick leave of absence at Providence, R. I., making an aggregate of 160.

On the 18th, we were ordered to move from near division headquarters to that of the artillery brigade headquarters, and encamped near the woods to give shade for the horses. Here tents were pitched in one line with the guns and caissons parked in front, the battery wagon and forge were near the woods where the horses were picketed, and the blacksmiths were kept busy shoeing the horses, for many were without shoes.

On the 19th, we were ordered to build an arbor covered with boughs of evergreen over our line of tents, for protection from the hot rays of the sun.

August 20th. There was a little excitement and activity to-day caused by an order to hitch up lively. The first section, under Lieut. C. A. Brown, left camp on the double quick and went a short distance beyond Morrisville to the cross roads on picket, remaining all night. The remainder of the battery stayed in camp. The weather for the past few days had been very warm, and at times was exceedingly hot.

August 21st. To-day a sad and painful duty was performed by the provost marshal guard, that of military execution. A deserter of the Seventy-first Pennsylvania regiment was shot at division headquarters. After the Gettysburg campaign there was a marked increase in desertions, many regiments became badly disorganized, and in a new phrase of the war "demoralized." The sympathy with criminals in 1861 and 1862 had made those of 1863 bold and audacious, and, combined with the special exigency created by the appearance of the "bounty-jumper," or professional deserter, sufficed to bring the administration to the alternative of executing the full measure of the law on all deserters. The execution of a score of bad men in 1862 would have saved the lives of many good men in 1863 and 1864. The right section returned to camp having been relieved by a section of Battery G, First New York Artillery. General Warren and staff inspected the camp and quarters of the battery in the afternoon, and complimented us on the sanitary condition of the camp.

On the 22d, a little life and activity was manifested in camp by orders to prepare for inspection. There had not been an inspection of Battery B since it left Fredericksburg in June, and, as the battery and equipments were all new, it did not take long to get ready. At eleven A. M. the battery was hitched up, but remained in park with the gun detachments at their posts. At 11.30 Capt. John G. Hazard, chief of the artillery brigade of the Second Corps, with his staff, inspected the battery, expressing his satisfaction of its appearance in a short address; the command was dismissed and returned to quarters with perspiration streaming from every pore, for the heat was very oppressive.

August 25th. The weather had been very warm for the past few days, but during the evening there was a shower which lasted from a half to three-quarters of an hour (the first rain for a month). It then cleared off cool, followed by high winds during the night.

At ten o'clock on the morning of the 28th, the monotonous routine of camp duty of the past few days was broken by an order for the command to assemble in line. All except camp guard and men on detail or fatigue duty were, under command of Lieut. W. S. Perrin, marched to division headquarters to witness the execution. Three men were to be shot for desertion. The division was drawn up in a square of three sides, with the provost guard and condemned men on the fourth. The troops had been ordered to witness this execution for its moral effect, especially on those bounty-jumpers who did not enlist to fight, but for the money value they received, and, deserting, would enlist again under assumed names. Unfortunately, the provost guard detachment did their work in a very bungling manner, owing to the novelty and the highly distressing nature of their duty. After the execution we returned to camp.

August 31st. Pleasant and warm. The month of August had passed quietly, the interval of rest being devoted to the reëquipment of the troops, to inspections, and surveys of unserviceable property which was condemned and replaced by new. But the month was not to end with the troops remaining in camp, although the occasion of the disturbance was so trivial and odd as to give the movement somewhat the air of a farce. To-day the Second Corps broke camp, and the several divisions took position covering the fords of the Rappahannock. The object of this movement was found in the purpose to destroy certain gunboats which the enemy had placed in the river, and which the cavalry, with such assistance as the infantry and artillery might be able to render, were to cut off and destroy. Whether the cavalry captured the gunboats no soldier in the Second Corps could ever ascertain, and, after three days of this new species of hunting, the corps returned to its old camps near Morrisville and Elkton.

At three o'clock on the morning of the 31st, the battery was aroused and ordered to prepare for light marching, placing three days' forage on the caissons and issuing three days' rations for the men to carry in the haversacks; the battery left camp at six A. M., leaving our tents standing and a detail of men to guard them. Moving southeast on the Falmouth road we passed Grove Church, also a small hamlet called Harwood Church, and encamped about a mile beyond the village on rising ground.

September 1st. Reveille at sunrise. The cavalry had been marching by the camp going southeast on the Falmouth road since two A. M. The battery remained bivouacked on the hill all day. All quiet along the lines.

On the 2d, the battery remained quiet, but some of the infantry made a reconnaissance towards the river, the result of which was not known, as there was no report from the gunboats. As night falls and closes her dark mantle around us, all is quiet on the Rappahannock.

On the 3d, there was a little stir of activity among the troops in the forenoon, as part of the cavalry returned and proceeded northwest up the river. The enemy must have received information of this movement, and concealed their gunboats for which the cavalry were looking. The battery remained in bivouac on the hill.

September 4th. Nothing of exciting interest had occurred since the battery left camp on this movement of hunting for gunboats in the woods, and few incidents of any description worth noting. The guns stood parked in grim silence ready to report when called upon. There was general commotion in the camps of the infantry, and, after the horses had been cared for and the men had partaken of a breakfast of hot coffee and hard-tack, a similar commotion was manifested in the battery by the order to pack and hitch up. At eight A. M. we moved out into the road and returned to Morrisville following the same route we came by; passing Harwood Church and Grove Church, two small hamlets of three or four houses and a church, we arrived at our old camp about noon. In the afternoon several of the horses were condemned and turned in to the quartermaster's department sick and unfit for artillery service.

On the 5th, the cannoneers cleaned the guns and equipments, while the drivers cleaned the harnesses which had become dirty on the march.

On the 6th, the battery had mounted inspection by the commander, First Lieut. W. S. Perrin. In the afternoon cannoneers' drill at the manual of the piece.

On the 7th, our cavalry was again on the move and we heard artillery firing on the right during the day. The cavalry were making a reconnaisance along the river beyond Rappahannock Station.

On the 9th, the battery received an ambulance complete, which in future was to accompany it on any movement. Five more horses were condemned, the weather and service being very hard on them. In the afternoon clothing was issued to those men who needed it.

On the 10th, several men who had been absent and in the hospital since July returned and reported for duty. John Leach, a bugler detached from Battery A, First Rhode Island Light Artillery, reported for duty. Stephen Boyle reported for duty as driver for the ambulance, detached from the Sixty-ninth Pennsylvania regiment. He had been at headquarters of artillery brigade on duty for some time.

On the 11th, the battery received seven new horses to replace those condemned and turned in to the quartermaster's department. For the past few days the camp of the battery had been a school for instruction in drilling and disciplining the recruits and the detached men. Battery drill and drill at the manual of the piece were held about every day, so that the recruits became quite proficient in the different manœuvres and were christened artillerymen, dropping the name of doe-boys, mud-mashers, and similar appellations given to the infantrymen.

At sunrise on the morning of the 12th Lieutenant Perrin received orders to prepare to move, tents were struck, the battery equipments put in place, three days' rations of forage strapped upon the caissons, and three days' rations of coffee and hard-bread were issued to the men. At nine A. M. the battery was ordered to hitch up. While we were awaiting further orders the chief of artillery of the corps, Capt. John G. Hazard, and staff rode into camp and presented to Lieut. William S. Perrin a new guidon for Battery B. The lieutenant acknowledged the gift in behalf of the men. Then Captain Hazard made a short address pertaining to duties while on the march and what was expected of us, ending with a few words of encouragement and withdrew amid cheers from his old command. Then followed the order from Lieutenant Perrin, "Right piece, forward — march!" and pulling out into the road we left camp going north. Crossed the Orange and Alexandria Railroad at Bealton Station, where a halt of an hour was made to make coffee, and at two P. M. resumed the march until dusk when a second halt was made, and we were ordered to park and bivouac for the night. During the evening there was a smart shower, and those who did not have their shelter tents pitched got a severe wetting.

CHAPTER XVIII.

ADVANCE TO CULPEPER.—FROM THE RAPIDAN TO CENTREVILLE.—BATTLE OF BRISTOE STATION.

WHEN the information which had been received at army headquarters that General Lee, pressed by the urgent necessities of the Confederate armies of the west, had dispatched nearly all of General Longstreet's corps to confront General Rosecrans's army at Chickamauga, had been confirmed it caused a forward movement of the Army of the Potomac, in which the cavalry and the Second Corps took the lead. It was hoped to prevent the withdrawal of any more of General Lee's troops holding the lines along the Rappahannock.

On the 12th of September Rappahannock Station was occupied by our cavalry. Surprising the enemy at early dawn they captured a number of prisoners, and rapidly advancing drove the rebel cavalry out of the peninsula lying between the Rappahannock and Rapidan Rivers. The Second and Sixth Corps were thrown forward to the Rapidan to hold the fords. The other corps followed in support, and occupied the ground so often skirmished over and fought for by the contending forces of both armies. The necessity of pressing General Lee's troops closely, lest he should send other troops to the west, led to constant demonstrations of a further advance by the Union army, until, in accordance with orders from the war department at Washington, the movement was suspended, and the Eleventh and Twelfth Corps were detached and sent to join the Army of the Cumberland in the west, reënforcing General Rosecrans.

Sunday, September 13th, at six o'clock A. M., the battery broke camp and moved down through Rappahannock Station, and crossing the river on the railroad bridge advanced to Brandy Station. Here we passed the artillery that General Kilpatrick's cavalry captured at Culpeper (three pieces of horse artillery of Stuart's rebel cavalry). As we moved along the effects of the cavalry engagements could be plainly seen. The torn trees, dead horses, saddles, and other equipments which were strewn along the road gave evidence of the strife which had taken place. In the afternoon the battery advanced with the Second Division to Culpeper, went into park near the town and bivouacked for the night.

On the morning of the 14th, the first section, under Lieut. C. A. Brown, was sent out on picket to the cross roads just beyond the town. At noon our teams came down to us with forage and rations, which the men and horses were very much in need of. Just at dusk the cars arrived from Warrington Junction bringing supplies.

On the 15th, the battery remained in camp near Culpeper, and the men were made happy by receiving their mail. In the afternoon the first section returned from picket duty, and orders were received to prepare to move.

On the 16th, at nine A. M., the battery broke camp, and passing through Culpeper advanced by the Orange turnpike to Robertson River (which flows into the Rapidan) where a halt was made for an hour; then we moved on again ascending to the summit of the mountain range. At dusk we halted on Cedar Mountain, and the guns were placed in battery guarding the turnpike. At nine o'clock we bivouacked for the night. The cavalry had quite a lively skirmish with the enemy along the river. The flash from their carbines could be plainly seen from our position, but we were not called upon to render any assistance so our guns remained silent. As Lieutenant Pierce was returning to camp from headquarters, he was thrown from his horse severely injuring his arm.

On the 17th, at nine A. M., the battery advanced to within one mile of the Rapidan, passed the camp of the First Rhode Island Cavalry at twelve o'clock, and at two P. M. went into camp to the right of Second Division headquarters. At four o'clock, the left section under Lieutenant Pierce was sent out on picket on the Orange Court House road.

On the 18th, the right section under Lieut. C. A. Brown relieved the left section which was on picket. There was heard heavy cannonading down on the left all the morning, and a lively cavalry skirmish was seen in our front at ten A. M. in favor of our forces. It rained severely last night and during most of the forenoon, but cleared at noon and was quite pleasant. There was another military execution at division headquarters in the forenoon, one more bounty-jumper was shot for trying to desert to the enemy.

On the 24th, Sergt. Albert Straight, who had been sick for some time and confined to his tent, was sent to the hospital where he died Nov. 19, 1863. In the afternoon the paymaster put in an appearance and the battery was paid for the months of July and August. Ten new horses were received to replace those which had been condemned.

On the 25th, Lieut. T. Fred Brown returned to the battery and resumed command, and on the 26th held an inspection; the first section was under Lieut. William S. Perrin, the left section under Lieut. Charles A. Brown, and Lieut. Willard B. Pierce was chief of caissons. While the battery was at the Rapidan it did picket duty by sections, and with us it was not a very arduous duty; if anything, we rather enjoyed it.

From the 15th of September until relieved the Second Corps extended itself along the Rapidan river, its picket line being nine miles long. Corps headquarters were established at Mitchell's Station on the Orange and Alexandria Railroad; the Second Division at Summerville Ford on the right; the Third Division extended to Crooked Run on the left, with the First Division in the centre. There was more or less picket firing between the two lines, and a number of prisoners were taken. The duty of inspecting the outposts was not as pleasant as sometimes; but nothing occurred of special interest until the 5th of October, when the corps was relieved by the Sixth, and the Second the next day withdrew to Culpeper.

On October 2d, Lieut. C. A. Brown was granted a sick leave of absence and started for Rhode Island, and Lieut. W. B. Pierce assumed command of the left section.

On the night of the 6th, the battery was relieved from picket duty, and went to the rear of artillery headquarters where we remained all night. At seven o'clock the next morning (October 7th) we moved with the artillery brigade to near Culpeper, parked and went into camp near our camping ground of the 13th of September. While here commander Lieut. T. Fred Brown made a general change of the non-commissioned officers. There were a number of sergeants and corporals absent, some in hospitals from wounds or other causes, and one was at artillery headquarters. First Sergt. John T. Blake being in the hospital, Sergt. Alanson A. Williams was acting as first sergeant; Quartermaster-Sergt. Charles A. Libbey was absent on detached service with the commissary department, and Sergt. Anthony B. Horton was acting quartermaster-sergeant of the battery; First Duty Sergeant John E. Wardlow was absent on detached service at headquarters, and Sergeant Williams had charge of the first gun detachment; Sergt. Edwin A. Chase was absent in hospital, and Corp. Pardon S. Walker in charge of his detachment, the second; Sergt. Richard H. Gallup was in charge of the third detachment, and Private John H. Rhodes, a driver, was promoted to corporal and placed in charge of the fourth detachment, as Sergt. Albert Straight was sick in hospital, and a number of corporals were promoted to gunners. This made some dissatisfaction among the non-commissioned officers and men who were seeking promotion, but the orders from headquarters were imperative and consequently had to be obeyed.

On the forenoon of the 10th, the brigade was called out and assembled on the plain near headquarters to witness a somewhat sad and novel scene, namely: the branding and drumming out of service of deserters from one of the batteries. The brigade was formed into a hollow square facing inward, with a battery forge in the centre, the blacksmith blowing the bellows. The deserters were brought into the square under an infantry guard and took position near the forge. The deserters were then partially stripped of their clothing, irons were heated, and the letter " D " was burned upon their left hip. Their heads were then shaved after which they were marched about the square under guard, led by a corps of fife and drummers playing the " Rogue's March." It was a painful and humiliating sight, but undoubtedly left its salutary impression, as was designed, upon all who witnessed it.

Upon the afternoon of the 10th, the battery was ordered to the left of the line, and moved with the Second Division to Stone Mountain three miles west of Culpeper, and went into park and bivouacked for the night. We were not allowed to rest long for at two o'clock on the morning of the 11th, we were routed out, ordered to hitch up and moved out into the road, where we halted until daylight, then marching back through Culpeper passed Brandy Station and crossed the river at Rappahannock Station on the railroad bridge, going back over the same route upon which we advanced on the forward movement in September. At three P. M. halting at

Bealton Station we went into park, and at night bivouacked by the pieces. The army was falling back across the Rappahannock.

We remained at Bealtown until noon of the 12th, when the battery was ordered back post haste. We recrossed the river at the old place and advanced to Brandy Station, where we expected an engagement with the enemy. But the only foe we saw was a squad of about fifty prisoners going to the rear, they were captured by our cavalry advance guards. At night the battery parked, but the horses remained in harness, and the men bivouacked by the pieces. At one o'clock the next morning (the 13th) the battery was aroused, the division having been ordered back across the river, we received orders to follow, and, passing over the same route, moved back to Bealton Station. In crossing one of the small but deep streams an accident happened to the first caisson, by the breaking of the stock. Lieutenant Perrin had it taken to one side of the road, and set about repairing damages by lashing a piece of railroad tie to the stock so the caisson could be moved, and joining the wagon train went to Warrenton Junction.

As the battery was approaching Bealton, there was heard what seemed to be rapid and persistent skirmish firing. Dame Rumor, who had already comprehended the general situation, concluded by this firing that General Lee's troops had gained our rear, and that another battle of Bull Run was imminent. On arriving at Bealton, however, it was learned that the noise was occasioned by the destruction of a large amount of small arm ammunition which could not be taken by the trains.

The troops were tired enough to sleep at Bealton, but the time for rest had not yet come, as the Second Corps was pushing northward to the support of the cavalry (General Gregg's). This movement upon which the corps had entered was to be among the most arduous in all its history. Fayetteville was reached about six o'clock A. M. A halt was made and the troops were ordered to prepare their breakfast. Hot coffee, broiled salt pork and hard-bread was the bill of fare. After only three-quarters of an hour's halt, however, the order to fall in was heard, and the tired men, who had scarcely been allowed time to prepare a cup of coffee, were again summoned to the march. The battery was more fortunate, they had ample time to prepare their coffee, and the horses to eat their grain. At seven A. M. the battery was again on the road moving north. The day's march was long and wearisome ; the distance traveled was not great but such were the delays and interruptions due to the presence of another corps (the Third) on the same road in front, that it was nine o'clock in the evening before the battery halted and bivouacked on the south side of Cedar Run not far from the little village of Auburn. Here Lieutenant Perrin rejoined the battery having left the broken caisson with the wagon train.

On the morning of the 14th we were aroused at four o'clock and the battery ordered to hitch up; at five o'clock in the midst of a heavy fog we moved out of park to the Warrenton Junction road marching toward the northeast. On arriving at the junction with the Warrenton road we turned to the east and crossed Cedar Run to Auburn, a little hamlet consisting of a post-office, saw mill, blacksmith shop and three or four residences. On entering the village the road turned sharply to the right toward the southeast, the route by which the corps was moving. The battery passed through this village at six A. M. with the Second Division.

General Caldwell with the First Division had taken position, after crossing Cedar Run, to the north of the village on high rising ground called "Coffee Hill" on which he had posted his artillery, the batteries of Arnold (A, First Regiment Rhode Island Light Artillery), Ames, and Rickett, to cover the crossing of the corps.

As the battery was approaching Cedar Run artillery firing was heard to the right in the same direction that the troops were moving. What was the meaning of this—who was the enemy thus appearing from a quarter where only friends were to be looked for, and barring the road by which the Second Corps was to move? The presence of this force in such a place and at such a time constituted one of the peculiarities of warfare. It was the rebel General Stuart, with his two cavalry brigades and a battery of seven pieces, caught by accident the previous night between two columns of the Union army. He did not dare to attempt a move at night, not knowing in which direction he might find the Union army the strongest; and so he quietly waited until morning willing to be let alone. With morning, however, came fresh audacity, drawing his troops up across the road from Auburn to Catlett's Station, and fronting the former place with guns in battery the rebel general awaited events. Suddenly, either by the lifting of the mist or the lighting up of the great fog-bank by the fires of the coffee makers, the position of General Caldwell's men on Coffee Hill was disclosed to the straining eyes of the Confederates. Instantly a score of shells were sent hissing among the camp-fires of the First Division. But there was something on the road which the rebel general and his cannoneers had not observed through the mist. Nearer than he supposed were the avengers of the dead of "Coffee Hill." General Hays's division (the Third) which had taken the lead, was already on the road and fast approaching its position as it marched toward Catlett's Station, and those missiles intended for the First Division flew over the heads of the men of the Third.

The rebel general did not seem to realize the proximity of the Union troops, whether because of the fog (now rapidly lifting) or because of his attention being absorbed by the tempting opportunity offered in the massed troops on the ridge. Astonished and amazed was the commander of the Third Division at the unexpected fire upon his men, from a direction which he had every reason to suppose was held by Union troops; nothing daunted, however, he dashed to the front while the men of the leading regiment were ordered to deploy as skirmishers and push forward against the unknown enemy. What the number or character of the force thus encountered might be General Hays could, of course, form no conjecture, but it was exactly what he proposed to find out in the shortest possible time. His skirmishers advanced rapidly to their work, and though unused to encountering cavalry they did not shrink from attacking the compact line formed across the road, but pushed forward to closer quarters, and opened a sharp fire on both horses and men. The enemy finally charged and drove the skirmishers back upon the battle line, which had rapidly formed and as it advanced poured a withering fire upon the rebels, and speedily sent their cavalry to the right about with no small loss.

Finally, observing General Hays's line of battle rapidly developing in his front, General Stuart concluding that he had played the game as long as it was safe withdrew, and putting his command at a gallop went down the road toward Catlett's Station. The skirmishers pushing forward ascertained to the great relief of officers and men, that no infantry force stood behind those audacious Confederates. While this was being enacted at the southeast the enemy's infantry, under General Ewell, was fast approaching from the northwest. For a time it seemed as if the Second Corps, through no fault of its own, was caught in a trap. The closeness with which the corps was environed can be judged from the fact, that the shot from Stuart's guns passed clear over our troops and fell among the advancing lines of Ewell actually checking their advance.

The disappearance of the enemy's cavalry (General Stuart's) removed one feature of the situation which for the moment had been appalling. General Warren knew well enough that the Second Corps could be relied upon, no matter what the situation might be, and, therefore, no sooner did General Hays report the way open than General Warren ordered General Webb to take the advance to Catlett's Station with the Second Division, followed by the Third Division. Meanwhile General Caldwell, with the First Division and General Gregg's cavalry, held the enemy (General Ewell) in check thus covering the movements of the corps. Whether deceived by our demonstrations and supposing the Union force on the Catlett's Station road greater than it really was, or in pursuance of a plan agreed upon, General Ewell, after feeling General Caldwell's position along its entire length, withdrew to the north in the direction of Greenwich. As soon as it was seen that the enemy had abandoned direct pursuit the line of battle was broken up, and the First Division, General Caldwell's troops, was again put in motion.

With the exception of six or seven hours's rest at Auburn, the troops of the Second Corps had been almost continually on the march or in line of battle since the morning of the 12th; notwithstanding this extra strain the troops filed rapidly and uniformly into the road, and again took up the route of march. An hour or more moved slowly by and Catlett's Station was reached. Here the Second and Third Divisions halted in position of battle. The trains of the corps joined by those of the cavalry had passed safely to the rear, headed for Centreville, by the Wolf Run Shoals road. Upon the arrival of General Caldwell, with his division, the whole corps was put in motion and marched up the Orange and Alexandria railroad. The Second Division, General Webb, with two batteries (B, First Rhode Island Light Artillery, and Battery F, First Pennsylvania) took the north side of the railroad, and the Third Division under General Hays the south side, the ambulances and artillery of the cavalry following. The First Division, General Caldwell, continued to act as rear guard to the Second and Third Divisions which were moving in two columns. As the corps was put in motion towards Bristoe Station each step of the ground was measured off by the weary troops under their unusual burdens. It was nearly three o'clock. Battery B, First Rhode Island Light Artillery led the van, and Colonel Morgan accompanied the advance to select a position and cover the crossing at Broad Run. General Warren and staff were at the rear of the column watching for the possible reappearance of the enemy (General Ewell), when suddenly firing was heard up the road some two miles distant which soon broke forth into a furious cannonade. Was the Fifth Corps, General Sykes, being attacked at Bristoe while waiting the arrival of the Second Corps? The spurs were sharply pressed against the flanks of the horses, and General Warren, followed by his staff, dashed out of the road that he might not hinder the troops nor be hindered by them, and through bush and timber made his way at a furious gallop to the front, the head of the column, and in a few moments he and his staff burst out from the bushes upon the plains of Bristoe. Here a sight greeted their eyes which might appal even older soldiers. The enemy, General Heth's Division of General Hill's corps, were on the hills from which Milford could be seen on the left and Bristoe Station in front.

The village of Bristoe was of even less importance as a place of residence than Auburn; the village which had once given name to the place had disappeared, only a few burnt chimneys remaining. One insignificant house, however, known as Dodd's, remained and constituted the sole human feature of the scene. This stood on the right of the road, running from Brentsville to Gainesville, about one hundred yards north of the railroad. The ground on the south side of Broad Run was more than usually diversified, a number of hillocks affording good positions for artillery. The enemy had reached this point in advance of the Second Corps, and looking toward Bristoe, Heth saw no Union forces confronting him. The Army of the Potomac had escaped! He looked to his left and there, across the plains a mile or so away, he beheld retreating troops evidently the rear-guard of the Union army — the prize was lost! Quickly he ordered a battery (Poague's) into position to rake the retreating column. It was the sound of Poague's guns opening on the rear of the Fifth Corps, which so startled General Warren as he rode with the rear guard, and which brought him at such a pace to the head of his column. Notwithstanding the swiftness with which he and his staff rode, before they had reached the clearing at Bristoe, answering guns were heard and the Confederates no longer had the music all to themselves. The answering fire was from the well-known, long-proved Battery B, First Regiment Rhode Island Light Artillery, under command of Lieut. T. Fred. Brown (recovered from the effects of his Gettysburg wounds) and told the enemy that they were not to have it all their own way.

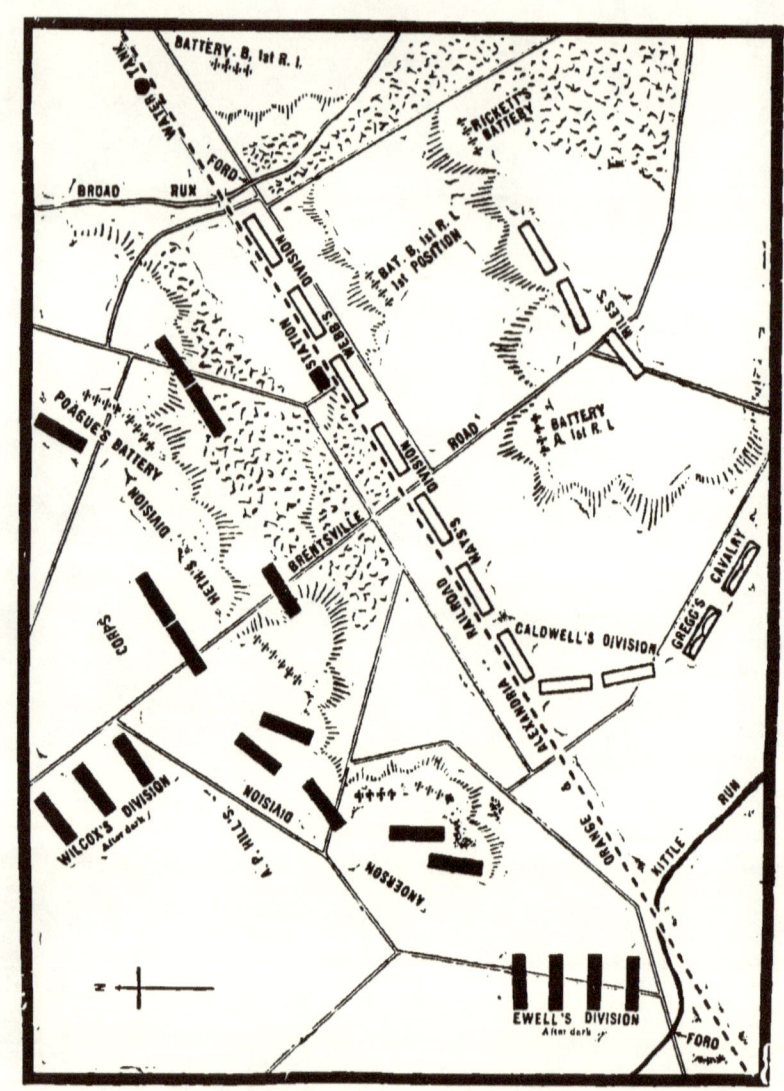

Bristoe Station, Oct, 14, 1863.

The battery after crossing Kettle Run was toiling slowly along, the men weighed down with unusual burdens and worn from loss of sleep, had no thought on their part that they were about to be thrown into the immediate presence of an enemy in full battle array. The booming of the guns startled the men. When the battery cleared the edge of a bit of woods through which it was moving, it perceived the enemy's battery on the left firing north and infantry moving northeast toward Broad Run. Discovering the enemy upon his left flank General Webb turned his division (the Second) sharply to the right and across the railroad, blocking for a time the path of General Hays's division (the Third) which had been moving in parallel column on the other side. The halt of the Third Division gave the lead to the Second Division. About three P. M. the men of Battery B were startled by the sharp bugle call of " Cannoneers mount!" followed by "Trot—march!" The battery dashed across the railroad and up to rising ground under fire of the enemy's skirmishers without loss. Wheeling to the left into battery we opened fire using spherical case with such effect as to cause the enemy to conceal itself, but not until as a parting salute they had delivered a volley which struck the ground in front of the battery like hail. Fortune favored us for the fire of the enemy being too low the men escaped unharmed.

By this time the infantry of the Fourth Brigade, holding the railroad, received orders to move further to the right, and two regiments were sent across Broad Run to hold the ford at the railroad bridge Battery B going with them. Limbering up, the cannoneers mounted and the battery dashed across the field, but owing to the nature of the ground it was obliged to proceed some distance down the stream before crossing, but finally went splashing through the water and up the bank on the other side turning to the left toward the railroad. Upon gaining rising ground it was discovered that the infantry, which had been sent over before us, had crossed back again. The battery was unable to recross as the road it had just passed over was fully commanded by the enemy. Moving up the railroad about two hundred yards to higher ground we wheeled into position and placing the guns in battery at once opened fire on the enemy's (Poague's) battery, and enfiladed its left flank. The Confederates' battery of light twelve-pounders and one rifled gun replied, and maintained a well directed fire for two hours when five of their guns were captured by our troops. The race for the ford had been a sharp one, with the Confederates moving squarely down on General Webb's left flank. But the goal was won by the Union troops. Part of the First Brigade, the Sixty-first New York and the Eighty-first Pennsylvania, crossed near the railroad to the opposite bank to hold and protect General Webb's right flank, aided by Battery B which was on the extreme right near the railroad.

There was literally not a moment to be lost. The enemy (Cooke's and Kirkland's brigades) was advancing from the woods on a charge for the railroad, and was more than half way across the open space when it was met by the fire of General Webb's men, whose line of fire was much shorter than that of the enemy. As regiment after regiment, however, dashed forward with loud shouts and took position along the railroad in the cut or behind the embankment, our fire spread rapidly from right to left, and when General Hays's men (the Third Division) were in position our line overlapped the front of the charging line. Meanwhile Battery B, First Rhode Island, from beyond the creek, and Rickett's Battery, F, First Pennsylvania, which had taken position on the ridge near the stream poured upon the rebels a rapid and most effective fire. "It is conceded," says Colonel Morgan, "that the finest artillery practice in the experience of the corps was witnessed here from these two batteries." A few minutes later Battery A, First Rhode Island, breaking through the brushes went into action behind General Owen's brigade, being near the road running from Brentsville to Gainesville. Thus far it had been simply a question of five minutes. Had these few minutes been lost the Confederates would have seized the railroad, and the Union troops would have been fortunate if they had so much as formed a line of battle on the ridge to the south, and abandoned the crossing of Broad Run to the enemy. As it was the five minutes saved the railroad, and those troops stationed in the railroad cut behind the embankment; it was still a question as to whether the advance of the enemy could be checked. Gallantly they pressed forward in the face of a withering fire which made large gaps in their ranks, and if a battle flag dropped from one hand it was instantly seized and held aloft by another. Valiantly they fought reaching Dodd's house near the railroad without halting or breaking, and continued pushing forward until they succeeded in gaining the railroad at two points, one of which was the crossing of the Brentsville road. Some of their bravest reached the embankment on General Webb's right about one hundred yards from the Run.

Excepting the momentary wavering of a company or two the Union troops had kept up their fire with unusual coolness and regularity, and showed no signs of a panic at seeing the enemy within our lines at two different points. The Confederates who reached the railroad in the centre were shot down by men of the Tammany regiment (Forty-second New York). On the right the Eighty-second New York changed front to the left, and killed, dispersed or captured all of the rebels who crossed the track near the Run. The enemy now at varying distances from our front halted, wavered and was finally forced back by the hail of musket shot poured into its ranks, and turning fled to the cover of the woods. Quick as thought amid loud cheers the men of half a dozen Union regiments (of the Second and Third Divisions) sprang across the railroad, and dashed forward after the retreating foe to gather up the trophies of the fight. They entered the woods in line of battle so lately held by the enemy, and taking 450 prisoners with two colors from under the very nose of the supporting brigade, and safely returned with them. Five guns of Poague's battery were captured and drawn across the track by the rollicking skirmishers.

It was related that at the time these prisoners were brought into the lines of the Second Division, and saw the white trefoil of their captors, they recognized their old antagonists of Gettysburg and exclaimed: "Those damned white clubs again!"

Battery B remained out on the flank beyond Broad Run near the railroad for two hours, and maintained a well directed fire on the enemy enfilading its right flank with such effect as to cause it to seek shelter.

At dusk the battery by orders recrossed Broad Run and joining the Second Division went into park in a hollow among small pines. Remaining only a short time, however, as we were soon ordered to the front to the ridge occupied by Rickett's battery; during the move we passed the captured prisoners and guns. As Battery B approached the ridge, Rickett's Battery, having been relieved, was limbering up to withdraw when the enemy opened fire on them, causing no little confusion as the shells burst in their midst wounding several men and horses. The nature of the ground was such that the enemy did not observe Battery B approaching, which upon gaining the crest of the ridge wheeled into position and opened fire on those guns which were firing upon Rickett's Battery. After using about twenty rounds we received orders to cease firing, and, strange to say, did not receive a shot from the enemy's battery which had caused Rickett's so much confusion.

The battery remained in this position until the corps withdrew and left the enemy in possession of the situation.

Battery B's casualties in the engagement at Bristoe Station Oct. 14, 1863 were: One man killed, Chester F. Hunt; and four wounded, Martin V. B. Eaton, Charles Clark and James B. Porter; John T. Gardiner slightly wounded. The last two were detached men from the One hundred and Fortieth Pennsylvania regiment. Joseph Cassen was again taken prisoner having returned only a short time previously to the battery from parole camp. Lieut. William S. Perrin was hit on the foot with a fragment of shell which took off the tap from the sole of his boot causing only a slight lameness to his foot.

During the engagement beyond the Run the battery expended one hundred and seventy rounds of ammunition.

Extracts from official records. From the report of General Warren, commanding Second Corps.

"The action had come upon us suddenly, and Lieutenant Brown's Battery B, First Rhode Island, though separated by a long interval from the infantry maintained itself on our extreme right, and poured a most destructive fire upon the flank of the enemy's line of battle during its advance and retreat."

From report of General Webb, commanding Second Division.

"Lieutenant Brown's Battery B, First Rhode Island, crossed Broad Run under general orders which I had given it, and obtained a position which completely enfiladed the enemy's line when it charged. The battery did good service, was without infantry support for a long time, but by its activity and boldness held its position without attack, except by artillery fire, since the enemy naturally supposed it was supported."

Report of Chief of Artillery Second Corps, Capt. John G. Hazard.

"At three P. M. the advance of the corps, while marching by the flank, was met at Bristoe Station by a column of the enemy moving in the same direction. The Second Division immediately secured the southern side of the Orange and Alexandria Railroad as a line of defense, and Brown's Rhode Island Battery temporarily attached to the division obtained a most fortunate position and opened fire with spherical case upon the advancing line of the enemy checking it, and causing it to seek shelter under the crest in its immediate front. Lieutenant Brown was then ordered into position on the eastern side of Broad Run by General Webb, whose division was about to make a similar move. After the crossing of the battery, it was seen that the division had recrossed the Run to its former position. The battery was unable to recross as the road it had just passed over was fully commanded by the enemy. So it moved up to the railroad, a distance of two hundred yards, to a position that enfiladed the enemy, and opened fire with good effect."

Report of Lieut. T. Fred. Brown commanding Battery B, First Regiment Rhode Island Light Artillery.

"CAPTAIN: I have the honor to submit the following report of the part taken by Battery B, First Regiment Rhode Island Light Artillery on the 14th of October. Was attached to Second Division Second Corps, Brig. Gen. A. S. Webb commanding, and at three P. M. on the 14th, was moving up the north side of Alexandria and Orange Railroad near Bristoe Station, Va. When the enemy's skirmishers suddenly opened upon the battery from the woods on the left, we moved forward on a trot and fortunately were soon enabled to cross to the south side of the railroad without loss and joined the advance of our column. General Webb ordered the battery into position with intentions to fire a few rounds at the enemy which was rapidly advancing in line of battle upon the railroad from the north side at a distance of about six hundred yards. General Webb further ordered the battery to cross Broad Run as soon as a similar movement on the part of his division began to take place.

Opened fire with spherical case with such effect as to cause the enemy to conceal itself. Observing that the movement of the troops across Broad Run had commenced proceeded to follow as ordered. From the nature of the ground was obliged to proceed some distance down the Run. After crossing, it was seen that the troops had all recrossed. The battery was unable to recross as the road it had just passed over was fully commanded by the enemy, so moved up to the railroad about two hundred yards to a commanding position that enfiladed the enemy, and immediately opened fire with good effect. A battery of four light twelve-pounder guns and one rifled gun replied, and maintained a well directed fire for two hours that was fully responded to. Was ordered to recross Broad Run, join division, go into park and wait orders. Was again placed in position and expended about twenty rounds. Withdrew at dark and moved with corps across Bull Run and encamped. Sustained a loss during engagement of one man killed, four wounded, two horses killed, and seven wounded. Expended about one hundred and seventy rounds of ammunition.

Bugler John F. Leach is especially to be mentioned for collecting thirteen stragglers (infantry), and disposing of them as skirmishers on the right flank of the battery on the north side of the railroad, at the time when the battery was wholly unsupported across the Run, without doubt preventing much annoyance from the enemy's skirmishers (who engaged his men) if not the capture of the battery."

Extract from report of Gen. A. P. Hill, C. S. Army, commanding Third Corps.

"Poague's battalion was ordered to take another position and open fire on the battery which was enfilading General Kirkland's line. This was not done as quickly as I expected and General Kirkland's line was exposed to a very deliberate and destructive fire. About this time Generals Cooke and Kirkland were both wounded, and their fall at this critical moment had a serious influence upon the fortunes of the contest. Brigadier-General Posey was seriously wounded by a shell * in the early part of the action."

Extract from report of Gen. H. Heth, C. S. Army, commanding division to which General Cooke's and Kirkland's brigades belonged.

"When in the railroad cut his men (Kirkland's) were exposed to an enfilading fire from the right, in addition to a severe fire from a battery on the north side of Broad Run. The position was untenable, and he was compelled to fall back."

From these reports, there is no doubt but that Battery B, First Regiment of Rhode Island Light Artillery, Lieut. T. Fred. Brown commanding, held an important position at the battle of Bristoe Station, as well as having the honor of opening the fight and preventing the enemy from gaining possession of the railroad and ford.

* From Battery B.

Great as was the relief of the corps commander when night closed down upon the field of Bristoe, all cause for anxiety had not disappeared as a great responsibility lay in withdrawing the corps from a superior force, and at the same time save it from being driven from the railroad to be captured or destroyed. It was in view of such possibilities that General Warren gave most punctilious instructions for the withdrawal, and, until the troops were fairly across Broad Run, no word of command was given above a whisper. The men prevented the rattling of their haversacks and canteens, and thus, in ghostly silence the corps stole away marching by the flank across the enemy's front within three hundred yards of their skirmishers, and in half range of their smooth bore guns. The little camp fires of the Confederates were seen burning at a hundred points across the plains still strewn with the dead where the enemy had charged, and up on the hill beyond new brigades were even then coming up to the expected battle of the morrow. Borne on every breeze were the voices of the Confederate soldiers in familiar talk around their camp fires, the challenging of sentinels or the low groans of their wounded.

Within the Union lines all was silence and darkness, no camp fires showed their flickering light, and no hum of voices was heard as Battery B, with the Second Corps of the Army of the Potomac, stole away from the presence of the great horde of the Confederate Army which had for hours held them at its mercy. Crossing Broad Run by the ford and railroad the infantry and artillery, not forgetting the five captured guns (which with some difficulty had been furnished horses), made their way over the great plains stretching towards Manassas, and between three and four o'clock on the morning of the 15th Battery B halted, and going into park bivouacked.

Sixty-nine hours had elapsed since leaving Bealton Station on the morning of the 12th, and the jaded troops, who had been either in column on the road, in line of battle, skirmishing or fighting with the enemy for more than sixty hours, were allowed at last to throw themselves upon the ground on the north bank of the Bull Run, near Blackburn's Ford, and for a time rest from their labors.

Well may Colonel Morgan say that this campaign, short as it was, " was more fatiguing than that of the Seven Days on the Peninsula, since the marches were much longer."

For its exertions and sacrifices the corps received a generous measure of praise, from its country, its comrades, and the commander of the Army of the Potomac. The following is General Meade's order of announcing the affair at Bristoe:

HEADQUARTERS OF THE ARMY OF THE POTOMAC,
October 15, 1863.

General Orders,
No. 96.

The major-general commanding announces to the army that the rear-guard, consisting of the Second Corps, was attacked yesterday while marching by the flank.

The enemy, after a spirited contest, was repulsed losing a battery of five guns, two colors, and four hundred and fifty prisoners.

The skill and promptitude of Major-General Warren, and the gallantry and bearing of the officers and soldiers of the Second Corps are entitled to high commendation.

(Signed,)
By command of   Major-General MEADE.
S. WILLIAMS, *Assis't Adj't General.*

Colonel Morgan justly said, that even the high credit which General Warren received for his conduct on this occasion, did not equal his deserts owing to facts not generally known. "General Warren had," he said, " not only to meet the enemy, but to change the formation made before he arrived on the field, and to effect this in the face of a powerful advance of the enemy. His quickness and decision inspired the troops with great confidence in him." This testimony was worth all the more because the first formation of General Webb's division, to which Colonel Morgan alludes, was one in which he had himself concurred as General Warren's staff officer.

If asked how it happened that Battery B and the Second Corps escaped annihilation on the 14th of October, it can only be explained by declaring that the Confederates were slower than they usually were on occasions of equal importance. General Hill was on high ground above Bristoe Station for more than an hour in advance of General Webb, and General Heth had four brigades deployed while Battery B and General Webb's troops were still toiling along the road, more or less straggled by the long march and the recent crossing of Kettle Run. There was nothing to prevent General Ewell, on the other hand, from following the Second Corps through Catlett's Station, up along the track to Bristoe Station, and to advance as fast as the troops of the Second Corps retired. Then as soon as the rear of the corps halted, he could have thrown out skirmishers on the rear guard's front, and followed with lines of battle which could have formed behind the skirmishers.

A most curious feature of this case was that not only had General Ewell fought General Hooker on this very field the year before, during the Second Bull Run campaign, but this was his own country home and he knew the ground well.

CHAPTER XIX.

CENTREVILLE TO THE RAPIDAN.—BATTLE OF MINE RUN.—WINTER QUARTERS.

OCTOBER 15th. It was quite late in the morning, nearly eight o'clock, before the men were called upon for camp duty. The rest and sleep they had been able to obtain were quite refreshing to both mind and body, and as a result performed their duties with a will. The empty limber chests were soon repacked with ammunition, horses fed and cared for, while the men received fresh rations.

About noon the camps of the infantry, to our right and front, were thrown into a state of confusion by a visit from some of General Stuart's cavalry (the enemy) on a reconnaissance to our line, and as a parting salute they threw some of those fiendish Hotchkiss shells into the camp, fortunately, however, without any great damage.

On the 16th, the weather was warm and showery during the morning. Just about noon the battery was ordered to the front, and advanced on the pike road about two or three miles only to retrace its steps in the afternoon, and return to camp in the old earthworks about Centreville.

On the 17th, being short handed the battery received fifteen volunteer recruits from the infantry, they were formed as a detachment and drilled at the manual of the piece, after which they were assigned to the gun detachments.

On the 18th, the battery received marching orders, and during the forenoon was busy preparing for the move. At noon the infantry recruits, received yesterday, were sent back to their regiment much to the disappointment of the men. In their stead the battery received detached men from Lieutenant Frank's Battery I; First United States, which had been relieved from the artillery brigade and mounted to perform duty with the cavalry corps of the Army of the Potomac. The men received were: William Bruce, Edward Curtis, Robert H. Cooper, William J. Cooper, John Fox, John H. Haller, William James, Ludwick Ling, John McGuire, David N. Minesinger, Henry Odell, John G. Pierce, Joseph Rhodenburg, and Washington Whitlock. The artillery brigade was reënforced by Lieutenant Weir's Battery C, Fifth United States Artillery, and Independent Battery C, of Pennsylvania.

On the 19th, the weather was quite cool, it rained most of the forenoon, but cleared at noon though still cool. At eight o'clock the battery broke camp and pulling out of park into the pike road, with the Second Division, commenced the march southward again after the rebel army. Forded Broad Run at the railroad near Bristoe Station. The enemy in its retreat had torn up the rails, and destroyed and burned the railroad bridge by which the troops crossed on the night of the 14th. We passed over the position occupied by the rebel battery (Poague's) with which we were engaged during the fight at Bristoe Station. The effect of our artillery fire could plainly be seen, there were four dead horses and a mule, a broken wheel, battered canteens, and broken rails strewn about; while the trees by their broken limbs and torn bark showed the effects of our shot. The division halted a short distance beyond Bristoe Station where the battery was ordered into park and bivouacked for the night.

At seven o'clock on the morning of the 20th, the battery resumed its march moving north to Gainesville, thence south to Greenwich and down to Auburn; no enemy appearing on the route of march the division was halted and ordered into camp. The battery was ordered into park on their old camping ground of the night of the 13th instant. We remained encamped during the 21st and 22d with the Second Division.

On the 23d, the Second Corps moved its camp from Auburn to the railroad crossing at Turkey Run, about half way between Warrenton and Warrenton Junction, where the corps remained nearly a fortnight.

The battery moved with the corps, and went into camp near the Run about a quarter of a mile from the crossing where we remained until the corps moved.

While encamped a number of changes took place with the commissioned and non-commissioned officers.

On the 24th, Sergt. John E. Wardlow was discharged to receive a commission as first lieutenant in Company E, Fourteenth Rhode Island Heavy Artillery (colored troops); and Second Duty Sergt. A. A. Williams was promoted to first duty sergeant, also acting as first sergeant in place of First Sergt. John F. Blake who was still in hospital.

On the 28th, Lieut.-Col. J. Albert Monroe, First Rhode Island Light Artillery, reported to the Second Corps for duty, and as senior officer of artillery relieved Capt. John G. Hazard who was chief of artillery of the corps. The captain subsequently returned to Battery B and assumed command.

On the 30th, at 11 o'clock A. M., the battery held mounted inspection by Lieut.-Col. Monroe, with Capt. John G. Hazard in command, First Lieut. T. Fred. Brown the right section, First Lieut. William S. Perrin the left section, and Second Lieut. Willard B. Pierce was chief of caissons, in place of Second Lieut. Charles A. Brown absent on sick leave. Everything passed off pleasantly.

On the 31st, the battery was mustered for the months of September and October, and the pay rolls signed, but when we were to be paid was another question not satisfactorily answered.

Sunday, November 1st, the usual inspection took place in the morning. The weather was pleasant and warm for the time of year. At noon a detail of men under Lieutenant Perrin and Sergt. Anthony B. Horton went to Warrenton Junction after horses, and late at night returned with seven.

The cars made their appearance passing in sight of our camp for the first time since our advance, the repairs to the railroad had been made thus enabling them to run.

On the 4th, Corp. John F. Hanson was promoted to fourth duty sergeant, a number of other sergeants were also promoted.

The weather for the past few days had been remarkably pleasant, and the time was spent in drill at the manual of the piece; proving of much benefit to the recruits, and making them quite proficient in the different manoeuvres.

On the 6th, the battery attended brigade drill, and was complimented on its promptness in executing the different movements, upon the fine appearance of its men, and the good condition of the horses and equipments. In the evening received marching orders, and at seven o'clock on the morning of the 7th the battery broke camp, and with the corps marched south passing through Warrenton Junction to

Bealton where a halt was made for coffee. Resuming the march we passed through Morrisville to the Rappahannock River, where the corps halted and the battery bivouacked near Kelly's Ford.

Cannonading had been heard in our front and away up to the right all the afternoon. Our advance troops were forcing the rebels to fall back, and in their retreat they were destroying the bridges, tearing up the railroad tracks and burning the sleepers in order to bend the rails; culverts were blown up, and in fact the destruction was carried out in a very systematic manner.

On the morning of the 8th the battery broke camp, and moving to the river crossed on the pontoon bridge which had been thrown across for the advance of the Third Corps, the Second Corps following up to the support of the Third. The battery after crossing turned to the northwest moving very slowly on account of the large number of troops on the road, about noon, however, the roads became less crowded and traveling much easier; at night we bivouacked near Brandy Station. On the road we passed a number of Confederate prisoners, and four pieces of artillery that were captured by the Sixth Corps.

Just before the battery halted we passed Batteries E and G, First Regiment Rhode Island Light Artillery, and many pleasant words were exchanged with friends and comrades from our mother state.

On the 9th, the battery remained quietly in camp all day, but on the morning of the 10th at eight o'clock it broke camp, and moving up nearer the railroad and station went into camp near corps headquarters. In the afternoon of the 11th orders about reënlisting and granting furloughs were read to the men.

November 12th, was hailed with joy. Dame Rumor had been busy with flying reports that the paymaster had arrived, and sure enough he was at headquarters for, at nine o'clock A. M., the battery was called into line, marched to the officers' quarters, and its men were paid for the months of September and October.

Captain Hazard, who had been confined to his quarters by sickness, went to the hospital up at corps headquarters to-day, and on the 21st was granted a sick leave of absence. Lieut. T. Fred. Brown is again in command of the battery.

On the 21st, the battery was ordered to move down to the Artillery Brigade encampment, and the next day preparations were made to lay out a camp which seemingly indicated that the battery was going into winter quarters.

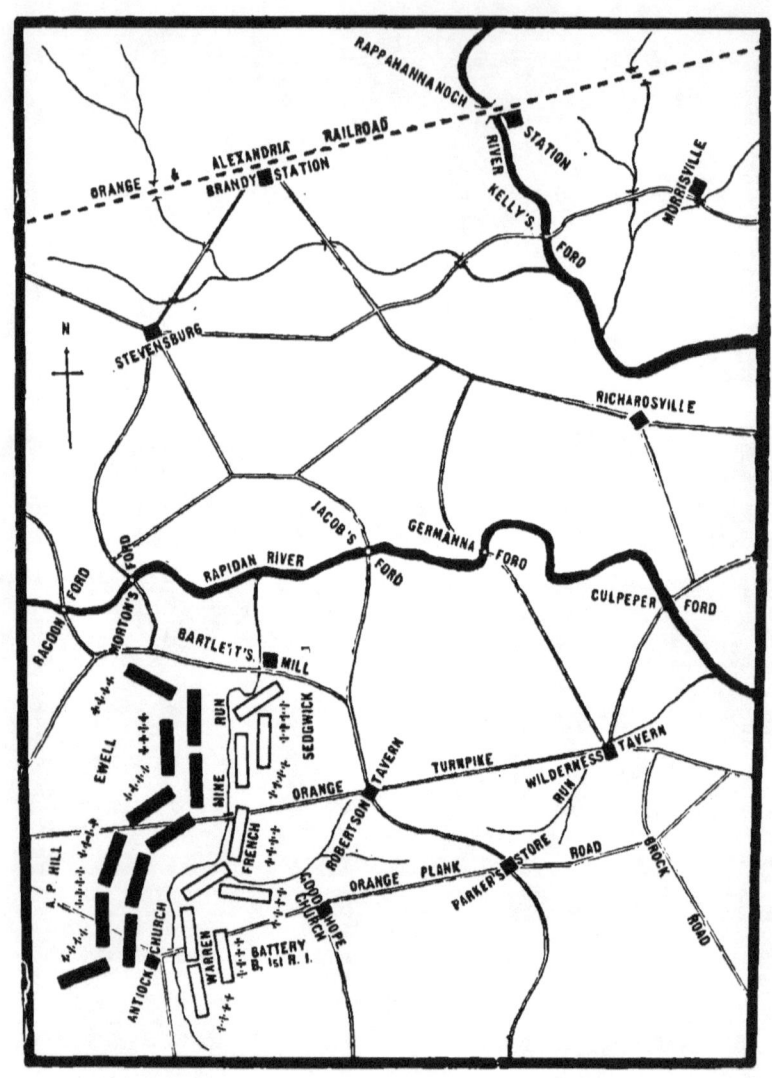

Mine Run, Nov. 8, 1863.

On the 23d, Bugler John Leach returned to Battery A, First Rhode Island Light Artillery, and John Doyle a detached man was promoted bugler.

On the 24th, Corp. John H. Rhodes was promoted to sergeant *vice* Sergt. Albert Straight deceased. Guidon Charles H. Adams was promoted to sergeant *vice* Richard H. Gallup resigned to go to artillery headquarters on detach service as butcher.

The past few days had been spent in drilling and holding inspections. No prospect of winter quarters being built.

On the evening of the 25th the battery received marching orders, and at sunrise on the 26th it broke camp marching all day until late in the afternoon, when it halted at the Rapidan River where it bivouacked for the night. Crossed the river at sunrise on the morning of the 27th by the pontoon bridge while the pieces, caisson, and wagons crossed by the Germania Ford; the water came up nearly to the bottom of the ammunition chests. We pushed on about four miles from the river when we halted, and were ordered into park bivouacking for the night near Flat Run Church.

The morning of the 28th was cold and rainy. The battery at an early hour had received orders to advance to the front with the Second Division, and moved out of camp to the Orange turnpike where a halt was made to allow the infantry to proceed as heavy firing from the skirmishers was heard in our front. After the infantry had passed the battery was ordered to advance at a double-quick with cannoneers mounted, and took position on a knoll covered with a young growth of shrubs. As the battery was unlimbering for action it had one horse killed and another wounded by the enemy's sharpshooters, but we did not become engaged as our infantry routed the enemy which retreated so fast that our services were not needed.

At three o'clock in the afternoon the corps was further advanced beyond Robertson's Tavern to the hills facing toward Mine Run. General Hays's division led, with General Webb's next in column. After advancing a short distance the Second Division turned sharply to the left, and fortunately General Webb led his troops forward at the double-quick, for as his leading brigade came up into line on the crest it came face to face with a line of rebel skirmishers followed by a battle line only a few yards distant, which was advancing to seize the same position. General Webb's men were just enough ahead in the race to gain the crest and open fire on the foe. The enemy was apparently not prepared for a contest, and fell back after a brief skirmish. Battery B which had been ordered up on the ridge came into position, and placing the guns in battery opened fire on the rebels as they retreated to the woods. During the remainder of the day the battery was engaged in shelling the enemy's lines. Although some of their shot and shell came remarkably close to us we sustained no casualties. At midnight we received orders, and, withdrawing from the front went back to Robertson's Tavern, and parked in an open field while the men bivouacked beside the guns.

On the 29th and 30th the battery remained encamped near the Orange turnpike, while the infantry of the division, to which we were attached, was sent down to the left of the line near Good Hope Church on the Orange Plank road.

Although the battery received marching orders at sunrise on the morning of December 1st it was noon before we broke camp. Pulling out into the turnpike we moved in an easterly direction until the Germania Ford road was reached, then moving up to the six corners, called the Cross Roads, we took the middle road going to the Rapidan River which we crossed at sunset by the Culpeper Mine Ford, and, going into park bivouacked a short distance from the river, the horses remained in harness all night.

At an early hour on the morning of the 2d the battery, with the division, was ordered back to Brandy Station where we arrived late in the afternoon and went into park at our camping ground of November 26th. We remained here until noon of the 4th when we moved to the edge of the woods near by, and preparations were begun to lay out a camp. In the afternoon, however, the battery received marching orders. The troops had returned to the north side of the Rapidan, and the flank movement on General Lee's right, at Mine Run, was at an end.

At eight o'clock on the morning of the 5th the battery with the corps left Brandy Station, and moving south to Stevensburg encamped. Corps headquarters was established at the Thorn House on Cole's Hill. The infantry were assigned a position on the plains for their winter camping ground, but the artillery was not assigned its position until after the infantry.

On the afternoon of the 5th, at roll call, an order was read which promoted Sergt. A. A. Williams to first sergeant *vice* First Sergt. John T. Blake discharged to accept a commission as second lieutenant in Battery A, First Rhode Island Light Artillery. Corp. Pardon

S. Walker was promoted to sergeant, *vice* Sergeant Williams promoted.

On the 8th, the battery was moved up to Cole's Hill near headquarters, and on the 9th again commenced preparations to lay out a winter camp. This place, however, was not destined to be our camping ground for at noon, on the 10th, we were again ordered to move to the southwest on rising ground near the edge of a belt of woods skirting the plains; this was a much better place for the protection of the horses than any we had thus far occupied.

On the 11th, the camp was finally laid out, and winter quarters of huts were built. The pieces and caissons were parked to the south on level ground, while on the rising ground north of the park the huts for the men were built in two lines; to the east of these were the artificers', quartermaster's, and cooks' huts. To the northeast of these was the stable stockade for the horses. North of the centre of the line of men's quarters was the first sergeant's hut, and north of the west end of the line was the duty sergeant's hut. North of the line of sergeants' quarters was an open space, called the parade ground, used for the assembly of the command at roll calls, and north of this space were the officers' quarters.

It took some eight or ten days to make the camp, but it was finally finished to the satisfaction of the officers. Then commenced a series of drills on pleasant days, while camp and mounted inspections with the daily camp duties occupied the time until the opening of the spring campaign.

After the return of the troops from the Mine Run campaign a policy was adopted for granting furloughs of ten days, to such of the men as were recommended by their officers, the number being limited to three in a battery. Later this policy was amended by only granting furloughs to those who had served two years or more, providing they would reënlist for another term of three years; under this order many of the old regiments were sent home to enjoy both their brief vacation of thirty days, and, if possible, to recruit their number for the coming struggle. Leaves of absence were also given to the commissioned officers.

On the 14th, Sergt. Anthony B. Horton and privates Benjamin A. Burlingame and James Bowe a detached man received furloughs of ten days and left for home. They were the first and last men who received a furlough without reënlisting, for on the 16th, the following order was read to the command, and no more ten days' furloughs were granted to privates:

STATE OF RHODE ISLAND,
EXECUTIVE DEPARTMENT,
PROVIDENCE, Dec. 15, 1863.

SOLDIERS OF RHODE ISLAND :

By General Orders No. 191, from the War Department, you are offered a bounty of four hundred dollars and granted certain privileges if you will reënlist for "three years, unless sooner discharged." To this Rhode Island desires to add her bounty of three hundred dollars, and so, in part, repay the debt that she owes those brave men who, at the commencement of this Rebellion, freely offered their lives without setting a price upon their services. Now an opportunity is given you to reënlist, and receive a liberal bounty from your State as well as your government.

The term for which you enlisted has not yet expired, but by enlisting for three years from the present time, unless sooner discharged, you can receive these bounties now held out to you.

Everything now indicates that your services will not be required three years longer, therefore, by reënlisting under this order you commence your new term before the expiration of your first one, and are also by General Orders No. 376, War Department, granted a furlough of thirty days before the expiration of your original term of enlistment.

These advantages are held out to you if you reënlist before the fifth day of January next, and it is evident that no better opportunity can occur for those who desire to again enter the service of their country.

Soldiers! the Union still needs your services! Now is the time to again offer yourselves for the preservation of that government which has so long protected you and your homes.

JAMES Y. SMITH.
By His Excellency the Governor.

CHAS. E. BAILEY,
Colonel and Private Secretary.

On the 21st, Capt. John G. Hazard returned to the battery and resumed command.

On the 26th, Lieut T. Fred Brown left for Rhode Island having been granted a furlough.

On December 31st, the muster rolls were signed for the months of November and December.

At noon thirteen men, the first squad of reënlisted men as veteran volunteers, left for Rhode Island on a thirty-five days' furlough. The happy men were : First Sergt. A. A. Williams, Sergt. Charles H. Adams ; Corps. Calvin L. Macomber, Nelson E. Perry, Charles W. Wood ; and Privates John Eatock, Calvin C. Fletcher, John Glynn, John Healy, John Kelly, William McCullum, Charles J. Rider and Francis Slaiger. With their furloughs safely placed in the inside pocket of their blouses they started on their way rejoicing. At Brandy Station they took the train for Washington.

January 1st. New Year's day came and passed as pleasantly as could be expected in the midst of civil war on rebel soil, and in front of a rebel army. The departure of the old gentleman with the venerable beard and ominous scythe, whose portrait has so often arrested attention, was not attended by any special demonstrations of nature, while his successor was ushered in with a cool, not to say freezing, reception. "All was quiet" along the Rapidan.

In the afternoon the battery received five detached men, recruits transferred from Battery G, First New York Light Artillery, namely: James Cavanagh, Peter Guinan, Timothy Lyons, Charles McGlocklin, and Fred Smith. Richard Fetthousen was to have come but was detained in the hospital.

On the 10th, the battery had a mounted inspection, and, for the first time since May, 1863, all of the commissioned officers were present, namely: Capt. John G. Hazard; First Lieuts. T. Fred. Brown and William S. Perrin; Second Lieuts. Charles A. Brown and Willard B. Pierce; 109 men were also present for duty, forty-eight men absent either on detached duty, sick in hospital, or on furlough.

On February 5th, Lieut. Willard B. Pierce was detailed, and went up to artillery headquarters on detached service as adjutant, where he remained until Lieut. G. Lyman Dwight returned from his furlough.

On the 6th, it was cold and rainy, but at three o'clock in the morning the battery was thrown into a state of excitement by receiving light marching orders to be in readiness to move at a moment's notice. Reveille was sounded and the camp was soon in a bustle, accompanied by the following exclamations: "What's up! What is it! have the rebs got in our rear?" No one could answer, Dame Rumor for once was quiet. The battery was soon in readiness waiting for further orders. Breakfast of hot coffee, hard-tack, and pork was soon disposed of, and then came an interval of tedious waiting for something to turn up. At daylight an order came for a detail of fifteen men, including one sergeant and two corporals, to report to Battery G, First New York Artillery, for duty. This detail (called because Battery G was short-handed, many of its men being absent) was soon made and the men left camp under guide of the aide who brought the order. During the day artillery firing was heard at intervals in the direction of the Rapidan.

Battery B was not called upon nor any of the smooth bore batteries, only those having rifle or long range guns went with the corps to Morton's Ford.

The men detailed from Battery B on arriving at the camp of the New York battery found it hitched up and ready for a move; they were assigned to the two gun detachments of the centre section and Sergt. John H. Rhodes was placed in command of the section.

All being in readiness Battery G, First New York Artillery, left its camp, and, with the Second Corps, took up the line of march on a flank movement. Reaching the Rapidan the battery was placed in position in an open field to the right of a dense strip of woods, while the enemy's intrenched lines could be seen on the opposite side. When the infantry advanced to carry the ford Battery G was ordered to open fire on the enemy's works.

The artillery on both sides answered promptly and continued firing while General Owen's brigade was thrown forward, and cautiously advanced until the situation could be clearly discerned, when it dashed through the ford capturing the entire picket line of the enemy. A strong skirmish line was then thrown out, and, though the enemy's skirmishers heavily reënforced firmly resisted, they were driven backward step by step into their works.

No active assault was made on the enemy's works, but a semblance was vigorously kept up during the day, and at night we bivouacked on the field. We remained here during the next day until sunset, when Battery G received orders to withdraw from the front and returned to their camp, thus relieving the men of Battery B who returned to their battery at noon on the 8th all safe and sound.

This break in the winter's rest of the corps was caused by a prearranged plan of the War Department at Washington. General Butler, commanding the Army of the James, was to move rapidly upon Richmond and seek to capture the city by surprise, while the Army of the Potomac was to coöperate by moving down to the Rapidan, and pretending to assume the aggressive in order to detain General Lee's army on the line of the Rapidan.

In pursuance with this plan the Second Corps on the morning of the 6th of February moved to Morton's Ford, under command of General Caldwell, and performed the part assigned it. It is needless to say that General Butler's movement on to Richmond amounted to nothing; the loss to the Second Corps, viz.: ten men killed, sixteen officers, and one hundred and ninety-three men wounded, and one officer and forty-one men missing (taken prisoners), was greater than that of the Army of the James, which admitted having lost six forage caps.

On February the 17th, our paymaster made us a welcome visit and the battery was paid for the months of November and December, 1863. The veterans (those having reënlisted) who had not been paid received, besides the two months' pay due for 1863 (which for a sergeant was $17 per month, a corporal $14, and for a private $13), their pay for January and February, in advance, amounting to $52 for the four months, $60 of the $400 bounty for reënlisting, and the $100 due at discharge, making a total of $212 for a private. This seemed a large sum for an enlisted man, yet it would pay a good mechanic for only about three months' work.

In the afternoon the second squad of nine veteran volunteers (the reënlisted men) left for Brandy Station on their way home on a thirty-five days' furlough. They were Sergt. Anthony B. Horton, Private Benjamin A. Burlingame (who had just returned from a ten days' furlough) Willliam Dennis, Solomon A. Haskell, William J. Kenyon, William Maxey, David H. Phetteplace, Charles G. Sprague, and Robert Wilkinson.

On the 19th, Lieut. William S. Perrin, having reënlisted, left for Rhode Island on a thirty-five days' furlough as a veteran officer.

On the 22d, privates Michael Butterfield and John Doyle having reënlisted were returned to their regiments as veteran volunteers, and three of our men returned from the hospital.

For a number of days details of men from the different batteries and regiments had been very busy erecting a large building at the headquarters of the Second Corps, for the purpose of holding a grand military ball. The loggers and lumbermen in the western and down-east regiments were in their glory, and the forests, which here abounded, were soon laid low by the wielding of their axes. The saw-mill on Mountain Run was run day and night, sawing logs into joists and boards for the building, which, when finished, covered an area of two hundred by one hundred feet, with a saloon fifty feet wide extending the entire length of one side of the building. The floor and sides were of lumber, while the roof was covered with tarpaulins (canvas) furnished by the batteries and quartermaster's department of the corps. Tarpaulins are used by the batteries to cover the pieces, caissons, and harnesses in stormy weather. On the 19th of February the building was about completed, and the work of draping the inside with flags, banners, and festoons of streamers was begun. Across one end of the building a platform was erected, on either side of which was mounted a brass light twelve-pounder Napoleon gun. These pieces belonged to the left section of Battery B to whom due honor was given, and Sergeants Rhodes and Walker superintended the placing of their pieces in position upon the platform.

The ball occurred on the evening of the 22d of Feburary, 1863, and was spoken of as a grand affair. A number of ladies from Washington, Baltimore, Philadelphia, and New York attended. Senator William Sprague and wife, of Rhode Island, were also present, and were the guests of Capt. John G. Hazard at Battery B's headquarters. The building was allowed to remain undisturbed for some time, and a number of vocal and musical entertaiments were given by men of the corps. Subsequently the building was stripped and the tarpaulins, flags, and other draperies were returned to their owners.

February 24th. First Lieut. T. Fred. Brown left Battery B on detached service, having been promoted to adjutant of the First Regiment Rhode Island Light Artillery, commanded by Col. Charles H. Tompkins.

On the 27th, the Second Corps moved down to Ely's Ford, on the Rapidan, in support of General Kilpatrick's cavalry which was starting on a raid toward Richmond. Battery B was not ordered to go with the corps, and consequently remained in camp.

On the 29th, the muster rolls were made out for January and February.

March 1st. Warm and rainy. All is quiet along the Rapidan. Three more men went home on a thirty-five days' furlough as veteran volunteers: Patrick Brady, Patrick Ford, and James McGunnigle.

On the 11th, Second Lieut. Willard B. Pierce returned to the battery from Artillery Brigade headquarters.

On the 12th, Capt. John G. Hazard and Corp. C. L. Macomber went to Washington, and the latter proceeded to Rhode Island on recruiting service. Lieut. Charles A. Brown was left in command of the battery.

On the 15th, the battery dismounted the pieces, and for three days we were busy painting the gun carriages and caissons a very dark green.

On the 18th, about noon, the battery was ordered to report immediately at headquarters for light marching. The pieces were quickly mounted, and hitching up we moved out of camp reporting at headquarters, after which the battery was ordered back to camp to await further orders. This proved to be a bluff on the battery for having its pieces dismounted so long. The order had been issued by Col. J. C. Tidball, of the United States Regulars, and now commanding the Artillery Brigade of the Second Corps.

On the 19th, the battery, with the other batteries of the corps, went up to headquarters for target practice. On the plains across a ravine, at the northwest of corps headquarters, were old shelter tents set up, and at these the batteries fired shot, shell, and spherical case; firing in rotation so as to note the effect of each. At the close of the practice there were no tents standing and many were torn in shreds. Battery B fired about twenty rounds to each piece, and was credited with making the best shots with shell and spherical case.

On the 22d, our paymaster put in his appearance and we were paid for the months of January and February.

On the 23d, we experienced a very severe snow storm—the worst we had ever witnessed in Virginia. On the second day after the storm it rained, and there was mud, mud, mud, everywhere.

On the 25th, Lieut. William S. Perrin returned to duty from Rhode Island where he had been on a furlough.

On the 27th, Corporal Macomber returned from Rhode Island with a number of recruits, but only one (Getz Leonard) for Battery B.

On the 29th, the detached men of the One Hundred and Fortieth Pennsylvania regiment, who were serving with our battery, were ordered to report to Battery C, First Pennsylvania Artillery, and the detached men serving in that battery came to Battery B to take their places. The detached men received from Battery C, First Pennsylvania Artillery, were: Peter Barry, Daniel Burch, Sidney Case, Dennis Daily, Henry Mason, Samuel Mason, James McCormick, Thomas McCormick, John Monroe, Ranford Riggs, Patrick Wardon, John Williams, and Josiah Williston.

April 1st. The army had been reorganized to lessen the number of corps, while the Artillery Brigade of the Second Corps had been increased and was comprised of Battery K, Fourth United States; Battery C, Fifth United States; Tenth Massachusetts Independent

Battery; Batteries A and B, First Rhode Island Light Artillery; Battery B, First New Jersey; Battery G, First New York; Twelfth New York Independent Battery; Battery F, First Pennsylvania; Sixth Maine Battery, and First Battalion (two companies) of the Fourth New York Heavy Artillery; Col. J. C. Tidball, United States Army, commanding the brigade.

On the 7th, Capt. John G. Hazard was promoted to major, and assigned to duty at Artillery Brigade headquarters.

On the 11th, Second Lieut. Willard B. Pierce resigned and left for Washington. In the afternoon the men who were absent on furloughs returned.

During the afternoon of the 12th we had mounted inspection by Col. J. C. Tidball. The battery was under the command of Lieut. W. S. Perrin, with only one other officer, Second Lieut. Charles A. Brown, present. The rest of our officers had been promoted and assigned to other positions, or had resigned and left the service. There was a total of 141 enlisted men, forty-five of whom were detached from the infantry. There were eighteen men serving on extra duty, some being at Artillery Brigade headquarters.

On the 13th of April Lieut. T. Fred. Brown, having been promoted to captain and assigned to Battery B, First Rhode Island Light Artillery, returned and assumed command.

On the 14th, the monotony of camp life was interrupted by a most pleasant affair not soon to be forgotten; the men of Battery B desirous of manifesting their esteem and regard for their late first lieutenant, now their captain T. Fred. Brown, presented him with a magnificent and costly sabre and belt. About three o'clock P. M. the men assembled in line in front of the officers' quarters, while at the right of line was the regimental band of the Fourth New York Heavy Artillery playing an overture worthy of its reputation. By request Captain Brown stepped in front of his command, while gathered at his rear were a large number of officers from headquarters, among whom were Col. C. H. Tompkins and Lieut.-Col. J. Albert Monroe; officers of batteries A and B were also present.

Capt. H. B. Goddard, of Col. J. C. Tidball's staff, made the presentation with the following speech:

CAPTAIN BROWN: A pleasing task falls to my lot to-day, sir, in attempting to express, in behalf of the non-commissioned officers and men of Battery B, some indication of their feelings towards yourself; al-

Capt. T. Fred. Brown.

though I have not the honor of being a member of the famous First Rhode Island Light Artillery, yet I have had the pleasure of knowing you, and knowing this and other batteries of your regiment. Accordingly, I deem it a high honor to be allowed to express the feelings of the men of one of the most famous batteries that "Little Rhody" ever gave to her country, towards as brave an officer and true a gentleman as ever drew a sabre in the great cause of the Union. Your history, sir, is known to all of us. We know how the "Little Corporal" of June, 1861, has worked his way up, winning his sergeant's stripes, after the First Bull Run, by attention to his duties all through the long tedious winter of 1861 and '62, when we were just beginning to discover that a soldier's life was not altogether a holiday affair. We know how he fought his way up through the weary mud-marches, and hard fights of the Peninsula Campaign. Worthily he won his second lieutenant's straps just before the short, swift, but glorious First Maryland Campaign with Antietam's blood won field as its noble reward. Then came the fearful assault on Fredericksburg, where this battery won lasting laurels, and the encomiums of the corps commander, for devoted gallantry in one of the most exposed positions in which a battery was ever placed. The bar of a first lieutenant was a fitting reward to you for that hard fight. During last year's campaign this battery was commanded by you at the Second Fredericksburg, or Marye's Heights, and at Gettysburg "the grandest of them all," where you were stricken from your horse by a rebel bullet, proving conclusively that in your country's cause limb nor life were held too dear to give. Right gladly did the men of this command ascertain that your wound, though severe, was not dangerous, and most happy were they all to see you resume command, which you did in time to lead them into the pretty little victory at Bristoe, where again your battery won laurels. Again, at Mine Run, the conduct of the "ever ready" battery was above fear and above reproach. Such a record is alike glorious to yourself and to the men now gathered about you. During all this period, sir, you have been singularly fortunate in the difficult task of performing your duties to the entire satisfaction of your superiors, at the same time winning the love and respect of your men.

Now, after receiving a third promotion as adjutant of your regiment, you return to us with the crowning wish of your and our hearts gratified, by your commission as captain of your own best-loved battery, the non-commissioned officers and men of its organization deem it a fitting opportunity to present a token of their esteem. In their behalf I prepresent you this sword and belt. Accept them, sir, as a fitting tribute from gallant men to a gallant officer."

The captain maintaining his reputation for coolness and self-possession replied earnestly and gracefully as follows:

"MEN OF BATTERY B: Two months ago, if made the recipient of this generous and elegant token of your esteem, I could only have expressed my gratitude by reiterating again and again my attachment to the men before me and to the memory of those who ever stood shoulder to shoulder with you, and who are now sleeping on every battle-field. But to-day it is far different. I can thank you far better than by words. My chief desire (that I expressed to you two months ago on my departure) has been granted, to be with you in the coming campaign. And my thanks shall be expressed in the making of every effort to prepare ourselves for the work before us, and making them in the hope of drawing this sabre in some crowning triumph—some second Gettysburg."

Three rousing cheers were given for Captain Brown, and the men broke ranks to drink his health, and listen to the band which played several pieces finely. The sabre was a beautiful piece of workmanship and did credit to the taste of the committee, Sergeants Charles H. Adams and Charles A. Libbey, Corporals Aborn W. Carter and Charles A. Rider, and Private Stephen Collins, who were entrusted with its selection. The blade was beautifully ornamented with emblematic designs raised upon the steel, while upon the scabbard was the Goddess of Liberty artistically engraved. The grip was of ivory on which was raised the artillery emblem of cross cannons and equipments, and the hilt was surmounted by a beautiful little gold eagle, with wings spread. Upon the scabbard was a silver plate on which was inscribed: "Presented to First Lieut. T. Fred. Brown by the members of Battery B, First Regiment Rhode Island Light Artillery, at Stevensburg, Va., April 1864.*

It was a most pleasant and successful affair, and will be remembered by those present as one of the most pleasing events in their military service.

April 17th. Lieut. C. A. Brown, and a detail of men, went to Brandy Station and returned with two new light twelve-pounder Napoleon guns and caissons complete. On the 18th the pieces and caissons were inspected, the equipments were found complete and the chests packed with ammunition. Two gun detachments were organized with Sergt. Charles H. Adams and Corp. C. W. Wood (acting sergeant) as sergeants of the new pieces.

On the 19th, the battery went up to headquarters for target practice. In the afternoon several detached men were received from the Fourth New York Heavy Artillery.

On the 20th, the artillery brigade of the Second Corps under command of Major John G. Hazard, who had returned from Rhode

* At the time the sabre was ordered it was not known to the men that Lieutenant Brown was to be made captain of the battery.

Island where he had been on recruiting service for the artillery, was reviewed by Major-General Hancock.

On the 21st, the battery received another squad of recruits for duty from Battery G, First Pennsylvania. The afternoon was spent in preparing for corps review.

April 22d. Pleasant and warm. Reveille at sunrise, and from that time until nine o'clock A. M. the men were busy with the duties of the day. At the above hour Battery B hitched up and left camp for the plains near headquarters, and arriving there it took position in line of the artillery brigade to the right of the infantry of the corps. For the first time since the consolidation and the reënforcement by the two veteran divisions of the ex-Third Corps, assigned to the Second, the troops were brought together. No change of camps was deemed advisable at the time of consolidation, and consequently the troops, although under the same command, found little more opportunity to form acquaintances than when they were in different corps.

The day was splendid, the first bright and sunny one after many days of storm and mud. The plain (the ground selected for the review) was so admirably adapted that, from the position of the reviewing stand, the eye could take in the whole corps without effort. The troops were arranged in four lines directly in front of the stand, the divisions being placed in their numerical order: General Barlow's division, the first; General Gibbon's division, the second; General Birney's division, the third; General Mott's division, the fourth.

The artillery brigade was formed on the right flank of and perpendicular to the infantry; the troops thus formed two sides of a square. The brilliant assemblage of spectators combined to make this the finest corps review ever seen in the Army of the Potomac.

Just before noon the reviewing officer, Lieut.-Gen. U. S. Grant, accompanied by his personal staff mounted the "stand," and took position in front while the bands played "Hail to the Chief." Among the spectators were Generals Meade, Humphreys, Williams, Hunt, and many from army headquarters. Generals Sedgwick and Warren commanders of the Sixth and Fifth Corps were also present. More than twenty-five thousand men actually marched by in review, and their appearance and bearing were brilliant in the extreme, while the scene was most exhilarating and the entire review admirably conducted. It proved a day of compliments, and none received more than the artillery of which Maj. John G. Hazard was chief. Two Rhode Island batteries A and B participated in the event, and in the judgment of many were not behind those longer in service (the United States batteries) regarding the details of their movements and fine appearance. Battery B returned to camp late in the afternoon hungry and very much fatigued, but nevertheless well satisfied with the work of the day.

The 23d was pleasant and warm. At ten A. M. had battery inspection by Captain Brown, and subsequently stretched the picket rope to the left of the quarters so as to give the horses a change of ground. The appearance of things in general indicated that the battery would soon move; and, sure enough, on the 26th at eleven o'clock A. M. the battery broke camp, packed up, and moved to Stevensburg within a quarter of a mile of corps headquarters, and going into park bivouacked.

On the 28th, moved our park about three hundred yards to the east on a knoll, and went into camp. In the afternoon there was a horse race at corps headquarters witnessed by a number of men in the battery, they having been granted passes to go and see it. During the past two months there were several races held on the plains near headquarters, and much interest was manifested in them; they served to determine which of the generals had the fastest horse, the division or brigade commanders.

Private Alfred G. Gardner.

CHAPTER XX.

GENERAL GRANT'S CAMPAIGN—FROM THE WILDERNESS TO COLD HARBOR.

SUNDAY, May 1st. Pleasant and warm. The battery had mounted inspection and the usual Sunday morning camp inspection by Captain Brown, followed by the granting of passes to those who made the best appearance in dress, and answered readily the questions asked by the inspecting officer.

The 2d was passed in drill at the manual of the piece. Late in the afternoon Captain Brown received marching orders, and the cooks were instructed to prepare and cook three days' rations of beef.

On the morning of the 3d, the caissons were parked and five days' rations of grain, with hard-tack, coffee, and sugar were strapped on the chests, and three days' rations were issued to each man to be carried in his haversack. At five o'clock P. M., tents were struck and packed, and the battery hitched up awaiting orders. On the eve of moving the battery received two additional officers, namely: First Lieut. James E. Chace, promoted from second lieutenant of Battery G, Rhode Isand; and Second Lieut. Gideon Spencer, promoted from sergeant of Battery D, Rhode Island. Thus Battery B was to start on the coming campaign fully officered, viz.: Capt. T. Fred. Brown, commanding; First Lieut. William S. Perrin in command of first or right section; First Lieut. James E. Chace in command of the third or left section; Second Lieut. Charles A. Brown in command of the second or centre section and Second Lieut. Gideon Spencer in command of battery train consisting of battery wagon, forge, army wagons (for baggage and forage), and spare horses. The total number of men present and on detached service at this time was 174, all well clothed and equipped for the coming campaign.

In the movement of the army now about to be made, it was generally known that it would be against General Lee's army, and not "On to Richmond," as had usually been the cry when the Army of the Potomac was about to move. To reach the field of operation the Second Corps, to which Battery B was attached, had by far the longest distance to traverse as it was to make a crossing at Ely's Ford, while the other corps were to cross at Culpeper Mine Ford and the Germania Ford; then all were to move in the direction of the Confederate army.

The first troops to move and resume the line of march were those of the Second Corps. In the afternoon of the 3d, the infantry stood massed on the road leading from Stevensburg to Richardsville, and, at half-past seven o'clock P. M., the order was given: "Forward, march!" and tramp, tramp the boys went marching on, all in good spirits and eager for the fray.

At eight o'clock P. M., Battery B broke camp, and moving with the First Division passed corps headquarters, and turning to the left marched all night. A halt was made at sunrise and Captain Brown received orders to park on the right of the road; then the horses were fed, and ample time was given for the men to make coffee. At seven o'clock A. M., of the 4th, the battery resumed the march to the river, and at eight o'clock we crossed the Rapidan at Ely's Ford by fording the river. After going a short distance we were forced to halt for an hour on account of the road being so crowded with troops and trains. At noon we arrived at Chancellorsville where we were ordered into position in battery with the First Division, which had been formed in line of battle to await the coming up of the rest of the corps.

The position occupied by the battery was on the same ground held by the Fifth Maine Battery on the 3d of May, 1863, at the battle of Chancellorsville. The ground was still strewn with the wreckage of that carnage in the form of torn knapsacks, haversacks, battered canteens and broken muskets. On this field Battery B bivouacked for the night.

On the morning of the 5th, the battery, with the division, took an early start, for at sunrise we were on the road moving south. With Lieutenant Perrin in command, the first section, with the fourth brigade, acted as rear guard. At the cross roads, called Three Fur-

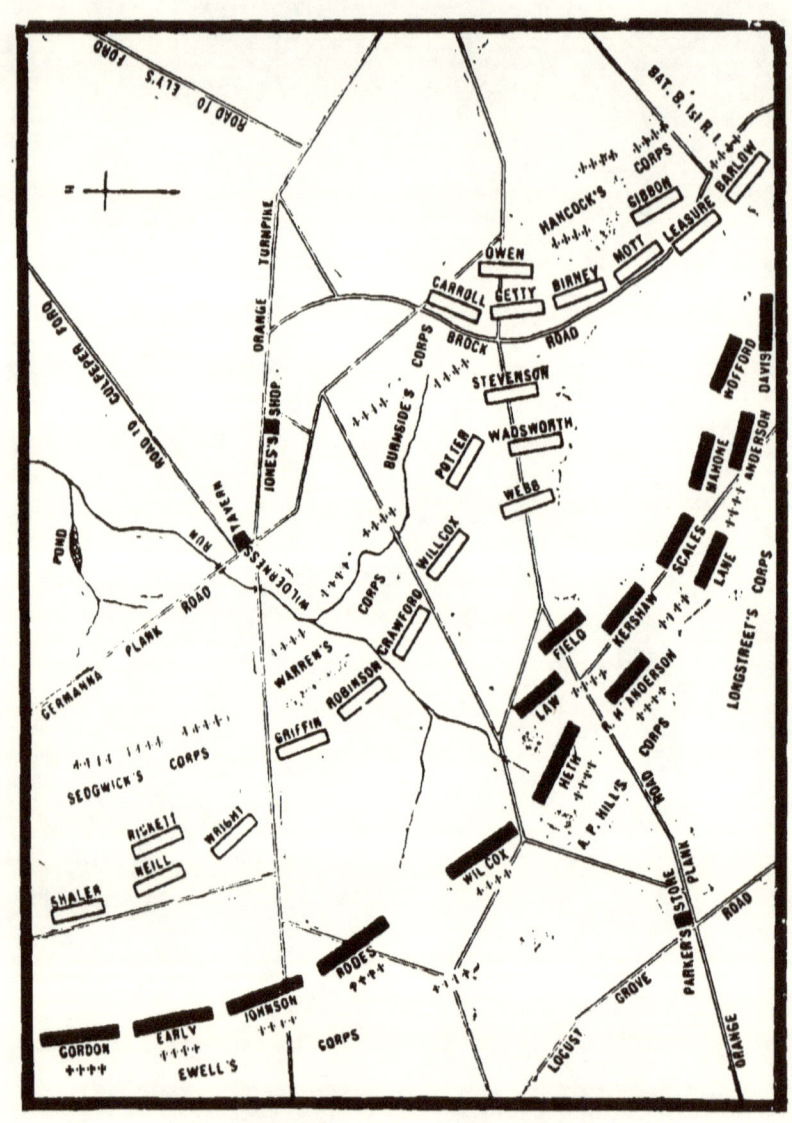

Wilderness, May 5-8, 1864.

naces, the battery was ordered into position on a knoll, to the left of the road, where we waited for an hour until Captain Brown was ordered to advance further to the front. Giving orders to limber to the front he led the battery along a very narrow road to the vicinity of Todd's Tavern where we halted. Upon our arrival firing was heard back to the right, and the division received orders to turn back and support those engaged. The battery, in countermarching, moved very slowly along the narrow road until the Brock road was reached, when it proceeded at a trot led by Colonel Tidball, and, at five o'clock P. M., took position on a ridge to the left of the road in rear of our main line of battle. Orders were immediately given to prepare for action, and we shelled the woods in our front for about half an hour. Captain Brown received orders to advance the battery still further to the left and front, and take position in the midst of some small scrub pines. With no little difficulty we placed the pieces in battery, and then fired a few round of shot in the direction of the enemy's lines located within the woods. The battery remained in position all night, the men bivouacking beside the pieces. This place was rightly named "The Wilderness," with its uneven ground and heavily wooded ravines and ridges, which, together with its tangled thickets of pines, cedars, and scrub oaks, greatly hindered the movements of the artillery, but nevertheless a number of batteries, including Battery B, were placed in good positions and did excellent service. The appalling rattle of musketry, the roar of the artillery, the yells of the rebels, and the cheering of our own men were constantly heard. At times our men, when firing, could not see the array of the enemy's lines less than fifty yards distant. The line of fire grew longer and longer, extending to right and left, proving that one of the fiercest battles of history had begun amid dense woods where the foemen could not see one another, where colonels could not see the whole of their regiments, and where captains could not see the left of their companies. Both armies thus suddenly brought into collision fought a desperate battle until night came and forced a halt in the strife. Neither side had gained any decided advantage, though the enemy (Hill's corps) had been driven some distance backward, and hundreds on either side had fallen. Many of those surviving had not yet seen the enemy.

The battery's casualties during the Battle of the Wilderness, on May 5th, were five men wounded: Corp. Charles B. Worthington; Privates Levi J. Cornell, Francis Slaiger, Peter Barry, and Dennis

Dailey; the last two were detached men. Three horses were disabled for further service.

At early dawn on the morning of the 6th, the battery was further advanced to the right and front, and took a position overlooking an unfinished railroad bed. At intervals during the forenoon we shelled the woods on our right front. In the afternoon the firing which had been going on down on the right extended up to the left, and, at about four P. M., broke out with renewed vigor. Captain Brown subsequently ordered the right half of the battery to change front, and it was turned to the west at right angles with the main line, giving us the impression that the enemy had broken through in that direction.

The direct cause, however, was the advance of the enemy in force along the Orange Plank road, while the Second Corps troops were being replenished with ammunition, causing part of the line to fall back. It was a most critical moment, particularly on account of the generally strained and tried condition of our troops, rather than from the actual number of the enemy who had thus gained an entrance; but startling as was the exigency it was promptly met. Carroll's brigade lay in reserve at the right of the Plank road, and this was sent forward. Putting his brigade into motion General Carroll, at the head of the column with bandaged arm, dashed across the road, and coming to a "front" charged forward encountering the exultant Confederates in the very moment of their triumph, thus averting the impending danger. The enemy was forced to retire to the woods, and firing soon died down along the left of the line.

The only part taken by Battery B was to throw a few shells into the woods at the retreating foe, and though the tangled forest had been alive with flying missiles and the whistling of the bullets through the air had been incessant we had no casualties. Many of those falling in the fight were still lying between the lines in the woods, which to our horror had taken fire in many places in front of the Brock road, and consequently no relief could be given to many who perished in the flames.

At dusk the battery was ordered to bivouac in the breastworks, but the men obtained little sleep on account of the picket firing, and being aroused several times to prepare for action though not engaging.

All day of the 7th, we remained quietly in position, though at intervals there was heavy skirmish firing in our front. At sunset the battery was withdrawn from the front, and went into park on the north side of the Brock road bivouacking for the night, while the horses remained in harness. The tumult made by the Fifth Corps, as they marched down to the left on a flank movement, was so great that sleep was next to an impossibility.

At eight A. M. on the 8th, the battery marched to Todd's Tavern and halted to feed the horses, but before they could eat their grain we were ordered to the front in line of battle. The place we were to occupy was covered with pine trees which had to be cut down before the pieces could be placed in position; after getting in battery we opened on the enemy's line with shot and shell at a distance of 1,300 yards. A rebel battery answered sending shell all around us, which cut off the tops of the trees in our front giving us a better view of their lines, and although their shot and pieces of shell came remarkably close no one was wounded. The men fortified their position and bivouacked for the night. At dusk our teamsters, Bob Niles and Welk Collins came up with forage and rations which were issued to the battery. The Second Corps at this time was holding the Catharpin road against any attempt of the enemy to cut the roads, by which the troops and trains were moving down to the left toward Fredericksburg, the place for the base of General Grant's supplies.

On the 9th, at early dawn, the battery was ordered to the rear, where the horses were fed and groomed while the men made coffee, and ate a hearty breakfast of fried salt pork and hard-tack washed down with hot coffee. In a short time Captain Brown received orders to move to the front again, and to send a section with the bearer of the order. By Captain Brown's orders Lieutenant Spencer took the centre section and went with the staff officer. The other sections were then ordered to hitch up and were sent to the right and front, where they were placed in position in the breastworks thrown up by the First Division (General Barlow's) where we remained until noon.

The centre section under Lieutenant Spencer was taken by the staff officer to a deep ravine, at the head of which the pieces were placed in position. The nature of the surroundings were such that, had the enemy made a charge at this point, there were grave doubts in the lieutenant's mind whether the guns could have been withdrawn, owing to a steep incline at his rear while the sides of the ravine were covered with low shrubs. Fortunately there was no attack made by the enemy at this place.

At noon the division (the First) was withdrawn and ordered down to the left. The battery left the breastworks, and, pulling out into the road, where the second section soon joined it, followed the division marching south to, and beyond the position occupied by the Second Division under General Gibbon the day before. Here three divisions of the Second Corps were drawn up in line on high ground overlooking the Po River.

While Battery B was getting into position in line, a wagon train of the enemy was seen passing along beside the woods on the opposite side of the river, and within easy range of our ten-pound rifle guns. Battery A, First Rhode Island, which with the troops (Brooke's brigade of Barlow's division) had been sent forward toward the river was ordered into position and soon opened fire upon the train. The first few shots created a wild stampede among the non-belligerents, and sent the wagons flying along the road toward the cover of the woods. Troops were ordered across the river to capture the train, which would perhaps have been effected if the teamsters had not been goaded into a wild flight by the shelling administered to them. We were not to have it all our own way, however, for soon a rebel battery retaliated, but by the random flight of shot and shell (which favored our troops and Battery A) its men seemed as thoroughly frightened as the teamsters; many missiles passed over Battery B which was half a mile in rear of Battery A.

The centre section had opened on the enemy's train with spherical case, and had fired but a few rounds when a rebel battery to its left across the river opened on it, and a shell bursting at one of the guns killed William Dennis and Ezra L. Fowles, the latter a detached man from the Nineteenth Maine regiment. Captain Brown ordered the other two sections of the battery down to the support of the centre section, and taking position they opened fire on the rebel battery, which after firing a few shot limbered up and withdrew out of our range. By this time the One Hundred and Forty-fifth Pennsylvania regiment had with much difficulty effected a crossing and climbed the steep and densely wooded banks overcoming all obstacles with energy. A pontoon bridge was soon thrown across the river which was about fifty feet wide, and the First Division (General Barlow) was soon on the south side.

About sunset Battery B limbered up, moved down to the river and crossed following the division to the left, and advancing about two miles halted on rising ground. Here we placed the guns in position and bivouacked for the night.

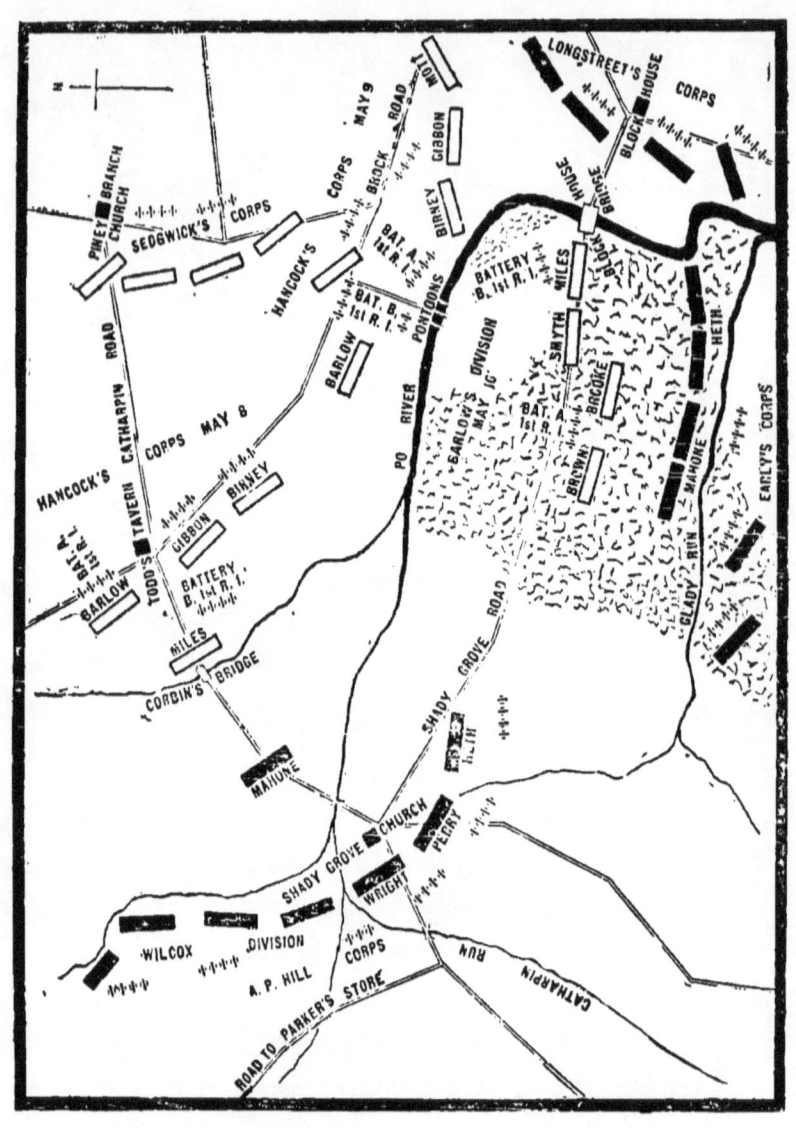

Todd's Tavern and Po River, May 8-10, 1864.

May 10th, was pleasant and warm. At sunrise the three divisions of the Second Corps were all across the Po River threatening General Lee's left flank. General Barlow's division was in advance, and facing to the east on the Shady Grove Church road near the Block House bridge. Battery B was in position on the road facing the bridge.

About eight o'clock A. M. a rebel battery showed itself on our left flank, and the third section, under Lieutenant Chase, opened fire upon it with spherical case; as a consequence it soon withdrew from sight without answering. About ten o'clock A. M. a column of rebel infantry was seen in our front moving to the southwest, upon which our battery opened a fire with shot and spherical case, so well directed that the column was broken in several places. To this a rebel battery answered, but its fire was so high and wild that most of its shot went over us making our casualties light, only one man being slightly wounded. The firing only lasted about ten minutes then all was quiet. The battery was subsequently ordered to the right where the enemy appeared to be in force, and, after placing the pieces in position, we threw up breastworks, working like beavers. About two P. M. we were ordered to retreat to the north side of the Po which we did without difficulty, crossing the river on the middle pontoon bridge, and afterward taking position on high open ground about four hundred yards from the river bank. This position was a fine one overlooking the valley of the Po, and commanding the approaches to and from the place of crossing by which our infantry was to recross when it withdrew, which it did in a cool and orderly manner. All the batteries except Battery A, First Rhode Island, under Captain Arnold, had withdrawn and ordered to recross to the north side of the Po, and take position along its bank so as to sweep with shot and shell the ground over which the enemy must advance in following up our men as they retreated. In the existing situation to fight seemed as easy as it was imminent, but to retreat with the river at our backs and the enemy in full advance in our front was a most critical matter, and such the general in command felt it to be. The infantry brigades, which had formed the advance line, were withdrawn and took position back of their support, while the enemy pressed rapidly on with a furious fire of musketry, under which our brigades of gallant veterans retired with the utmost coolness reaching the position assigned them in perfect order. Thus the first step in the critical operation was accomplished, and the next was to withdraw the second line (now the front by the withdrawal of the first) to the ridge in front of the bridges. This was rapidly and skillfully done while the troops, the moment they were in position, sought to protect themselves by throwing up rails and such material as they could lay hands upon.

The enemy, doubtless deeming the withdrawal of our lines a sign of fear, pressed forward and fell upon the troops of Brown's and Brooke's brigades. The combat now became close and bloody while the enemy, flushed with the anticipation of an easy victory, was apparently determined to crush the small force opposing it, and, rushing forward with loud yells, forced its way close up to our line delivering a terrible musketry fire as it advanced. Our brave troops resisted this onset with an undaunted determination to stand their ground, and made the fire along our whole line so continuous and deadly that the enemy abandoned its stand, and breaking retreated in wild disorder.

During this repulse the woods in the rear and right of our troops caught fire, and the flames rapidly approached our lines, rendering it almost impossible to retain the situation longer. General Barlow directed Brown and Brooke to abandon their positions and retire, and recross to the north side of the Po. The withdrawal was attended with extreme difficulty and peril, as the men were nearly enveloped in the burning woods while their front was assailed by an overwhelming force of the enemy. They displayed wonderful coolness and nerve, however, such as was rarely seen or exhibited in the presence of dangers so appalling; indeed, it seemed as if those gallant soldiers were doomed to destruction. The enemy perceiving that our lines were again retiring advanced, but was again promptly checked by our troops, who then fell back through the burning forest with admirable order; though in so doing a large number were killed and wounded, while many on both sides perished in the flames.

In retiring the terrified horses attached to one of the pieces of Battery A, First Rhode Island Light Artillery, became unmanageable and dragged their piece between two trees where it became so firmly wedged that it could not be moved, and had to be abandoned to its fate. This was the first piece of artillery lost by the Second Corps in battle.

The troops after emerging from the woods had to traverse an open plain, lying between Shady Grove Church road and the river, which was swept by the enemy's artillery stationed on the heights above the Block House bridge on the east side of the river. As the last troops, Miles's brigade, were about to withdraw the enemy opened a tremendous artillery and musketry fire, from left and front, across this open space directly in front of Miles's troops. Our artillery was too numerous and too well placed to allow this to long continue, and, the enemy, after having one or two of its limbers or caissons blown up, was silenced. The advance of its infantry having been checked at the first outbreak of its fire, General Miles took advantage of the repulse and withdrew by the bridges, crossing rapidly but in perfect order. When the troops were again back on the north side of the river Po the pontoons were at once taken up.

Battery B's position was directly north in line of the middle bridge covering the retreat of the infantry, and when our troops began to retreat we opened fire with spherical case on the enemy's line which was advancing. We fired rapidly but with deliberate aim and good effect. Meanwhile the enemy opened upon us with a battery on our left flank wounding four men and one horse. The left section then turned and delivered a fire upon the foe, but after firing a few rounds in the direction of the enemy's battery we ceased firing, and turned our fire again on the enemy's infantry which was crowding our troops on the ridge south of the bridges. At this time Sergeant Rhodes observed that the shots from his piece (the sixth gun) were going away to the right toward our own troops; upon making an examination he discovered that the iron axle was broken, having been hit with shot or shell in the middle where the bolt passed through to fasten it to the wooden stock. This caused the middle, the axle now being in two pieces, to settle down from the stock bringing the top of the wheels nearer together, and causing the gun carriage to lean to the right, throwing the windage too much to the left side of the shot sending them to the right, and not in the direction aimed. Sergeant Rhodes ordered his gunner to cease firing, and reported his piece as disabled to chief of section Lieutenant Chace. Captain Brown upon learning of the accident ordered Lieutenant Spencer, who had just come upon the field, to have the piece taken to the rear. In charge of Sergeant Rhodes it was withdrawn from the line of battle, and under direction of Lieutenant Spencer taken to the rear where the battery train was parked. The blacksmith Joseph B. Place was ordered to try and weld the axle, but before he had time to build a fire in the forge the train received orders to move, and the attempt to weld the axle was abandoned. The broken axle was strapped up and the gun moved along with the train.

Battery B remained in position until after the taking up of the pontoons when it was ordered to withdraw and move to the rear. Notwithstanding that the battery had been under fire all day the casualties were light, one horse being killed and four men slightly wounded. The battery was again ordered into position on a hill about half a mile from the river, near the road which passed to the left of the first position. On getting into battery it opened fire, throwing a few shell into the woods across the river. After a few rounds were thrown we received orders to cease, and bivouacked in this position for the night.

Just after midnight we were routed up and ordered to build breastworks in front of the pieces, as it was expected that the enemy would try to cross the river, it being reported that a large force was massed on the south side of the Po. By daylight we had our breastworks finished and then we laid down to get a little rest if possible.

On the morning of the 11th, the horses which had remained in harness all night were unhitched, unharnessed, taken to water, fed, and groomed. The pieces remained at the breastworks, and during the day the cannoneers occasionally sent the compliments of Battery B, in the shape of solid shot, to the enemy who could plainly be seen throwing up earthworks on the south side of the Po River. Our compliments were not returned. At night the men bivouacked in the breastworks under arms. At eleven o'clock P. M. we were routed up and withdrawing from the front line marched to near corps headquarters, where we halted until three o'clock on the morning of the 12th, when we moved east to the left of the line, and at daylight took position in rear of Brooke's brigade (General Barlow's division, Second Corps) south of Brown's house. There was a clearing here from three to four hundred yards wide and extended to the left toward the Landrum house, thence curving to the right toward the earthworks now occupied by the enemy, and our next point of attack. The rest of the ground was thickly wooded and a heavy fog was spread over the scene. Just about sunrise the troops began to move forward to the charge, the First and Third Divisions, General Barlow's and Birney's leading, supported by the Second Division, General Gibbon.

General Birney's troops met some difficult ground in their advance, but pushed on with superhuman exertions and again came up abreast of the First Division. On reaching the Landrum house the enemy's picket reserve opened fire on the left flank of General Barlow's column which was swiftly passing by. This fire our troops disdained to notice, but continued moving steadily forward. As soon as the curve in the clearing was reached, and the troops saw the red earth of the enemy's line they (General Barlow's men) broke into a wild cheer, and starting on the double-quick rushed against the works. Tearing away the abattis the troops sprang over the intrenchments, shooting, bayoneting, and beating down those who opposed them. Almost at the same time General Birney's troops entered the works on his side making the charge a success, and the salient was won. Crazed with excitement and success the men could not be restrained, but followed the flying enemy until its second line of works was reached. Here the now disorganized mass of Birney's and Barlow's troops was brought to a stand by the resolute front of the enemy's reserve. As soon as the enemy's line had been carried General Hancock ordered up the artillery, and Battery B on a double-quick went trotting to the front as fast as the nature of the ground would permit, and, taking position in battery, within three hundred yards of the captured works, opened on the flying enemy with shot and spherical case shell, firing over the heads of our pursuing troops into the space traversed by the rebels. Rain was falling in torrents, and clouds of smoke hung over the scene obscuring the surrounding country from view.

Thus far the attack had been a grand success, but on account of the failure of connection, and the delay in the arrival of reënforcements (caused by the rain, mud, and smoke) our men were forced back to the first line of earthworks. Everything that General Hancock and his commanders could do to prepare for a new advance was done. The reserve division was ordered to a man to the captured works, and the leading brigades, broken by the fury of the assault, were assembled as well as possible under the furious fire now poured in from the enemy's second line. The Sixth Corps coming up had taken position on the right of the Second, occupying the line to the southwest. The troops were at once set to work preparing the captured intrenchments for use against those who had constructed them. The fortifications at this point were elaborately constructed of heavy timber banked with earth to the heighth of nearly four feet, above which was placed what was known as a head log, raised just high enough to enable the muskets to be inserted between it and the lower work. Pointed logs formed an abattis, in front of which was a deep ditch. The work of changing the front of the breastworks was soon made and there was not a moment to spare, for into that bloody space were advancing hundreds of stout soldiers desperately determined to retrieve their defeat of the morning.

During the successive encounters all those troops who had crossed over the breastworks into the space enclosed by the salient, had been driven out, and the Second Corps now held only the outer side of the intrenchments which they had captured in the assault. The Sixth which had gained the enemy's works at the right of the Second Corps, opened a terrible fire of musketry into the space traversed by the enemy, and the conflict became the closest and fiercest of the assault. The enemy was determined to recover its intrenchments at whatever cost, and for nearly a mile, amid a cold drenching rain, the combatants were literally struggling across the breastworks, firing directly into each other's faces, while bayonet thrusts were given over the intrenchments, and the men even grappled with each other across the piles of logs, the strongest pulling his antagonist over the work to the victor's side to be carried to the rear as prisoner. The contest had settled down to a struggle for the recovery of the apex of the salient between the east and west angle. If any comparison can be made between the sections involved in that desperate contest, the fiercest and deadliest fighting took place at the west angle ever afterward known as "The Bloody Angle." As General Grant was preparing for an assault at different parts of the line with the corps of Generals Burnside and Warren, General Meade's order was to "Tell Hancock to hold on." And Hancock held on with his men, four ranks deep, keeping their furious assailants at bay and from retaking their lost line. He even ordered artillery up to the intrenchments (a section of Battery C, Fifth United States, and one of Battery B, First Rhode Island Light Artillery) and, though the muzzles protruded into the very faces of the charging enemy, the begrimed cannoneers continued to pour canister into the woods and over the open ground on the west of the McCool house. This was, I believe, the first if not the only instance in the history of the war, where artillery charged on breastworks.

After the capture of the Confederate works Battery B was ordered to the front, and, taking position just under a hill among small pine trees, to the left of those already mentioned, opened fire with spherical case. Of course we could not see the enemy's line, but we elevated our pieces so as to clear our own infantry. While the battery was thus engaged a staff officer rode up to Capt. T. Fred.

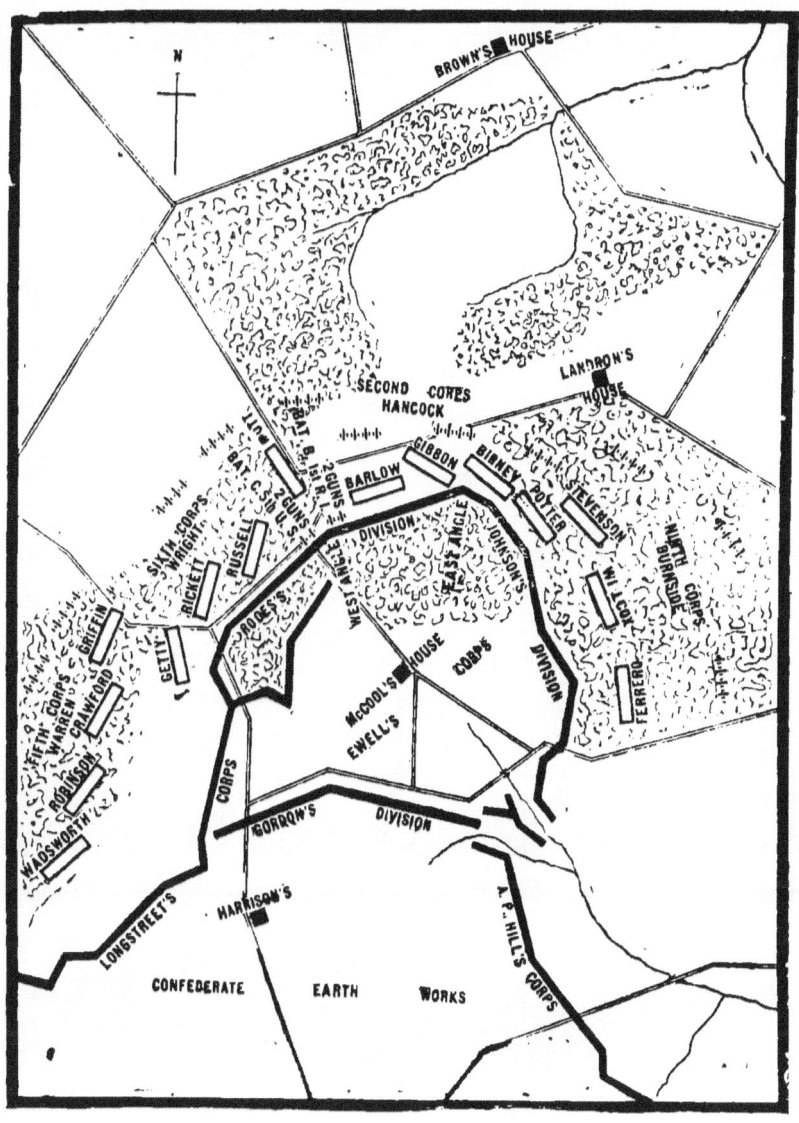

Bloody Angle at Spottsylvania May 12, 1864.

Brown and engaged in conversation. Captain Brown nodded and ordered the battery to cease firing. Then turning to Lieut. Charles A. Brown he ordered him to advance with his section. The lieutenant then gave the command: "At-ten-tion!—drivers mount—limber to the front—cannoneers mount—caissons rear—forward—trot—march!" and away they went, up hill and down, to the very earthworks, and wheeling into position commenced firing canister at the flying enemy as it left its intrenchments. Being some distance in front of our infantry, it was a matter of fact that artillery at short range could not live long under such a fire as the enemy was pouring in upon it. The cannoneers went down in short order, but the pieces did not cease sending their compliments to the rebels until the limber chests were empty of ammunition. The effect of our canister and spherical case upon the enemy was terrible, as it was evidently trying to strengthen its first line from its second when our pieces opened fire on it, and one can imagine the execution at such short range.

The battle was now at white heat, and to our right was one continual roar of musketry. The rain continued to fall, and clouds of smoke hung over the scene. Like leeches our infantry stuck to the earthworks, determined by its fire to keep the enemy from rising up, but as it began to shrink in numbers it backed off from the works, though still keeping up a fusilade; soon, however, it closed up its shattered ranks, and being reënforced settled down again to its task of holding the captured line. As the centre section of Battery B was being withdrawn from the breastworks some of the horses of each team were wounded, thus becoming unmanageable, and cannoneers from the right section were sent to their relief, drawing the pieces back to the hollow by hand, then, with fresh horses, the section returned to the battery. Leaving the caissons in the hollow the battery advanced to the left and front to the breastworks which had been turned by our infantry. Upon the trenches, filled with the dead and covered with pine boughs and earth, stood our pieces in position, sending shot after shot into the enemy's lines in the woods.

In the afternoon Sergeant Rhodes returned to the battery, and was given command of the fourth gun in the centre section, which had been under charge of Corporal Wood. As night approached the men made shed roofs from the top of the breastworks with poles and pine boughs covered with earth, making a very fair protection for the cannoneers at the pieces. Those at the limbers dug holes and made a roof over them of the same material, in which rude structures the men bivouacked for the night. The battle lasted all day long and even into the night, for it was not until after twelve o'clock midnight, twenty hours after the command of "Forward" had been given, that the firing slackened and the rebels, relinquishing their attempts to retake their lost works, commenced under cover of the darkness to construct a new line. So ended this bloody day, and those that slept after its tremendous labor and its fierce excitement had in them, for the time, hardly more of life than the corpses that lay around on every side. A chilling rain still fell upon that ghastly field.

May 13th. Cold and still raining. At daybreak it was found that the rebels had retired from the salient and constructed intrenchments, which cut off entirely that portion of their line our troops had captured from them.

Battery B remained at the breastworks on Laurel Hill all day, but did not fire a shot. The enemy's sharpshooters, however, made it quite lively and interesting for us, and we were compelled to have our wits about us taking care not to expose ourselves needlessly, for the zip and ping of the sharpshooter bumble bees flew in all directions. At night the men again bivouacked in their earth huts.

May 14th, showery and cold. The battery withdrew from the breastworks and went to the rear, where the caissons were parked, and encamped. Here the horses were fed and groomed, while the men had a royal good time preparing something for the inner man, consisting of hot coffee, fried salt pork, and hard tack. Sharp skirmish firing had been going on all the forenoon on the right and front. About two P. M. the battery was ordered to hitch up, and the pieces, with the caisson limbers going to the right and front, took position in battery in the breastworks of the picket line of General Miles's brigade. The sharpshooters on both sides were quite busy in our front, for between the two lines lay two brass guns, light twelve-pounders, both very near our skirmish line. These guns were in the works which were captured from the rebels on the 12th, and had been run out by our men toward our line, but had been abandoned at the time of the fight at the bloody angle, and had since stood there in plain view of both lines of skirmishers, though neither side would allow the other to approach the guns. The rebels desired to retake them, but we also wanted them, and having run them so near to our lines we determined if possible to gain their possession. Battery B was ordered to open fire on the rebel skirmish line, and sending spherical case into the tops of the trees made things very unpleasant for the enemy's sharpshooters. The battery fired from fifteen to twenty rounds to a piece in quick succession, causing a cloud of smoke to form between the two lines which served to cover our actions from the enemy. Under cover of our fire Corp. Josiah McMeekin and Stephen Collins, who had volunteered, went out to the rebel guns and attaching prolonges to the trails of each, a company of infantry of the Sixty-first New York regiment drew them within our lines, the cannoneers of Battery B helping to get them over the breastworks. This dangerous enterprise was successfully accomplished amid the loud cheering of the brigade. The fruits of our capture were two guns, one limber, and two caissons, which by Lieut. W. S. Perrin with drivers of the caisson limbers were taken to the rear near headquarters of Artillery Brigade, and Captain Brown returned to camp with the battery.

Early on the morning of the 15th, the battery was routed out to hitch up, and at half-past three o'clock A. M. moved to the left about two and a half miles, where it halted for two hours beside the Spottsylvania and Fredericksburg road, near the Ny River, to allow the infantry to pass, when it again moved forward to the right of the road and went into park bivouacking on Hart's farm near General Grant's and army headquarters. The First and Second Division of the Second Corps, which came with us, went to the front, while the Third Division remained at the breastworks on the right of the Ninth Corps. During the day the enemy, with a number of pieces of artillery, opened fire on the breastworks evacuated by the Second Corps, but did little damage.

On the 16th, the weather was still cloudy with frequent showers, while affairs remained unchanged at the front. Battery B remained encamped near headquarters and enjoyed a day's rest. The corps to-day received about eight thousand reënforcements from the defenses of Washington, comprised of Gen. R. O. Tyler's Division of Heavy Artillery and the Corcoran Legion.

May 17th. Reveille at sunrise, the weather was pleasant and warm. At eight o'clock A. M. the battery broke camp near headquarters, and, moving to a strip of woods on the right went into park, while the men bivouacked on a field in front, and the horses were picketed in the woods. Our supply wagons came up to camp, and fresh rations of coffee, sugar, pork, and hard-tack were issued, also boots and clothing to those in need. Orders were received that all batteries were to be reduced to four guns on account of the limited number of men and horses. Captain Brown turned over to the ordnance department of the corps two pieces, one with the broken axle and the other with a damaged trail. The two extra caissons, with Corp. C. L. Macomber in charge, were sent to the ammunition train.

Lieut. Charles A. Brown, in charge of the captured guns with those turned in from the batteries, left for Belle Plain where the pieces were to be turned over to the ordnance department depot. Lieut. Gideon Spencer, by orders, went on detached service with the Second Corps ammunition train.

At noon Captain Brown received marching orders, and by one o'clock all tents were struck, everything packed, and the battery hitched up ready for a move, with Lieut. W. S. Perrin in command of the right section, Lieut. James E. Chace the left section, and First Sergt. A. A. Williams in charge of the battery train.

At three P. M. the battery moved down to the left near the Sixth Corps at Clark's Mills, halted and went into park as we supposed for the night, but at ten P. M. we were ordered to hitch up, and moved back to Hart's farm where we had been encamped on the night of the 16th. Halting here only a short time we again moved up to the right, marching until two o'clock on the morning of the 18th, when the battery went into position in the old breastworks on Laurel Hill which we had occupied on the 13th. Another attack on the rebel line by the Second Corps had been ordered; the First and Second Divisions under Generals Barlow and Gibbon were moved to the Landrum House, while General Birney was already in position. On moving forward at daybreak the enemy was found strongly posted in rifle-pits, its front completely covered by heavy fallen pines, while a powerful artillery fire opened upon our advancing column which was promptly answered by our batteries. Our assaulting brigades could not penetrate the dense slashings in the face of such severe musketry and artillery fire, though they made most gallant efforts and displayed great steadiness, scarcely a man going unwounded to the rear.

The men of General Gibbon's division succeeded in getting possession of an advanced line of rifle-pits, but were unable to hold them long. Becoming satisfied that persistence was useless General Hancock advised a discontinuance of the assault, and General Meade thereupon instructed him to withdraw his troops.

Battery B on taking position had opened a vigorous fire of shot and spherical case on the enemy's works continuing for some twenty

Lieut. Charles A. Brown.

minutes, then slackened down firing only at intervals during the day. In this engagement only one man was wounded, Corp. Stillman H. Budlong. The battery remained at the breastworks under fire of the enemy's sharpshooters, whose fire was not to be compared with the effect of the stench, on our nerves and nostrils, which arose from the old battle-field. A large number of the dead were still unburied and these, with the bodies which had been washed nearly bare by the rain and subsequently exposed to the hot sun, presented a hideous sight, making many of the officers and men deathly sick, and tending to dishearten rather than to encourage the men.

At dusk we were relieved to hear the welcome and promptly obeyed order: "Attention — drivers mount — limber to the rear by piece from the right — forward into line — march — head of column to the right!" Battery B turned its back upon and left those breastworks without any regret, marching back to its camp of last night near the Fredericksburg road, and going into park bivouacked for the night at Clark's Mills.

May 19th. Reveille at sunrise, cloudy with showers. First Sergeant Williams came up with the battery train and rations were issued, and at noon the camp was moved into the woods. In the evening the last squad of veterans who had been at home on a furlough returned to duty. At dark the battery was ordered to hitch up and the horses were kept harnessed all night.

On the 20th, reveille at four A. M., pleasant and warm. After the usual camp duties three days' rations were issued to be carried in the haversacks. At nine o'clock the battery received its mail, and nearly every one had a letter, some receiving three or four. Two got the lion's share, one receiving six and the other nine. The mail was a large one, it being the first received by the battery since leaving its winter quarters at Stevensburg on May 3d.

At ten o'clock we received marching orders, and the battery train was sent to the rear. Tents were struck and packed, the battery hitched up and everything was in readiness for a move. Just before starting we received word of the capture of our senior second lieutenant, Charles A. Brown, on the 18th, by guerrillas (Mosby's men), while returning to the battery on the Fredrickburg road leading from Belle Plain.

At five o'clock P. M. the battery broke camp and, marching southeast, traveled all night, crossing the Fredericksburg and Richmond Railroad at Guinea Station just after sunrise on the morning of the

21st. The firing of our cavalry videttes was heard as they approached the enemy's pickets, and the movement was therefore no longer to be concealed. The troops went pushing on, and as the battery passed through Bowling Green about 10.30 A. M., a number of the F. F. V. ladies (southern belles) were seen at the windows or on the porches viewing the northern troops as they marched by, but no men were visible. They were probably in the cellars on guard. Continuing the march we passed through Milford Station, on the above-mentioned railroad, and halted taking position on the right bank of the river. The advance guard (the cavalry) found a force of rebel pickets located in rifle-pits on the north side of the Mattapony River, and by a vigorous dash dislodged them capturing sixty or more prisoners, and saving the bridge from serious injury secured an easy crossing of the river. General Barlow's division crossed as soon as it reached the bridge, followed by General Gibbon's division on the left, and a line of battle was soon formed about a mile from the river. Battery B, after crossing, took position with General Barlow's troops, and at three P. M. threw up breastworks for the pieces. General Tyler's division of heavy artillery held the left of the line, while General Birney's division remained in reserve. The cavalry was pushed well to the front to give timely notice of any advance of the rebels, while necessary preparations were made to attack them vigorously in case they showed themselves. The intrenched lines of General Hancock's troops, which had been thrown up in a few hours, were marvels of skill and industry, and General Burnside, upon his arrival, expressed astonishment at their massive character, scarcely believing that it had not required days instead of hours for their construction. The troops, worn by the long march (twenty miles) and the subsequent labor, were still further harassed by the groundless alarm of some of the new regiments, which compelled the troops to remain under arms nearly all night. Fortunately the next day was one of complete rest for the Second Corps while waiting for the arrival of the other troops.

On the 22d, the battery remained quietly in the breastworks all day and the men thoroughly appreciated the rest. Our mail came again to-day, much to the joy of those fortunate ones who received a message from home. At night the battery bivouacked in the works, supported by Colonel Byrne's brigade (the Second) of General Barlow's division (the First). All was quiet on the picket line.

On the 23d, at daybreak, the troops were moving to the left and

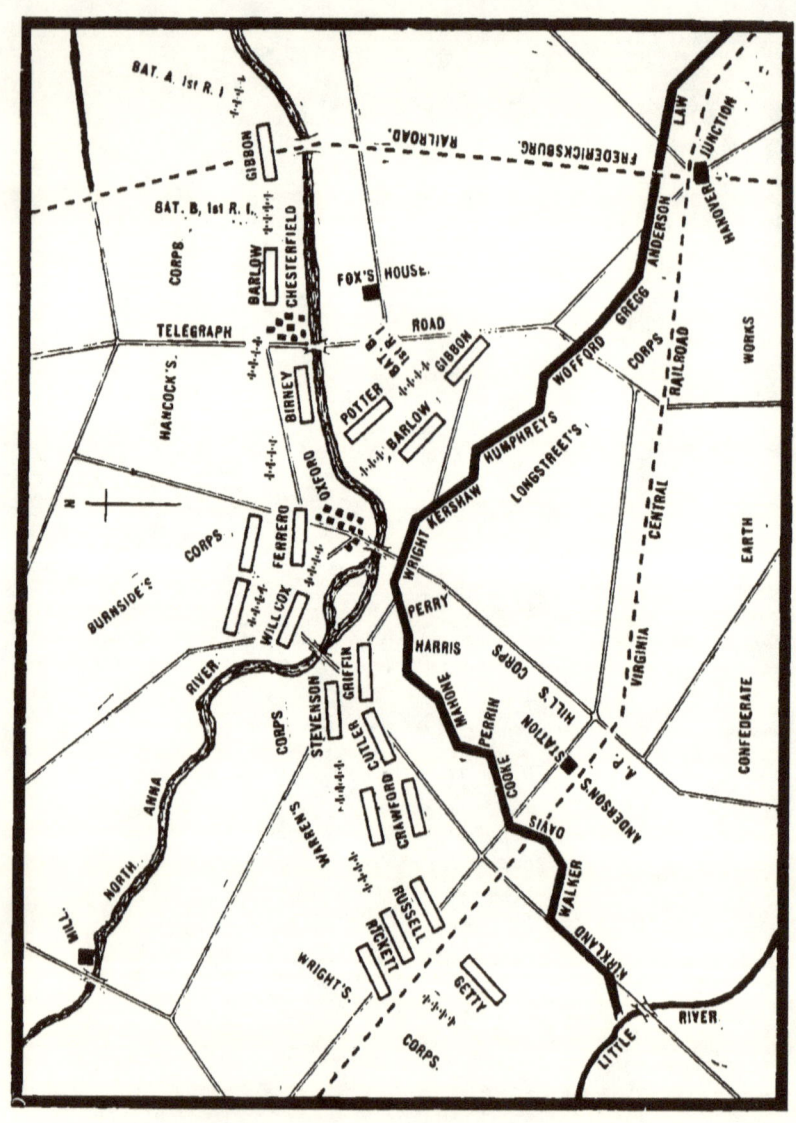

North Anna River, May 23-27, 1864.

front, but it was nine o'clock before Battery B left the breastworks to follow the Second Brigade. About four P. M. we met the rebel videttes on the north side of North Anna River. Battery B took position in battery near the Richmond and Fredericksburg Railroad, opening fire on the enemy's troops who were forming on the south side of the river. The long lines of jaded rebel troops could be seen coming into position on the opposite bank and forming simultaneously with our men. The sharp artillery fire which we opened compelled them to seek cover in the woods at their rear, or in the intrenchments which they had already prepared with a view to this contingency. The rebels still held a small earthwork on our (the north) side of the river, thus covering the county road bridge. Our advance (General Birney's troops) steadily pushed the enemy backward until all its skirmishers were driven to the works at the head of the bridge, which General Hancock determined to carry and hold, and for this purpose two brigades were brought up. They advanced rapidly in splendid style over open ground, and carried the intrenchments without a halt. The rebels were driven pell-mell across the river, and the bridge seized and saved from destruction. Some prisoners were captured. During this engagement the advance portion of the Artillery Brigade (consisting of Battery B and two other batteries) were warmly engaged with the enemy. The rebels had made desperate efforts to burn the bridge as they retreated, and not succeeding renewed their attempts during the night, but were foiled and beaten off. They succeeded, however, in partially destroying the railroad bridge of the Richmond and Fredericksburg road.

On the 24th, the infantry crossed the North Anna at eight o'clock A. M., succeeded in driving back the enemy's skirmishers, and captured the first line of works which it occupied. Our artillery assisted from the north bank of the river. Battery B during the forenoon shelled the enemy's line, and although the rebel batteries answered no one in our battery was wounded. About five o'clock in the afternoon the battery hitched up, and leaving the breastworks crossed the river below the railroad bridge by means of the pontoon bridge, by which the First and Second Divisions had crossed; we then advanced about a mile and took position in partially constructed breastworks, which we finished. From this position we could plainly hear the cars running within the rebel lines. The enemy's sharpshooters were quite troublesome until dark, but no one in the battery was hit by them. We had a shower in the evening which continued nearly all night. The men bivouacked beside the pieces.

On the 25th, the battery was ordered to change its position, and therefore advanced to the right and front crossing the Richmond and Fredericksburg Railroad to within six hundred yards of the rebel picket line. Here we again threw up works in front of our pieces, and were supported by Colonel Byrne's brigade. We fired a few shot at the rebel works causing their pickets to remain quiet for the rest of the day. Another shower passed over but it did not last long. At dusk the battery withdrew from the breastworks about two hundred yards to the rear, and parked, with the caissons in a hollow, under cover of a ridge upon which the reserve line of infantry was in position. Here the men bivouacked for the night enjoying a good rest, not being called upon to build breastworks as had been the case for the past three nights.

On the 26th, at daybreak, the battery again took its position at the breastworks of the picket line, but everything was quiet. The enemy's line and the men moving about could be plainly seen, but no firing occurred, and thus we lay all day watching each other. Just at dark the rebel skirmishers opened a sharp fire upon our skirmish line as it was about being relieved. Our men formed in double lines were not slow in answering, and the Confederates received a return fire such as they were not looking for; as a consequence they were forced to fall back, and some of our men following them up captured a few prisoners. At this outbreak the cannoneers sprang quickly to their posts at the pieces, but being so close to the lines dared not fire for fear of killing their own men in the dark. The firing did not last more than ten minutes when all was quiet again. Our pickets learned that the assault was unintentional on the part of the Confederates, being caused by a bold comrade who wished to make himself conspicuous. He accomplished his purpose, but paid the penalty with his life. It was said that he had three bullet wounds in his head from the first fire of our infantry, killing him instantly.

At eleven o'clock P. M. the order was given for the battery to hitch and pack up quietly. At 11.30 we withdrew from the front to the rear, moving by the same route of our advance. At twelve, midnight, the battery recrossed the North Anna and the railroad, back to the breastworks we had occupied on the 23d, and bivouacked after the pieces had been placed in position.

Early on the morning of the 27th, the rebel pickets came down to the opposite bank of the river, and their sharpshooters were somewhat troublesome, but no one in the battery was hit. At noon the battery was packed and broke camp, moved by the left flank and marched until sundown, and bivouacked for the night having marched ten miles beyond Concord.

On the 28th, after the usual morning duties, the battery resumed the march at seven o'clock, moving southeast to Perry's Ford on the Pamunkey River, crossed at nine o'clock, and moving forward for about a mile went into position in battery on a ridge, with the infantry and a few rods in front. Here the cannoneers threw up little half circle works in front of each piece. The caissons were parked in a hollow some three hundred yards to the rear. At dark we bivouacked for the night.

May 29th. Reveille at sunrise. A beautiful Sunday morning. The weather was as pleasant as could be asked for, but a little rain to settle the clouds of dust would have been appreciated. At ten o'clock received marching orders. The battery was soon packed and hitched up, and at noon left the breastworks and advanced with the First Division, General Barlow having been ordered to make a reconnaissance in his front and right towards the Totopotomoy River. We passed over the ground of the cavalry fight of the preceding afternoon, and at Hawe's shop a number of dead rebel cavalrymen were seen. These were buried by our men. Barlow did not strike the enemy until he reached the junction of the Cold Harbor and Hanover Court House road with the county road. Here some rebel cavalry disputed his passage, but were speedily dispersed and the division moved on. On reaching Shallow Run, a tributary of Totopotomoy, we found breastworks well manned. The division formed line of battle and Battery B took position on the ridge in rear of the infantry, throwing up breastworks in front of the pieces, working nearly all night. By morning the other two divisions of the corps formed on our right and left, with the Sixth Corps well up and in support.

On the 30th, the morning opened fine, and at sunrise Brooke's brigade, of Barlow's Division, moved forward against the rebel line of skirmishers and rifle-pits, and carried them in handsome style. They immediately converted the pits into cover and protection for themselves, as the enemy's artillery had opened fire on its lost lines. Battery B could not long remain inactive when a rebel battery was at work in its vicinity. Receiving orders we opened fire, sending our compliments by shot and shell and firing about forty rounds. The other batteries of the brigade came up, and took position to our right along the ridge where stood a handsome mansion which was riddled by shot and shell during the firing. After a fierce duel of about one hour our artillery succeeded in silencing the rebel guns. Our line of fire had been very short, but we were again fortunate in having no casualties. After the artillery firing had ceased the battery was ordered to advance, and moved forward about a thousand yards to the captured line. After placing the guns in position we were ordered to strengthen the earthworks for our protection. The horses were taken to the rear where the caissons were parked, and the cannoneers bivouacked at the breastworks.

On the 31st, as morning dawned, the activity of the enemy's sharpshooters commenced, then the pickets of both sides took a hand, and the result was quite a lively skirmish. The rebels, not being satisfied in the loss of their lines, advanced on a charge and attacked in force. They were met by a steady fire from our troops which brought them to a halt. Our men then countercharged and the enemy was driven back within its lines closely followed by Barlow's and Gibbon's men, but the position was found too strong to afford a successful assault.

While the infantry were reconnoitering the position Battery B vigorously shelled the enemy's line, and their artillery made it quite hot for us, compelling us to carry the ammunition up by hand, as it was not safe to have horses bring up the caisson limbers. After the repulse of the enemy, and the return of our troops to their own lines, the sharpshooters remained quiet. The remainder of the day, however, was passed in heavy and incessant skirmishing by the pickets, in which the battery took no part. At night the cannoneers bivouacked in the breastworks by the pieces.

Wednesday, June 1st. Weather pleasant but very warm. After the horses had been cared for, the piece horses were taken to the front and hitched to the limbers. The sharpshooters and pickets on both sides were quite active all day, and bullets flew thick and fast. We had one horse wounded which was taken to the rear and replaced by one of the spare horses. There were no other casualties. The battery remained at the front all day, but suffered greatly from the heat, it having been very hot. Two of the cannoneers were overcome by the heat and taken to the rear.

At dusk the pieces were withdrawn from the breastworks to where the caissons were parked, and everything was packed ready for another move. At nine o'clock P. M. we moved with the First Division marching south all night, passed in rear of the Eighteenth Corps near Beulah Church and halted at Cold Harbor. The night had been intensely hot and breathless, and our march was through roads deep with dust, which rose in suffocating clouds as it was stirred by the feet of men and horses. In the darkness much confusion arose throughout the column as the road, on which we were moving, gradually narrowed until finally the hubs of the wheels would strike the trees on either side. One piece became firmly wedged, and we were obliged to cut down a tree in order to obviate the difficulty. This mishap was occasioned by the error of one of General Meade's aides, a faithful and excellent officer of engineers, who undertook to conduct the leading column of the Second Corps by a short cut through a wooded road, which proved too narrow to move with the expediency desired. This misadventure prevented General Hancock from reaching Cold Harbor at the appointed time (daybreak of June 2d). Instead it was not until between six and seven o'clock that the troops began to arrive, and then in an extremely exhausted condition.

On the 2d, Battery B passed through Cold Harbor at eight A. M., and parked in an old cornfield in the suburbs of the town. The horses were unhitched, unharnessed and taken to water, and if beasts ever enjoyed water those poor horses did. They plunged into the brook sinking their heads up to their eyes, and, after drinking, many laid down in the stream and rolled over much to the discomfiture of their riders. At noon the battery was again packed and hitched up already for the march, and at one o'clock we moved for the front, passing some five hundred rebel prisoners who had been captured by the Sixth and Eighteenth Corps.

We took position in battery on a high ridge overlooking sloping ground upon which the First Division lay in line of battle. We had no more than got into position when the enemy opened fire from a battery, and shelled our line vigorously for a few minutes. We promptly replied, sending shot and shell with such effect that the rebel battery soon ceased firing. We could see only the smoke of the enemy's battery, as it was hidden in the edge of some woods, while we were in plain sight with only small earthworks in our front. Again the battery was fortunate in having only one horse wounded. We remained at the front until dark then withdrew the battery to the rear under cover of the hill, and after going into park unhitched and unharnessed, and bivouacked for the night. The intense heat of the day, and the fire of the sharpshooters had made it exceedingly hot for us.

On the 3d, reveille was sounded not by our bugler but by the enemy's pickets who opened a sharp fire on our lines. Orders were given to move, the horses were soon harnessed and hitched to the pieces, and away we went for the front on the double-quick. On reaching our position of last evening we wheeled into battery in the earthworks, which had been strengthened during the night, and prepared for action. On arriving at the breastworks we found the division under arms preparing for an assault on the enemy's works. The brigades of Brooke and Miles deployed, leading the attack supported by Byrnes, in the immediate front of Battery B's position. At the signal General Barlow's division advanced, and found the enemy strongly posted in the sunken road, from which it was driven after a severe struggle, and followed into its intrenchments under a heavy fire of musketry and artillery. Between two and three hundred prisoners, a stand of colors, and three pieces of artillery fell into the hands of Barlow's troops. The captured guns were turned on the enemy by men of the Seventh New York Heavy Artillery, Col. L. O. Morris, and the most strenuous efforts were made to hold the position.

An enfilading fire of the rebel artillery swept down the line captured by our men, while the enemy in the second line of works opened on it, and, after being reënforced by fresh troops, advanced upon our men with the utmost determination to retake its lost position. Our infantry supports were slow in going forward on account of this enfilading artillery fire of the enemy's guns, and though Barlow's men held on with great stubbornness they were finally forced out. Colonel Brooke was severely wounded, and Colonels Byrnes and Morris killed. Though compelled to retire our men did not fall back far, but intrenched themselves by piling up rails, sticks, broken limbs from the trees, loosening the earth with their bayonets, and scraping it up with their hands or tin plates; and here, at little more than pistol range from the enemy's line of works, they remained throughout the day.

As our troops advanced to the assault Battery B opened fire, with shot and spherical case at long range, on the enemy's artillery to draw its fire from our infantry, but without much success, as it only

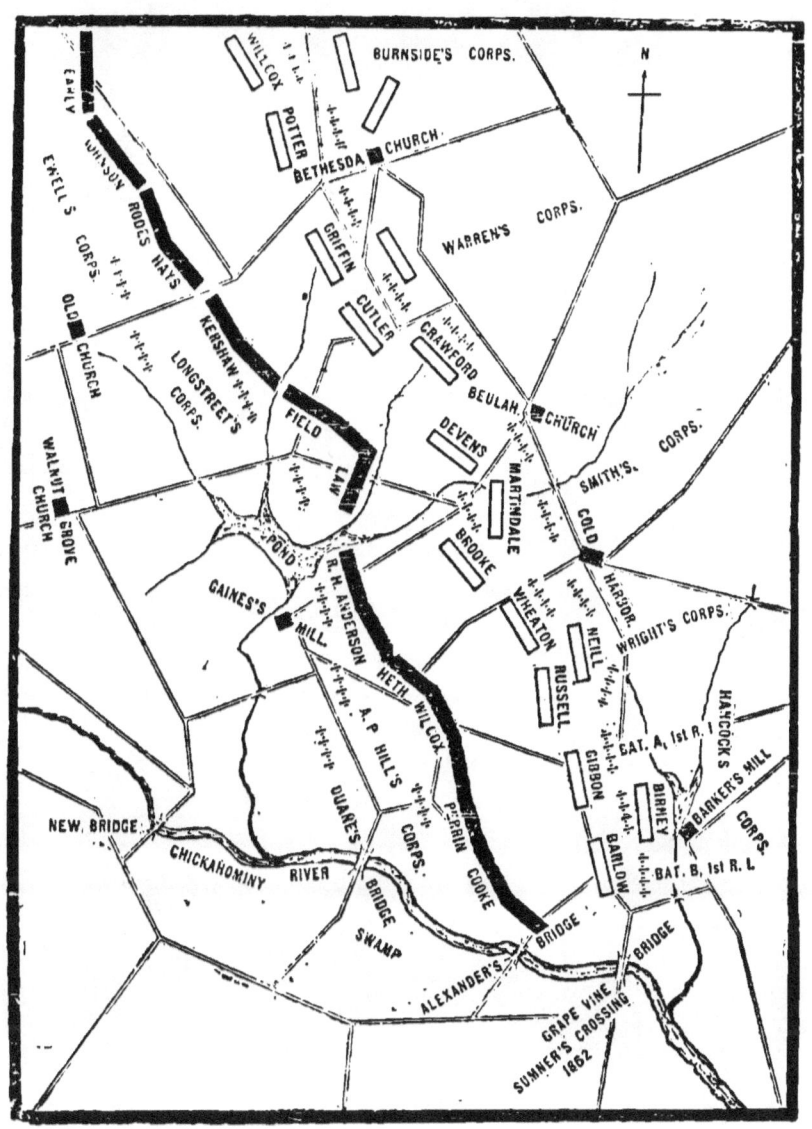

Cold Harbor, June 2-12, 1864.

sent us its compliments now and then, many of them went over us much to the discomfort of those in our rear. The battery continued its fire for some ten or fifteen minutes, when suddenly the enemy's shells burst in our midst and about us like a tornado, followed by solid shot, sending the dirt and debris of the earthworks in every direction, and blinding the cannoneers for a time. Crack—would go a report overhead and the shells rushing to the rear would cause the non-combatants to think that the rebels were after them. It looked to us as if it were going to be another Gettysburg. Had the enemy got our range, and was it trying to knock us out? But no! it only lasted a few moments, when the shells, which had only been chance shots, went wild, much to our relief, and its fire ceased. We kept up our fire for some minutes, but receiving no reply we were ordered to cease firing. The fire of the enemy's artillery and musketry, which Battery B endured for some thirty minutes was terrific.

Again I am happy to write that the battery was most fortunate. Though a dozen or more shell burst in and around our breastworks, our casualties were very light; only one cannoneer, Francis Slaiger, was wounded, being hit in the foot, and two drivers slightly injured. After the firing had ceased the cannoneers set to work repairing and strengthening their breastworks. As evening came on a furious infantry fire broke out along the two lines; now so near together, being in many places only thirty yards apart, that no pickets could be thrown out by either side. The firing indicated to us that the enemy, under cover of the clouds of smoke, would make an attempt to rush out on our lines and capture them by a sudden dash; our men, however, were on the alert and gave the rebels as good a fire as they sent, which so satisfied them that they remained quiet for the night. The Second Corps intrenchments so rapidly constructed, under heavy fire at an almost incredibly short distance from the enemy's line, had by this time been sufficiently strengthened to make them as formidable to the rebels as theirs were to us. In this critical and painful situation the two armies settled down to watch each other. The battery bivouacked at the breastworks, and the night was made comfortable by a refreshing shower.

June 4th. The morning opened with a brisk firing by the sharp-shooters. Whenever a head appeared above the works for an instant it became a target for a score of shots. At eleven o'clock the rebel batteries opened a heavy fire on our lines, being promptly answered by our artillery, Battery B using only solid shot. The firing was kept up for about an hour, then came an interval for lunch of hardtack and salt pork. About half-past one P. M. the battery was ordered to commence firing at intervals of two minutes for an hour; then we ceased firing. No casualties.

First Sergt. A. A. Williams received his commission of second lieutenant in Company C, Fourteenth Rhode Island Heavy Artillery (colored), and was ordered to report to artillery headquarters. This commission he had been expecting for some time. Sergt. John F. Hanson was promoted to first sergeant *vice* A. A. Williams discharged to accept commission.

For better protection from the enemy's artillery fire, we dug into the ground and constructed bomb-proofs with logs covered with bushes and earth, and when not at work at the pieces we were like the ground hogs burrowed in the earth. The approach of night brought another outburst of infantry firing. The battery did not fire any but remained quietly at the front all night.

The 5th and 6th of June were essentially a repetition of the 4th, with this exception, we received our mail. In active campaign, whether in battle, on the march, or at a halt for a day, the forwarding of the mails was an uncertainty.

June 7th. This morning orders were issued to save all bags and boxes, this looked as if we were to settle down for a siege. Our caissons were ordered up to the front, and parked in the hollow within two hundred yards of the pieces, and the men who came up with them were set to work building bomb-proofs, as the men at the pieces had done. It was very quiet in our front all day; the sharpshooters were taking a rest. In the afternoon flags of truce were seen along the lines, Generals Grant and Lee having made arrangements for a cessation of hostilities from six to eight in the evening, in order to bury the dead and remove the wounded. Five days had elapsed since the deadly engagement on the morning of the 3d, and through all this dreadful interval scores of desperately wounded men were lying in that narrow space between the two lines, uncared for and without water. All who could crawl in on the one side or the other had done so, hundreds had been brought in at great risk to their rescuers, but there were still those who lay where it was simply death for one to attempt their rescue.

During the time of the truce the men of both armies at the entrenchments stood up and viewed each other. Some sat on top of the works calmly smoking their pipes, while others held up bags of

First Sergt. John F. Hanson.

coffee, beckoning to the Confederates to come over and get some. The rebels held up plugs of tobacco signaling to us the same, but these invitations were not accepted. Just before eight o'clock the detail which had been out between the lines returned, and strange to say they reported that there were more Confederate than Union dead lying there. They gave their attention to burying the Union dead, as General Lee had replied to General Grant's first request, that " he had no dead or wounded not attended to." But facts proved to the contrary as the field was examined for our dead. Very few were found wearing the Union blue, while those of the butternut gray were more numerous.

At eight o'clock not a head could be seen above the works on either side, all had retired behind their breastworks each watching for the careless one to show his hat for an instant, and if he did so it became the target for the sharpshooters, and *zip* would be heard in that vicinity.

At nine o'clock occurred the usual outburst of musketry with some artillery fire, which soon rose to the greatest fury. The troops in the trenches were comparatively safe, but the plain behind was swept by shot and shell. At corps headquarters Capt. A. M. McCune, Seventy-fourth New York, the assistant provost-marshal, was killed by a solid shot while standing at the door of General Hancock's tent. No one exposed to the fury of that storm will ever forget how the horrors of battle were heightened by the blackness of the night.

On the 8th of June the morning was very warm, and the pickets were quiet, probably it was hot enough for them and they did not want to make it any hotter. It was quiet along the lines all the forenoon for a change, but in the afternoon the Confederates opened fire with artillery doing little damage. We did not answer.

Battery A, First Rhode Island Light Artillery, was relieved from the front as the term of service of many of the men had expired. They had been with the Second Division of the corps in this campaign while we were with the First.

The morning of the 9th was a little cooler than several preceding ones, and the sharpshooters heralded the rising sun by peppering each other, keeping it up during the day. The usual cannonading was dispensed with, and at dusk all was quiet along the line. We bivouacked in our bomb-proofs in quietude, having a good night's rest.

The 10th and 11th of June were similar in their essential character, and the battery remained quiet at the front waiting orders.

CHAPTER XXI.

GENERAL GRANT'S FLANK MOVEMENT TO THE SOUTH OF THE JAMES.—FROM COLD HARBOR TO PETERSBURG.

JUNE 12th. The usual salute of the pickets and sharpshooters was fired at sunrise. The cannoneers were ordered to their posts, but the battery did not fire as the pickets soon quieted down, and the cannoneers were dismissed from their pieces, leaving only a guard on duty.

At noon the caissons, with all surplus baggage, were sent to the battery train, three miles to the rear, in charge of First Sergeant Hanson. Dame Rumor was again busy, and it was whispered around by those coming up from the rear that another flank movement was on foot. If so, it must be for some distance to the south or north, for Richmond was directly ahead of us with General Lee's army between.

At sunset the battery quietly withdrew from the intrenchments and moving to the rear where the battery train was parked halted. Here we waited for the division to withdraw, it having been relieved. We did not have to wait long for at nine o'clock we moved out of park into the road, and moved along with the Third Brigade of the First Division (General Barlow) marching all night. We passed Black Creek Church, and crossed the Richmond and York River Railroad near Summit Station at two o'clock on the morning of the 13th. Continued marching until eleven o'clock, then halted and fed the horses, the men in the meantime making coffee. At noon we resumed the march and crossed the Chickahominy River at Long Bridge, passed Charles City Court House and halted at dark near Wilcox Landing on the James River. Here the battery parked and bivouacked for the night. The lights of the gunboats and transports could plainly be seen.

On the 14th the battery remained in park all day, and had a good rest after the long and fatiguing march of about twenty-four hours. We were waiting for the infantry to cross the river, which it had been doing all day on transports. It was a slow process there being so many troops to cross over. At sunset the battery hitched up and moved down near the road leading to the river, so as to be in readiness to cross when its turn came, remaining here all night.

June 15th. It was ten A. M. before the battery moved down to the landing, and commenced to embark on the transports which were to take us over. We disembarked at Wind Mill Point, and moving up the river a few rods went into park. It was slow and tedious work conveying the troops across, the facilities were very inadequate, and the landing places, wharves, and roads were incomplete. The weather was very warm and pleasant, and after camp duties the men were given permission to bathe in the James River, which they greatly enjoyed. At night we received marching orders and hitched up, the horses remaining in harness all night. The men bivouacked beside the pieces and caissons.

On the 16th, the battery moved at an early hour, marching some fifteen or sixteen miles toward Petersburg. Heavy firing was heard in front, our forces were making an attack on the redoubts. We passed some rebel prisoners and captured pieces of artillery, which had been taken by General Smith's men. One of his colored regiments made a splendid charge yesterday, in which the men proved themselves good soldiers, for they took and occupied the first line of the enemy's works, captured a great number of prisoners, and sixteen pieces of artillery.

As the firing became sharper the battery was ordered to move forward on the double-quick, the cannoneers were ordered to mount, and we went down the road on a gallop; turning to the right into an old cornfield, we took position in battery and prepared for action on a ridge, in front and at the foot of which ran a small creek. We did not fire as we were not engaged. Here we bivouacked for the night.

On the 17th, things remained quiet until two o'clock in the morning, when we were routed out of our slumbers and ordered to pack and hitch up as soon as possible. We moved by the left flank down into the road then advanced to the front to the breastworks, on the left of the Prince George Court House and Petersburg road, and, taking position, about nine hundred yards from the rebel works, relieved Captain Dorr's battery. The caissons were parked some distance in the rear. At sunrise we were troubled by the enemy's sharpshooters. The battery fired shot and spherical case at intervals during the day. We could plainly see the rebels throwing up earthworks, but made it quite warm for them, causing them to hustle around lively. At dusk the enemy made an attack on our line at our right and front, but was repulsed and driven back within its own works. The battery fired about forty rounds, mostly spherical case. Our casualties were two horses wounded which had to be killed. We bivouacked at the breastworks all night.

On the 18th, after a good night's rest, we were routed up at daylight. The enemy's pickets made an attack at sunrise, were repulsed and driven back into their intrenchments. A part of their works were captured and occupied by our men. Battery B was ordered to limber up and moved out of the breastworks advancing to the front, to again relieve Captain Dorr's battery at the picket line intrenchments. While getting into position we had one horse wounded by the fire of the enemy's sharpshooters. As soon as the pieces were in battery we opened fire with solid shot, and then a few shell. The enemy was at such short range that we were ordered to have the horses taken to the rear where the caissons were parked. At night the cannoneers strengthened the breastworks in front of the pieces for better protection.

Sunday, June 19th. At daylight every man was up and moving about, looking over the grounds and taking in the situation. There was to our right and rear a once splendid mansion (the Hare house) now nearly destroyed by shot and shell, being completely riddled with rifle-balls. The lawn had been ruthlessly torn up by pickaxe and shovel, and converted into earthworks by the troops, while the once level fields were now covered with long ridges thrown up here and there. A man by the name of Hare formerly resided here, but did not stay to form our acquaintance : though the enemy's sharpshooters did, and kept up a steady fire at anything that moved. As time hung heavily on our hands some of the men obtained rifles which had been left on the field by the wounded, and getting ammunition from the infantry of our support, tried their skill at sharpshooting with the result of soon being ordered to cease in the work they had undertaken, or they would be sent to the skirmish line where they would get all the rifle practice they desired. This threat proved effective.

They threw down the rifles, preferring to stay where they were instead of going any nearer to the front.

At two o'clock on the morning of the 20th, the right piece of the battery was advanced about fifty yards to a knoll, where heavy earthworks were thrown up in a half circle about the piece, and at sunrise when the enemy's sharpshooters began their work, a fire of spherical case sent into a clump of trees in our front quieted them for most of the forenoon, and when they did begin again there were not so many shots sent in our direction as there had been. At dark Battery B withdrew from the front, and moving back to the rear about a mile went into park bivouacking for the night.

The Second Corps had been relieved by the Ninth Corps, though it was said that the Second Corps was to be in reserve. The old men of the Second knew what that meant, they had not forgotten the remark of a member of the Irish brigade when General Caldwell formed his division in line of battalions behind General Sickles at Gettysburg, and the men were told that they were to be in reserve. " In resarve is it? Yis, resarve for the heavy fightin!" And such it proved.

On the morning of the 21st, at eight o'clock, the battery was hitched up and moved down to the left several miles with the First Division, General Barlow. Crossing the Norfolk and Petersburg Railroad and the Jerusalem Plank road, we advanced toward the Weldon Railroad and were placed in position on rising ground near the woods. The Second Corps formed on the left of General Warren's line (the Fifth Corps) extending the line further to the left. In this new position the First Division, General Barlow, held the left flank, which was within two miles of the Weldon Railroad. As the division was advancing it encountered the picket line of the enemy and a lively skirmish ensued, when the enemy was driven back and our lines were established. Battery B remained all night at the reserve picket line, while the division held on to the lines established. The left was formed at nearly right angles to the main line. During the night the Sixth Corps arrived and formed taking position on our left.

On the 22d, at sunrise, Battery B withdrawing from the picket line moved to the rear and went into park near the Sixth Corps batteries. Here we met some old friends and acquaintances of our youth, the members of Battery C, First Rhode Rhode Island Light Artillery. Their battery was parked a few rods to our left.

In the afternoon heavy musketry firing was heard on our right, and at three o'clock Battery B was ordered to the front on a double-quick. On reaching the infantry's line of battle we took position in rear of the First Brigade, General Miles, and threw up breastworks in front of the pieces. In the advance movement which had been undertaken, the Sixth Corps, on account of the woods, the nature of the ground, and the long distance it had to cover, could not keep up with the Second Corps, which being pushed rapidly forward caused the left to break away from the right of the Sixth making a gap. The advance soon met the enemy, and the left of the division was thrown into confusion by a sharp attack of the enemy in force. The Sixth Corps being still behind, General Barlow halted his line and made a stand, waiting for it to come up. The falling back of each successive body of troops uncovered the left flank of the one next to it. When the left flank of General Gibbon's (the Second Division) was reached, a resolute attack was being made on his front, which, combined with that upon the left, drove his line back in some disorder, due to the suddenness rather than to the severity of the assault.

The disorder proved most disastrous to the division for the enemy captured the four pieces of the Twelfth New York (McKnight's) battery and several hundred prisoners, while the Second Corps was defeated almost without being engaged. There had been very little fighting, and only the extraordinary quickness and precision of the enemy's movement at the time could have produced such a result. At the outburst Battery B was ordered to the front, as were other batteries of the corps, but it was all over before they could be brought into position. We bivouacked in line of battle all night. There was heavy firing at intervals until morning.

On the 23d and 24th, Battery B remained at the front in the earthworks which the cannoneers had thrown up on the 22d, but was not called upon to do any firing, as the infantry pickets did all that was required in that line.

On the 25th, the battery withdrew from the front, and moving to the rear parked on a level plain in front of a wooded hill. Water was very scarce in this vicinity, and the drivers were obliged to go nearly two miles to water their horses. The weather had been exceedingly warm, and the roads and fields were extremely dusty. Our troops on the march looked more like the graybacks of the Confederacy, than the blue coats of the Union.

Sunday, June 26th. Moved our camp into the woods on the hill. The weather was close and muggy in the morning and the sun very hot at noon, the thermometer registering 104° in the shade. This intense heat seemed to keep the Confederates quiet during the day, but at night they were as lively as owls. At nine o'clock P. M. they attacked our picket line, but our boys were ready for them and gave them all they wanted, and our batteries kept up a heavy firing all night. Battery B was not engaged, but for a wonder remained in camp.

On the 27th, the weather was somewhat cooler, we had a shower in the afternoon which was quite refreshing. Received our mail to-day which was the largest that had been received for some time. It had been held back somewhere, as some of the letters received were over a month old. At dark the battery was ordered to hitch up, and moved to the front line relieving the Tenth Massachusetts Battery, Captain Sleeper. We are still in *reserve* as usual, but in the front lines awaiting a visit from the Confederates. We waited all night, the horses remained harnessed, and the men bivouacked at their posts. The enemy did not try to surprise our lines as we expected they would. All was quiet throughout the night.

On the 28th and 29th, the battery remained at the breastworks, having nothing to do but to watch the rebels in their works. Firing was heard in the distance on the right though all was quiet in our front. Our wagons with forge came up from the train, and parked with the caissons in our camp on the hill. The sutlers made their appearance, none having been seen since last April. One had conveniently located his tent near our camp. How our boys longed to return to their camp and patronize that sutler. They would have bought him out regardless of cost, for they never let the matter of price stand between them and good things if they were to be had. Money was plenty in Uncle Sam's pocket-book, but alas, not in our's which were flat, not having been paid since March. So much excitement had been going on for the past two months that we had almost forgotten there was such a thing as "greenbacks."

June 30th. The weather was cool and comfortable though cloudy. There was a little picket firing early in the morning, just to let us know that the rebels were still there and as lively as ever. The battery was mustered for the months of May and June. We may get our pay next week and perhaps not until next month, there is nothing certain about it. The paymaster would make us exceedingly happy if he would put in his appearance shortly with a carpet-bag of greenbacks, now four months due.

Friday, July 1st. A light shower this morning was hailed with pleasure, as it cooled the air making it quite comfortable. Colonel Tidball, of the United States Army, who had been in command of the Artillery Brigade of the Second Corps, was relieved and ordered to West Point for duty. Later he returned and commanded the artillery of the Ninth Corps. On the retirement of Colonel Tidball Maj. John G. Hazard was appointed to the command of the Artillery Brigade of the Second Corps, comprised of fourteen batteries of fifty-six guns.

On the 2d, the pickets of both armies were quiet and remained so throughout the day. At noon we were surprised by the issuing of potatoes, tomatoes, pickled onions, lemons, and tobacco. These had been sent to the Rhode Island troops by the Sanitary Commission, whose relation to the army was vital. The value of such work could not be overestimated, and the commission, which carried it on so vigorously, deserved the hearty and liberal support of the patriotic and humane, whom it so faithfully represented. Its experience in everything pertaining to the sanitary welfare of the troops, whether on the field or in the hospital was invaluable, and while the Rebellion continued found ample scope for its disinterested labors.

At sunset the enemy's pickets opened a lively skirmish fire along the line and kept it up for quite a while, as if determined to make up for lost time in remaining quiet all day. During the night several outbursts of a like nature occurred, but the services of the battery were not required.

Sunday, July 3d. This morning Battery B was relieved by Lieutenant Roder's Battery K, Fourth United States, and we returned to the camp on the hill. After parking and caring for the horses the men began to look for the sutler, but he was nowhere to be found in the vicinity of our camp, much to the regret of Battery B's men. It was said that he had pulled up stakes and moved the day before, upon hearing that the battery was to return to its old camping-ground. Dame Rumor had been gossipping, and, as the sutler was not anxious to sell out just then regardless of cost, he thought he would move and take up his abode near the camp of troops who had just been paid.

On the 4th, there was a mounted inspection of the battery by Captain Miller, of the Artillery Brigade, at five o'clock in the afternoon. Everything was found to be in tip-top condition.

On the 5th, we received more vegetables from the Sanitary Commission such as were issued on the 2d instant. This was a second treat of fresh vegetables, etc. For the past month the beef (fresh) ration had been from cattle nearly exhausted by long marches through a country scantily provided with forage. As a result men died of flesh wounds, who, otherwise, would have been afforded a welcome excuse for a thirty days' sick-leave. An outburst of the enemy's pickets, although met promptly by a return fire from our men, failed to show any trace of that enthusiasm which characterized the earlier days of the campaign.

July 6th. Water being scarce and having to go a great distance for it, the men were set to work digging a well, one squad working for an hour and then being relieved by another.

July 7th. William S. Perrin, our senior first lieutenant, was ordered to Battery A, First Rhode Island Artillery, to take command, as Captain Arnold had resigned having been mustered out of service. This left Battery B with only two commissioned officers present for duty, namely: Capt. T. Fred. Brown and First Lieut. James E. Chace. Second Lieut. Gideon Spencer was absent on detached service with the corps ammunition train, and Second Lieut. Charles A. Brown was a prisoner in the hands of the enemy.

July 8th. Hot and muggy, and the rebels made it still hotter at sunrise by opening a sharp picket fire extending along the front of the line. At one place they left their works and advanced on a charge, but were driven back with some loss, our men capturing 150 prisoners. This made them mad, and to vent their spite they kept up a sharp fire the greater part of the forenoon. Battery B at the outburst of the firing was ordered to hitch up and await orders; and we did wait, with horses in harness and cannoneers at their posts, until nine A. M., when we received orders to unhitch and unharness the horses, and take them to water.

July 9th, was a warm pleasant day with no firing on either side to speak of. During the day the Sixth Corps was relieved from the front, and the Second Corps took its place in the intrenchments, and for a wonder Battery B was not ordered to the front, but allowed to remain in camp. Lieut. Gideon Spencer returned to the battery from detached service with the ammunition train of the corps.

Sunday, July 10th. The morning was very muggy, but the day was pleasant though very hot, and the roads were very dusty. The Sixth Corps was withdrawn yesterday and dispatched in haste to Washington to reënforce the troops there, to meet the invasion of General Early.

At ten o'clock the battery had its usual Sunday inspection, and clothing such as pants, blouses, shirts, socks, and boots were issued to those who wished them. The day passed quietly without any unusual excitement.

July 11th. Another fine day. At sunrise the battery was hitched up and remained harnessed until nine A. M., when orders were given to take the horses to water, but before the drivers could get their horses unhitched and into line they were ordered to hitch up again, and at 9.30 Battery B left camp, moving down on the left it crossed the Jerusalem Plank road, and going on about half a mile halted at the right of the country road on rising ground. We moved forward and placing the pieces in battery in the breastworks bivouacked. The horses were taken to water later in the afternoon. All was quiet throughout the night. The detached men of the Fifteenth Massachusetts were relieved from duty, and sent to the regiment to be mustered out of service, their time (three years) having expired.

On the 12th, at sunrise, the battery, with the First Brigade under General Miles, moved down to the left in support of the cavalry, which had been sent out on a reconnaissance to the Weldon Railroad. We advanced about three miles and took position on the brow of a hill overlooking the plains toward the railroad. Here the battery went into bivouac awaiting orders. In the afternoon our ration wagon came out to us and rations were issued. They were to have been issued the afternoon before, but having been on the move since yesterday morning the wagon could not get to us, and now did not remain long, but returned to the trains at the rear. Toward midnight the cavalry began to return and reported all quiet on the left. This last move had been made upon the report that the rebels, under Gen. A. P. Hill, were moving down on our left flank to give us a surprise. At midnight the battery limbered up and started on the march back, and after crossing the Jerusalem Plank road halted until daylight.

At sunrise the battery was ordered to move up toward the right of the line. We had expected that we were going to City Point on the James River. After crossing the Norfolk and Petersburg Railroad we turned to the left and moved up toward the intrenchments in front of Petersburg. On reaching the Norfolk pike the battery went into camp in the woods on a ridge to the right of the road, the infantry moved further on to the plains in front. While the battery and the First Brigade were down to the left on a reconnaissance, the

Second Corps had been withdrawn from the intrenchments, and had gone into camp behind the Fifth Corps. General Hancock made his headquarters in the shot-riddled mansion on the Petersburg and Norfolk town road known as "The Deserted House." Here the troops of the Second were destined to remain and rest undisturbed for more than a fortnight.

July 14th. Reveille at sunrise. After morning roll-call the cannoneers were set to work clearing a space, about two hundred by one hundred and fifty yards square, of brush, briers, and small trees, leaving the larger ones for shade. This was called the "parade," where the men formed in line for roll-calls or to receive or hear orders read. On the east side the officers' tents were pitched, while on the west were the men's formed in two rows with an arbor of pine boughs erected over them. At the north and in front of the ridge was level clear ground, upon which the pieces and caissons were parked. Here the drivers erected poles on crotches placed in the ground in front of the limbers on which the harnesses were hung. At the south of the camp the ground sloped to a hollow or small ravine, in which were many tall pine trees, and by the thrifty appearance of these it was thought a good locality in which to dig a well as water was still scarce in the vicinity of the camp. The drivers went to work and dug a circular hole, eight feet in diameter and about ten feet deep. When it was brought to the depth of seven feet there was a squad of men who kept the water down by bailing it out with pails. In this way it was sunk until there was three feet of water in the well, and then it was covered first with logs then boughs of pine, and then the clay which had been dug out was packed on top. There was a hole four feet square left in the centre, and with the use of a prolonge attached to a pail the water could readily be obtained, which proved to be very clear, cool, and plentiful, so that we used it for watering the horses, instead of going with them one and a half miles to a small creek.

On the 15th, in the afternoon, the drivers of the baggage wagons, Welcome Collins and Robert A. Niles, brought to camp a watering trough about eight feet long, for the use of the horses; its use was very convenient as it did not take so long to water them, and kept the ground dryer and cleaner around the well. Yesterday Battery A arrived and encamped on the ridge to the west of us, and to-day they were busy making their camp comfortable. It was very pleasant to have friends and acquaintances, or men from the same town as yourself for neighbors, to talk over old times, and to converse on matters in which all were mutually interested.

July 20th. For the past few days the weather had been fine, but the roads being dry and dusty we hailed with delight the frequent showers which visited us, for they cooled the air giving us a fresh breathing spell. Our time was spent in repairing equipments, cleaning and oiling the harnesses, shoeing the horses, and performing general camp duties, and last if not least, eating, drinking, sleeping, and growing fat and lazy, for we artillerymen did not have any of the fatigue duty to perform during the siege operations that were going on. The battery remained quietly in camp recruiting both in health and strength, as well as in numbers. Nothing of importance occurred until the afternoon of the 25th when Captain Brown received orders to prepare for light marching. Then activity began again. Five days' rations for men and horses were packed on the caissons, all surplus baggage put into the wagons, and all equipments put in their proper places.

On the 26th, reveille was sounded at 4.30 A. M., and after the usual morning duties were performed three days' rations were issued to the men to be carried in the haversacks. At two o'clock P. M. the battery was hitched up ready for the move. But it was four before we pulled out of park and left camp, and moving up toward the right of line crossed the City Point and Petersburg Railroad, and going in a northeasterly direction to the Appomattox River, crossed at Point of Rocks on pontoon bridges guarded by the cavalry. Pushing forward with the infantry the battery arrived on the bank of the James at 2.30 on the morning of the 27th, and halted for the infantry to cross. After the First Division of infantry had crossed, the battery then moved down to the pontoon and crossing the river proceeded up to Deep Bottom. The advancing column met the rebels in force behind some breastworks on the New Market and Malvern Hill road, where they became sharply engaged and reenforcements were sent forward to rout the enemy. Battery B was also sent forward, and, after taking position on a hill behind the line of battle, opened on a rebel battery with solid shot and spherical case. A few shot from the enemy's guns passed through the battery between the pieces, while others went wild, going high in the air. We, however, by a careful and well-directed fire, landed our shot directly in the midst of the rebel battery making it rather uncomfortable for them and their position untenable. As they limbered up

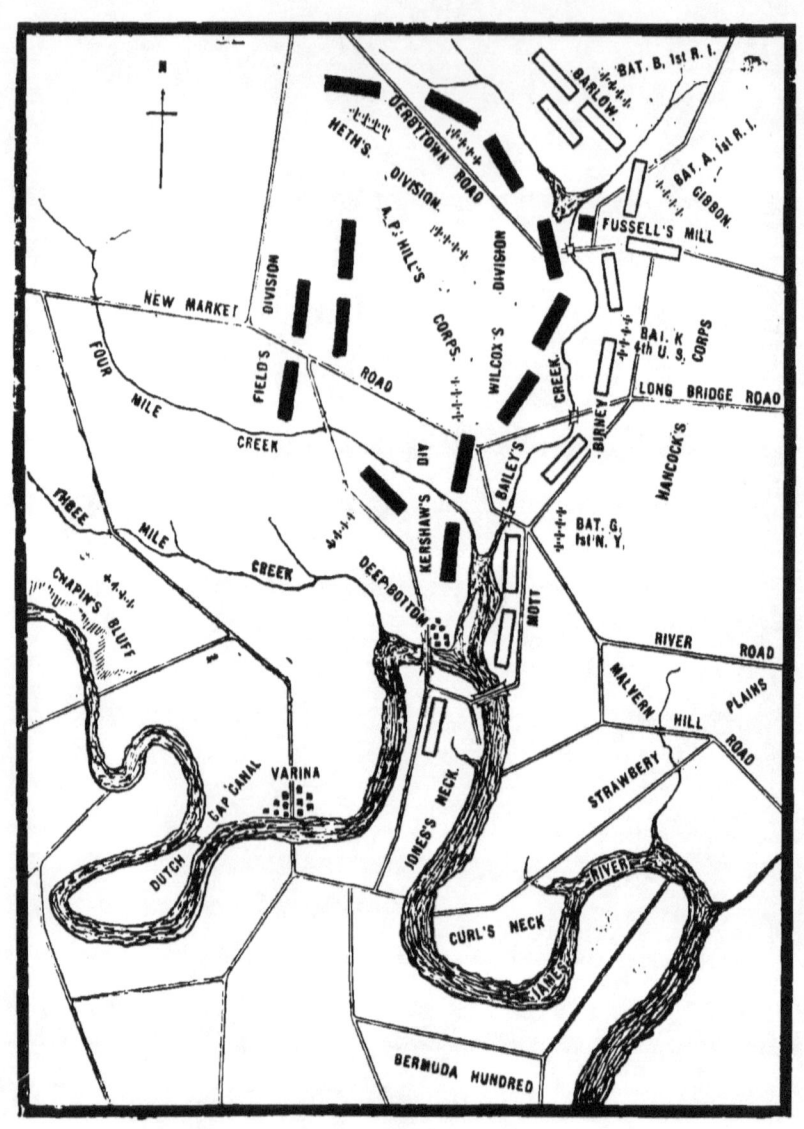

Deep Bottom, July 27-29, 1864.

and galloped to the rear on the double-quick we fired a parting salute. During this time General Barlow's skirmish line had been steadily advancing against the breastworks along the New Market road. The enemy's intrenchments were held by both infantry and artillery, but so spirited was the advance, and so skillful were the dispositions made, that the works were actually carried by the skirmishers alone. Some prisoners were taken, though the retreat of the Confederates was too hasty to allow of many captures; but, nevertheless, four splendid twenty-pound Parrotts with limbers and caissons became the trophies captured in the brilliant charge of our skirmishers. Our men knew the ten-pounder Parrotts by their shells, but twenty-pounder Parrotts seemed altogether different, and, as these great engines of war were one after another hauled out of the enemy's works and brought down the road on the run, they were greeted with loud cheers, and regarded as a full compensation for those four twelve-pounder Napoleons, of Captain McKnight's Twelfth New York Battery, lost on the 22d.

So fortunate a beginning promised a successful day. The troops of General Gibbon's division were thrown forward in pursuit of the retreating enemy, who withdrew behind Bailey's Creek. When, however, our advance reached the creek, the Confederates were found in well constructed works, apparently well manned and covered with abattis. The position as developed was one of great natural strength, the creek itself being an obstacle that could not be passed by a line of battle, which indicated that the termination of an assault would be doubtful, hence no attempt was made to charge the enemy's works; instead everything was bent to turning its left flank if possible.

The cavalry had come up, and gained, by several spirited charges, some high ground on the right, and infantry was sent to its support to hold the position gained. While General Gibbon's division held the front, Mott's and Barlow's divisions were moved up to the right to operate with the cavalry. At noon Battery B limbered up and moved out on the right to the infantry line of battle, and took positions in its rear placing the pieces in battery on an open level plain. The infantry of the division (General Barlow's) made a vigorous reconnaissance to the right; it did not succeed in finding the extreme flank of the enemy, but did discover that its flank bent sharply toward its rear at Fussell's Mill, and had been largely reënforced. At night the troops bivouacked in line on the field.

On the 28th, at daybreak, reveille was sounded by a sharp picket fire on our right and front. Our men were ordered to their posts at the pieces, expecting an outbreak or advance of the Confederates, but the firing did not extend along the line down to us, it being only against the advanced cavalry, which was driven from the ridge upon which it was posted. Dismounting his men, General Sheridan met the enemy's charge with stubborn resistance, and driving the rebels back captured over two hundred prisoners and reoccupied his position on the ridge. Battery B remained quietly in position all day watching the enemy's lines. At night the horses were unharnessed and taken to water of which they were greatly in need, not having had any since the evening before.

On the 29th, at an early hour in the morning, Battery B was ordered out to the front line toward the Charles City road, and took position in an open plain on rising ground overlooking a small ravine; beyond this was an extensive cornfield and still further a wooded ridge. Everything was quiet about the battery, and the day being warm the men were lying idly about the pieces and limbers in what shade they could find, thinking no doubt of the five months' pay due them, when their reveries were disturbed by a sharp report and a shell burst over their heads. Instantly everyone was on his feet and quickly came the order from Captain Brown: "Attention—cannoneers to your posts" (the men were already there), followed by orders to commence firing with solid shot and spherical case, and right lively did those pieces, under willing hands, belch forth in angry tones a reply to the challenge of the rebel battery that was in position on the ridge beyond the cornfield. A spirited fire was kept up for some minutes, when the rebels were seen to limber up and scatter out of sight, pursued by shots from our guns. This was the second rebel battery that had withdrawn from the fire of Battery B since we had crossed to the north side of the James, the cause of which could only be conjectured. Each time during the duel both batteries were without any earthwork protection and in plain sight of each other. While the shot and shell of the rebels did us no material damage, our shell, by carefully handling the guns, was landed and burst directly in their midst. Although Battery B was all the time at the front in the main lines of battle and under fire during General Hancock's demonstrations along Bailey's Creek north of Deep Bottom, we had no casualties from the enemy's fire.

On the 29th, at sunset, Captain Brown received orders to withdraw

Battery B from the battle line, and at once gave orders to quietly limber to the rear. Going by left piece into column we withdrew to the road by which we had advanced, and followed the Second Division (General Gibbon's) back to the James River which we crossed at midnight. We kept on the move until we had crossed the City Point and Petersburg Railroad, when we halted in a grove of pines on the south side, and went into park at three o'clock in the morning and bivouacked. The men tired and weary threw themselves upon the ground rolled up in their blankets hoping to get a few hours sleep. They were doomed to disappointment, however, for about four o'clock all were startled by a loud "boom" which shook the very foundation of the earth. Instantly every one was upon his feet, and speculation ran wild. What was it, an earthquake or the firing of Burnside's mine, which had so unceremoniously aroused us from our needed slumber? Oh, no! it was only the report of the railroad mortar; the squad in charge was sending its morning's greeting into Petersburg in the shape of a 100-pound shell. As there was no reply it was not known how the salute was appreciated. A few minutes past five o'clock, however, a terrific sound like great peals of thunder burst forth upon the morning air, the ground heaved and trembled, and toward the front lines could be seen huge masses of earth thrown high in the air mingled with cannons, garrison equipage, and human bodies. It seemed like a volcanic eruption, a mountain enveloped in clouds of smoke, sand, and dust. It was, however, the explosion of tons of powder in what was known as "Burnside's Mine." After the smoke and dust had subsided it was found that a pit 170 feet long, sixty feet wide, and from twenty to thirty feet deep, was all that remained of the enemy's great fort at Elliott's salient, which had had a battery of six guns and a garrison of over two hundred men.

No sooner had the sound of this explosion reached the ears of our artillery commanders than they opened fire with nearly two hundred guns and mortars from the front lines. It was a scene never to be forgotten by those fortunate enough to witness it, and beggared description. The effect upon the rebel troops was astounding; to the right and left they fled through fear of other explosions which they expected would follow. Had our troops promptly advanced, as ordered, they would no doubt have reached the crest of the hill with little or no opposition. At this time Battery B was, with the other batteries of the corps, held in reserve at supporting distance, and would have been sent forward had occasion required. From a hill in front of the battery's camp a fair view of the enemy's works about the mine could be obtained, and many went to inspect the scene.

July 30th. Battery B remained parked near the railroad all day with other batteries of the Artillery Brigade; the infantry had been sent to the front in support of those troops who were to make the charge on the enemy's works after the explosion of the mine. The batterymen passed the forenoon in watching the gun detachment load and fire the railroad mortar. To us it was a novel sight, we knew the workings of light artillery in every detail, but knew little about the handling of heavy ordnance and of mortars especially, as we had had no practice with them. This mortar was mounted on a large open flat car, the floor of which had been strengthened with railroad iron. In loading a very short sponge staff was used, to which was attached at one end a rammer head; after first swabbing out the mortar, the charge, thirty-five pounds of powder, was inserted and rammed down, then four men, by means of a pair of tongs made for the purpose, lifted the shell and placed it in the muzzle of the mortar; then a sharp pointed wire was inserted into the vent to make a hole in the cartridge bag, and next the primer was inserted into the hole, to which the lanyard was attached by means of a hook to the looped wire in the top of the primer tube. At the command of—"Ready!" the man drew the lanyard tight, and at the command—"Fire!" gave the lanyard a quick pull by throwing his hand and arm down behind him. This drew out the wire in the primer causing a friction, which ignited the powder in the tube and cartridge, and *boom* would ring out from the mouth of the mortar, sending on its aerial flight the messengers of death and destruction.

At one o'clock the assembly call was sounded and the men formed into line, remarking to each other, "What's up?" "What's in the wind now?" To these and similar questions, no satisfactory answers could be given. For once Dame Rumor was caught napping, and we were forced to await further developments.

As the line was forming First Sergeant Hanson ordered the non-commissioned officers to form on the right of the line, and when thus formed gave the order: "Right face, forward—march!" Going to the officers' quarters we were made happy by receiving a ration of greenbacks from Uncle Sam. The battery was paid, by Major Webb, for the months of March, April, May, and June. We much regretted the absence of the sutlers, as we would willingly have parted with our hard earned scrip, paying one dollar a pound for butter, fifty cents for cheese, twenty-five cents a dozen for molasses cookies, and other luxuries at corresponding prices.

Sunday, July 31st. Reveille at sunrise. The weather was warm but pleasant, and, after the usual morning duties, Captain Brown received orders to return to the camp he had left on the 26th. At nine o'clock we took up the line of march back to the left. On arriving at his old camp Captain Brown found it occupied by a part of the ambulance corps of the Second Corps. After parking the pieces and caissons in the places they had formerly occupied, orders were given to unhitch and unharness, and then our captain went to see the officer in command of the ambulances about evacuating the battery's camp. At first the officer did not seem inclined to vacate, but, after a short conversation with Captain Brown, finally gave orders to his men to hitch up, and they moved out leaving the vicinity. It was well for them that they left before the wrath of our drivers found vent.

The appearance of our camp was forlorn, it looked as if a cyclone had struck it. The arbors which had covered the men's tents were laid flat and heaps of rubbish covered the parade, while the well, which the drivers had taken so much care to keep clean, was now a sight to behold, for the ambulance drivers had washed their teams so near that the ground around it was all soft and muddy, making the water in the well unfit to drink. There was no help for it now but to try and repair damages, and the men went to work cleaning and putting the camp in order, rebuilding the arbors and pitching their tents. By sunset the camp was made quite respectable again. It had commenced raining late in the afternoon, causing the men to hurry and get their tents set up, securing them to stakes firmly driven into the ground. Those who did not take this precaution had the pleasure of setting them up again, for at night a terrible rain-storm burst over us, the rain falling in torrents for some minutes; then it cleared off pleasant and warm for the remainder of the night.

August 1st. Reveille at sunrise. After the usual morning duties the men were kept busy in finishing the work of putting the camp in proper order, and, as the water in our well did not settle clearly, arrangements were made with Battery A (our next door neighbor) to get water from their well for culinary and drinking purposes. They in return obtained water for their horses from our well, which relieved them of the necessity of going a long distance for water. Battery A, First Rhode Island Light Artillery, was encamped at the right of Battery B along the same ridge, and had dug a well twenty-five feet deep, rigging a well sweep to the crotch of a tree set for the purpose, and a pole and rope with bucket attached. The water was cool, clear, and sparkling.

From the 1st to the 12th of August Battery B remained encamped on the ridge near the Norfolk town road. The time was occupied in drilling new recruits, a number having been received to take the places of those infantrymen who had been returned to their regiment, their term of service having expired. Only a few incidents of importance occurred during this time.

On the 4th, the battery horses were inspected and a number of unserviceable ones were condemned by Captain Miller, and turned in to the quartermaster's department. On the 5th, the battery received six new horses to replace them.

Late in the afternoon of the 9th, we were startled by the report of what was thought to be heavy firing upon the right, but we learned later that a large barge loaded with ammunition, while being unloaded at the wharf at City Point had blown up, killing and wounding 175 of the colored troops who were performing the work of unloading the supplies for the army. It was thought, at the time, that General Butler's troops were being attacked by the Confederates at Dutch Gap.

On the 10th and 11th of August, the battery clerk, William J. Kenyon, was busy making out the muster rolls and discharges of the men whose three years' term of service was about to expire.

Friday, August 12th. The day was pleasant and warm. Just before noon Captain Brown received orders to have his battery ready to march at a moment's notice. At twelve o'clock noon, "Boots and saddles" call was sounded. The horses were harnessed and the battery was soon hitched up. The cannoneers were ordered by detachments in line in rear of the pieces. Artificers and spare men formed in line on the left of the battery wagon, in charge of First Sergt. John F. Hanson.

Capt. T. Fred. Brown then rode out in front of the battery, and gave the orders of: "At-ten-tion—drivers—mount!" Upon these orders being given the chiefs of sections, First Lieut. James E. Chace of the right, and Second Lieut. Gideon Spencer of the left, and chiefs of detachments, Sergt. Charles H. Adams of the first, Sergt. John H. Rhodes of the second, Sergt. Edwin A. Chase of the third, and Sergt. Pardon S. Walker of the fourth, took their respective stations. Then Captain Brown ordered: " Attention !" and read an order which formally relieved those whose term of service had expired, and appointed other men to fill the offices left vacant. The following were those who were relieved to be mustered out of the service of the United States, viz.: First Sergt. John F. Hanson; Quartermaster-Sergt. Charles A. Libbey; Line Sergts. Edwin A. Chase, John H. Rhodes, and Pardon S. Walker; Corporals Stillman H. Budlong, John Delevan, Josiah McMeekin, John B. Mowry, Charles H. Paine, Charles B. Worthington, and Edward B. Whipple; Artificers: William H. Cornell, blacksmith; Edwin M. Peckham, saddler; Albert H. Cornell and James A. Sweet, wheelwrights; Privates Mowry L. Andrews, John A. Arnold, Russell Austin, Arthur W. Brickley, Allen Burt, Napoleon B. Clarke, Stephen Collins, Welcome Collins, Charles Cornell, Levi J. Cornell, Michael Duffy, Richard H. Gallup, Edward Howard, John Kendrick, Robert A. Laird, George R. Matteson, Henry A. Mason, Nelson B. V. Maine, Robert A. Niles, David Phetteplace, William B. Remington, Charles G. Sprague, Clark L. Woodmansee, and Albert J. Whipple.

Besides these there were a number absent in the hospitals, and others transferred to the Veteran Reserve Corps who were discharged at the same time.

The following were those promoted to fill the vacancies of the non-commissioned officers, viz.: Sergt. Charles H. Adams, to first sergeant; Sergt. Anthony B. Horton, to quartermaster-sergeant; Corp. Charles J. Rider, to first duty sergeant; Corp. Calvin L. Macomber, to second sergeant; Corp. Aborn W. Carter, to third sergeant; and Corp. John Fox, a detached man, acting sergeant; Privates Patrick Brady, Samuel H. Collington, William Maxey and Francis Priestly were promoted to corporals. The gun detachments were then reorganized and drivers appointed. Then Captain Brown gave orders to unhitch, unharness, and prepare for light marching. The men who had been relieved on returning to their quarters packed their luggage and prepared for the march to City Point.

To the batterymen three days' rations were issued, and five more packed on the caissons with five days' rations of grain for the horses. To the men who had been relieved one day's ration of hard-tack was issued. The officers' tents were struck and packed in the baggage wagon along with the other battery baggage, the shelter tents of the men were struck and rolled and packed with their blankets, while the blankets of the cannoneers were carried on the foot boards of the gun limbers and caissons, and those of the drivers were strapped to the rear of their saddles. The canteens and haversacks were carried by the men slung from their shoulders.

At four o'clock P. M. the assembly call was sounded and the relieved men were ordered to fall into line, and, as their names were called, they were given their discharge papers, which showed they had been lawfully relieved from the service of the United States.

The discharge papers, which the men received, had not been signed by the commissary of musters, Capt. E. B. Brownson. This was known to Captain Brown, but as the battery was to move with the corps on another expedition to Deep Bottom, he thought it best to give the papers to the men rather than to keep them in his possession until they could be sent to headquarters, for there was a possible chance of getting them signed at City Point.

At five o'clock " Boots and saddles" call was sounded. The battery was hitched up and remained in park awaiting orders. While waiting the men filled their canteens with water from the well in Battery A's camp. Our camp was not destroyed, as it was not known whether the battery would return or not. At six o'clock the order was given: " By piece from the right—forward into column—march ! " Battery B moved out of park and left its camp, marching north by the same road it had traveled to Deep Bottom on the 26th of July. At midnight it crossed the Appomatox River at Point of Rocks on the pontoon bridge, and marched until morning when it halted and bivouacked on Jones's Neck near the James.

As the Artillery Brigade of the Second Corps moved toward the Point of Rocks, the infantry was moving down toward City Point, followed by the baggage and supply trains. As the squad of discharged men left camp with the battery, many placed their roll of blankets in the baggage wagons, saving themselves the trouble of carrying them. A few of the favored ones were allowed to ride (the writer being one) while the rest footed it, all moving in the direction of City Point, marching nearly all night, at least those with the wagons. We halted at three A. M., when a short distance from the river, and had a good sleep until sunrise on the morning of the 13th. As the wagons were not going any further the travelers bade their comrades, the drivers, good-bye, and resumed the march to the Point on foot. On arriving there they went to the provost marshal's office, at the head of the wharf, to get permission to leave the lines of the army, as no one could leave without being arrested as a deserter unless such permission was obtained. It was not time for the officer to be at the office so we could do nothing but wait. At nine o'clock the provost marshal put in an appearance, but, on presenting our discharges he shook his head saying: "No good." Our papers had not been signed by the commissary of musters of the corps to which we had been attached, and his signature must be affixed to the discharge papers before the provost marshal would grant us permission to leave. We were surely in a dilemma now. Quartermaster-sergeant Charles A. Libbey, on learning of the trouble, came to the rescue, having been on duty (by request) with the trains last night he still had his horse, not having sent it back to headquarters, and said: "Give me all your discharges and I will go back and get them signed." As this was the best thing that could be done, the papers were soon in his possession and away he galloped to where the infantry of the Second Corps had halted, and inquired for corps headquarters. After considerable trouble and inquiry he finally succeeded in finding the person he was in search of, and made known his object. Capt. E. B. Brownson, upon learning Sergeant Libbey's errand said: "Certainly," and, seating himself beside the road, then and there affixed his signature to each of the discharge papers. Sergeant Libbey upon receiving them thanked the captain for the courtesy shown, and hastened to return to the Point.

To those awaiting his return the time passed all too slowly. Would he return in time for the mail boat which would leave at ten o'clock, and was now due in fifteen minutes? The suspense began to increase as the time passed, and still the sergeant failed to appear. The steamer's bell began to ring, warning us that the boat was about to leave. Our one thought was, would it sail without us? It looked very much as though it would; and that meant a wait of twenty-four hours on the wharf, until ten o'clock the next day. As the first bell ceased ringing, there came a shout from those watching, and—"Here he comes! Here he comes!" Looking up the road leading from the wharf the sergeant was seen with his horse on the dead run. Arriving at the provost marshal's office he sprang from his horse (which one of the comrades grabbed by the bridle) and rushed into the office presenting the papers to the marshal. Then the routine of examining the discharges commenced, but, by the courtesy and consideration of that officer, who took in the situation, they were approved in double-quick order, and returned to the men, who made for the boat as fast as their legs could carry them. The bell of the steamer was tolling, and the captain was giving orders for casting off. The men on a run made for the gangway, and passed on to the steamer as the sailors were about to draw the gang-plank on board. And thus, after intense suspense and excitement, the discharged men of Battery B, First Rhode Island Light Artillery, were safely embarked on board the mail boat *Charlotte Vanderbilt* bound for Washington, D. C., on their way home.

It was five minutes past ten o'clock before the steamer left the wharf and that five minutes' delay was favorable to us, and we appreciated it. We were not allowed to go up on the upper deck as we desired, but had to remain between decks abaft of the main shaft. Through the windows, however, in the side of the boat glimpses of the Virginian shore could be had as the steamer sailed along winding her way down the James River. We passed Harrison's Landing, where we had encamped through the month of July and part of August, 1862, under General McClellan. Further down we passed Windmill Point, where the Army of the Potomac had crossed the river in June, and then we passed the mouth of the Chickahominy. Here the river began to widen to twice its width at City Point. On nearing the flats between Jamestown Island and Hog Island the steamer ran very slowly, but after passing the flats her speed was increased and we began to run at a lively rate. Passing Newport News we entered Hampton Roads, where the duel was fought between the famous Yankee cheese-box, the *Monitor*, and the rebel ram *Merrimac*. On passing Fortress Monroe, at Old Point Comfort, the steamer entered Chesapeake Bay; sailing along we viewed the distant shore and calm water, and our thoughts went back to the time of our withdrawal from the Peninsular Campaign in August, 1862. Then our passage up the bay was made in a rain-storm, and the angry sea lashed our frail crafts as if eager for their destruction; but now there was only a slight ripple on the water's mirror-like surface, offering no resistance to the steamer which was bearing us on our homeward journey. Darkness soon veiled from our view the Virginian shore, and shut out the surrounding scenes. We lay on the deck rolled in our blankets to sleep and dream of our friends at home or our comrades left behind.

At daybreak, on the 14th, we were up and stirring about our limited quarters on the steamer. We borrowed a pail from one of the sailors, and gave our face and hands a salt water bath which was quite refreshing, after which, for want of some better occupation, we viewed the distant shores along the river. The passage up the Potomac was not distinguished by any extraordinary occurrence. We passed Mount Vernon, Fort Washington, Alexandria, and arrived at the wharf on Water street, near the foot of Seventh Street, Washington, at seven o'clock A. M. We immediately disembarked, and, under guidance of a friend, were piloted to the rooms of the Sanitary Commission. Here we were permitted to finish our morning toilet, and fully improved the opportunity, brushing our clothes, blacking boots, and combing our hair. The washing of our faces and hands, and drying them on nice, new, clean towels two yards long, was a luxury to many, for at the front we were fortunate if we had a piece of a grain sack. After finishing our toilet we were each given a pocket handkerchief by the person in charge of the Sanitary Rooms. Probably by the appearance of some of us he thought we were in need of such articles.

It being Sunday and not wishing to be encumbered with our knapsacks we were permitted to leave them in one of the rooms. There were no accommodations for board and lodgings at the Sanitary Rooms, so we thanked those in charge for the courtesy shown us, and left to seek such accommodations as suited us. Many went to the Willard Hotel, while others, not so "high-toned," sought rooms where charges were less exorbitant. After securing quarters many of us took a stroll about the city.

On the morning of the 15th, at nine o'clock, the men assembled (as agreed upon) at the rooms of the Sanitary Commission, and at ten o'clock went to the Treasury Department, where, after a little delay, we received our pay for the month of July and twelve days of August. To those who had not overdrawn their allowance for clothing (forty-two dollars per year) was paid the balance of the amount; but those who had overdrawn had the amount for clothing deducted from their monthly pay. We also received the one hundred dollars bounty promised at the expiration of our term of service. Instead of giving us free transportation to Rhode Island, we were paid mileage, receiving about twenty-six dollars. As each received the greenbacks and shinplasters (as the fractional currency was called) which squared his account with Uncle Sam, his discharge paper was stamped with a circular stamp, viz.: "Paid in full. Washington, D. C., Aug. 15, 1864. C. TAYLOR, Paymaster. U. S. A."

After receiving our money we returned to the rooms of the Sanitary Commission, where many of us bought tickets for Providence, R. I., at a discount from regular railroad prices. Taking our baggage we went to the Adams Express office to have it forwarded home. On finding that it would be cheaper to send it collectively, Comrade Welcome Collins procured a large dry-goods box, into which we packed our knapsacks, haversacks, canteens, and blankets. This box was sent to Providence, R. I., from Washington, D. C., at a cost of six dollars.

At six o'clock P. M., on the 15th, we boarded the train at the Baltimore and Ohio station for the north, and traveling all night passed through Baltimore and Philadelphia, arriving at Jersey City about six A. M. on the 16th. Here we left the cars, and embarking on a ferry boat crossed the Hudson River landing at Courtland Street, New York City. Disembarking we took an omnibus which carried us to the railroad station at Forty-second Street, arriving there at seven o'clock. At eight o'clock we boarded the Shore Line train of the New York and New Haven Railroad for Providence, R. I., and arrived in that city at four P. M., after an absence of three years. As we alighted from the cars, the veterans scrutinized the throng of people passing to and fro with anxious eyes, hoping some dear friends might be waiting to receive them. The time of our arrival had not been made known to the State officials and consequently there was no formal reception. By request the writer reported on arrival to the Governor, Hon. James Y. Smith, who said he felt sorry that he had not been informed in time to prepare a reception for us; however, if we would meet at the station on the following morning at nine o'clock we should have a formal welcome. This information being imparted to the veterans they said they would be on hand.

On Wednesday morning, August 17th, at the appointed hour, the veterans of Batteries A and B, First Rhode Island Light Artillery, who had returned from the service, were received at the railroad station, Exchange Place, by the Mechanics Rifles, Col. Stephen C. Arnold, and, with a drum band, were escorted to the armory of the Marine Corps of Artillery on Benefit Street, where the veterans were pleasantly welcomed in behalf of the State by His Honor Lieut. Gov. Seth Padelford, Brig. Gen. W. W. Paine, and others. We were entertained by a few pleasant remarks, and a collation, prepared by L. H. Humphreys, was then partaken of with a hearty zest by the veterans and their escorts.

CHAPTER XXII.

SECOND EXPEDITION OF DEEP BOTTOM—BATTLE OF REAMS'S STATION.

THE veterans having arrived safely in Providence, R. I., we will now return to Battery B which we left encamped on the James River, at Jones's Neck, with the other batteries of the brigade on the morning of August 13th, awaiting the arrival of the infantry which had proceeded to City Point, where it had taken steamers and other transports and sailed down the James, to create the impression upon the Confederates, who were certain to learn of the movement, that the corps was bound for Washington to resist Early. Under cover of night, however, the steamers and transports were to return up the James (sixteen miles above City Point) to Deep Bottom, there make a landing, and after rapidly debarking press up the several roads to Richmond ; thus making the second attempt to turn the enemy's line on Bailey's Creek.

But while the Second Corps was effecting by elaborate operation a surprise of the enemy at this point, it was not to act alone. General Gregg's division of cavalry, followed by his artillery and trains, had moved by way of Point of Rocks on the Appomattox, and with the Tenth Corps, General Birney's, at Deep Bottom were all placed under General Hancock's command.

While the second expedition to Bailey's Creek was transpiring Battery B remained encamped on the south side of the James.

Sunday, August 14th. At noon the battery was ordered to hitch up and left camp, and marching about a mile toward the crossing halted. After waiting about an hour Captain Brown received orders to return to the camp near the river, where we arrived about four o'clock and parked. The tents were soon pitched again, and by sunset no one would have thought by the appearance of the camp that the battery had been out of it.

On the 16th, Lieut. John T. Blake, of Battery A, reported to Captain Brown with sixty-four men for duty. Lieut. W. S. Perrin, commanding Battery A, received orders on the 15th to turn in the battery to the ordnance department at City Point; the horses to the quartermaster of the Artillery Brigade of the Second Corps, and the men to Battery B. Their names appear in the accompanying roster.

On the 17th, the gun detachments were reorganized, and the men from Battery A were mostly assigned to the left section. Rations were then issued, the gun equipments inspected, and also the horses, three of which were condemned, and ordered to be turned in as unfit for further service.

On the 18th, our senior First Lieut. William S. Perrin, who had been on detached service, commanding Battery A, returned to Battery B for duty.

On the 19th, Lieut. John T. Blake, by his own request, was mustered out of service, and, bidding us an adieu, left for Rhode Island.

On the 20th, at reveille it rained quite hard, and, as it had been raining all night, the air was very chilly. The men were kept busy trying to light fires from well soaked wood: not an impossibility, for little fires soon grew larger and were seen to spring up here and there about the camp. In the afternoon Captain Brown received orders to be in readiness to move at a moment's notice. The tents were struck, battery equipments and baggage were soon packed, and at sunset the battery hitched up and moved back to its old camp in rear of Petersburg, where we arrived about nine o'clock and parked.

On the 21st, when reveille was sounded heavy firing was heard down on the left. There was no Sunday morning inspection, but instead orders were given to prepare for a move. The battery was soon under marching orders, and at nine o'clock moved near to Second Division headquarters and parked. The Artillery Brigade was here massed and awaiting orders. Maj. John G. Hazard, having returned from Rhode Island, resumed command of the Artillery Brigade. He brought with him four recruits for Battery B, Joseph Fisher, Samuel H. Greene, Patrick Kelly, and Charles Stephens. These were assigned to the right section. Three days' rations were issued to the men, and other preparations were made for a movement down toward the left of line.

On the 22d, at sunrise, things looked lively, the infantry was on the move bright and early. At 9.30 "Boots and saddles" call sounded, the battery packed and hitched up, and at ten o'clock moved out into the road taking up the line of march with the Artillery Brigade toward the left. After passing the Jones house on the Jerusalem Plank road we halted and went into park on the right of the road. Here Capt. T. Fred. Brown left his command, having been ordered home to Rhode Island on recruiting service. The battery was turned over to First Lieut. William S. Perrin, upon Captain Brown leaving for City Point.

There was a hard shower in the evening, and most of the men were wet through, especially those who had not pitched their shelter tents. Many thought they would risk lying under the tarpaulins of the pieces and caissons, and had the usual experience of being completely drenched.

On the 23d, there was battery inspection by Lieut. W. S. Perrin, the right section being in command of Lieut. James E. Chace, and the left section, under Lieut. Gideon Spencer. After inspection the men spread their blankets and clothing out in the hot sunshine to dry. In the afternoon the battery received marching orders from General Gibbon to follow his division as soon as it should move. Embodied in this order were instructions to have all corps or state insignia removed from hats, caps, and clothing, so, if captured, the enemy could not tell to which corps of the army the prisoner belonged; and also to prevent the enemy from learning that the Second Corps was down on the left of the line, instead of being up on the right in the intrenchments in front of Petersburg.

At six o'clock the battery left camp and moved down the Jerusalem Plank road. On arriving at Shay's Tavern the column turned to the right moving toward the Weldon Railroad. On the way we passed two pieces and a caisson which were stalled in dry quicksand, blocking the road and causing slow progress. At ten P. M. the battery halted and parked. At midnight Lieutenant Perrin received orders to move to Reams's Station (twelve miles south of Petersburg) and report to General Miles (First Division). The battery, proceeding alone, had not marched far before it found the road blocked by fallen trees, which the enemy had cut in order to retard the approach of our troops on its flank. After some delay a road was cut and cleared, and the battery proceeded on its way, arriving at the station a little before three o'clock on the morning of the 24th. Lieutenant Spencer's left section was ordered out to the Halifax road to the right of the station, and took position fronting northwest with only the cavalry videttes in support. Lieutenant Perrin with Lieutenant Chace's right section went south down the railroad, about three-quarters of a mile below the station.

On taking position one piece was placed on the railroad bed, and the other was placed a few yards to the right in the field, both fronting south in order to cover and protect the infantry, which was still destroying the railroad by tearing up rails and ties. As soon as the pieces were placed in position the cannoneers were set to work, and by sunrise had thrown up around the pieces substantial earthworks. The left section, however, was not destined to occupy the works it had constructed, for at nine o'clock, by General Gibbon's orders, it joined the right below the station. By this time the Second Division and three batteries of the Artillery Brigade had arrived. When the left section joined the right, Lieutenant Spencer's right piece was placed in position on the Halifax road to the left of Lieutenant Chace's left piece. Lieutenant Spencer's left piece was placed in the field to the right of Lieutenant Chace's right piece. The third and second pieces thus placed formed the left section of the battery, and was under the command of Lieutenant Chace, while the first and fourth pieces formed the right section of the battery and was under the command of Lieutenant Spencer. Lieutenant Perrin was in command of the battery which was fronting southwest, overlooking the railroad and the fields west of the Halifax road. The battery's present position was about two hundred yards south of the junction of the Dinwiddie stage road with the Halifax road. A force of cavalry under General Gregg, which was posted along the stage road, had been sharply attacked and repulsed early in the day by the rebel cavalry under General Butler. No infantry had appeared as yet to oppose our troops engaged in tearing up the railroad. On the arrival of General Gibbon's division (the Second) it was posted in the intrenchments, which had been constructed by either the Sixth Corps or the cavalry on the occasion of General Wilson's fight near this point some weeks previously. During the day the work of destroying the railroad was continued by General Miles's troops, proceeding as far as Malone's Crossing, three miles below the station. At dark General Miles's Division (the First) was drawn back within the intrenchments, and General Gregg's cavalry held the approaches in the direction of the Petersburg and Dinwiddie stage road.

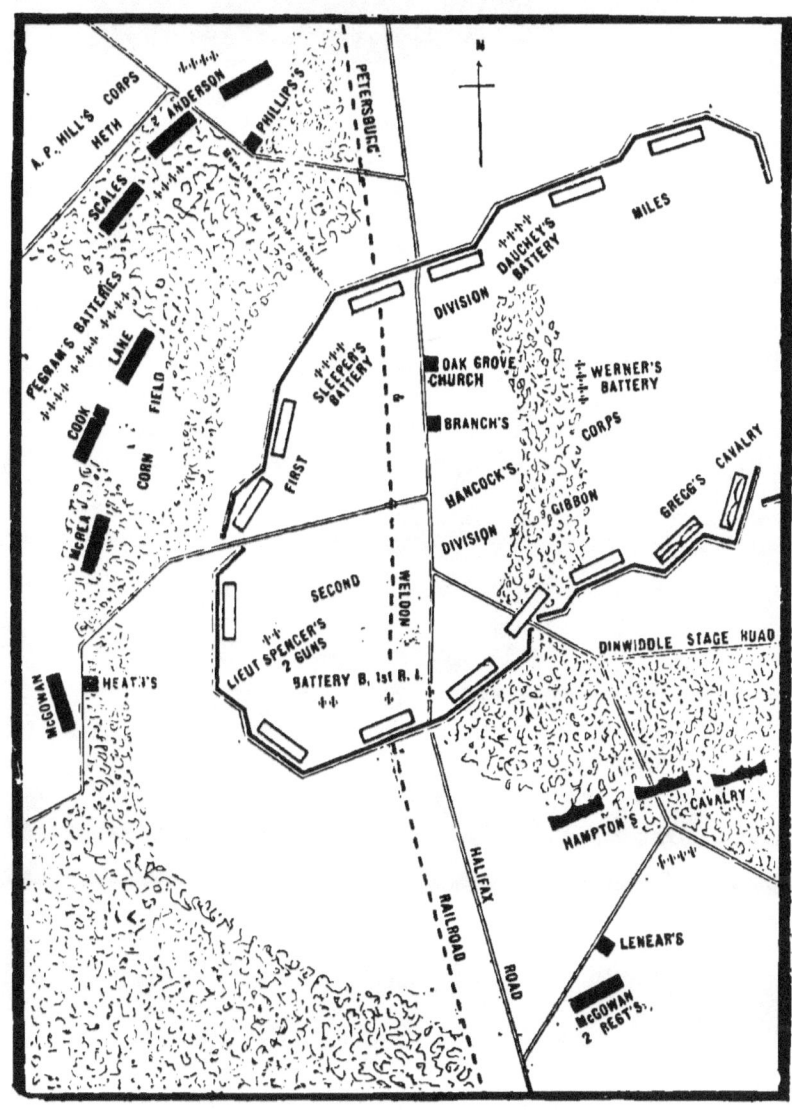

Reams's Station, August 25, 1864.

Battery B bivouacked in the intrenchments all night without being disturbed. At daylight on the morning of the 25th, the men were aroused from their slumbers by the infantry going out of the works to the support of the cavalry, which had been ordered out to make an extended reconnaissance to the south. Reports were received that the enemy's pickets had been repulsed at two points without developing any increase of strength. General Hancock determined, therefore, to continue the work of destroying the railroad, and General Gibbon's troops were ordered out for that purpose. Hardly had they got well out from the intrenchments when the head of the column, which had reached Malone's Crossing and commenced work, was attacked by a strong force of the enemy and driven back. General Gibbon was obliged to deploy a strong skirmish line to check the enemy's advance, effected after a smart and lively skirmish of a few moments' duration. The division held its ground though not advancing on the enemy. It was now evident that Gibbon's division had more serious business on its hands than tearing up railroads, and it was ordered back within the breastworks taking the left of the line. At ten o'clock A. M. the men were back in the intrenchments which extended across the Dinwiddie stage road.

During this time Battery B was not idle, for the enemy had shown itself in force on our right. This obliged Lieutenant Perrin to change front, and Lieutenant Spencer's pieces, the first and fourth, which were in the field to the right of the railroad, swung around to the right and rear about one hundred yards nearer to the traverse of the breastworks. Lieutenant Chace's right piece, which was on the railroad bed, was swung around to the front and right. By these changes three pieces were facing nearly west with one of Lieutenant Chace's pieces facing nearly southeast on the Halifax road. The breastworks west of the railroad extended parallel with the same several hundred yards, then turned to the east at both the south and north flanks with Battery B at the southwest angle, while the Tenth Massachusetts, Captain Sleeper's battery, was at the northwest angle. Further to the right was the Twelfth New York, Lieutenant Donchy's battery. In the centre of the position, behind the Oak Grove Church, was the Third New Jersey, Lieutenant Werner's battery. Such was the position of the artillery at Reams's Station on the morning of the 25th. The ground immediately in front of the battery was comparatively clear of large timber, though covered with brush sufficiently high in many places to conceal the movement of the troops. To the right and front (northwest) were heavy timber, in which the enemy's infantry was massed.

During the forenoon the enemy's sharpshooters began to pick off both men and horses, and soon several men and two horses were killed; thereupon Lieutenant Perrin, who was with Lieutenant Spencer's section, which was now in an advanced position, gave orders to shell the enemy's line. After firing a few rounds an order to cease firing was given by an aide from brigade headquarters, who said we were firing upon our own men. It was observed that he did not dismount nor make a long stay, bullets were flying thick and fast, and he had more urgent business which called his attention to the rear, in which direction he went at double-quick time. Lieutenants Perrin and Spencer, as well as the men, knew better than to credit the aide's report for they could see the enemy aim and fire, it having crept up so close to our lines. As there had been no general engagement with our pickets, which should have been in our front, brigade headquarters was mistaken as to the situation of things. But orders had been received from higher authority to cease firing, and they were rigorously obeyed. During this time the First Division had repulsed several attacks of the enemy on its lines, which were not pushed with much vigor. Soon after the battery had ceased firing it became evident that the enemy was preparing for another attack upon the right, for a commotion could be seen going on in a cornfield within their lines. About 5.30 P. M. a strong column of the enemy appeared, directing its assault against the northeast angle to the right of the Tenth Massachusetts Battery. Unfortunately our troops at this point gave way, and the enemy rushing forward leaped the breastworks and swarmed into our lines. As our lines were being broken the enemy opened a terrific fire from twenty pieces of artillery, which they had massed in the cornfield on our right and front in order to demoralize our troops holding the west intrenchments. The enemy's guns were served with vigor and determination. Their fire not only swept the whole space enclosed by the intrenchments west of the railroad, but took portions of General Gibbon's line upon the left and rear in reverse. Our artillery was not dumb, but quickly answered the enemy's first shot. Battery B and the Tenth Massachusetts Battery, occupying the low ground west of the railroad, found themselves in an unpleasant position. Both men and horses were completely exposed to the volleys of the enemy and the fire of its sharpshooters. One by one our horses had fallen, until every one was killed, some being riddled by dozens of bullets. Several men had been severely wounded and taken to the rear. As the enemy's artillery fire broke out furiously Batteries B and the Tenth Massachusetts, notwithstanding their severe loss, pluckily responded, while the Twelfth New York Battery, upon the right, shelled the woods on the northwest where the enemy's infantry were massed.

The attacking rebel force consisted of the brigades of General Cooke, McRae, Lane, and Scales, with Anderson's and three of McGowan's regiments in support.

In charging, the rebels encountered serious obstructions from the slashing of the woods which had been made at this point, and they were not a little shaken by the fire which greeted them. Four times they charged up to our breastworks and were repulsed. Five minutes more of good conduct and staying qualities on the part of our infantry, which occupied the lines between the Tenth Massachusetts and the Twelfth New York batteries, would in all probability have ended the strife with a victory for our arms. But it was not so to be. In a moment of panic our infantry gave way, and the enemy closely pursuing gained our rear.

At the time our line was broken, and the enemy opened its artillery fire from the cornfield, Battery B could bring only three guns into use, as its fourth on the Halifax road was on lower ground than the railroad, across which it could not fire to the west. We responded, however, from our three serviceable guns sending shot and shell into the cornfield and woods, but were not able to fire upon the charging column at the breastworks for fear of firing into our own troops, as the intrenchments curved so sharply to the right.

In the height of this cannonading an aide on Major Hazard's staff, Lieutenant Fairchilds, rode down to the battery and shouted: "Why in h—— do you not fire upon the charging column?" Lieutenant Spencer replied, that he could not unless he fired across the Massachusetts battery. The lieutenant did not stop to argue the point in the midst of the enemy's deadly shot and shell, but quickly decamped. Lieutenant Chace could neither fire on the charging column, nor on the woods where the rebels were formed without firing across Lieutenant Spencer's two pieces as well as the Tenth Massachusetts Battery.

Under this heavy fire our gun detachments were pretty well reduced, in consequence of which Lieutenant Perrin took charge of

Spencer's left piece, which was Sergeant Rider's, his gunner, Corp. William Maxey, being disabled by a wound in the arm sustained from a sharpshooter in the early part of the engagement, but with the injured member tied up in a handkerchief he stubbornly refused to leave his post.

Lieutenant Spencer gave his attention to his right piece, which was in charge of Acting Sergt. John Fox. Sergeant Macomber had been hit by a sharpshooter while trying to get his piece out of the soft ground into which it had settled. When struck the sergeant fell back into the arms of Lieutenant Spencer, who, with the help of two cannoneers, carried him to the left of the gun and placed him under the breastworks. Lieutenant Spencer had finally got his right piece forward upon hard ground when a shell, in passing over the men at the gun, exploded, and a piece struck No. 6 in the side almost cutting his body in half, killing him instantly. He was a detached man whose time was about out.

About this time, just as the enemy opened a heavy fire upon the battery, First Sergeant Adams went from the caissons down to the limbers to see if he could be of any service there. He was mortally wounded and carried a short distance to the rear, where after being placed beside a tree he soon expired.

Lieutenant Perrin was with Sergeant Rider's piece only a short time, before he also was wounded by a piece of shell, which broke his leg below the knee. He was helped to the rear by some of Sergeant Rider's men. About this time Lieutenant Spencer observed that his left piece was not firing, and going to find out the cause, discovered Sergeant Rider and Corporal Maxey sitting on the trail of the piece played out, having no men to help them. Lieutenant Spencer asked an officer of the New York Heavy Artillery regiment for men to assist in working the pieces, who replied that he did not know what men to detail not knowing which ones understood how to work light guns. Lieutenant Spencer said: "Give me men, they can do something," and becoming impatient called for volunteers himself, and several came forward, doing good service as long as the ammunition lasted.

Notwithstanding that the enemy, after breaking through our lines, was making toward our rear, the regiment of infantry in support of the battery remained inactive, not firing a round in self-defence. This seemed wrong to Lieutenant Spencer, and, in the excitement of the moment, he went up to the colonel of the regiment and asked him why he did not march his men into the opening. The enemy was now moving around toward our left leaving the captured guns of the Twelfth New York Battery, and the angle of intrenchments without any troops. The colonel replied that he had had no orders and could not do it. Lieutenant Spencer impetuously replied: "To h—ll with orders!—march your men in there and cut off the enemy from getting back!" But the colonel would not accept an order from a second lieutenant of artillery; no! not he! he would be captured first! And sure enough before the battle was over he and his whole regiment, nearly fourteen hundred strong, including thirty-two officers, were taken without firing a gun.

Lieutenant Spencer finding it useless to argue with the colonel went back to his section, and assisted with his right piece in shelling the enemy, remaining on the outside of the work until only two men were left to help him, while the wheels of the gun carriage and trail had settled so far into the ground (which was soft and spongy) that he could not work the gun to advantage without endangering the Union troops. The guns had become so hot, by the rapid fire, that they could not be handled. For the lack of ammunition Lieutenant Spencer ceased firing, and looking toward his left piece again saw Sergeant Rider and Corporal Maxcy sitting on the trail, there being no men nor ammunition. The lieutenant realized that the case was hopeless, and his men who had so unflinchingly stood fire, remaining at their posts with no signs of neglecting their duty, had showed their mettle, and were worthy of a chance to escape if it were possible, without being kept there to be slaughtered. They had been under fire all day long and still survived the conflict. He ordered his men to retire and take care of themselves, and started with them in the direction of Lieutenant Chace's section under a heavy fire of shot and shell.

As Lieutenant Spencer was crossing the railroad, which was about six feet above the level of the field in which his section had been stationed, a solid shot from the enemy came so close as to cause him to fall to the ground, with nothing more serious than a good shaking up. Proceeding on his way he met Lieutenant Chace, on the Halifax road, leading his horse, and as he hailed him a shot from the rebels passed through the horse's body killing him instantly, the last horse of Battery B that went into the fight. Lieutenants Chace and Spencer then discussed the situation. Chace said there were three rounds of canister in one of his limbers, and thought they had better go back and use it up, they concluded to do so, and had started to go back to the pieces when a rebel major with some fifty or sixty men came out of the woods in their rear and demanded their surrender. He took them into the opening, left vacant by our troops, where the enemy had passed through into our lines near the Tenth Massachusetts Battery. As the major and his men, with the prisoners of Battery B were passing over the intrenchments into the enemy's line, one of Battery B's guns, of Lieutenant Chace's section, was fired by some one of our men. It had been loaded with canister and cut a swath in the enemy's ranks, killing and wounding a great number who were swarming into the field where the guns of Lieutenant Spencer's section were silently standing. But on swept the rebels, not only capturing the guns of Battery B, but also the entire New York Heavy Artillery regiment, which was supposed to have been placed there in support of the battery.

As Battery B's men were taken into the rebel line, the enemy showed Lieutenant Spencer the trenches which it had dug up to our picket line early in the morning in front of the Tenth Massachusetts Battery and where it had captured our pickets, and stationed rebel men in their places, attired in Union clothes taken from our captured men. This explains the reason why there was no picket firing in our front before the charge of the enemy.

Battery B's casualties at the Battle of Reams's Station on the 25th of August, 1864, were as follows: First Lieut. William S. Perrin commanding, wounded, struck by a piece of shell in the leg below the knee, and taken prisoner. First Lieut. James E. Chace and Second Lieut. Gideon Spencer were taken prisoners. Killed: First Sergt. Charles H. Adams and Private John Glynn. Wounded: Sergeants, Aborn W. Carter, Calvin L. Macomber, and Charles J. Rider; Corp. William H. Maxcy, and Private Thomas Donnelly. The following with those above were taken prisoners: Corp. Samuel H. Collington, who deserted taking the oath of allegiance to the Confederacy; Privates, William Costin, Samuel J. Goldsmith, John Hampston, Frederic G. Herman, Thomas McNamara, Charles F. Riley, Irving W. Tallman, Benjamin W. Walker, Henry A. Wellman, and William W. Winsor. Of the detached men two were killed, wounded and taken prisoners, twenty-nine. Killed in action four, wounded and taken prisoners, forty-eight; a total of fifty-two officers and men. There were also fifty battery horses killed and wounded. Our four pieces and four caissons were lost. Only one limber was saved. The enemy had dearly paid for our lost pieces in blood, for never were guns served more faithfully or held on to with greater tenacity. As long as ammunition lasted they belched forth an angry reply to the enemy located in the cornfield. The battery lost trophies, but not honor.

It was nearly midnight when the last squad of men from the battle field arrived at the camp of the battery's train, which was parked on the left of the road between the Norfolk Railroad and the Jerusalem Plank road. In the morning it was learned that one limber and a gun had been brought from the field into camp. At first it was thought to be one of Battery B's guns, and the men of that battery were quite pleased to think that one gun had been saved. Subsequent investigation proved, however, that the gun belonged to the Twelfth New York Battery, whose men proved their ownership by its number, and were allowed to take it to their camp after they had obtained permission from Major Hazard, chief of Artillery Brigade.

On the 26th, First Sergt. William D. Child, of Battery A, by orders from corps artillery headquarters, was placed in command of the remaining remnants of both batteries A and B, and ordered to make a report of the battle of Reams's Station for headquarters. The sergeant faithfully performed the duties assigned him. The men of Battery B, though somewhat insubordinate to his orders, were nevertheless courteous in other respects.

Corp. William P. Wells.

CHAPTER XXIII.

THE WINTER SIEGE OF PETERSBURG—THE BATTERY REORGANIZED.

AFTER the return of the Second Corps from Reams's Station, the First and Second Divisions were chiefly engaged, during the remainder of August, in completing a formidable line of defensive earthworks, which General Grant had ordered to be constructed to protect his left flank. The Third Division occupied the lines of intrenchments from Strong's house to the Norfolk Railroad. Meanwhile the men of the two batteries, under the command of First Sergt. W. D. Child, lay in camp awaiting orders.

On Sunday, September 4th, Capt. T. Fred. Brown returned and resumed command. The men were pleased to see him back.

On the 6th, the pioneer corps built a railroad which passed in rear of the camp, and ran from City Point Railroad to corps headquarters, facilitating the transportation of troops and supplies.

On the 7th, the two caissons which had been with the trains were returned to the battery.

On the 8th, Captain Brown ordered a general policing of the camp. This was the first time the grounds had been cleaned since the return of the men from Reams's Station.

On the 9th, the corps advanced and obtained possession of the enemy's rifle-pits at the point known as "The Chimney's," on the Jerusalem Plank road. This proved to be one of the most creditable operations of the siege.

On the 10th, a detail of men under command of First Sergeant Child, with Quartermaster-sergeant Horton, returned from City Point with rather a poor lot of horses for the battery. They were fortunate in securing as many as were required, for the demand was greater than the supply.

On Sunday, September 18th, Captain Brown received a park of six new Napoleon brass guns, light twelve-pounders, and four caissons. For the fifth time the battery was now fully equipped and ready for action.

On the 20th, Captain Brown commenced a series of mounted drills twice a day, weather permitting, as many new men and horses had been added to his command.

On the 23d, the two batteries A and B, which had been operating together since the 17th of July, were officially consolidated as one command, known as Battery B, First Regiment Rhode Island Light Artillery. This act terminated a distinctive history marked by the brilliant deeds of one of the first batteries of Rhode Island.

On the 24th, Captain Brown received marching orders. The prospects of a change stimulated the men to renewed activity, tents were soon struck, the battery equipage packed, and at dusk we pulled out of camp moving up to the right. The night was very dark, and we moved along slowly through the galleries and valleys to the intrenchments. The caissons and wagons were left and parked in a hollow in front of Meade's Station on the military railroad. Captain Brown with the pieces proceeded to the front line, and was assigned position in Fort Stedman. While going up to the fort in the dark we were much annoyed by the enemy's artillery fire. We remained under arms during the night, but as the enemy's fire was mostly to our right we did not become engaged.

On the 25th, a camp was laid out where the caissons were parked, the ground being cleared of shrubs, tents were pitched, and then the picket-rope for the horses was stretched.

At noon we were made happy by the appearance of the paymaster to settle Uncle Sam's account. The battery was paid for the months of July and August.

September 27th. The enemy had been remarkably quiet for the past few days, and we had improved the time by cleaning up the fort and making ourselves as comfortable as possible. At dusk, as if to make up for lost time, the enemy opened three batteries and shelled the fort vigorously. Battery B responded with telling effect, while the batteries on our right and left also opened, continuing the fire for more than an hour. The shells from the enemy's batteries swept the knoll at our rear clean of shrubs and small trees. Many of our tents in the fort were destroyed, but the casualties among the cannoneers were of a slight nature. During the night the battery kept up an occasional fire, so that there was no sleep for the men.

About nine o'clock on the evening of the 28th, the enemy again opened fire on us, and about the same programme was enacted as on the preceding night.

On the 29th, at dusk, the enemy opened fire again. The mortar batteries on both sides, stationed in our vicinity, seemed to take special delight in engaging each other at night, thus disturbing the peace of every one. Between the fire of the mortars at night and the necessity for instant readiness at the guns during the day, sleep for any length of time was impossible, and what we did obtain was greatly appreciated.

On the 30th, the battery received eleven recruits, detached from the Fourth New York Heavy Artillery.

Saturday, October 1st, at dawn, there was brisk firing of the pickets in our front, to which the battery had no chance to respond as the rain suddenly began to pour down. Soon everything was drenched and many of the bomb-proofs of the men were flooded, causing great discomforture to the occupants. It rained all day and part of the next night so that the troops were glad to remain quiet.

On the 6th, the men whose time of service had expired were discharged and they left for home. Quartermaster-Sergeant Anthony B. Horton was promoted to first sergeant *vice* William D. Child discharged. As sergeant Horton was absent on detached service with the supply trains, Company Clerk William J. Kenyon was promoted sergeant and to acting first sergeant.

On the 8th, by orders of the chief of artillery, Lieutenant Clarke, of the First New Jersey Battery, reported for duty. At this time all of Battery B's lieutenants were in the hands of the enemy as prisoners of war.

On the 18th, Lieutenant Bull, an engineer from corps headquarters, made a general inspection of Fort Stedman, the battery, and camp quarters. He complimented Captain Brown in regard to the good condition of the fort and his men.

On the 20th, the battery fired a salute of twenty guns in honor of General Sheridan's victory.

On the 26th, the Second and Third Divisions of the Second corps were sent on an expedition, to the left, to Boydton Plank road at Hatcher's Run. By the withdrawal of these two divisions, the First occupied in length about three and a half miles of the intrenchments.

On the afternoon of the 27th, our troops made an advance movement on our left, and the enemy countercharging pressed our men back to their support. On being reënforced our men held the enemy in check, while we gave the rebels a vigorous shelling causing them to return to their intrenchments, when their artillery opened and sent us their compliments by a few solid shot which did us no damage. We remained under arms all night expecting an attack, but all was quiet along the lines until dusk of the 28th, when the enemy gave us another shelling to which we responded.

On the 31st, Second Lieut. William B. Westcott, of Battery H, First Rhode Island Light Artillery, reported to Battery B for duty relieving Lieutenant Clarke, who then returned to his battery the "First New Jersey."

Tuesday, November 1st, the weather was very pleasant, and, as the enemy had been very quiet for the past few days, time hung heavy on our hands with nothing to do but watch the rebel lines.

On the 5th, at midnight, we were called to our posts and prepared for action. The rebels had charged our lines upon our left and captured four picket posts. This brought on a sharp engagement between the enemy and General Mott's division, joined in by the batteries. The heavens were lighted up by the flashing fires of burning fuse and bursting shells, while the discharge from the mortars streaked the sky with a seeming shower of falling stars. In this Battery B took no part, other than to enjoy the magnificent sight of the ærial fireworks.

On the 10th, at dark, a rebel mortar battery engaged in a duel with one of ours upon our right, which lasted for more than an hour resulting as far as we could discern in only a waste of ammunition, for the shelling of the enemy did our mortar battery no material harm.

On the 15th, Second Lieut. Nathaniel R. Chace, promoted from sergeant of Battery G, First Rhode Island Light Artillery, reported for duty.

On the 22d, at dark, sixty rebel prisoners passed the fort on their way to headquarters, they had deserted the Confederate cause having become tired of the war.

On the 23d, the drivers finished a bush fence around the camp of the battery's train, this was to keep the horses from straying off at night should they become loosened from the picket-rope.

On the 26th, Maj.-Gen. A. A. Humphreys succeeded General Hancock in the command of the Second Corps.

On the 29th, the Second Corps was relieved from its position in front of Petersburg by the Ninth Corps and marched to the extreme left, where it took up the lines formerly held by the Ninth. Headquarters were established at the Peebles house.

At early dawn the battery quietly withdrew from the intrenchments and arrived at the camp of the caissons without any casualties. Captain Brown ordered the tents to be struck, and forage and equipments packed for a move.

At one P. M. the battery broke camp and left Meade's Station, moving with the First Division toward the left of the line we passed the Jones house and halted, bivouacking near the Southwell house.

On the 30th, we resumed the march to Patrick's Station, the end of the Military Railroad near Poplar Spring Church, and encamped.

First Sergt. A. B. Horton, having been discharged received the commission of second lieutenant in Battery H. Sergt. William J. Kenyon was promoted to first sergeant.

Thursday, December 1st, Captain Brown received orders to prepare camp quarters, and the men were kept quite busy until the camp was finished.

On the morning of the 7th, the rain poured in torrents, but nevertheless at seven o'clock the battery was ordered to hitch up and leave camp. Moving back toward the right we crossed the military railroad and took position in a new fort which the infantry was building. We remained until dark when upon being relieved by Battery B, First New Jersey, we returned to camp.

On the 9th, the First Division was ordered out on a reconnaissance, and Battery B followed along the Vaughan road near to Hatcher's Run. Here our infantry encountered the enemy's pickets and drove them across the stream. The battery was ordered into position, but, after shelling the enemy's line for about twenty minutes, we were ordered to cease firing. No reply was received from the enemy's artillery during the demonstrations made by our infantry. We remained in position all day and at dark withdrew to the rear, then parked and bivouacked for the night.

On the morning of the 10th, the division moved forward to Armstrong's Mill. The advance guard had a slight brush with the enemy's pickets who retreated without bringing on an engagement. At dark the division was ordered to return, and the battery reached camp at ten o'clock.

On the afternoon of the 11th, the centre and left sections, under

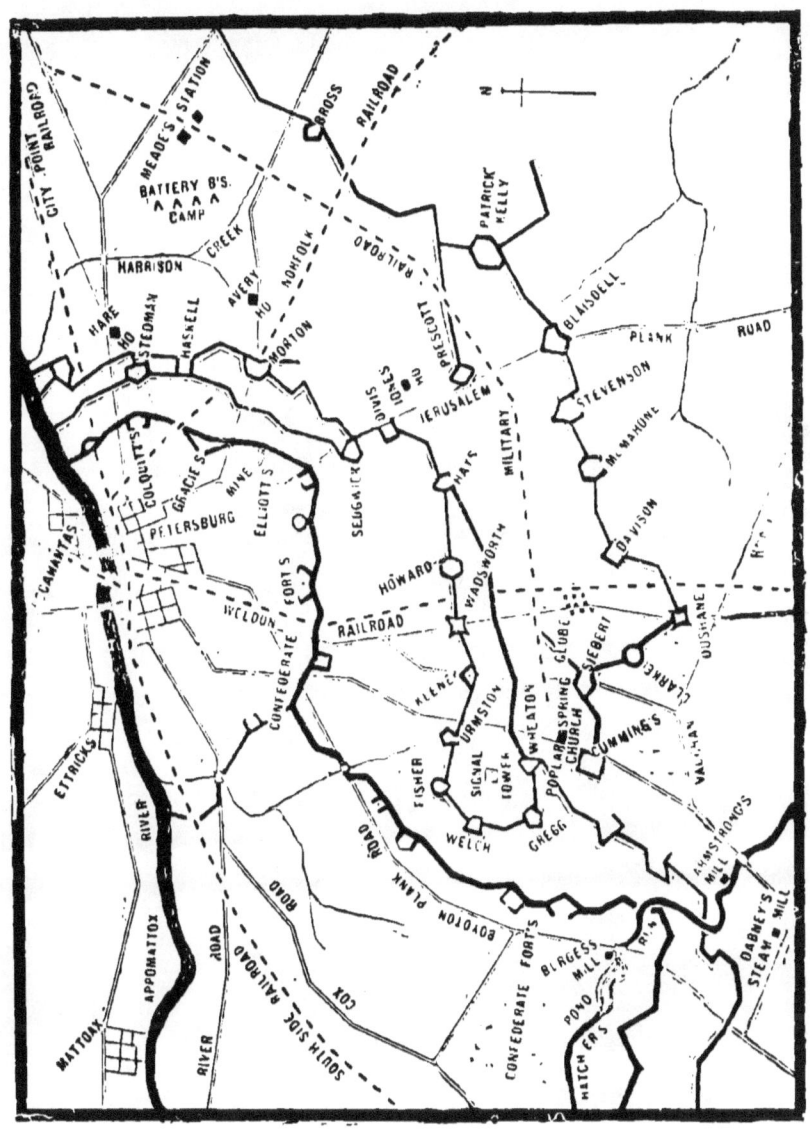

Siege of Petersburg, June 15, 1864-April 2, 1865.

Lieutenants Chace and Westcott, were sent to the front. After crossing the Weldon Railroad they were ordered into position in Fort Davidson. The Fifth Corps was sent out on a reconnaissance, and succeeded in destroying the Weldon Railroad beyond the Nottoway River to Hicksford. On the 14th, the Fifth Corps returned and the two sections were relieved and sent back to camp.

On the 17th, the battery fired a salute in honor of General Thomas's victory.

On the 18th, we commenced to build huts and stable stockade, also a bush fence around the camp. Upon the completion of winter quarters the men were given an opportunity to rest and recuperate. Before the year closed Capt. T. Fred. Brown was breveted major, to date from Dec. 3, 1864, for meritorious service, remaining with the battery as commander.

Sunday, Jan. 1, 1865. The New Year opened with a fierce snow storm, followed during the day by a cold wave. The month of January, weather permitting, was occupied in drilling the large number of temporarily attached men. Foot and mounted drills, and manual of the piece were practiced regularly.

On the 7th, the battery was paid for the months of September, October, November and December, thus settling accounts for 1864.

Nothing of consequence occurred to the battery while encamped at Patrick's Station.

On February 3d, Major Brown received marching orders to have his battery ready to move at a moment's notice, the gun and caisson equipments were all replaced, and three days' rations of grain strapped on the chests.

On the 4th, Major Brown with the right and centre sections, under Lieutenant Westcott, left camp and moved out to the front and going into Fort Cummings relieved Battery K, Fourth United States. The First Division of the Second Corps was left to hold the intrenchments, while the other two with the Fifth Corps and General Gregg's cavalry went on an expedition across Hatcher's Run.

On the 5th, Lieut. N. R. Chace was ordered to report with the left section and caissons to Lieut. J. W. Roder, Battery K, Fourth United States, and with that battery and the Second Division moved down to Hatcher's Run. During the afternoon heavy skirmish firing was heard at the front.

On the 7th, the three sections returned to camp, the left from the front, the first and centre from Fort Cummings. The result of the expedition, on the 5th and 6th, was to extend our lines of intrenchments to Hatcher's Run at the Vaughan road crossing.

On the 11th, upon Major Brown receiving marching orders, the tents were struck and all camp equipage packed in the wagons, then the battery was ordered to hitch up, and at noon broke camp and pulled out into the road leaving our winter quarters at Patrick's Station. Marching westward toward Hatcher's Run we moved down by the Vaughan road, and at dusk halted at the Tucker house where we parked and bivouacked.

On the 12th, Major Brown ordered a camp to be laid out, and after the ground was cleared of shrubbery, the tents pitched, and during the remainder of the month we remained quietly in camp the time being occupied in drilling.

On the 21st, Lieut. W. B. Westcott, who was on detached service from Battery H, was granted a furlough and left for home. While in Providence, R. I., he was promoted, receiving the commission of first lieutenant of Battery B, and on the 11th of March he returned and reported for duty.

On the 15th of March, the battery was reduced for light marching, all surplus baggage and camp equipage were sent to the quartermaster's department.

On the 18th, the battery received twenty-one recruits from Rhode Island.

On the 19th, Battery B with the Artillery Brigade was reviewed by General Humphreys, commander of the Second Corps.

On the 23d, the Second Corps was reviewed by General Grant. In the afternoon the left section, under Lieut. N. R. Chace, was sent to the front to relieve Battery B, First New Jersey.

On the 24th, our infantry advanced and formed new lines.

On the 25th, the left section returned to camp. At noon we heard of the capture of Fort Stedman by the rebels, but it was subsequently retaken by our troops who captured nearly two thousand prisoners and nine stands of colors. About three o'clock the battery was sent out to the picket line, and went into position near the Watkins house. There were several heavy skirmishes in our front. During the time that the battery shelled the rebel lines it received no reply from their artillery. At midnight being relieved we returned to camp.

On the 26th, the left section, Lieut. N. R. Chace, went to the front and relieved one of the Fifth Corps batteries.

On the 28th, the battery being relieved from picket duty returned to camp. The Second Corps was relieved at the intrenchments by General Gibbon's Twenty-fourth Corps.

In the afternoon Major T. Fred. Brown left the battery to fill the position to which he had been promoted on the staff of Col. John G. Hazard, Chief of Artillery. The command of the battery was turned over to First Lieut. William B. Westcott.

Charles A. Libbey, our late quartermaster-sergeant, was in camp to-day on a visit to his comrades-in-arms; he was given a hearty welcome, and on leaving said if we would call on him he would return the compliment. He was connected with the sutler's department, therefore, it is needless to say that many called. At dusk the battery received twenty-nine recruits from Rhode Island.

On the 29th, at seven A. M., we broke camp at the Tucker house and followed the Second Division; crossing Hatcher's Run at eight o'clock we advanced about a mile and went into position. Heavy firing was heard to our right, it was the engagement of the Fifth Corps on the Quaker road.

On the morning of the 30th, the battery advanced about one mile to the Crow house, and took position at short range in front of a rebel fort. The day passed without anything of importance transpiring; the operations of our troops were delayed by a fearful downpour of rain which had commenced the night before and continued through the next day, flooding the low swampy country, and rendering the miry roads almost impassable until they were corduroyed.

On the 31st, while our infantry was assaulting the enemy's line between Hatcher's Run and the Boydton Plank road, Battery B vigorously shelled the rebel fort in its front, and at night bivouacked in the same position.

Saturday, April 1st, at early dawn the left section, under Lieut. N. R. Chace, was advanced to the right and front about three hundred yards, to a redoubt which the cannoneers had built during the night. The battery was under orders to open on the enemy's line upon the firing of a signal gun. Thus the men were under arms all day and part of the following night. It was not until two o'clock on the morning of the 2d, that the signal gun was fired, then Battery B opened on the rebel fort. At the same time all of our artillery opened fire on the enemy's line, and a heavy cannonading was kept up until sunrise. Then our infantry made a charge, and the rebel lines, from in front of Fort Sedgwick to our extreme left, were captured and occupied by the troops of the Second, Sixth, Twenty-fourth, and Twenty-fifth Corps. This brilliant victory resulted in the fall of Petersburg.

At ten o'clock the battery left the intrenchments and advanced, marching up the Boydton Plank road to the Cox road, along which we advanced about five miles, then halted and encamped for the night.

Sergt. Albert Straight.

CHAPTER XXIV.

THE PURSUIT OF THE CONFEDERATE ARMY—GENERAL LEE'S SURRENDER AT APPOMATTOX.

ON the 3d of April the battery made an early start and marched all day and night, moving toward the west we crossed the Namozine Creek, and halted at three o'clock in the morning to feed the horses. Lee's army was now in full retreat followed by the Army of the Potomac. One of the most eventful days in the history of this country, was Monday, April 3, 1865, when the Confederates evacuated both Richmond and Petersburg, resulting in the fall of the rebel capital and seat of war. The Confederates unwilling that the victorious army should have as spoils the tobacco stored in their warehouses, set them on fire. They also fired the bridges which spanned the James River. The wind spread the flames far and wide, burning a large portion of the houses in the centre of the city. The conflagration was checked by the Union army after its occupancy of the place.

On the 4th, at five o'clock we resumed the march toward Burkeville, crossed the Nintercomac Creek and marched all day until eight P. M., when we halted and bivouacked for the night.

On the 5th, at daybreak, we were again on the road following Lee's army. At night we camped near Jetersville.

On the morning of the 6th, at six o'clock, we resumed the march going westward, on reaching rising ground and looking across the field we could see, to the front and right, columns of weary rebel troops toiling along endeavoring to escape in a flank movement by way of the Danville road. Our artillery was ordered into position and Battery B opened with shot and shell, firing about forty rounds, while our infantry was sent forward in hot pursuit. This was the last shelling that Battery B gave the rebels. At noon we limbered up and resumed the march, crossed Flat Creek, and at nine P. M. halted and parked for the night. The country through which we passed was broken, its open fields alternating with forests having a dense undergrowth and numerous swamps, over and through which the lines of battle followed the retreating foe.

On the 7th, we left camp at sunrise and still moving westward halted at Farmville. Here the enemy made a stand, and the battery was placed in position overlooking the railroad, but did not do any firing. The infantry of the corps was smartly engaged at High Bridge, and forcing the enemy back saved the wagon road bridge from destruction, also capturing nineteen guns and 130 army wagons. Among the prisoners captured during the day was General Lewis, of Gordon's Corps, severely wounded.

On the morning of the 8th, we heard that General Grant last night sent to General Lee, by way of the Second Corps lines, a letter demanding the surrender of the Confederate army. As anticipated the enemy's forces had moved off during the night, and the pursuit was accordingly taken up by the Second Corps. At seven o'clock the battery left camp and moving along the Lynchburg stage road marched all day. At midnight we halted, parked beside the road and bivouacked.

While the Second Corps was in hot pursuit along the north bank of the Appomattox, General Grant's second letter to Lee was sent through the lines. Late in the afternoon our cavalry under General Custer captured Appomattox Station, and the trains loaded with supplies for Lee's famishing troops, together with a large park of artillery and many prisoners. Inspired by the prospect of a final victory, the cavalry still pushed forward and by nightfall had gained a position west of the Appomattox Court House, thus cutting off the enemy's retreat to Lynchburg as it had done before at Danville.

On the morning of the 9th, before we broke camp three days' rations were issued, after which the battery was inspected by Lieut. W. B. Westcott, with a view to having the battery in readiness to perform any duty whether marching or fighting. At nine o'clock we left camp and took up the chase moving at a slow pace until eleven o'clock, when a halt was made by the roadside. While waiting the couriers, with dispatches from Lee to Grant, crossed the path of Battery B, passing under its guidon on their way to headquarters.

Lieut. Gideon Spencer.

Firing was heard at the front. The infantry had been pushed steadily forward by General Humphreys, and had come upon the skirmishers of General Longstreet's rear guard. Preparations were at once made to attack the enemy, which was found in position, by sending troops forward, and at noon Battery B resumed its march onward.

At four o'clock in the afternoon we received the glad news of General Lee's surrender at Appomattox Court House. The long struggle to maintain the union of the States was virtually ended. Of the magnanimity with which the conqueror bore his triumph, and hastened to lift his fallen foe it is not necessary to speak. The world knows the story well, and in both sections of the united country this will ever be one of his chiefest titles to fame.

As the glad tidings spread among the troops the enthusiasm of the men knew no bounds, cheer upon cheer went up, hats and caps were flung high in the air. The soldiers could hardly restrain their feelings, being nearly overcome with joy as the picture of home presented itself to their minds.

At six P. M. the battery parked and encamped near Clover Hill, where it rested all day on the 10th.

On the 11th, Lieutenant Westcott received marching orders, and preparations to return to the James River were at once begun. At ten o'clock the battery broke camp and moving toward the east marched ten miles to New Store where we parked for the night. The roads were very muddy as it had rained all day.

On the 12th, we marched back near to Farmville, crossed the Appomattox River and bivouacked for the night.

On the 13th, the battery moved three miles beyond the Lynchburg Railroad, and on the 14th, marched near to Burke Station on the Danville Railroad and encamped. While here Lieuts. James E. Chace and Gideon Spencer returned to duty, having been exchanged in March. As senior officer Lieut. James E. Chace was given command of the battery, while Lieutenant Westcott resumed command of the right section, Lieutenant Spencer the left section, and Lieut. N. R. Chace the centre section.

On the 19th, by orders issued from the war department, the battery as well as the entire army performed no work during the funeral service of our late President, Abraham Lincoln.

On the 21st, had battery inspection by Lieut. James E. Chace, and on the 22d the Artillery Brigade was reviewed by Col. John G. Hazard for the last time while in the field.

On Sunday, the 23d, had battery and camp inspection by Maj. T. Fred. Brown.

On the morning of the 25th, by General Orders No. 66, from Artillery Brigade, Battery B, First New Jersey fired a salute of thirteen guns, then one gun at intervals of half an hour during the day in token of bereavement of the nation's loss, "the death of President Lincoln."

Battery B had the honor of firing the national salute of thirty-six minute-guns at sunset.

On the 28th, the troops were made quite jovial by the news that General Johnson of the rebel army had surrendered to General Sherman.

Monday, May 1st, the battery received marching orders, but as the roads were very muddy and in a bad condition for traveling, on account of recent rains, the ammunition chests were taken to the station, on the morning of the 2d, and shipped to City Point on cars, and from there they were shipped by transports to Alexandria. Corporal Burlingame with a detail of cannoneers went with them.

At 3.30 o'clock Lieut. James E. Chace ordered the battery to pack and hitch up. About four o'clock we broke camp and left Burke Station passing through Burkeville; we marched until eight P. M., then halted and parked for the night.

At an early hour on the morning of the 3d, we resumed the march eastward, and passing through Jetersville and Amelia Court House crossed the Appomattox River, at dusk we halted and bivouacked by the wayside, having marched twenty-seven miles during the day.

On the 4th, we resumed the march, and on the morning of the 5th, arrived at Manchester where we were encamped all day.

On the 6th, we crossed the James River to Richmond and passing through the city encamped five miles beyond.

The business portion of Richmond, between the canal basin and Capitol Square, was a heap of ruins. Household furniture which had been brought to the square during the conflagration had disappeared piece by piece, being appropriated by the colored population. The doors of Libby Prison stood wide open, and as we passed the negroes about the place greeted us with: "Dey's all gone, massa." Yes, Belle Island was deserted.

On the morning of the 7th, we again set out, marching north and crossing the Chickahominy River we passed through Hanover Court House, and crossing the Pamunkey River encamped for the night.

On the 8th, we were on the march all day, crossed the Richmond and Fredericksburg Railroad at Chesterfield Station and parked for the night at Old Chesterfield.

On the evening of the 9th, we encamped three miles beyond Massaponax Church.

On the 10th, the battery passed through Fredericksburg, crossed the Rappahannock River to Falmouth, and at night parked near Stafford Court House.

On the 11th, we went into camp at four P. M. on the bank of the Quantico Creek.

On the 12th, we halted for the night near the Occoquan River.

On the 13th, left camp at four A. M., crossed the river at Wolf Run Shoals, passed through Fairfax Station and Court House, and encamped at Bailey's Cross Roads.

On the 15th, we moved up near to Munson's Hill and encamped, remaining there during the rest of the month.

On the 16th, the battery went to Alexandria and returned with the ammunition chests which had been shipped from Burkeville.

On the 19th, the caissons were taken to Washington and left at the arsenal. Brevet Captain William S. Perrin visited the battery in the afternoon, and the men were glad to see him looking so well though minus a leg.

The 22d, was a busy day in preparing for inspection and review.

On May 23d, occurred the grand review of the Army of the Potomac by the President. Early in the morning Battery B left its camp, and proceeding to Washington took the position assigned it. At the appointed time the head of the column, led by General Humphreys and staff, moved up Pennsylvania Avenue. On the reviewing stand, in front of the White House, were the President and his Cabinet, and all foreign ministers, together with the governors of the loyal states and many other distinguished people invited to be present. The parade of the troops was magnificent. In dress, in soldierly appearance, in precision of alignment and in marching it could not be surpassed, was the decisions made by those who witnessed it. At five P. M. the battery returned to camp, the men somewhat tired but well pleased that they had had the honor of taking part in the final scene of the war.

The next day occurred the review of General Sherman's army. One of the pleasing features of this was the following after each brigade of "the foragers," known as "Sherman's Bummers," as they appeared on the march through Georgia.

These reviews were probably never surpassed on the American continent.

On the evening of the 25th, there occurred a most beautiful sight, the regiments and batteries throughout the army lighted bon-fires composed of every material at hand that would burn, besides thousands of lighted candles flaming from the ridge-poles of the tents. As the din of cheers from the delighted troops rose with the evening air, it might be said that the enthusiasm of the soldiers was going up in smoke.

On the 27th, Lieut. Gideon Spencer, having received a first lieutenant's commission in Battery F, then stationed at Richmond, left Battery B and proceeded to the late rebel capital.

On the 30th, the battery took part in the review of the Second Corps, by Generals Meade, Hancock, and Humphreys, on the plains at Bailey's Cross Roads. Soon after these reviews the troops were ordered into the various camps, where they received a final visit from the paymaster, and where they separated, some never to meet again.

CHAPTER XXV.

THE RETURN TO RHODE ISLAND AND MUSTER-OUT OF SERVICE.

IT was now known that the men of Battery B were soon to be sent home, and we awaited with impatience that happy hour. Lieut. James E. Chace had received orders to make an inventory of all the battery equipments and supplies. The guns and carriages were cleaned, the harnesses washed and oiled, and everything was put in readiness to be turned in. All attached men were sent to their regiments, and all of our detached men returned to the battery.

On the 31st of May the battery was taken to Washington, and parked near the Arsenal grounds having been turned in to the ordnance department. The most serviceable horses were turned over to Battery K, Fourth United States Artillery.

On June 1st, all government property was turned over to the quartermaster's department, and the horses were taken to the corral. In the afternoon the last inspection of the men was held, after which we were informed that we had been ordered to Rhode Island.

On the morning of the 3d, after partaking of our last army breakfast of hard-tack, pork, and coffee, tents were struck, and with our few articles of clothing packed and slung upon our shoulders we broke camp, and turning our backs on Virginia marched to Washington, D. C. Here we had to wait and passed the time as best we could until six P. M. At that hour we boarded the cars and left for Baltimore, where upon our arrival we marched to the Pennsylvania and New Jersey Railroad station taking the cars from there for Philadelphia. Upon our arrival at the Quaker City, we were taken to the " Cooper Union " rooms and served with an ample repast. Again boarding the cars we left for Jersey City, at which place we embarked on a ferry-boat and crossing the North River to New York city again took cars for Rhode Island, arriving in Providence about nine o'clock on the morning of the 5th. We were welcomed with a salute fired by the Marine Artillery, and escorted by the Mechanic Rifles, Colonel Arnold, to Washington Hall, where we were regaled with an abundant collation, after which we were marched to the Silvey barracks on the Cove lands west of the railroad station. Here the men were quartered until they were discharged. In due time the muster-out rolls were completed and signed and the men paid.

Battery B was formally mustered out of the service of the United States, Monday, June 12, 1865, with a record of three years and eleven months' service in the War of the Rebellion. Its reputation made in actual service was of the highest. There was nothing connected with its organization to particularly impress the minds of the people of the State it represented, but those connected with it, and particularly those who were with it from the beginning, have always been proud of their membership. It is with much gratification that its members, when asked the question " What did you serve with? " reply : " Battery B, First Rhode Island Light Artillery."

After receiving their discharge papers the men separated with farewell words and hearty good-byes, many never to meet again. Others on Memorial Day, the 30th of May of each year, meet to honor the memory of comrades who gave their lives for their country's cause. At the annual reunions of veteran associations they assemble to renew the ties of comradeship formed during the struggle of more than four years duration ; a struggle which cost hundreds of thousands of lives and as many millions of treasure, but which has conferred, even upon the defeated South, blessings that more than compensate the country for all her losses.

By order of General Meade, March 7, 1865, the following names of the battles in which Battery B had borne a meritorious part were directed to be inscribed on its colors :

BALL'S BLUFF,	MINE RUN,
YORKTOWN,	WILDERNESS,
FAIR OAKS,	PO RIVER,
MALVERN HILL,	SPOTTSYLVANIA,
ANTIETAM,	NORTH ANNA,
FIRST FREDERICKSBURG,	TOLOPOTOMOY,
SECOND FREDERICKSBURG,	COLD HARBOR,
GETTYSBURG,	PETERSBURG,
BRISTOE STATION,	DEEP BOTTOM,
REAMS'S STATION.	

ROSTER.

[THE names are recorded in the order of the highest rank while in service in the battery. The missing dates are owing to the unfinished records, now being compiled at the Adjutant's-general's office of Rhode Island.]

Captains.

THOMAS F. VAUGHN. First lieutenant, Battery A, June 6, 1861; captain, Battery B, Aug. 21, 1861; resigned Dec. 2, 1861; discharged Dec. 11, 1861.

WALTER O. BARTLETT. First lieutenant, Battery E, Sept. 28, 1861; captain, Battery B, Jan. 30, 1862; resigned Aug. 13, 1862; discharged Aug. 19, 1862.

JOHN G. HAZARD. Mustered Aug. 6, 1861, as regimental hospital steward; first lieutenant, Battery C, Aug. 8, 1861; transferred to Battery A, Sept. 17, 1861; captain, Battery B, Aug. 18, 1862; major April 7, 1864; brevet lieutenant colonel Aug. 1, 1884; lieutenant-colonel April 13, 1865; brevet colonel May 3, 1865; colonel June 12, 1865; breveted brigadier-general to date, May 3, 1865; mustered out July 1, 1865.

T. FRED. BROWN. Mustered June 6, 1861, as corporal; sergeant, Battery A; second lieutenant, Battery C, Aug. 13, 1862; first lieutenant, Battery B, Dec. 29, 1862; wounded July 2, 1863, at Gettysburg, Pa.; adjutant Feb. 17, 1864; captain, Battery B, April 13, 1864; brevet major to date, Dec. 3, 1864; brevet lieutenant-colonel April 9, 1865; major June 2, 1865; mustered out lieutenant-colonel June 12, 1865.

First Lieutenants.

RAYMOND H. PERRY. First lieutenant, Battery B, Aug. 12, 1861; honorably discharged Oct. 11, 1862.

GEORGE W. ADAMS. Mustered Aug. 12, 1861; first lieutenant, Battery B; captain, Battery I, Feb. 6. 1863, to date Jan. 30, 1863; transferred to Battery G, April 22, 1863; brevet lieutenant-colonel April 2, 1865; major June 12, 1865; mustered out June 24, 1865.

HORACE S. BLOODGOOD. Second lieutenant, Battery B, Aug. 12, 1861; first lieutenant Oct. 13, 1862; captain, Battery G, Dec. 29, 1862; resigned; discharged April 22, 1863.

T. FRED. BROWN. See captain.

WILLIAM S. PERRIN. Mustered Aug. 25, 1861, as corporal; sergeant March 25, 1862, Battery C; second lieutenant, Battery B, Nov. 11, 1862; first lieutenant March 20, 1863; wounded Oct. 14, 1863, at Bristoe Station; reënlisted Feb. 12, 1864; wounded and taken prisoner Aug. 25, 1864, at Reams's Station, Va.; paroled Sept. 12, 1864; brevet captain Dec. 2, 1864; discharged for disability from wounds Feb. 4, 1865.

JAMES E. CHACE. Mustered Dec. 2, 1861, as sergeant; second lieutenant, Battery G, March 12, 1863; first lieutenant, Battery B, April 26, 1864; taken prisoner Aug. 25, 1864, at Reams's Station, Va.; paroled Feb. 22, 1865; mustered out June 12, 1865.

WILLIAM B. WESTCOTT. Mustered Dec. 2, 1861, as sergeant; quartermaster-sergeant, Battery G, June 9, 1862; second lieutenant, Battery H, April 26, 1864; first lieutenant, Battery B, March 2, 1865; mustered out June 12, 1865.

Second Lieutenants.

HORACE S. BLOODGOOD. See first lieutenant.

FRANCIS A. SMITH. Mustered June 6, 1861, as sergeant Battery A; second lieutenant, Battery B, Aug. 12, 1861; discharged Nov. 28, 1861.

G. LYMAN DWIGHT. Mustered June 6, 1861, as corporal Battery A; second lieutenant, Battery B, Nov. 29, 1861; first lieutenant, Battery A, Nov. 4, 1862; adjutant to May 23, 1863; mustered out July 17, 1864.

WILLIAM S. PERRIN. See first lieutenant.

JOSEPH S. MILNE. Mustered Sept. 30, 1861, as sergeant Battery E; second lieutenant, Battery B, Nov. 11, 1862; attached to Cushing's Battery A, Fourth United States Artillery, June 9, 1863; mortally wounded July 3, 1863, at Gettysburg, Pa.; died in hospital July 8, 1863.

CHARLES A. BROWN. Mustered Sept. 30, 1861, as corporal; quartermaster-sergeant March 14, 1862, Battery E; second lieutenant, Battery B, March 20, 1863; taken prisoner May 18, 1864, returning to Fredericksburg, Va.; escaped Nov. 4, 1864, from prison at Macon, Ga.; first lieutenant, Battery G, Oct. 21, 1864; never mustered; discharged Jan. 31, 1865.

WILLARD B. PIERCE. Mustered June 6, 1861, as private; first sergeant, Battery A; second lieutenant, Battery B, July 27, 1863; discharged April 11, 1864.

GIDEON SPENCER. Mustered Sept. 4, 1861, as private; sergeant; reënlisted Jan. 30, 1864, Battery D; second lieutenant, Battery B, April 26, 1864; taken prisoner Aug. 25, 1864, at Reams's Station, Va.; paroled Feb. 22, 1865; first lieutenant, Battery F, May 16, 1865; mustered out June 27, 1865.

NATHANIEL R. CHACE. Mustered Dec. 2, 1861, as private; corporal; sergeant June 9, 1862; first sergeant Nov. 3, 1864; reënlisted Dec. 19, 1863, Battery G; second lieutenant, Battery B, Oct. 21, 1864; mustered out June 12, 1865.

First Sergeants.

ERNEST STAPLES. Mustered Sept. 11, 1861, as first sergeant; transferred to Rhode Island, Dec. 2, 1861.

GEORGE W. BLAIR. Mustered Aug. 13, 1861, as sergeant; first sergeant Dec. 2, 1861; discharged Feb. 7, 1863; first lieutenant, Battery I, to date from Feb. 2, 1863; transferred to Battery H, April 23, 1863.

JOHN T. BLAKE. Mustered Aug. 13, 1861, as sergeant; first sergeant Feb. 7, 1863; wounded July 2, 1863, at Gettysburg, Pa.; discharged Dec. 4, 1863; second lieutenant, Battery A, Dec. 5, 1863; discharged Aug. 19, 1864.

ALANSON A. WILLIAMS. Mustered Aug. 13, 1861, as private; corporal Oct. 15, 1862; wounded Dec. 13, 1862, at Fredericksburg, Va.; sergeant Feb. 5, 1863; first sergeant Dec. 4, 1863; reënlisted Dec. 18, 1863; discharged May 18, 1864; second lieutenant, Company C, Fourteenth Regiment Rhode Island Heavy Artillery, June 6, 1864.

JOHN F. HANSON. Mustered Aug. 13, 1861, as private; wounded Dec. 13, 1862, at Fredericksburg, Va.; corporal Feb. 5, 1863; sergeant Nov. 4, 1863; first sergeant May 18, 1864; mustered out Aug. 12, 1864.

CHARLES H. ADAMS. Mustered Aug. 13, 1861, as sergeant; reënlisted Dec. 23, 1863; first sergeant Aug. 12. 1864; killed Aug. 25, 1864, at Reams's Station, Va.

WILLIAM D. CHILD. Mustered Oct. 5, 1861, as private; first sergeant; transferred from Battery A, Sept. 23, 1864; discharged Oct. 3, 1864.

ANTHONY B. HORTON. Mustered Aug. 13. 1862, as private; corporal March 25, 1863; sergeant Dec. 1, 1862; reënlisted Feb. 8, 1864; first sergeant Oct. 3, 1864; discharged Dec. 19, 1864; first lieutenant, Battery H, to date from Nov. 29, 1864.

WILLIAM J. KENYON. Mustered Aug. 13, 1861, as private; reënlisted Feb. 4, 1864; sergeant Oct. 6. 1864; first sergeant Dec. 19, 1864; second lieutenant May 16, 1865; not mustered; mustered out June 12, 1865.

Quartermaster-Sergeants.

WILLIAM S. DYER. Mustered Aug. 13, 1861, as quartermaster-sergeant; discharged for disability Dec. 1, 1862.

CHARLES A. LIBBEY. Mustered Aug. 13, 1861, as corporal; sergeant Dec. 15, 1861; quartermaster sergeant Dec. 1, 1862; mustered out Aug. 12, 1864.

AMOS M. C. OLNEY. Mustered June 6, 1861, as private; sergeant; reënlisted Dec. 19, 1863; transferred from Battery A, Sept. 23, 1864; quartermaster-sergeant Aug. 12, 1864; mustered out June 12, 1865.

Sergeants.

JACOB B. LEWIS. Mustered, Aug. 13, 1861, as sergeant; acting first sergeant until Sept. 11, 1861; discharged for disability Dec. 13, 1861.

JOHN McCOMB, OR McCOOMBS. Mustered Aug. 13, 1861; discharged for disability Dec. 13, 1861.

SILAS G. TUCKER. Mustered Aug. 13, 1861; wounded Oct. 21, 1861, at Ball's Bluff, Va.; discharged for disability from wounds Oct. 22, 1862.

RICHARD H. GALLUP. Mustered Aug. 13, 1861, as private ; corporal Oct. 1, 1861 ; sergeant Dec. 15, 1861 ; resigned to private Nov. 24, 1863, and attached to Artillery Brigade Headquarters as butcher ; mustered out Aug. 12, 1864.

JOHN E. WARDLOW. Mustered Aug. 13, 1861, as private ; sergeant Dec. 15, 1861 ; discharged Oct. 24, 1863 ; second lieutenant, Rhode Island Volunteers, Oct. 24, 1863 ; first lieutenant, Company E, Fourteenth Regiment Rhode Island Heavy Artillery, Dec. 3, 1863.

LEONARD J. WHITING. Mustered Aug. 25, 1861, as corporal; transferred from Battery C, Jan. 1, 1862 ; sergeant March 16, 1862 ; discharged March 29, 1862 ; second lieutenant, Sixth Regiment Rhode Island Volunteers, to date March 27, 1862 ; transferred to Company E, First Rhode Island Cavalry.

ALBERT STRAIGHT. Mustered Oct. 2, 1861, as private : lance corporal Nov. 20, 1861 ; corporal Dec. 15, 1861 ; sergeant May 12, 1862 ; died Nov. 16, 1863, at Fairfax Cemetery Hospital, Virginia.

EDWIN A. CHASE. Mustered Aug. 13, 1861, as corporal ; sergeant Jan. 26, 1863 ; wounded July 2, 1863, at Gettysburg, Pa. ; mustered out Aug. 12, 1864.

JOHN H. RHODES. Mustered Aug. 13, 1861, as private ; lance corporal Nov. 18, 1862 ; corporal Oct. 7, 1863 ; sergeant Nov. 24, 1863 ; mustered out Aug. 12, 1864.

PARDON S. WALKER. Mustered Aug. 13, 1861, as private : corporal Oct. 1, 1861 ; sergeant Dec. 4, 1863 ; mustered out Aug. 12, 1864.

CALVIN L. MACOMBER. Mustered Aug. 13, 1861, as private ; corporal March 24, 1863 ; reënlisted Dec. 18, 1863 ; sergeant Aug. 12, 1864 ; wounded and taken prisoner Aug. 25, 1864, at Reams's Station, Va. ; paroled Sept. 1, 1864 ; mustered out June 12, 1865.

CHARLES J. RIDER. Mustered Aug. 13, 1861, as private ; reënlisted Dec. 20, 1863 ; corporal May 12, 1864 ; sergeant Aug. 12, 1864 : taken prisoner Aug. 25, 1864, at Reams's Station, Va. ; paroled Sept. 1, 1864 ; mustered out June 12, 1865.

ABORN W. CARTER. Mustered March 24, 1862, as private ; corporal May 27, 1862 ; sergeant Aug. 12, 1864 ; wounded Aug. 25, 1864, at Reams's Station, Va. ; mustered out March 24, 1865.

ROBERT L. JOHNSON. Mustered Aug. 16, 1862, as private; corporal; sergeant; transferred from Battery A, Sept. 23, 1864; mustered out June 12, 1865.

AMOS H. ARMINGTON. Mustered May 22, 1862, as private; sergeant; transferred from Battery A, Sept. 23, 1864; mustered out May 21, 1865.

CHARLES E. SMITH. Mustered July 17, 1862; transferred from Battery A, Sept. 23, 1864; mustered out June 12, 1865.

Corporals.

WASHINGTON C. HASKINS. Mustered Aug. 13, 1861, as corporal; wounded Oct. 21, 1861, at Ball's Bluff, Va.; discharged for disability from wounds Sept. 22, 1862.

LUTHER C. OLNEY. Mustered Aug. 13, 1861, as corporal; wounded Oct. 21, 1861, at Ball's Bluff, Va.; died Oct. 22, 1862, in hospital at North Providence, R. I.

DAVID B. PATTERSON. Mustered Aug. 13, 1861, as corporal; ran over June 29, 1862, fracturing both legs, and taken prisoner at White Oak Swamp, Va.; paroled Aug. 1, 1862; discharged for disability March 25, 1863.

CALVIN W. RATHBONE. Mustered Aug. 13, 1861, as corporal; wounded July 1, 1862, at Malvern Hill, Va.; wounded Dec. 13, 1862, at Fredericksburg, Va.; discharged for disability from wounds June 24, 1864.

EDWARD B. WHIPPLE. Mustered Aug. 13, 1861, as corporal; mustered out Aug. 12, 1864.

WILLIAM M. TANNER. Mustered Aug. 13, 1861, as private; corporal Oct. 1, 1861; missing Oct. 21, 1861, at Ball's Bluff, Va.

CHARLES B. WORTHINGTON. Mustered Aug. 13, 1861, as private; corporal Oct. 1, 1861; wounded July 2, 1863, at Gettysburg, Pa.; wounded May 5, 1864, at Wilderness, Va.; mustered out Aug. 12, 1864.

WILLIAM A. DICKERSON. Mustered Aug. 13, 1861, as private; corporal March 3, 1862; died Nov. 1, 1862, in hospital at Harper's Ferry, Va.

WILLIAM HAMILTON. Mustered Aug. 13, 1861, as private; corporal March 13, 1862; died Dec. 4, 1862, in hospital at Frederick, Md.

WILLIAM P. WELLS. Mustered Aug. 13, 1861, as private; corporal March 25, 1862; wounded Dec. 13, 1862, at Fredericksburg, Va.; discharged for disability from wounds March 27, 1863.

JOHN ASPINWALL. Mustered Aug. 13, 1861, as private; wounded Oct. 21, 1861, at Ball's Bluff, Va.; corporal May 12, 1862; discharged Oct. 25, 1862, on surgeon's certificate.

WILLIAM W. PEARCE. Mustered Aug. 23, 1862, as private; corporal Oct. 1, 1862; mustered out June 12, 1865.

JOHN DELEVAN. Mustered Aug. 13, 1861, as private; corporal Oct. 1, 1862; lance sergeant Aug., Sept., Oct., 1863; mustered out Aug. 12, 1864.

SAMUEL J. GOLDSMITH. Mustered Aug. 11, 1862; corporal Dec. 1, 1862; lance sergeant Sept. 1, 1863; resigned to private May 12, 1864; taken prisoner Aug. 25, 1864, at Reams's Station, Va.; paroled Nov. 26, 1864; discharged May 23, 1865.

HENRY H. BALLOU. Mustered Aug. 13, 1861, as private; corporal Jan. 31, 1863; lance sergeant May 16, 1863; mortally wounded July 2, 1863, at Gettysburg, Pa.; died of wounds, July 4, 1863, in field hospital.

NELSON E. PERRY. Mustered Aug. 13, 1861, as private; corporal March 24, 1863; reënlisted Dec. 20, 1863; deserted while on furlough; arrested and sentenced March 27, 1865, to hard labor on government works.

CHARLES W. WOOD. Mustered Aug. 13, 1861; corporal April 8, 1863; reënlisted Dec. 18, 1863; lance sergeant April 17, 1864; reduced to private May 19, 1864; mustered out June 12, 1865.

STILLMAN H. BUDLONG. Mustered Aug. 13, 1861, as private; corporal May 12, 1864; mustered out Aug. 12, 1864.

BENJAMIN A. BURLINGAME. Mustered Aug. 13, 1861, as private; reënlisted Feb. 4, 1864; corporal May 12, 1864; mustered out June 12, 1865.

CHARLES H. PAINE. Mustered Aug. 13, 1861, as private; wounded July 2, 1863, at Gettysburg, Pa.; corporal May 12, 1864; mustered out Aug. 12, 1864.

JOHN B. MOWRY. Mustered Aug. 13, 1861, as private; corporal May 12, 1864; mustered out Aug. 12, 1864.

JOSIAH McMEEKIN. Mustered Aug. 13, 1861, as private; corporal May 12, 1864; mustered out Aug. 12, 1864.

PATRICK BRADY. Mustered Feb. 11, 1862, as private; reënlisted Feb. 11, 1864; corporal Aug. 12, 1864; mustered out June 12, 1865.

SAMUEL H. COLLINGTON. Mustered Jan. 5, 1862, as private; corporal Aug. 12, 1864; taken prisoner Aug. 25, 1864, at Reams's Station, Va.; enlisted in rebel army Oct. 12, 1864; dropped from battery rolls as deserter.

WILLIAM H. MAXCY. Mustered Aug. 13, 1861, as private; wounded July 2, 1863, at Gettysburg, Pa.; reënlisted Feb. 4, 1864; corporal Aug. 12, 1864; wounded and taken prisoner Aug. 25, 1864, at Reams's Station, Va.; paroled Sept. 1, 1864; mustered out June 12, 1865.

FRANCIS F. PRIESTLY. Mustered March 19, 1862, as private; reënlisted March 25, 1864; corporal Aug. 12, 1864; mustered out June 12, 1865.

FRANCIS H. ANGELL. Mustered Aug. 1, 1862, as private; corporal; transferred from Battery A, Sept. 23, 1864; mustered out June 12, 1865.

WILLIAM H. HUNTER. Mustered Aug. 5, 1862, as private; corporal; transferred from Battery A, Sept. 23, 1864; mustered out June 12, 1865.

MICHAEL KEAN. Mustered June 16, 1862, as private; corporal; transferred from Battery A, Sept. 23, 1864; mustered out June 12, 1865.

JAMES MALANY. Mustered Aug. 2, 1864, as private: corporal; transferred from Battery A, Sept. 23, 1864; mustered out June 12, 1865.

FRANCIS E. PHILLIPS. Mustered Aug. 13, 1861, as private; wounded Sept. 17, 1862, at Antietam, Md.; reënlisted Feb. 15, 1864; transferred from Battery A, Sept. 23, 1864; mustered out June 12, 1865.

Buglers.

EBEN S. CROWNINGSHIELD. Mustered Aug. 13, 1861, as first bugler; wounded July 2, 1863, at Gettysburg, Pa.; discharged Aug. 12, 1864.

HENRY COKELY. Mustered Aug. 13, 1861, as second bugler; discharged Jan. 5, 1863, on surgeon's certificate.

JOHN F. LEACH. Temporarily attached Sept. 10, 1863, as bugler; returned to Battery A, Nov. 23, 1863.

JOHN DOYLE. Attached from Twentieth Massachusetts May 2, 1863; bugler Nov. 23, 1863; reënlisted Feb. 2, 1864; returned to his regiment.

JAMES F. JERROLLMAN. Mustered Aug. 29, 1862, as bugler; transferred from Battery A, Sept. 23, 1864; mustered out June 12, 1865.

Artificers.

DANIEL B. THURSTON. Mustered Aug. 13, 1861, as blacksmith; discharged for disability March 19, 1863.

WELCOME C. TUCKER. Mustered Aug. 13, 1861, as blacksmith; discharged Feb. 25, 1862, on surgeon's certificate for disability.

WILLIAM H. CORNELL. Mustered Aug. 13, 1861, as private; wounded Dec. 3, 1862, at Fredericksburg, Va.; blacksmith Aug. 1, 1863; mustered out Aug. 12, 1864.

JOSEPH B. PLACE. Mustered Aug. 13, 1862, as private; transferred from Battery G, Feb. 28, 1863; blacksmith March 1, 1863; mustered out June 12, 1865.

EDWARD M. PECKHAM. Mustered Aug. 13, 1861, as harness maker; mustered out Aug. 12, 1864.

DANIEL C. TAYLOR. Mustered Aug. 13, 1861, as harness maker; transferred to Veteran Reserve Corps Nov. 15, 1863; discharged Aug. 12, 1864.

ISAAC W. SLACK. Mustered Aug. 13, 1861, as wheelwright; discharged Dec. 1, 1861, for disability.

ALBERT H. CORNELL. Mustered Aug. 13, 1861, as private; wheelwright Dec. 15, 1861; mustered out Aug. 12, 1864.

JAMES A. SWEET. Mustered Aug. 13, 1861, as private; wheelwright Jan. 2, 1862; mustered out Aug. 12, 1864.

GEORGE O. SCOTT. Mustered Aug. 13, 1861, as farrier; reduced to private Nov. 21, 1862; mustered out Aug. 12, 1864.

ROBERT S. NILES. Mustered Aug. 7, 1862, as private; stable sergeant Nov. 21, 1862; mustered out June 12, 1865.

WELCOME A. COLLINS. Mustered Aug. 13, 1861, as private; wagoner, Oct. 31, 1861; mustered out Aug. 12, 1864, as private.

JOHN EATOCK. Mustered Aug. 13, 1861, as private; wagoner Sept. 7, 1861; reënlisted Dec. 18, 1853; mustered out June 12, 1865.

HENRY E. GUILES. Mustered Oct. 2, 1861, as private; wagoner Feb. 7, 1862; discharged Oct. 3, 1864.

ROBERT A. NILES. Mustered Aug. 13, 1861, as private; wagoner Oct. 31, 1861; mustered out Aug. 12, 1864.

Privates.

ADAMS, CHARLES H. See first sergeant.

ADLINGTON, HENRY. Mustered Aug. 13, 1861; discharged for disability, Dec. 18, 1861, at Poolesville, Md.

ANDERSON, JOHN. Mustered Aug. 18, 1864; transferred from Battery A, Sept. 23, 1864; mustered out June 12, 1865.

ANDREWS, ALBERT. Mustered Aug. 13, 1861; discharged for disability Sept. 5, 1861, at Camp Sprague, Washington, D. C.

ANDREWS, MOWRY L. Mustered Aug. 13, 1861; wounded July 2, 1863, at Gettysburg, Md.; mustered out Aug. 12, 1864.

ANGELL, FRANCIS H. See corporal.

ARMINGTON, AMOS H. See sergeant.

ARNOLD, JOHN A. Mustered Aug. 13, 1861; brigade butcher July 18, 1863; mustered out Aug. 12, 1864.

ASPINWALL, JOHN. See corporal.

AUSTIN, GEORGE H. Mustered March 6, 1865; mustered out June 12, 1865.

AUSTIN, GEORGE R. Mustered Oct. 5, 1861; died Aug. 31, 1862, in hospital at Hampton, Va.

AUSTIN, RUSSELL. Mustered Aug. 13, 1861; wounded July 2, 1863, at Gettysburg, Pa.; mustered out Aug. 12, 1864.

ALDRICH, GEORGE N. Mustered April 8, 1864; transferred from Battery A, Sept. 23, 1864; mustered out June 12, 1865.

BAKER, GEORGE C. Mustered March 6, 1865; mustered out June 12, 1865.

BAKER, LEANDER. Mustered March 2, 1865; mustered out June 12, 1865.

BALLOU, HENRY H. See corporal.

BARBER, HENRY J. Mustered April 1, 1862; died Dec. 2, 1862, in hospital at Warrenton, Va.

BARBER, THOMAS J. Mustered March 24, 1862; mustered out March 24, 1865.

BARTLETT, FREDERICK F. Mustered Aug. 13, 1861; discharged for disability Dec. 18, 1861, at Poolesville, Md.

BARTLETT, GEORGE O. Mustered Aug. 23, 1862; discharged for disability Aug. 12, 1864.

BENNETT, SAMUEL A. Mustered Feb. 21, 1865; mustered out June 12, 1865.

BOUDEN, CHARLES H. Mustered Aug. 24, 1864; mustered out June 12, 1865.

BOYLE, JOHN L. Mustered Jan. 1, 1863; wounded July 3, 1863, at Gettysburg, Pa.; deserted July 17, 1863.
BLAIR, GEORGE W. See first sergeant.
BLAKE, JOHN T. See first sergeant.
BRADY PATRICK. See corporal.
BRAGG, WILLIAM A. Mustered July 8, 1864; transferred from Battery A, Sept. 23, 1864; mustered out June 12, 1865.
BRAYTON, FREDERICK. Mustered March 7, 1865; mustered out June 12, 1865.
BRICKLEY, ARTHUR W. Mustered Aug. 13, 1861; mustered out Aug. 12, 1864.
BRIGGS, ERASTUS D. Mustered March 27, 1862; discharged March 27, 1865.
BROMLEY, HENRY W. Mustered Aug. 13, 1861; wounded Oct. 21, 1861, at Ball's Bluff, Va.; lance corporal Jan. 1, 1862; reduced May 27, 1862; discharged for disability March 11, 1863.
BROWN, DAVID. Mustered Jan. 3, 1863; deserted Jan. 17, 1863.
BROWN, FENNER A. Mustered Aug. 13, 1861; disabled by cars Aug. 15, 1861, at Camden, N. J.; transferred to Veteran Reserve Corps Oct. 22, 1863; returned to battery Feb. 1, 1864; died Aug. 6, 1864, in hospital at David's Island, N. Y.
BUCKLIN, JOHN. Mustered Feb. 23, 1865; mustered out June 12, 1865.
BUDLONG, LORENZO D. Mustered Aug. 13, 1861; wounded Dec. 13, 1862, at Fredericksburg, Va.; discharged for disability from wounds, April 12, 1863.
BUDLONG, STILLMAN H. See corporal.
BURLINGAME BENJAMIN A. See corporal.
BURT ALLEN. Mustered Aug. 13, 1861; mustered out Aug. 12, 1864.
BURTON, HAZARD W. Mustered March 24, 1862; died Oct. 15, 1862, in hospital at Fort Ellsworth, Va.
BURTON, JOSEPH C. Mustered March 26, 1862; died Dec. 17, 1862, in hospital at Falmouth, Va.
BUTCHER, WILLIAM. Mustered Feb. 21, 1865; mustered out June 12, 1865.
BUTLER, JEREMIAH. Mustered Feb. 13, 1365; mustered out June 12, 1865.
BUTTS, CHARLES P. Mustered Aug. 13, 1861; discharged for disability April 29, 1862.

CAPRON, DANIEL. Mustered Feb. 19, 1862; transferred to Veteran Reserve Corps, Oct. 22, 1862; mustered out May 17, 1865.

CARLTON, CHARLES. Mustered Feb. 16, 1865; mustered out June 12, 1865.

CARMICHAEL, MORRIS. Mustered Aug. 13, 1861; lance corporal Dec. 15, 1861; reduced March 13, 1862; wounded Dec. 13, 1862, at Fredericksburg, Va.; discharged for disability from wounds, May 16, 1863.

CARR, HUGH. Mustered Aug. 10, 1864; mustered out June 12, 1865.

CARROLL, JOSEPH. Transferred to battery May 27, 1865; mustered out June 12, 1865.

CARTER, ABORN W. See sergeant.

CASSEN, CHARLES H. Mustered Aug. 13, 1861; discharged for disability Oct. 23, 1862.

CASSEN, JOSEPH S. Mustered Aug. 13, 1861; taken prisoner July 2, 1863, at Gettysburg, Pa.; paroled on field; taken prisoner Oct. 14, 1863, at Bristoe Station, Va.; exchanged Nov. 27, 1864; discharged Jan. 8, 1865.

CHASE, EDWIN A. See sergeant.

CHAMPLIN, WILLIAM H. Mustered Aug. 12, 1864; mustered out June 12, 1865.

CHAPPELL, ADOLPHUS A. Mustered March 7, 1865; mustered out June 12, 1865.

CHAPPELL, EDWARD H. Mustered July 18, 1862; transferred from Battery A, Sept. 23, 1864; mustered out June 12, 1865.

CHILD, WILLIAM D. See first sergeant.

CLARANCE, JOHN. Mustered Aug. 13, 1861; discharged for disability March 21, 1863.

CLARK, CHARLES. Mustered Dec. 19, 1862; died Oct. 21, 1863, in hospital at Washington, D. C.

CLARK, JOHN H. Mustered March 24, 1862; reënlisted March 25, 1864; mustered out June 12, 1865.

CLARK, GEORGE P. Mustered May 4, 1864; transferred from Battery A, Sept. 23, 1864; mustered out June 12, 1865.

CLARK, NAPOLEON B. Mustered Aug. 13, 1861, as corporal; reduced Sept. 7, 1862; mustered out Aug. 12, 1864.

CLARK, WILLIAM O. Mustered March 24, 1862; discharged for disability March 11, 1864.

COKLEY, HENRY. See bugler.

COBURN, ANDREW S. Mustered Aug. 17, 1862; transferred from Battery A, Sept. 23, 1864; mustered out June 12, 1865.
COLE, JOSEPH A. Mustered Aug. 13, 1861; discharged for disability Sept. 14, 1863, on surgeon's certificate.
COLLINGTON, SAMUEL A. See corporal.
COLLINS, STEPHEN. Mustered Aug. 13, 1861; mustered out Aug. 12, 1864.
COLLINS, WELCOME A. See artificer.
COOK, JOSEPH. Mustered March 27, 1864; transferred from Battery A, Sept. 23, 1864; mustered out June 12, 1865.
COOKE, JOHN. Mustered March 6, 1865; mustered out June 12, 1865.
COOPER, BENJAMIN. Mustered Aug. 31, 1864; mustered out June 12, 1865.
CONLIN, OWEN. Mustered Feb. 15, 1865; mustered out June 12, 1865.
CORNELL, ALBERT H. See artificer.
CORNELL, CHARLES. Mustered Aug. 13, 1861; taken prisoner Oct. 21, 1861, at Ball's Bluff, Va.; exchanged; wagoner three months in 1863; mustered out Aug. 12, 1864.
CORNELL, LEVI J. Mustered Aug. 13, 1861; wounded May 5, 1864, at Wilderness, Va.; mustered out Aug. 12, 1864.
CORNELL, WILLIAM H. See artificer.
CONNERS, MICHAEL. Mustered Feb. 13, 1865; mustered out June 12, 1865.
COSTIN, WILLIAM. Mustered Oct. 4, 1862; wounded and taken prisoner Aug. 25, 1864, at Reams's Station, Va.; transferred from Battery A, Sept. 23, 1864; paroled April 28, 1865; mustered out June 12, 1865.
COTTRELL, CHARLES. Mustered Aug. 13, 1861; discharged for disability Sept. 8, 1861, at Washington, D, C.
COWEN, JOHN. Mustered Jan. 28, 1863, at Falmouth, Va., by Capt. John G. Hazard. Deserted March 20, 1863.
CRAVEN, JOHN F. Mustered Feb. 15, 1862; mustered out Feb. 18, 1865.
CROWNINGSHIELD, EBEN S. See bugler.
CRUIKSHANK, JAMES. Mustered Sept. 12, 1864; mustered out June 12, 1865.
CUMMINGS, MARTIN. Mustered Jan. 5, 1863; transferred from Twentieth Massachusetts Regiment; deserted May 13, 1863.

DELEVAN, JOHN. See corporal.
DENNIS, WILLIAM. Mustered Aug. 13, 1862; reënlisted Feb. 11, 1864; killed May 9, 1864, at Po River, Va.
DEMPSTER, THOMAS. Mustered Oct. 15, 1862; transferred from Battery A, Sept. 23, 1864; mustered out June 12, 1865.
DERMONDY, PATRICK. Mustered Feb. 2, 1864; transferred from Battery A, Sept. 23, 1864; mustered out June 12, 1865.
DEVENS, CHARLES S. Mustered March 7, 1865; mustered out June 12, 1865.
DICKERSON, WILLIAM A. See corporal.
DODGE, ROWLAND L. Mustered Aug. 13, 1861, as company clerk and guidon; discharged March 11, 1863; second lieutenant, Company L, Third Regiment Rhode Island Heavy Artillery, March 2, 1863.
DONNELLY, THOMAS. Mustered Feb. 29, 1864; wounded and taken prisoner, Aug. 25, 1864, at Reams's Station, Va.; transferred from Battery A, Sept. 23, 1864; (no later record).
DORE, DANIEL C. Mustered April 29, 1864; transferred from Battery A, Sept. 23, 1864; discharged July 13, 1865.
DOYLE, BERNARD. Mustered Aug. 13, 1861; wounded July 3, 1863, at Gettysburg, Pa.; taken prisoner Oct. 14, 1863, near Bristoe Station, Va.; paroled Nov. 24, 1864; discharged Jan. 11, 1865.
DUFFY, MICHAEL. Mustered Aug. 13, 1861; wounded July 2, 1863, at Gettysburg, Va.; mustered out Aug. 12, 1864.
DUGAN, EDWARD. Mustered Feb. 22, 1865; mustered out June 12, 1865.
DUNBAR, FRANCIS. Mustered Feb. 13, 1865; mustered out June 12, 1865.
DYER, WILLIAM S. See quartermaster-sergeant.
EATON. MARTIN V. B. Mustered Aug. 18, 1861; wounded and taken prisoner, Oct. 14, 1863, at Bristoe Station, Va.; paroled on field; mustered out Aug. 12, 1864.
EATOCK, JOHN. See artificer.
ENGLAND, SAMUEL. Mustered Aug. 13, 1861; discharged for disability Jan. 26, 1862.
FALVEY, JAMES. Mustered Feb. 16, 1865; mustered out June 12, 1865.
FELT, DANIEL W. Mustered Jan. 5, 1863; wounded July 3, 1863, at Gettysburg, Pa.; transferred to Veteran Reserve Corps, Nov. 15, 1863; discharged Sept. 15, 1865.

FISHER, JOSEPH. Mustered July 26, 1864 ; mustered out June 12, 1865.
FLEMING, JAMES. Mustered Feb. 13, 1865 ; mustered out June 12, 1865.
FLETCHER, CALVIN C. Mustered Aug. 13, 1861 ; reënlisted Dec. 20, 1863 ; mustered out June 12, 1865.
FORD, PATRICK. Mustered Aug. 13, 1861 ; reënlisted Dec. 20, 1863 ; mustered out June 12, 1865.
FORD, MARTIN C. Mustered April 5, 1864 ; mustered out June 12, 1865.
FRANKLIN, GEORGE A. Mustered June 6, 1861 ; transferred from Battery A, Sept. 10, 1861 ; deserted Oct. 27, 1862, at Bolivar, Va.
FRIED, CHARLES. Mustered Jan. 5, 1863 ; mustered out June 12, 1865.
GALLUP, RICHARD H. See sergeant.
GALLUP, WILLIAM H. Mustered Aug. 13, 1861 ; deserted July 3, 1863, at Gettysburg, Pa.
GARDNER, ALFRED G. Mustered Aug. 12, 1862 ; killed July 3, 1863, at Gettysburg, Pa.
GARDNER, HENRY A. Mustered Aug. 13, 1861 ; wounded Dec. 13, 1862, at Fredericksburg, Va. ; discharged for disability from wounds, Sept. 10, 1863.
GILMORE, ALBERT T. Mustered Feb. 18, 1865 ; mustered out June 12, 1865.
GODFREY, EDWARD L. Mustered Aug. 13, 1861 ; discharged for disability, Dec. 1, 1862.
GOFF, JOSEPH B. Mustered Aug. 13, 1861 ; transferred to Veteran Reserve Corps, Oct. 22, 1863.
GOFF, RUFUS. Mustered Aug. 13, 1861 ; discharged for disability, Oct. 26, 1862.
GOLDSMITH, SAMUEL J. See corporal.
GLOVER, JAMES. Mustered March 2, 1865 ; mustered out June 12, 1865.
GLADDING, ARTHUR M. Mustered March 3, 1865 ; mustered out June 12, 1865.
GLYNN, JOHN. Mustered Aug. 13, 1861 ; reënlisted Dec. 21, 1863 ; killed Aug. 25, 1864, at Reams's Station, Va.
GREEN, CALEB H. H. Mustered Oct. 5, 1861 ; wounded Dec. 13, 1862, at Fredericksburg, Va. ; transferred to Veteran Reserve Corps, Oct. 9, 1863 ; discharged Oct. 24, 1864.

GREEN, JOHN. Mustered Feb. 13, 1862; wounded slightly July 1, 1862, at Malvern Hill, Va.; wounded July 3, 1863, at Gettysburg, Pa.; died of wounds July 16, 1863, in hospital.
GREEN, JOHN. Mustered Aug. 16, 1862; transferred from Battery A, Sept. 23, 1864; mustered out June 12, 1865.
GREEN, WILLIAM. Mustered March 6, 1865. Mustered out June 12, 1865.
GREENWOOD, WILLIAM H. Mustered Feb. 13, 1865; mustered out June 12, 1865.
GRINNELL, GEORGE A. Mustered Feb. 13, 1865; mustered out June 12, 1865.
GUILES, HENRY E. See artificer.
HAAK, CLAUDIUS H. Mustered March 8, 1865; mustered out June 12, 1865.
HALL, HERBERT H. Mustered March 30, 1864; mustered out June 12, 1865.
HAMILTON, WILLIAM. See corporal.
HAMMOND, JOSEPH. Mustered Jan. 1, 1863; wounded July 3, 1863, at Gettysburg, Pa.; deserted July 17, 1863.
HAMPSTON, JOHN. Mustered March 16, 1864; taken prisoner Aug. 25, 1864, at Reams's Station, Va.; transferred from Battery A, Sept. 23, 1864; released April, 1865; mustered out June 12, 1865.
HANSON, JOHN F. See first sergeant.
HARE, DANIEL. Mustered Dec. 30, 1862; deserted April 28, 1863, at Falmouth, Va.
HARRISON, JAMES 'M. Mustered Oct. 6, 1862; wounded July 2, 1863, at Gettysburg, Pa.; transferred from Battery A, Sept. 23, 1864; mustered out June 12, 1865.
HART, BARTHOLOMEW. Mustered Aug. 13, 1861; wounded Dec. 13, 1862, at Fredericksburg, Va.; mustered out Aug. 12, 1864.
HASKELL, SOLOMON A. Mustered Aug. 13, 1861; reënlisted Feb. 4, 1864; mustered out June 12, 1865.
HASKINS, WASHINGTON C. See corporal.
HATHAWAY, GEORGE. Mustered Aug. 6, 1862; transferred from Battery A, Sept. 23, 1864; mustered out June 12, 1865.
HAWKINS, CHARLES E. Mustered Oct. 2, 1862; mustered out Oct. 3, 1864.
HAVENS, HARRIS. Mustered March 7, 1865; mustered out June 12, 1865.

HEALY, JOHN. Mustered Aug. 13, 1861; taken prisoner July 18, 1863, in Loudon Valley, Va.; exchanged; reënlisted Dec. 18, 1863; mustered out June 12, 1865.

HENDERSON, ROBERT. Mustered March 7, 1865; mustered out June 12, 1865.

HENDRICK, ALBERT E. Mustered Oct. 2, 1862; wounded Dec. 13, 1862, at Fredericksburg, Va.; died of wounds Dec. 23, 1862, at Falmouth, Va.

HENDRICK, ASA F. Mustered Aug. 9, 1864; transferred from Battery A, Sept. 23, 1864; mustered out June 12, 1865.

HERMAN, FREDERICK G. Mustered Oct. 14, 1862; wounded and taken prisoner Aug. 26, 1864, at Reams's Station, Va.; transferred from Battery A, Sept. 23, 1864; died Nov. 4, 1864, at Salisbury, N. C.

HOLLAND, JOHN. Mustered Aug. 12, 1864; transferred from Battery A, Sept. 23, 1864; mustered out June 12, 1865.

HOLMES, HENRY S. Mustered March 6, 1865; mustered out June 12, 1865.

HORTON, ANTHONY B. See first sergeant.

HOUSTON, CHARLES. Mustered Sept. 1, 1864; mustered out June 12, 1865.

HOWARD, EDWARD. Mustered Aug. 13, 1861; mustered out Aug. 13, 1864.

HOYLE, JOSEPH. Mustered Feb. 24, 1864; transferred from Battery A, Sept. 23, 1864; mustered out June 12, 1865.

HUGHES, JAMES. Mustered March 8, 1865; mustered out June 12, 1865.

HUNT, CHESTER F. Mustered Aug. 13, 1861; killed Oct. 14, 1863, at Bristoe Station, Va.

HUNT, WALTER S. Mustered Aug. 13, 1861; discharged for disability Feb. 7, 1863.

HUNTER, WILLIAM H. See corporal.

IDE, SYLVESTER G. Mustered Aug. 13, 1861; corporal Oct. 1, 1861; lance sergeant Dec. 15, 1861; reduced March 1. 1862; discharged for disability Oct. 22, 1862.

INGALLS, GEORGE. Mustered Aug. 13, 1861; transferred to Veteran Reserve Corps, Oct. 22, 1868.

IRONS, LEWIS W. Mustered March 9, 1865; mustered out June 12, 1865.

JENCKS, HEZEKIAH. Transferred from Battery D, Jan. 20, 1862; discharged for disability Aug. 12, 1862.

JERROLLMAN, JAMES F. See bugler.

JOHNSON, GILBERT. Mustered Aug. 18, 1862; transferred from Battery A, Sept. 23, 1864; mustered out June 12, 1865.

JOHNSON. JOSIAH. Mustered Aug. 17, 1864; mustered out June 12. 1865.

JOHNSON, ROBERT L. See sergeant.

JONES, WILLIAM. Mustered Aug. 13, 1861; lance corporal Dec. 15, 1861; reduced Sept. 7, 1862; killed July 3, 1863, at Gettysburg, Pa.

JORDAN, WILLIAM T. Mustered Aug. 13, 1861; reënlisted March 25, 1864; guidon Jan. 1, 1865; mustered out June 12, 1865.

KANE, JOHN. Mustered Dec. 20, 1862; deserted April 28, 1863, at Falmouth, Va.

KEAN, MICHAEL. See corporal.

KELLY, JOHN. Mustered Aug. 13, 1861; reënlisted Dec. 21, 1863; mustered out June 12, 1865.

KELLY, PATRICK. Mustered July 27, 1864; mustered out June 12, 1865.

KENDRICK, JOHN. Mustered Aug. 13, 1861; mustered out Aug. 12, 1864.

KENNEY, MICHAEL. Mustered Aug. 13, 1861; reënlisted Dec. 19, 1863; transferred from Battery A, Sept. 23, 1864; mustered out June 12, 1865.

KENYON, WILLIAM J. See first sergeant.

KIMPTON, GEORGE H. Mustered Feb. 28, 1865; mustered out June 12, 1865.

KINE, JAMES. Mustered April 18, 1864; transferred from Battery A, Sept. 23, 1864; mustered out June 12, 1865.

KING, DAVID B. Mustered Aug. 13, 1861; killed July 2, 1863, at Gettysburg, Pa.

KNOWLES, EDWIN H. Mustered Aug. 13. 1861, as corporal; reduced Sept. 7, 1862; wounded Dec. 13, 1862, at Fredericksburg, Va.; mustered out Aug. 12, 1864.

LAIRD, ROBERT A. Mustered Aug. 13, 1861; lance corporal Dec. 15, 1861; reduced March 26, 1862; mustered out Aug. 12, 1864.

LARKIN, PATRICK. Mustered Aug. 6, 1862; transferred from Battery A, Sept. 23, 1864; mustered out June 12, 1865.

LEACH, JOSEPH. Mustered Aug. 13, 1861; discharged for disability May 12, 1862.

FIRST RHODE ISLAND LIGHT ARTILLERY.   369

LEE, RALPH.   Mustered Oct. 3, 1864; mustered out June 12, 1865.
LEONARD, GETZ.   Mustered Feb. 2, 1864; discharged for disability July 22, 1865.
LEWIS, JACOB B.   See sergeant.
LEWIS, THOMAS S.   Mustered March 8, 1865; mustered out June 12, 1865.
LIBBEY, CHARLES A.   See quartermaster-sergeant.
LUTHER, JOSEPH.   Mustered Feb. 9, 1862; died Feb. 24, 1863, in hospital at Washington, D. C.
MACOMBER, CALVIN L.   See sergeant.
MAHRE, FREDERIC.   Mustered Jan. 5, 1862; deserted Jan. 17, 1863, at Falmouth, Va.; arrested Feb. 14, 1863; sentenced to hard labor on government works.
MAINE, NELSON B.   Mustered Aug. 13, 1861; mustered out Aug. 12, 1864.
MALANY, JAMES.   See corporal.
MARTIN, THOMAS J.   Mustered Aug. 13, 1861; discharged for disability Dec. 18, 1861.
MASON, HENRY A.   Mustered Aug. 13, 1861; mustered out Aug. 12, 1864.
MASON, LUCIUS M.   Mustered Aug. 13, 1861; taken prisoner Nov. 23, 1862, near Warrenton, Va.; exchanged July, 1864; mustered out Aug. 12, 1864.
MATTESON, BENJAMIN W.   Mustered Aug. 13, 1861; wounded Oct. 21, 1861, at Ball's Bluff, Va.; discharged for disability from wounds Aug. 21, 1862.
MATTESON, GEORGE R.   Mustered Aug. 13, 1861; wounded Oct. 21, 1861, at Ball's Bluff, Va.; lance corporal Sept. 7, 1862; wounded July 3, 1863; reduced to private May 12, 1864; mustered out Aug. 12, 1864.
MATTESON, WILLIAM F.   Mustered Aug. 13, 1861; taken prisoner Oct. 21, 1861, at Ball's Bluff, Va.; exchanged May 28, 1862; mustered out Aug. 12, 1864.
MAXCY, WILLIAM H.   See corporal.
MCALLEN, ARTHUR J.   Mustered Aug. 13, 1861; discharged for disability Dec. 18, 1861, at Poolesville, Md.
MCCANN, MICHAEL.   Mustered Feb. 13, 1865; mustered out June 12, 1865.
MCCARNEY, MICHAEL.   Mustered Feb. 13, 1865; mustered out June 12, 1865.

McConney, Edward. Mustered March 6, 1865; mustered out June 12, 1865.
McComb, John. See sergeant.
McCullum, William. Mustered Aug. 13, 1861; reënlisted Dec. 18, 1863; transferred to the United States navy April 6, 1864.
McDonald, Owen. Mustered Aug. 6, 1862; transferred from Battery A, Sept. 23, 1864; mustered out June 12, 1865.
McFarlin, John. Mustered March 4, 1865; mustered out June 12, 1865.
McGovern, John. Mustered March 6, 1865; mustered out June 12, 1865.
McGuinness, Edward. Mustered Aug. 13, 1861; discharged for disability March 12, 1863.
McGunnigle, George. Mustered Aug. 13, 1861; wounded July 3, 1863, at Gettysburg, Pa.; transferred to Veteran Reserve Corps, June 17, 1864.
McGunnigle, James. Mustered Aug. 13, 1861; reënlisted Dec. 22, 1863; mustered out June 12, 1865.
McMeekin, Josiah. See corporal.
McNamara, Thomas. Mustered March 19, 1864; taken prisoner Aug. 25, 1864, at Reams's Station, Va.; transferred from Battery A, Sept. 23, 1864; paroled Feb. 20, 1865; mustered out June 12, 1865.
Meredith, Alexander. Mustered Feb. 23, 1865; mustered out June 12, 1865.
Mitchell, Sidney R. Mustered Aug. 8, 1864; transferred from Battery A, Sept. 23, 1864; mustered out June 12, 1865.
Moffett, Thomas. Mustered March 12, 1864; died Nov. 8, 1864, in hospital at Washington, D. C.
Moofler, Horace S. Mustered Aug. 24, 1864; mustered out June 12, 1865.
Morris, Albert. Mustered Feb. 15, 1865; mustered out June 12, 1865.
Morris, Charles. Mustered Feb. 15, 1865; mustered out June 12, 1865.
Morris, William H. Mustered Aug. 13, 1861; discharged for disability April 11, 1863.
Mowry, John B. See corporal.
Newell, John. Mustered Feb. 28, 1865; mustered out June 12, 1865.

NICHOLS, GEORGE W. Mustered Aug. 5, 1864; transferred from Battery A, Sept. 23, 1864; mustered out June 12, 1865.
NICHOLS, JOSEPH S. Mustered Aug. 5, 1864; transferred from Battery A, Sept. 23, 1865; mustered out June 12, 1865.
NILES, ROBERT A. See artificer.
NILES, ROBERT S. See artificer.
OLNEY, AMOS M. C. See quartermaster-sergeant.
OLNEY, LUTHER C. See corporal.
O'SULLIVAN, CORNELIUS. Mustered Feb. 21, 1865; mustered out June 12, 1865.
PAINE, CHARLES H. See corporal.
PATTERSON, DAVID B. See corporal.
PEARCE, HARVEY. Mustered March 24, 1862; discharged for disability March 20, 1863.
PEARCE, WILLIAM. Mustered March 24, 1862; sent to hospital at Yorktown, Va., April, 1862; no further record.
PEARCE, WILLIAM W. See corporal.
PECKHAM, EDWARD M. See artificer.
PECKHAM, ISRAEL H. Mustered Feb. 27, 1862; transferred from Battery A, Sept. 23, 1864; mustered out Feb. 28, 1865.
PELL, JABESH. Mustered Feb. 17, 1865; mustered out June 12, 1865.
PERKINS, CHARLES H. Mustered March 4, 1865; mustered out June 12, 1865.
PERRY, NELSON E. See corporal.
PHETTEPLACE, DAVID. Mustered Aug. 13, 1861; mustered out Aug. 12, 1864.
PHETTEPLACE, DAVID H. Mustered Aug. 13, 1861, as corporal; reduced March 4, 1863; reënlisted Feb. 4, 1864; mustered out June 12, 1865.
PHILLIPS, ALBERT A. Mustered Aug. 13, 1861; died Dec. 15, 1862, in hospital at Alexandria, Va.
PHILLIPS, FRANCIS E. See corporal.
PHILLIPS, THOMAS W. Mustered Aug. 13, 1861; wounded July 3, 1863, at Gettysburg, Pa.; transferred to Veteran Reserve Corps July 21, 1863; mustered out Aug. 12, 1864.
PLACE, JOSEPH B. See artificer.
PRIESTLY, FRANCIS T. See corporal.
PRESTON, HENRY A. Mustered Aug. 14, 1862; transferred from Battery A, Sept. 23, 1864; mustered out June 12, 1865.

RAMSDEN, JOHN. Mustered March 7, 1865; mustered out June 12, 1865.
RATHBONE, CALVIN W. See corporal.
REMINGTON, WILLIAM B. Mustered Aug. 13, 1861; mustered out Aug. 12, 1864.
REYNOLDS, WILLIAM F. Mustered Aug. 13, 1861; wounded Dec. 13, 1862, at Fredericksburg, Va.; discharged for disability Feb. 18, 1863.
RIDER, CHARLES J. See sergeant.
RILEY, CHARLES F. Mustered March 19, 1862; taken prisoner Aug. 25, 1864, at Reams's Station, Va.; transferred from Battery A, Sept. 23, 1864; paroled Feb. 20, 1865; mustered out March 30, 1865.
RHODES, JOHN H. See sergeant.
RYAN, PETER. Mustered Dec. 30, 1862; deserted April 28, 1863, at Falmouth, Va.
SANFORD, HERBERT D. Mustered Aug. 13, 1861; wounded July 2, 1863, at Gettysburg, Pa.; sent to hospital at White Plains, Va., July 30, 1863; mustered out Aug. 12, 1864,
SAYLES, ALBERT A. Mustered Aug. 12, 1864; mustered out June 12, 1865.
SCOTT, GEORGE O. See artificer.
SCOTT, LEWIS W. Mustered Aug. 13, 1862; wounded Dec. 13, 1862, at Fredericksburg, Va.; transferred to Veteran Reserve Corps, Sept. 1, 1863. Discharged Aug. 13, 1865.
SEAMANS, EZEKIEL W. Mustered Aug. 13, 1862. Died Dec. 16, 1862, in hospital at North Providence, R. I.
SIDDERS, CHARLES. Mustered March 7, 1864; transferred from Battery A, Sept. 23, 1864; mustered out June 12, 1865.
SISSON, JOHN J. Mustered Aug. 13, 1861; wounded Dec. 13, 1862, at Fredericksburg, Va.; transferred to Veteran Reserve Corps, Aug. 18, 1863; mustered out Aug. 12, 1864.
SKIFER, CARL. Mustered Jan. 3, 1863; mustered out June 12, 1865.
SLACK, ISAAC W. See artificer.
SLAIGER FRANCIS. Mustered Aug. 13, 1861; reënlisted Dec. 20, 1863; wounded May 5, 1864, at Wilderness, Va.; wounded June 3, 1864, at Cold Harbor; discharged Sept. 11, 1865.
SMITH, CHARLES E. See sergeant.
SMITH, GEORGE E. Mustered Feb. 16, 1865; mustered out June 12, 1865.

SMITH, JOHN. Mustered Feb. 16, 1865; mustered out June 12, 1865.

SPRAGUE, CHARLES G. Mustered Aug. 13, 1861; wounded July 3, 1863, at Gettysburg, Pa.; reënlisted Feb. 4, 1864; mustered out June 12, 1865.

STACY, HERBERT. Mustered Aug. 28, 1862; transferred from Battery A, Sept. 23, 1864; mustered out June 12, 1865.

STAPLES, ERNEST. See first sergeant.

STEERE, THOMAS P. Mustered Aug. 4, 1862; transferred from Battery A, Sept. 23, 1864; mustered out June 12, 1865.

STINSON, JAMES. Mustered Aug. 13, 1861; transferred to Battery D, Jan. 1, 1862.

STEPHENS, CHARLES. Mustered July 29, 1864; mustered out June 12, 1865.

STONE, ALMANZO S. Mustered March 7, 1864; transferred from Battery A, Sept. 23, 1864; mustered out June 12, 1865.

STONE, ALPHEUS R. Mustered Jan. 2, 1863; discharged for disability March 27, 1864.

STRAIGHT, ALBERT. See sergeant.

SWEET, JAMES A. See artificer.

TABOR, GEORGE. Mustered April 12, 1864; transferred from Battery A, Sept. 23, 1864; mustered out June 12, 1865.

TALBOT, GEORGE H. Mustered Aug. 13, 1861, as corporal; reduced Sept. 7, 1862; discharged for disability March 28, 1863.

TALLMAN, W. IRVING. Mustered March 7, 1864; taken prisoner Aug. 25, 1864, at Reams's Station, Va.; paroled Sept. 24, 1864; mustered out June 12, 1865.

TANNER, WILLIAM M. See corporal.

TAYLOR, DANIEL C. See artificer.

TAYLOR, WILLIAM H. Mustered June 6, 1861; reënlisted Dec. 18, 1863; transferred from Battery A, Sept. 23, 1864; mustered out June 12, 1864.

THAYER, ZIBA C. Mustered Aug. 13, 1861; corporal Dec. 15, 1861; reduced March 2, 1862; discharged for disability Feb. 7, 1863.

THOMPSON, JAMES. Mustered Aug. 13, 1861; discharged for disability Oct. 23, 1862.

THOMPSON, WILLIAM. Mustered July 27, 1864; transferred from Battery A, Sept. 23, 1864; mustered out June 12, 1865.

THORNTON, JAMES D. Mustered March 14, 1865; mustered out June 12, 1865.

THORNTON, JOHN A. Mustered Aug. 4, 1862; transferred from Battery A, Sept. 23, 1864; mustered out June 12, 1865.

THURBER, DARIUS N. Mustered Aug. 13, 1861, as corporal; reduced Sept. 30, 1861; discharged for disability Oct. 23, 1862.

THURSTON, DANIEL B. See artificer.

TILLINGHAST, JAMES A. Mustered Oct. 5, 1861; discharged for disability Dec. 19, 1862.

TILLINGHAST, MERRITT. Mustered Oct. 2, 1861; discharged Oct. 3, 1864.

TRESCOTT, JOHN F. Mustered Aug. 13, 1861; died March 29, 1862, at Providence, R. I.

TUCKER, SILAS G. See sergeant.

TUCKER, WELCOME C. See artificer.

VICKERY, OTIS. Mustered March 10, 1862; transferred from Battery A, Sept. 23, 1864; mustered out March 13, 1865.

WALKER, BENJAMIN W. Mustered Aug. 15, 1862; taken prisoner Aug. 25, 1864, at Reams's Station, Va.; paroled Oct. 8, 1864; mustered out June 12, 1865.

WALKER, JOSEPH. Mustered March 8, 1865; mustered out June 12, 1865.

WALKER, PARDON S. See sergeant.

WARDLOW, JOHN E. See sergeant.

WAGNER, WILLIAM. Mustered Feb. 29, 1864; transferred from Battery A, Sept. 23, 1864; mustered out June 12, 1865.

WARREN, CHARLES. Mustered Jan. 5, 1863; deserted Jan. 17, 1863.

WEEKS, JEROME. Mustered March 24, 1862; discharged March 24, 1865.

WELLMAN, HENRY A. Mustered Sept. 4, 1862; taken prisoner Aug. 25, 1864, at Reams's Station, Va.; transferred from Battery A, Sept. 23, 1864; paroled March 10, 1865; mustered out June 12, 1865.

WELLMAN, GEORGE A. Mustered June 6, 1861; deserted Feb. 26. 1863; arrested; transferred from Battery A, Sept. 23, 1864; mustered out June 12, 1865.

WELLS, WILLIAM P. See corporal.

WILBUR, WILLIAM B. Mustered Aug. 3, 1864; transferred from Battery A, Sept. 23, 1864; mustered out June 12, 1865.

WILDER, ABEL. Mustered Aug. 13, 1861; reënlisted Feb. 9, 1864; transferred from Battery A, Sept. 23, 1864; mustered out June 12, 1865.

WILKINSON, ROBERT. Mustered Aug. 13, 1861; reënlisted Feb. 4, 1864; mustered out June 12, 1865.
WILLIAMS, ALANSON A. See first sergeant.
WINSOR, WILLIAM W. Mustered Aug. 8, 1862; taken prisoner Aug. 25, 1864, at Reams's Station, Va.; transferred from Battery A, Sept. 23, 1864; died Feb. 22, 1865, on the cars near Salisbury, N. C.
WHIPPLE, ALBERT J. Mustered Aug. 13, 1861; wounded July 2, 1863, at Gettysburg, Pa.; mustered out Aug. 12, 1864.
WHIPPLE, EDWARD B. See corporal.
WHITFORD, JOHN U. Mustered Feb. 16, 1864; transferred from Battery A, Sept. 23, 1864; discharged for disability Sept. 26, 1864.
WHITING, LEONARD J. See sergeant.
WOOD, CHARLES W. See corporal.
WOOD, WILLIAM B. Mustered Feb. 6, 1862; discharged for disability Sept. 19, 1862.
WOODBURY, THOMAS. Mustered March 6, 1865; mustered out June 12, 1865.
WOODMANSEE, CLARK L. Mustered Aug. 13, 1861; mustered out Aug. 12, 1864.
WORTHINGTON, CHARLES B. See corporal.

Q. M. Sergt. Charles A. Libbey.

ROLL OF MEN TEMPORARILY ATTACHED.

From *Battery B, First New Jersey Artillery*, from Sept. 23, to Oct. 31, 1864: Second Lieut. Robert Fairchild.

From the *Thirty-fourth New York Regiment*, Dec. 23, 1862, to June 9, 1863: Charles Flynn, George Hobby, Charles Powers, James Reddan, David Smith, Thomas Sandford.

From the *Fifteenth Massachusetts Regiment*, from Feb., 1863, to ——: Ethan Allen; Amos Broad, wounded July 3, 1863, at Gettysburg; Mitchel Butterfield; Dyer Cady, wounded July 2, 1863, at Gettysburg; Michael Flynn, killed July 2, 1863, at Gettysburg; Winthrop Maynard, Oliver W. Moore.

From the *Nineteenth Maine Regiment*, from April, 1863, to ——: James Bean; Ira Bennett, killed July 2, 1863, at Gettysburg; James Bowe, Elliott Collins; Ezra L. Fowles, killed May 9, 1864, at Po River; Charles Goodwin, Henry C. Goodwin, Morrison Heal, William Kitridge, Summer Merrill; Louis Moulton, wounded July 2, 1863, at Gettysburg; Peleg Staples, wounded July 2, 1863, at Gettysburg; George Tibbetts, blacksmith; James Tyler, John Weinburg, Randall K. Whitten.

From the *Seventy-second Pennsylvania Regiment*, from May, 1863, to ——: John Gray, wounded at Gettysburg July 3, 1863; Michael Kelley, Albert Neinburg.

From the *One hundred and fortieth Pennsylvania Regiment*, from May 26, 1863, to March 29, 1864: James Baird, wounded July 2, 1863, at Gettysburg; Joseph Brackell, J. W. Dill; J. M. Dye, lance corporal; James B. Foster; Jacob Frazee, wounded July 3, 1863, at Gettysburg; John F. Gardner, Thomas Glennon; Thomas Hardusty, lance corporal; Stephen C. Harris, Joseph Hemphill, James Miller, James L. Noah; Peter Phillips, wounded July 3, 1863, at Gettysburg; Joseph B. Porter, John H. Seiples, Peter Shevlin, Simon S. West, John D. Wishart, James Young.

FIRST RHODE ISLAND LIGHT ARTILLERY. 377

From the Sixty-ninth Pennsylvania Regiment, from Sept. 10, 1863: Stephen Boyle, ambulance driver.

From Battery I, First United States Artillery, from Oct. 19, 1863: William Bruce, Robert H. Cooper, William T. Cooper, James Crooks, Edward B. Curtis; John Fox, lance sergeant; John H. Huller, William James, Ludwick Ling, John McGuire, David N. Minesinger, Henry Odell, John G. Pierce, Joseph Rhodenburg, Washington M. Whitlock.

From Battery G, First New York Artillery, from Jan. 1, 1864, to ———: James Cavanaugh, Richard Fetthousen, Peter Guinan, Timothy Lyons, Charles McGlocklin, Fred. Smith, Patrick Staer.

From Battery C, First Pennsylvania Artillery, from March, 1864, to ———: Peter Barry, Daniel Burch, Sidney Case, Dennis Dailey, James McCormick, Thomas McCormick. Henry Mason, Samuel Mason, Simon Mason, George Monroe, John Monroe, Ranford Riggs, Patrick Wardon, John Williams, Josiah Williston.

From Battery F, First Pennsylvania Artillery, from April to July, 1864: William Ammons, George W. Augstadt, Samuel B. Baker, Christian Benneville, Charles Briner, Henry W. Call, William H. Decker; Isaac Grimes, wounded May 9, 1863, at Po River; Patrick Gimley, William Halligan, Charles Hauck, Samuel Hofmaster, Isaac Humrell, Lewis Katzantz, Henry Kisel, William Kline, Milton Lehman, Peter McKinney, William McKinney, George A. Messno, Lewis Midner, John Moore, Jacob F. Morton, Patrick Nealon, Timothy O'Brien. Samuel Perry. Edwin H. Peters, Thomas W. M. Potter, George Roland. John Rooney, Joseph Ruth, Adam Schwalb, John Stevenson, David Stout, Eli Trine; Charles T. Wathline, wounded May 9, 1863, at Po River; Lewis Weibner, Edward Williston, Franklin Young.

From Fourth New York Heavy Artillery, from July 15, 1864, to ———: Charles H. Bacon, Morris Bartell, Thomas Batters, Henry Birch, William Bissell; Henry Blake, taken prisoner Aug. 25, 1864, at Reams's Station; Thomas Blanchard, taken prisoner Aug. 25, 1864, at Reams's Station; Martin Briton, Peter Guidan, John B. French, Thomas Healy, John F. Hogland; William A. Livingston, taken prisoner Aug. 25, 1864, at Reams's Station; Michael Muffy, James Murphy; Joseph Rockwell, taken prisoner Aug. 25, 1864, at Reams's Station; E. S. Roe, Henry Smith; James Smith, taken prisoner Aug. 25, 1864, at Reams's Station; Isaac Stewart, William Stoneburner, Albert Tyler, Frederick Vanderhide, James Weller,

Francis B. Whitman, Abel Wickfet, Henry Williams, A. Wright; Charles E. and John B. Wright, both taken prisoners Aug. 25, 1864, at Reams's Station.

From Battery B, First New Jersey Artillery: Alfred Hartreane, as Lieutenant Fairchild's servant.

There were thirty-nine men from different regiments who served from one to two weeks whose names were not carried on the rolls, of which there is no record, so their names are not obtainable.

Corp. Calvin W. Rathbone.

APPENDIX A.

THE GETTYSBURG GUN.

THE brass field piece which stands on the granite pedestal at the south side of the State House parade has a history unequaled perhaps by any other gun that did service in the war for the Union. An honorable history it is, for it was the prize for which, in that terrible battle of Gettysburg, brave men on both sides contended in a deadly hand to hand encounter. The batterymen, backed by the brave Sixty-ninth Pennsylvania, finally won the prize, but a dearly bought one it was, for it was paid for by the sacrifice of the lives of many gallant men.

The Gettysburg gun was one of the park of six brass field light twelve-pounder Napoleons which the battery received at Harrison Landing, Va., in exchange for the ten-pounder Parrotts with which the battery was equipped during the Peninsular Campaign. (See page 109, July 31st.)

In 1870 the surviving members of the battery held a reunion at Rocky Point, R. I., on the thirteenth day of August, that being the anniversary of the date of their muster into the United States service, and there formed a veteran association to hold annual reunions upon that day. At the reunions held afterward the subject of this gun has been an animated matter of discussion. Through efforts of the members of the Association, the citizens of Rhode Island, and Hon. Henry B. Anthony, late senator from this State, Congress honored the Association with the privilege of placing this memento of the battle of Gettysburg in the care and protection of the State of Rhode Island.

In 1874, Daniel C. Taylor, then president of Battery B, Veteran Association, was largely instrumental in having the gun turned over from the general government to the State, and, with Lieut. James E. Chace and Jacob B. Lewis, was appointed a committee to go to

Washington, D. C., to receive the gun; also a copy of the act of Congress giving the gun to the State. This copy was obtained by Senator Henry B. Anthony, who had it suitably engrossed and presented to the Association.

The following is a copy of the act of Congress:

AN ACT AUTHORIZING THE SECRETARY OF WAR TO DELIVER TO THE STATE AUTHORITIES OF RHODE ISLAND A CERTAIN GUN.

Be it enacted by the Senate and House of Representatives of the United States of America in Congress assembled:

That the Secretary of War be and he is hereby authorized to deliver, if the same can be done without detriment to the government, to the proper authorities of the State of Rhode Island, a certain gun marked Battery B First Regiment of Rhode Island Light Artillery, battle of Gettysburg, for the purpose of being placed among the archives of that State.

JAMES G. BLAINE,
Speaker of House of Representatives.

[SEAL.]

MATT. H. CARPENTER,
President of the Senate pro tem.

Approved Feb. 19, 1874.

U. S. GRANT.

At Providence, R. I., on May 21, 1874, there was a grand military demonstration on the reception of Battery B's relic, and the delivery of the gun to the State, which took place under very trying and moist aspects of the weather, with the following committees in charge, viz.:

Governor Henry Howard, Gen. Charles R. Dennis, Hon. J. M. Addeman in behalf of the State; Mayor Thomas A. Doyle, Col. N. Van Slyck, Henry R. Barker, in behalf of the city; Col. A. C. Eddy, George R. Drowne, Lieut. James E. Chace, John F. Hanson, Finance Committee; Col. J. Albert Monroe, Col. E. H. Rhodes, Jacob B. Lewis, Programme Committee; Gen. Charles R. Dennis, Edwin Metcalf, Silas G. Tucker, Reception Committee; Lieut. James E. Chace, Daniel C. Taylor, Jacob B. Lewis, Gun Committee; Col. J. Albert Monroe, Chief Marshal; Col. E. H. Rhodes, Chief of Staff.

The patter of the rain Thursday morning was anything but merry music to the men of Battery B who heard it, and to the veterans and militia who were to join them in the parade and demonstration.

Everything looked blue to the veterans except the sky, and that was dull enough, while the rain poured as if it had set in for a long storm and was taking it easy. Old Probabilities was anxiously consulted, but he had no encouragement to offer. But in spite of the weather flags were thrown to the breeze from public and private flag-staffs as if to encourage us.

In front of the Soldiers and Sailors Monument on Exchange Place a stand had been erected for the formal exercises, with a national flag flying at each corner, and in the centre a banner bearing the clover leaf (Trefoil) of the Second Corps, under which in a scroll was the thrilling word, "GETTYSBURG." There was little evidence that this stand would be wanted or used that day.

The marshal and commanding officers of various organizations met together to consult about postponement. Postponement meant almost certain failure, while if carried out the demonstration, if not what was expected and wished, would at least have the merit of spirit and punctuality, and show that when the veterans take hold of anything they mean business.

Before a decision was reached the cars arrived from Westerly bringing the Westerly Rifle Battalion of one hundred and three men, under command of Col. A. N. Crandall, who, undaunted by the weather, had come to parade. This was encouraging certainly, and before the enthusiasm created by this had subsided, the boat arrived from Newport with two bands and the Newport Artillery and Veteran Association. More encouragement and matters began to assume more life.

Lieut.-Col. Bullock of the First Light Infantry Regiment on being asked what his command would do, quickly replied, "We shall parade if you do." And the same reply was received from the United Train of Artillery, the Marine Artillery, and many of the other organizations. With all this encouragement and the fact that most of the men had come prepared to parade, the matter was decided and the order given: "Prepare for Parade."

The rain, however, caused some changes in the proceedings, the route of march was cut short, and Music Hall was engaged for the exercises intended for Exchange Place.

An arrangement was made for an artillery signal at two o'clock to inform the different organizations what to do. At half-past one o'clock it let up somewhat, and just about two o'clock the Marine Artillery marched into Exchange Place and fired the signal gun, which said to those in waiting—Parade!

At this time a large force of the umbrella brigade lined the sidewalks, while every window on Exchange Place was crowded to the utmost, and matters soon began to assume a lively aspect.

The militia was promptly on hand, soon followed by the other organizations arriving from different directions, and all were assigned positions.

THE LINE.

Col. J. Albert Monroe, Chief Marshal.
Col. Elisha H. Rhodes, Chief of Staff.

First Division, Mounted Troops.

Lieut.-Col. Stephen Brownell, Assistant Marshal.
Providence Horse Guards, Col. J. Lippitt Snow commanding, and staff of six field officers.
Company A, Capt. George B. Inman, three officers and fifteen men.
Company B, Capt. David Lester, two officers and fifteen men.
Pawtucket Horse Guards, Maj. J. W. Leckie commanding, staff and line officers, thirty-five men.
Tower Light Battery, Pawtucket, Maj. Daniel Briggs commanding, one officer and sixteen men.

Second Division, Mounted Light Battery.

Adjt. J. M. Hull, Assistant Marshal.
Providence Marine Corps of Artillery, Lieut.-Col. Robert Grosvenor commanding, eight officers and six pieces and caissons fully manned.

Third Division, Veteran Associations.

Lieut. James E. Chace, Assistant Marshal.
Platoon of Police, Sergeant Warner.
American Band, D. W. Reeves, leader, twenty-eight pieces.
First Regiment Rhode Island Veteran Association, thirty men.
Second Regiment Rhode Island Veteran Association, Col. Horatio Rogers, President, fifty men.
Third Regiment Rhode Island Veteran Association, Gen. Charles R. Brayton, President, sixty men.
Ninth Regiment Rhode Island Veteran Association, J. T. Pitman, President, twenty men.
Eleventh Regiment, Rhode Island Veteran Association, Robert Fessenden, President, twenty men.
First Regiment Rhode Island Light Artillery Veteran Association, I. R. Sheldon, Vice-President, forty men.
Ives Post, No. 13, G. A. R., R. F. Nicola, commander, twenty-five men.
Battery B, First Rhode Island Light Artillery Veteran Association, Daniel C. Taylor, President, forty men.

FIRST RHODE ISLAND LIGHT ARTILLERY. 383

Gun detachment with the Gettysburg Gun.
Lieut. Gideon Spencer, commanding.
Sergt. John F. Hanson, orderly.
Edwin A. Chase, sergeant of piece.
Corporal Edward B. Whipple, gunner.
No. 1. Benj. A. Burlingame. No. 2. Josiah McMeekin.
No. 3. Joseph Cassin. No. 4. Charles D. Worthington.
No. 5. John Delevan. No. 6. Charles Cornell.
No. 7. Charles J. Rider.
Drivers, Joseph A. Cole, lead; Levi J. Cornell, swing; Stephen Collins, wheel.
John Healy, with the old headquarters flag of the Artillery Brigade of the Second Corps.

The Fourth Division, Invited Guests.

Sergt. Silas G. Tucker, Assistant Marshal.
Governor Henry Howard, Lieut.-Governor C. C. Van Zandt, Adjt.-Gen. H. LeFavour, in carriage.
Colonel Waterman, Colonel Barstow, Colonel Nightingale.
Colonel Robinson of Governor's staff, mounted.
Maj.-Gen. William R. Walker, Colonels Jenks and Fisk, Majors Tillinghast, Deming and Pierce, of his staff, in carriage.
Quartermaster-Gen. Chas. R. Dennis, Surgeon-General King, in carriage.
Brigadier-General Burdick, Chaplain Jones, Surgeon Turner, Captains Marvel and Sisson of his staff, mounted.
Brig.-Gen. Frederick Miller, and Capt. A. E. Greene, Capt. W. B. Vincent, of his staff, in carriage, all in new uniforms.
Maj.-Gen. G. K. Warren, U. S. A., commander of Fifth Army Corps.
Major-General Averill, U. S. A., commander Cavalry Division.
Col. A. P. Blunt, Quartermaster, U. S. A.
Brig.-Gen. John G. Hazard, U. S. Volunteers.
Col. W. H. Reynolds of First Regiment Rhode Island Light Artillery.
Brev. Lieut.-Col. J. H. Rice, U. S. A., Maj. C. E. Rice, U. S. A.
Capt. C. E. Bowers, Massachusetts Volunteers.
Capt. N. N. Noyes, Boston Light Infantry.
Capt. T. L. Harlow, Company C, Fourth Battalion of Infantry, and H. E. Hotchkiss, of New Haven, Conn.
James Foley, of New York, and C. E. Tucker, Blackstone, Mass., all in carriages.

Fifth Division, State Militia.

Capt. C. Henry Barney, Assistant Marshal.
Drum corps of eight pieces.
Westerly Rifle Battalion, Col. A. N. Crandall commanding, with eight field and staff officers.
Co. A, Capt. A. B. Dyer, four officers and forty-eight men.
Co. B, Capt. J. A. Brown, four officers and thirty-five men.

Burnside National Guards, Maj. George H. Black commanding, three
field and staff officers.
Co. A, Capt. W. H. Scott, three officers and twenty-six men.
Co. B, Capt. Thomas Brinn, three officers and thirty men.
Co. C, Capt. Lewis Kenegee, three officers and thirty-two men.
Newport Brass Band, J. E. O. Smith, leader, twenty-six pieces.
United Train of Artillery, Col. Oscar Lapham commanding, six field
and staff officers.
Co. A, Capt. G. A. Dodge, three officers and twenty men.
Co. B, Capt. F. S. McCausland, two officers and twenty-two men.
Co. C, Capt. C. G. Cahoone, two officers and twenty men.
Gilmore's Pawtucket Band, T. J. Allen leader, twenty-two pieces.
Rhode Island Guards, Col. J. Costine commanding, three staff and field
officers.
Co. A, J. H. McGann, three officers and thirty-eight men.
Co. D, Capt. J. E. Curren, three officers and thirty men.
Co. G, Lieut. William McPherson, two officers and thirty-six men.
Co. H, Capt. James Leary, three officers and thirty-two men.
First Light Infantry Drum Corps, G. W. Lewis, leader, twelve men.
First Light Infantry Regiment, Col. R. H. I. Goddard commanding, four
field and staff officers.
Co. A, Capt. J. H. Kendrick, three officers and twenty-eight men.
Co. B, Capt. E. F. Annable, three officers and twenty-seven men.
Co. C, Capt. William Frankland, three officers and thirty-five men.
Co. D, Capt. A. H. Hartwell, two officers and twenty-five men.
Drum Major Charles Whitters, of Hartford, Conn.
National Band, William E. White, leader, twenty-seven pieces.
Slocum Light Guards, Lieut.-Col. Benjamin P. Swarts commanding, two
staff officers.
Co. A, Capt. W. B. W. Hallett, three officers and twenty men.
Co. B, Lieutenant B. McSoley, two officers and twenty men.

The First Light Infantry Regiment wore their fatigue uniforms, with red blankets belted at the waist. They had as their guests, Col. B. B. Martin, Maj. J. B. Childs, Adjt. B. M. Bosworth, Jr., and Quartermaster F. E. Dana, of the Warren Artillery, Col. Julius Sayles, Lieut.-Col. J. D. Seabury, Maj. Howard Smith, Capt. Silas De Blois, Q. M. Benjamin Marsh, Surgeon Henry E. Turner, Paymaster George H. Wilson of the Newport Artillery Veteran Association, and Lieut.-Colonel Sherman of the Newport Artillery. The United Train of Artillery were attired in fatigue uniforms, with dress caps and pompon, and had for their guests the Westerly Rifle Regiment, the Newport Brass Band, and the field and staff officers of the Pawtucket Light Guards. The Slocum Light Guards were in fatigue dress and overcoats, and their guests were Capt. Morse, of Company G, Third Regiment Mass. Volunteer Militia, the Taunton Guards, of Taunton, Mass.; Capt. N. N. Noyes, of Boston Light Infantry, and Captain Hanlon and Lieut. Fallon of the Boston Tigers, Fourth Massachusetts Volunteer Militia.

A pleasant feature to the Battery men was the presence in the Association line of the old headquarters flag of the Artillery Brigade of the Second Corps Army of the Potomac.

At 3.15 P. M. the column moved in good order through the following streets: Dorrance, up Westminster, Mathewson, Washington, Franklin, down High to Broad, Weybosset to Market Square, countermarching over the bridge through Washington Row to Exchange Place, Dorrance to Westminster, up to Music Hall, which was reached at four o'clock, and though the rain was then falling briskly the streets were lined with interested spectators. The line was a fine one all things considered, and gave evidence of what the demonstration would have been had the weather been more favorable.

At Music Hall the American Band, D. W. Reeves, leader, was stationed in the seats between the organ and the platform. On the platform were His Excellency Gov. Henry Howard and staff, Lieut.-Gov. C. C. Van Zandt, Maj.-Gen. A. E. Burnside, Maj.-Gen. W. R. Walker and staff; Brig.-Gen. F. Miller and staff; Rev. Carlton A. Staples, Orator of the Day; Rev. D. H. Greer, Chaplain of the Day; Daniel C. Taylor, President of Battery B Veteran Association, Brig.-Gen. John G. Hazard, as presiding officer, and the different committees of arrangements.

After music by the American Band and prayer by Chaplain Greer, the Chairman, General Hazard, introduced Daniel C. Taylor, President of Battery B Veteran Association for the delivery of the gun to the State, which he said should make every Rhode Islander proud.

President Taylor, who was warmly received upon coming forward, then formally delivered the gun to the State authorities in the following address:

YOUR EXCELLENCY: As presiding officer of Battery B Veteran Association, the duty devolves upon me to place in your custody and keeping, as chief executive officer of this State this piece of ordnance, consecrated to liberty, and baptized in the blood of Rhode Island's sons. And to impress more fully upon your heart, if possible, the sacredness of this honored relic to us, I desire to give you a brief history of this gun from the time of its reception by us as a part of our battery until the present.

During the Peninsular campaign the battery consisted of four Parrott guns and two brass howitzers. After the terrible seven days battle which terminated at Malvern Hill, and the Army of the Potomac found rest at Harrison's Landing, on the James River, Va., the vents of our guns were found to be in such a condition as to render the guns unfit for service. They were therefore condemned, and their places supplied upon the 31st of July, 1862, by a park of new guns, consisting of six brass twelve-pounder Napoleons, of which this gun was one.

Upon the organization of the Army of the Potomac Battery B was attached to the Second Brigade, General Gorman; Second Division, General Sedgwick; Second Corps, General Sumner, which position they held during the war, notwithstanding the various changes which took place of commanders of brigade, division or corps. The battery with this piece and others, was at the shelling of the town of Fredericksburg, Va., Dec. 11, 1862. Stationed at the right of the Lacy House, on a bluff overlooking the town, it fired 384 rounds of shot and shell upon the town and the rebel rifle-pits, when the pontoon bridge was being laid. On the morning of December 12th, at seven o'clock, we crossed the bridge and entered the town, being the first battery to cross at this place.

At the battle of Fredericksburg, December 13th, the battery was at four o'clock in the afternoon ordered to the front, and took position on the left of the road at the brick house in front of the stone wall, and here did good service. The battery did similar service at the second battle of Fredericksburg or Marye's Heights.

About the 18th of June commenced the skirmishes which terminated in the great struggle of Gettysburg.

July 1st the battery with the Second Corps arrived within three miles of the town, and July 2d was assigned position in battery about ten o'clock in line of the Second Corps and to the left of Cemetery Hill, our line being joined by the Third Corps on our left. In the afternoon while the Third Corps was engaged, the battery was advanced to the right and front, and engaged a rebel battery at once, and in this position the battery was charged upon, and forced to retire to the rear of the lines of infantry.

On the 3d of July the battery and this gun took part in that great artillery duel just before Pickett's grand charge, and it was in this fierce storm of shot and shell that this piece was struck by a shell which exploded and killed two men in the act of loading it. This shell disabled the gun so that it could not be loaded. It was condemned and sent to Washington, D. C. At the Arsenal it was placed on exhibition, where it remained until this time; and, sir, I am proud to say that to me has been accorded the privilege of obtaining through our honored senator, Henry B. Anthony and others, this valued memento for the people of Rhode Island, and as an ever pleasant reminder to our children of that loyalty and fidelity to duty that actuated their sires, and may they learn and profit by the experience of their fathers. And in behalf of my comrades I desire to express the wish that this piece of ordnance may be deposited upon the green in front of the State House in this city within an appropriate enclosure, and that it be protected during the inclement season by a suitable covering. And with the strong conviction that our wishes will be carried out, I leave the piece in your possession and care.

The address was very attentively listened to, and at its close was very earnestly applauded.

Governor Howard who remained standing during President Taylor's address responded as follows:

Mr. President: Rhode Island accepts the honorable trust which you confide to her. She takes into her faithful keeping this mute witness, this interesting memento of the most decisive and glorious struggle known to the annals of freedom. More than this, reminded by its presence of the eventful scene which attended that triumph of our arms, of the heroic devotion and valor of her own ever honored sons, recalling the noble and resolute ardor of patriotism which impelled them to stand an impregnable barrier between a flushed and superior force and the menaced firesides of the North, she assumes with the trust the higher guardianship of the holy memories and associations which this occasion revives, recognizing in the inspiration of the hour a lesson and a mandate for the future, she dedicates herself to the pious care of guarding with the reverent tenderness of a mother's love, the fair fame of those who stood for her and the nation on the ensanguined crest of Gettysburg. Survivors of the field, your State folds you in its grateful arms to-day. Spirits above who poured out your young lives in availing though costly sacrifice for us, receive the inadequate homage of our saddened remembrance and our eternal gratitude.

The governor's remarks elicited another spirited manifestation of approval.

The chairman, General Hazard, then introduced the Orator of the Day, Rev. Carlton A. Staples, late Chaplain United States Volunteers, who delivered the following eloquent oration:

REV. C. A. STAPLES'S ORATION.

The occasion which has brought us together is one of no ordinary interest. This gun which has now been delivered up to the State of Rhode Island is a sacred relic of the war which saved the Union. By the valor of your sons it did good service in that war, and in the blood of your sons it was baptized. Let us call it then a precious, a sacred memento. For suffering borne in a noble cause, sacrifice cheerfully made for the highest interest of man, life yielded up heroically in defence of honor, of country, of freedom, make any object or spot sacred to the human breast. Hence the undying interest which gathers about every place where martyrs have suffered or heroes have died for the truth. Hence the reverence with which we trace the footsteps of the first settlers on this wild New England shore. Hence the solemn feeling that steals over the soul at Thermopylæ and Marathon, at Bannockburn and Marston Moor, at Bunker Hill and Valley Forge. The heroism, suffering, and blood of men in behalf of country and right sanctify the meanest object and glorify the humblest place.

What but a life like Christ's, laid upon the altar of a love for man so broad, sweet and high, could have changed an instrument of torture and shame like the cross into an object of inspiration and of beauty. Since the war we have felt a new respect for the musket, the cannon, and the soldier. Not that war seems less dreadful, or, when waged in behalf of injustice and for territorial conquest, less wicked. No pen has ever adequately pictured its horrors. No Christian heart but shrinks from it as from the fires of hell. No real soldier who has been in one battle ever desires to be in another. But horrible as war always is and must be, there are things worse than war—national disgrace and dishonor are worse ; national indifference to principles of justice, to the inalienable rights of man, and all the interests of his higher nature, are worse. Better war with all its suffering agony and loss, than a peace of moral stagnation and decay. We are fond of saying that "The pen is mightier than the sword." But when the pen is enlisted in the cause of robbery and oppression, it produces a state of society at last which only the sword can purify. Thought may be a weapon stronger than cannon balls. But wrong thinking, and wrong acting, to which it so often leads, sometimes necessitates the use of cannon balls to beat down the falsehood and let in the light of truth. It is right thinking, and what is nobler, right living, that are to sheathe every sword at last, and stop the mouth of every gun. Unless the pen, therefore, be guided by an intelligent mind, and an honest and good heart, these instruments of destruction will be needed to undo its baleful work.

Looking at the War of the Rebellion from this point of view, and in this connection, as we stand around this sacred memento, we feel toward it something of the tenderness and respect of the Arab for the noble steed that has saved him from his mortal foe.

For this gun, manned by our brothers and sons on many a battlefield, has beaten back the hosts that sought our country's ruin. At Gettysburg it saved our Northern cities from being sacked and burned, and our homes from devastation and death.

With its hundred fellows it kept our line firm and strong on that momentous day, and broke to pieces the ranks of the advancing foe. Those guns and bayonets in the hands of our valiant men knocked the shackles from the limbs of three million slaves, and made the Declaration of Independence something more than a glittering generality in this land. They swept away as in a whirlwind of flame a thousand old falsehoods and wrongs, and let in the light which pulpit, platform and press had resolutely barred out. They made it possible for an American citizen to call his country a land of equal rights and privileges without a flush of shame.

Take this gun, then, and place it among the proudest archives of the State. Cherish it as a precious legacy from the men who bore it into the forefront of the battle, and laid down their lives in serving it there. Tell your children and your children's children the story of its triumph: a triumph not of men over men, but of truth over error; right over wrong; freedom over slavery. And bid them remember that whenever they cling to false principles and base practice in the conduct of the government, embody the idea in law that any class, condition or sect may have superior privileges or power, and array themselves against the reform of any injustice or corruption in the State, they are building up a condition of society, which, at last will surely let loose the dogs of war. For so deep in the soul has the Almighty planted the love of justice, and of equality before the law, that no community can outrage that sentiment even in its treatment of the lowest members without kindling in its own bosom the fire of ceaseless strife, and destroying the fabric of its own peace and power, "First pure, then peaceable," says the Apostle. It is as truly the divine order in social and political life as it is in the experience of the individual soul.

Of the history of the battery to which this gun belonged, it does not need that I should speak. The story of its organization, its long marches, its fierce and bloody conflicts with the foe, its faithful service and its heroic sacrifice, has been already told by one who bore a part in these things, and by whom they are much better understood.

Among those who lost their lives in this engagement we would mention Second Lieut. Joseph S. Milne, a gentleman and a soldier, who is said to have endeared himself to the hearts of his brother officers, and commanded the love and respect of every member of the battery. He was born at Fall River, Mass., his father being a minister of the Gospel, and at the time of his death his mother was engaged in teaching a contraband school at Hilton Head. A short time before he was employed at the *Post and Herald* office in this city, and was the only officer the battery lost during the service.

The men shot at this gun were William Jones, a native of Boston, Mass., one of the original members of the battery, and Alfred G. Gardner, a recruit, a native of Swansea, Mass.

All this has passed into history, and occupies an honorable place in the record made by the State of Rhode Island during the war.

But there is an unwritten history lying behind these external events which gives them their real significance and glory. Though this gun be forever silenced, though its voice will never again be heard in thunders of war, yet it speaks to us and those who are to come after us in tones that cannot be misunderstood. It tells us of what manner of men they were who came forth at the call of their country, and bared their bosoms to shield her from death. Its dumb lips are eloquent to minds that can grasp and hearts that can feel the real nobility of their spirits. Truer, braver souls never went up to God in the fiery chariot of battle than they. I know that they came from humble homes, that their hands were hardened by the toil of the workshop, the factory and the farm. I know that thousands of them had no expectation of rising above the humblest place in the ranks, and were content to stand there and to bear on their shoulders the awful burdens of war that their country might be saved. But in the main they were men of royal stuff. They went out from good homes. They had been trained in the common schools and taught to reverence the principles of justice and of truth. They knew what was at stake in the war. They were thoughtful men. They were reared in the love of peace. All their aspirations and plans in life belonged to peaceful arts and industries.

But when the call came how grandly they responded to it, and through the long dreadful years of the war, in camps, in hospitals, in rebel prisons, under delay and defeat, how patient, how true and how firm they were. In victory how magnanimous, in suffering how heroic, in death how peaceful! As I call to mind the scene on the Plains of Abraham when Wolfe died in the moment of victory, saying, "I am content," and Nelson, on the deck of his ship, expiring just as the awful battle had been won, serene and happy, I see the glory of that spirit in man which rises above the horrors of war, and is mightier than death. But I have seen a spirit as high, serene and happy in the humblest man of our armies, dying in dreary hospitals and camps, well knowing that no monument would ever be raised to their memory, nor mother, wife, nor friend look upon their graves. "Tell my wife and children," said a dying soldier shot down on picket duty at night, "That I have done the best I could." "You are dying for your country," said one who knelt beside him. "That is what I came here for," was the reply, and so he fell asleep.

And what can be more glorious than the spirit of Alfred Gardner, who stood beside this gun under that terrific fire at Gettysburg, and placed that shot in its muzzle which a rebel shell caused to be sealed there forever? He fell at his post, his arm and shoulder torn from his side; but with the other arm he drew from his pocket a Testament and a little book which he carried with him to press flowers, and handing them to his sergeant said, "Give these to my wife, and tell her that I died happy —glory, glory, hallelujah!" Nelson when dying remembered his mistress, and commended her to the care of his country. Gardner remembered his Testament, his herbarium and his wife, and departed shouting, "Glory, hallelujah," amid the roaring of two hundred guns.

Do not such men deserve to be remembered with prayers and tears of gratitude? Thousands as heroic, as faithful, as grand, fell in that awful strife. Call them "hirelings," "the refuse of our cities?" Shame on such words and all who utter them!" Call them kings and priests of liberty. Call them the saviors of republican institutions and the servants of the living God. On such an occasion as this it is well for us to remember what it has cost to save republican institutions in this land, and free our country from the curse of slavery. I speak not of the millions of treasure swallowed up and lost in the war; of the mountains of debt heaped upon us and the burdens of taxation laid upon our industry and our wealth; nor of the suffering and agony which it carried to ten thousand homes, filling them with loneliness and gloom, but of the cost in valuable lives, in men who added something to the intelligence, the patriotism, the conscience, the moral integrity of the country. We have lost not only countless millions of money and property, but an aggregate of moral character and influence a thousand times more valuable. The best blood of the country was poured out on the battlefields of the war. No man can tell how much poorer we are as a people, in conscience, in honor, in manliness for its loss. There is less political integrity among us; less care that high public offices be filled by competent and worthy men; less fidelity to principle in the use of the ballot; less vigilance in protecting the sacredness of the ballot. There is greater greed for riches, and less scruple about the means used to gain them. There is a lower sense of honor in the discharge of sacred trusts, and a deeper craving for sensational excitement and extravagant display; a lower tone in social and political life, due largely to the loss of moral character incurred by the death of so many thousands of our noblest men. We miss them sorely in our homes and in all the pleasant walks of life. But more than this, we miss them in the pulse of the public conscience, of mercantile honor, of legislative purity, of corporate and municipal faith. An approximate estimate can be made of the money cost, but who can guage the moral cost of saving the Union?

And is it not well that we should be reminded in the presence of such a relic as this of what remains to be done in the work of our country's salvation?

The nation was saved in that awful crisis by a great valor and terrible sacrifice.

And we are all too ready to cry out, "It is finished," and shut our eyes in security and peace, forgetting that it needs a continual saving. We think the cannon and the bayonet closed up the work forever at Appomattox Court-House, leaving us all free to pursue our private schemes of gain or pleasure. But I tell you a greater peril than rebel armies will soon be upon us if we yield ourselves up to this false sense of security. "A government of the people, by the people, and for the people," requires the constant interest and vigilant activity of the people. Without them it must soon fall a prey to the machinations of bad men. Without them the filth of the gutters will rise up to the high places of power in its cities, its halls of legislation and its courts. If eternal vigilance be the price of liberty it is also the price of purity and safety in a republican government. And if we care so little for this grand heritage, received from the fathers and preserved at the cost of so much treasure and blood, that we will not give a day in the year from our business to prevent bribery at the polls and help elect good men to all offices of trust and responsibility; if we care so little what kind of men represent us in the City Council, in the Legislature and in Congress, what kind of sentiments they utter or laws they make, that we never look into their private life or hold them to account for the course they pursue in their public actions; if we are too indifferent or too busy to pay any regard to the country's welfare in such vital matters as these, who will say we deserve to have a country, or that we are worthy of the great legacy that has been bestowed upon us, or the tremendous sacrifices that have been made for us? I see cause for alarm in this growing neglect of political duties, and the consequent corruption in official life. I see a more insidious, a more deadly foe to the country's welfare in this easy, indifferent spirit which sits content by the fireside, while bad men worm their way into power, than in rebel bayonets and cannon.

It is the stronghold of base measures and corrupt men. It is a poor tribute we pay to the memory of our dead heroes, when we scatter a few flowers on their graves, if we are careless and thoughtless in the exercise of our political rights.

May I not appropriately on this occasion use the thought of our martyr president in that sublime speech at Gettysburg? It is not our poor words and prayers which make this gun a consecrated memento. It has been already consecrated by our brothers' suffering and blood. But let us here consecrate ourselves to political fidelity, purity and justice, that we may carry on the work which they began, and transmit untarnished to our children what they died to save.

With one other thought I will close. It has already been explained to you how this gun was loaded, and why it can never be discharged. Brave men have struggled for it in the carnage and madness of battle. Once it was lost and then recaptured. Its voice is now forever silenced, and its place is to be amid the great enterprises and busy industries of this beautiful city.

It symbolizes, as we proudly hope, the future history of our country and the final destiny of the world. The strife in which it played so noble a part is over. Its lesson must never be forgotten, but its animosities must be buried in mutual helpfulness and kindness. They were our brothers; as honest, as brave, and as conscientious as we.

On those battlefields the Bible was met by the Bible, and prayer by prayer. They believed in their cause as firmly as we, and sacrificed even more unselfishly.

They lost and we won, because they were wrong and we were right, and they were poor and we were rich. The cause of the strife was a mutual sin. Scarcely less was our guilt than theirs, and scarcely less have we suffered than they.

One thing we must insist upon, cost what it may, that this is a land of equal rights and privileges for all its people. Holding that as forever sacred, let us bear and forbear, give and forgive, scatter flowers on our dead and on their dead, for they were equally heroic, equally true to what they believed was right, and they perished for a common crime. Every point that justice requires let it be yielded cheerfully and promptly, and let all our conduct towards them be inspired, as I think in the main it has been, by magnanimity and Christian kindness.

A glorious era will it be when all nations shall lay down their arms, and a code of international law shall bind them to everlasting peace. We catch glimpses of the dawning of that day in a growing public sentiment for a congress of nations before which all the differences of nations shall be tried. The example of England and the United States in the Geneva arbitration has deepened that sentiment throughout the world. It is sure to prevail at last. For all the forces of civilization and Christianity are on its side. The telegraph, the steam engine, the printing press, are fast binding all races and nations together, creating a common interest by causing them all to suffer together or rejoice.

War of nation upon nation will become a universal calamity by this interlinking of interest and sympathy; and the doctrine of Christ become a visible reality in a brotherhood of nations. When that glorious day has come, as come it surely will, may this gun again find voice to speak, and in thunder tones utter the people's joy.

The interesting occasion was brought to a close with music—"Auld Lang Syne"—by the American Band.

There was no re-formation of the line as a whole. The several veteran associations and the militia proceeded separately to their respective quarters, and thus ended the great demonstration, which was nobly carried out despite the disagreeable weather. At the close of the parade the Gettysburg gun was placed on exhibition in the *Journal* office on Weybosset street by the battery men, where it attracted much attention from crowds of persons who eagerly thronged to more closely view the great war relic and curiosity. The storm cleared away after the parade, but that was not much comfort to the participants in the day's demonstration. But the rain, however, was not allowed to dampen the ardor and enthusiasm of our Rhode Island veterans, and during the entire movements of the afternoon their general deportment was excellent.

Corp. David B. Patterson.

Battery B's Monument at Gettysburg.

APPENDIX B.

THE GETTYSBURG MONUMENT AND DEDICATION.

THE subject of erecting a monument to the Rhode Island heroes who fell at Gettysburg, Pa., when first conceived was that the State should erect one stately monument on the field of battle in honor of all the Rhode Island soldiers who fell there. But the committee to which the legislature referred the matter, after investigation and discussion on the subject, concluded that it would be better to erect a special monument for each regiment and battery from the State engaged in the battle, and upon the report of this committee the following resolution was passed by the General Assembly of Rhode Island, April 14, 1885, viz.:

RESOLVED, That the sum of $3,000 is hereby appropriated to perpetuate the participation of the Rhode Island troops at the battle of Gettysburg, to be expended under the supervision of Messrs. Horatio Rogers, Elisha H. Rhodes, Amos M. Bowen, Second R. I. Volunteers; D. Coit Taylor and Charles Cornell, Battery "B"; William Millen and Pardon S. Jastram, Battery "E"; Benjamin H. Child and James P. Rhodes, Battery "A"; in manner following, that is to say: One thousand dollars thereof to be paid to the president and directors of the Gettysburg Battlefield Memorial Association, to be expended in the purchase of additional grounds of special interest upon said battlefield, and especially for a site for the memorial of Battery E, First Rhode Island Light Artillery, hereinafter mentioned, and in acquiring rights of way in constructing roads and avenues, in the preservation of natural and artificial defences, and in the erection of such memorial structures as are contemplated by the charter of said Association; also a sum not exceeding five hundred dollars each, to be paid to the Second Rhode Island Veteran Association, Battery A, Battery B, Battery E, Veteran Associations of the First Rhode Island Light Artillery, respectively, whenever it shall be shown to said committee that said respective Veteran Asociations have caused to be erected on the battlefield of Gettysburg a memorial of their respective regiments or batteries satisfactory to the Superintendent of Tablets and Legends of said Gettysburg Battlefield Memorial Association, etc.

The persons named in the resolution were appointed committees by their respective associations* at the reunions held in the summer of 1885, to procure suitable memorials and cause them to be erected on the battlefield of Gettysburg, and before the end of June, 1886, all had been placed in position ready for dedication.

The memorial of Battery B was the workmanship of John Flaherty, of Niantic, R. I., and is composed of seven pieces of Westerly granite weighing four and a half tons, and is seven and a half feet high. It is square in form, the base being fifteen inches deep and three feet eight inches square, and the finish is a combination of "rustic," that is, giving the appearance of roughly-hewn natural rock — and hammered work, the capstone being fine hammered. The whole is surmounted by a granite representation of a cannon ball resting on a die, which bears the Second Corps badge, "the trefoil," or clover leaf. The shaft, which is three and a half feet high, bears the inscription on the front side, "Brown's Battery B, First Rhode Island Light Artillery"; on the reverse side, "Second Brigade, Second Corps, Army of the Potomac." The monument stands upon ground occupied by the battery during the third day's fight, at the left of the famous clump of little trees which the Confederate commander, General Pickett, took as the point of direction in his desperate charge of July 3d.

On Wednesday, Oct. 13, 1886, the several Rhode Island memorials were dedicated. The party on arriving at Battery B's were addressed by Corp. John Delevan, who served as a gunner at the battle of Gettysburg.

MR. CHAIRMAN, LADIES AND GENTLEMEN, AND MY OLD COMRADES OF THE WAR:

I feel more like sitting down and bowing my head and letting memory take its sway at this time and place, than in attempting to speak. Although the surroundings and the face of the country have a familiar look, still there seems to be something missing, which memory all the while is trying to fill with regiments, brigades, divisions, batteries, and all the paraphernalia of the grand old Army of the Potomac engaged in desperate battle. I find it very difficult to realize the present while the recollections of the past crowd themselves in serried columns, as it were, on the mind. At the first glance backward it seems hardly possible that

---

*The veterans of Battery B at their annual reunion on the 13th of August, 1885, appointed John Delevan a committee to represent the Association at the dedication of its memorial.

twenty-three years and upwards have been added to our lives since our first visit to this spot, when we marched up in column across those fields to take our position in line and share with the old Second Corps the destinies of battle, and also to secure a spot for this monument. It is but natural that a small company like ours, continually in the face of danger, should become intimately acquainted with one another and as strongly attached as one family under one roof, for we had shared alike together the dangers and excitement of battle and skirmish, the suffering of hunger and thirst, the fatigues of the long and tedious march by day and by night, in sunshine and rain, the longing for home and loved ones, and often in the lone hours of night when on post, we would meet at the end of our beats and converse in low tones of our homes, and tell to one another our plans and what we intended to do if we lived to arrive safe at home. Many of them never lived to enjoy the realization of their cherished plans and desires, but have passed hence on this and other fields, or from lingering disease, or from wounds received. I feel that we the survivors, have much to be thankful for, that we have been spared from the sad casualties of war, and our hearts should be filled with gratitude to a kind Providence which has guided our marches by day and by night, and permitted us to gather here after so many years. As I stand on this sacred spot, I cannot help comparing the occasion of this visit with that of our first visit so many years ago. We have a duty to perform to-day; we had a duty to perform then; but what a vast difference in those duties! To-day we are here to dedicate the monument contributed by the State of Rhode Island in grateful recognition of our services in that desperate battle. Well might Rhode Island be proud of her soldiers, for they fought side by side with the best troops of other States, and have met in battle array the choicest troops of the Confederacy, and on no field, under no circumstances, has the honor of Rhode Island suffered at their hands, especially her artillery. We are here to-day to dedicate this monument, sacred to the memory of our unfortunate and revered comrades who fell at this place, dying in the full vigor of manhood. Death, under the most favorable circumstances, is terrible to contemplate; but to the soldier on the field of carnage—torn, mangled, bleeding, dying in the full vigor of manhood and health, with all the bright prospects of future glory blotted out forever! O! cruel, cruel war! . . .

I feel that we are here to-day to dedicate this monument to the memory of Battery B, the pride of our hearts, and the grandest, choicest recollections of our lives. Battery B was mustered in at Providence, R. I. Aug. 13, 1861, for the period of three years. . . .

One day in June we received orders to pack up and be ready to move, but not to strike tents till dark, as we were camped in sight of the enemy across the river.* That night our tents were struck, and then commenced our march for Gettysburg. But we were not then aware of our destination. We marched by day or by night, and formed lines of battle so as to be prepared to receive the enemy if they should attempt to follow. . . .

*At Fredericksburg, Va.

On the afternoon of July 1st, we heard distant firing of artillery, and, as we reached the top of the hill, we saw away in the distance the smoke of battle. Then we know the Army of the Potomac was in time. At dark we arrived near the field. The next morning we started for the front line. As we marched across these fields there were columns at the right of us, and columns at the left of us. Behind us were our homes and all we held dear; above us the starry flag, which, next to Heaven, we most revered; on front of us, our old adversary, the Army of Northern Virginia, with its skillful leader, and its bravest and most experienced corps commanders, flushed with the knowledge of previous victories, and joyous in expectations of present success. Between the two armies, on an open field and no favors, nearly equal in numbers, there was about to take place a struggle of giants, on the issue of which hung the destiny of this continent. Well might the soldiers of the Army of the Potomac be silent and thoughtful.

The battery occupied three positions on this field; first, in the morning, at our left, where you see those shocks of corn, but we were not engaged there, but moved to the right and front, to the second position on that small ridge in front of the line of battle and forming a spur from the main line, facing at right oblique and firing left oblique—a very awkward position, especially for the left of the battery. The third and last position was on the ground where we now stand. On our approaching this field, the steeples, the chimneys, and roofs of houses in the distance could be seen. We asked what town it was, and soon word was passed,—Gettysburg! We had never heard of such a place before, but, soon, thousands of hearts, North and South, would throb in anguish at the mention of Gettysburg.

In conclusion, I wish to thank the ladies and gentlemen who have been to the trouble and expense of accompanying us here, and I bid them welcome to this sacred and historic spot, the high-water mark of the great Rebellion.

PRESENTATION ADDRESS BY DANIEL C. TAYLOR, WHO SERVED AS AN ARTIFICER IN BATTERY B.

MR. KRAUTH: And now it becomes my pleasant duty, as a representative of the State and the battery, to place in your keeping this granite tablet. And may its summit point up to Heaven for generations, its base be watered by the dews of the returning seasons, the sun light up its side with its golden rays, and the tears of angels keep ever green this hallowed spot, made sacred by the blood of heroes of a common and now united country.

Response by Secretary Krauth.

Mr. Chairman, Veterans of Batteries A and B, Ladies and Gentlemen :

I can add nothing to what I have already said at the memorial of the Second Rhode Island, as to the purpose and desires of the Association I represent, to carefully guard the monument. The ground on which we stand is hallowed and sacred, if there be any ground on the continent that is so. It was here that the Confederate chieftain made the last attempt on Northern soil to restore the waning fortunes of his cause. I think that these men of Rhode Island should esteem it a great good fortune to have been on this spot at that time, as it was their guns, double-shotted, which could repel the enemy from this field. It is especially fitting that Rhode Island should have monuments on this field, since that ancient commonwealth was the first organized government in the world to establish impartial religious toleration. In conclusion, I assure you that our Association will preserve these monuments, and all others upon this field, confided to us, from the hand of the spoiler, and that nothing but the corroding finger of time shall ever molest or disturb them.

Benediction by Rev. Samuel H. Webb, chaplain.

By request of the State Monument Committee from Battery B, the local Board of Trustees of the Gettysburg Battlefield Memorial Association, has purchased a site on Codori's field, where the battery held position on the 2d of July, and there erected the granite marker contributed by Col. T. Fred Brown.

Marker on Codori's Field.

First Sergt. John T. Blake.

First Sergt. A. A. Williams.

INDEX.

Acquia Creek Landing, 115, 157, 161, 163, 179, 185, 188, 190.
Adams Express Co., 322.
Adams, George W., Lieut. and Capt., 8, 15, 19, 23, 30, 31, 35, 37, 38, 39, 47, 48, 53, 54, 57, 58, 64, 67, 70, 76, 77, 79, 85, 86, 89, 93, 112, 115, 118, 127, 131, 134, 137, 139, 142, 144, 150, 154, 169, 170, 177.
Adams, Mrs. Seth, 8.
Adams House, 89, 90, 91.
Adams, Charles H., Sergt., 15, 31, 34, 35, 36, 53, 100, 222, 259, 262, 270, 316, 317, 330, 332.
Alexandria, 68, 115, 117, 321.
Allen, Captain, 76.
Allotment Commission, 80, 165, 231.
Ammunition, 22, 23.
Andrews, Mowry L., 204, 317.
A Nightmare Alarm, 190.
Appearance of a Battlefield, 123.
Apple Pedler, 116.
Appomattox C. H., 344, 345.
Arlington Heights, 21, 24, 25.
Armstrong's Mill, 338.
Arnold, John A., 48, 317.
Arnold, Stephen C., Col., 322, 350.
Arnold, Wm. A., Capt., 177, 179, 180, 207, 221, 224, 228, 279, 307.
Artillery Brigade, 153, 177, 199, 213, 267, 270, 291, 306, 314, 318, 324, 326, 340, 345, 346.
Artillery Horses, 21.
Aspinwall, John, 35.
Auburn, 243.
Austin, Russell, 204, 317.

Bailey's Creek, 311, 323.
Baird, James, 204.
Baker, Edward D., Col., 31, 35, 41, 42, 45.
Balloon Ascension, 75.
Ballou, Henry H., Corp., 263.
Bathing, 175.
Barbour, Alfred M., 61.
Bartlett, Walter O., Capt., 57 58, 76, 77, 78 ,86, 89, 96, 99, 107, 109, 112, 113.
Barlow, Francis C., Maj. Gen., 271, 280, 293, 303.
Barry, Peter, 275.

Battle of Balls Bluff, 33-46.
Battle of Fair Oaks and Seven Pines, 89-92.
Battle of Peach Orchard and Savage's Station, 97.
Battle of White Oak Bridge, 98.
Battle of Glendale, 99.
Battle of Malvern Hill, 101.
Battle of 1st Fredericksburg, 137-145.
Battle of 2d Fredericksburg, 169-174.
Battle of Gettysburg, 200 to 216.
Battle of Bristoe Station, 246-254.
Battle of Mine Run, 259, 260.
Battle of Wilderness, 275.
Battle of Po River, 278, 281.
Battle of Spottsylvania, 282-286.
Battle of North Anna, 291.
Battle of Totopotomoy, 293.
Battle of Cold Harbor, 295-299.
Battle of Deep Bottom, 310-312.
Battle of Reams's Station, 325-332.
Battle of Hatcher's Run, 336.
Battery No. 8, 81.
Battery A, Rhode Island, 20, 28, 51, 52, 56, 77, 89, 118, 132, 135, 139, 157, 166, 167, 177, 179, 180, 207, 216, 221, 231, 232, 236, 243, 248, 259, 260, 278, 279, 280, 299, 307, 309, 316, 322, 324, 333, 335.
Battery C, Rhode Island, 19, 61, 136, 155, 160, 303.
Battery D, Rhode Island, 273.
Battery E, Rhode Island, 57, 135, 164, 258.
Battery F, Rhode Island, 49, 348.
Battery G, Rhode Island, 56, 79, 150, 167, 169, 170, 171, 177, 258, 273, 337.
Battery H, Rhode Island, 337, 338, 340.
Battery A, 4th U. S., 166, 177, 194, 199, 207, 208, 214, 221.
Battery B, 1st New Jersey, 338, 340, 346.
Battery B, 1st New York, 207.
Battery G, 1st New York, 122, 234, 263, 264.
Battery K, 1st U. S., 339.
Bean, James, 195.

Bennett, Ira L., 203, 213.
Bethel, Big and Little, 73.
Birney, David B., Maj.-Gen., 207, 271, 282, 288, 323.
Bishop Clarke, 8.
Blackberries, 228.
Blake, John T., Sergt., 15, 53, 154, 189, 199, 204, 240, 257, 260, 324.
Blair, George W., Sergt., 15, 53, 54, 57, 86, 114, 150, 153, 154.
Bloodgood, Horace S., Lieut., 15, 33, 36, 47, 48, 49, 56, 58, 76, 89, 93, 112. 118, 127, 131, 137, 141, 149, 150.
Bloody Angle, 284.
Bolivar Heights, 61, 63, 64, 126, 129.
Bomb Proofs, 298, 336.
Bon-fires, 54, 348.
Bounty, 3, 8.
Boyle, Stephen, 236.
Bowe, James, 261.
Brackell, Joseph, 212, 213.
Brady, Patrick, 266, 317.
Bramhall, Walter M., Lieut., 33, 34.
Branding Deserters, 241.
Bromley, Henry W., 35, 56.
Brooke, J. R., Brig.-Gen., 79, 280, 293, 296.
Brown, Charles A., Lieut., 164, 189, 199, 210, 221, 224, 231, 233, 239, 240, 257, 263, 266, 268, 270, 273, 285, 288, 289, 307.
Brown, Fenner A., 9.
Brown, T. Fred, Lieut. and Capt., 154-157, 162, 164, 167, 169, 170, 173, 178, 180, 183, 185, 189, 194, 199, 200-204, 233, 240, 246, 257, 258, 262, 263, 266, 268, 270, 272-278, 281, 285, 287, 288, 307, 310, 312, 315-318, 323-325, 334, 335, 339-341, 346.
Brownson, E. B., Capt., 318, 319.
Budlong, Lorenzo D., 141.
Budlong, Stillman H., Corp., 78, 289, 317.
Bugle Calls, 16, 18, 29.
Burke Station, 345.
Burlingame, Benj. A., Corp., 140, 261, 265, 346.
Burnside, A. E., Maj.-Gen., 23, 109, 121, 131, 151, 152, 284, 290.
Burnside's Mine, 313.
Burt, Allen, 317.
Butler, Benj. F., Maj.-Gen., 264, 316, 326.
Butterfield, D., Maj.-Gen., 160, 163.
Butterfield, Michael, 265.
Byrne, Richard, Col., 290, 292, 296.

Cady, Dyer, 204.
Caldweld, J. C., Brig.-Gen., 243, 245, 303.
Cameron, Hon. Simon, 12.
Camp Amusements, 160, 163.
Camp at Falmouth, 135, 146.
Camp Life, 178, 193.
Camp at Petersburg, 309.

Camp at Poolesville, 28, 50.
Camp Sprague, 14, 49.
Canteens of Water, 204.
Capitol Hill, 64.
Capron, Daniel, 99.
Carmichael, Morris, 53, 140, 141.
Carter, Aborn W., Sergt., 270, 317, 332.
Cassen, Joseph, 204, 250.
Casualties, 34, 39, 99, 101, 140, 194, 203, 214, 250, 275, 278, 289, 297, 332.
Centreville, 192.
Chace, James E., Lieut., 273, 279, 281, 288, 307, 316, 325, 326, 327, 331, 332, 345, 346.
Chace, Nathaniel R., Lieut., 337, 339, 340, 341, 345.
Chase, Edwin A., Sergt., 204, 241, 316, 317.
Chaplain Penry, 150.
Charlotte Vanderbilt, 320.
Chickens and Potatoes, 129.
Child, Wm. D, Sergt., 333, 334, 336.
Christ Episcopal Church, 115.
Christmas, 54, 55, 148.
Clark, Charles, 250.
Cogswell, Milton, Col., 33.
Cokely, Henry, Bugler, 16.
Cold Harbor, 87, 105, 295.
Collins, Elliott, 232.
Collins, Stephen, 270, 287, 317.
Collins, Welcome, 277, 309, 317, 322.
Collington, Samuel H., Corp., 317, 332.
Conrad's Ferry, 33, 52-57.
Cooking Utensils, 17.
Cooper Union, 10, 349.
Corduroy Roads, 93.
Cornell, Albert H., 317.
Cornell, Charles, 34, 317.
Cornell Levi J., 140, 216, 275, 317.
Cornell, Wm. H., 141, 317.
Costin, William, 332.
Corps Badges, 159.
Couch, D. N., Maj.-Gen., 126, 130, 149, 152, 154, 187, 196.
Courtney's House, 89.
Cowan's Battery, 211.
Crab Fishing, 116.
Crossing the Antietam, 122.
Crossing the Chickahominy, 88, 113.
Crossing the Shenandoah, 62, 129.
Crow House, 341.
Crowingshield, Eben S., 15, 153, 204.
Cumberland Landing, 86.
Curting, A. G., Gov. Pa., 160.
Custer, G. A., Maj.-Gen., 344.

Dame Rumor, 58, 65, 111, 153, 162, 179, 180, 183, 185, 231, 242, 258, 263, 300, 306, 314.
Dana N. J. T., Maj.-Gen., 99.
Deep Bottom, 310, 318, 323.
Delevan, John, 135, 204, 317.
Dennis, William, 265, 278.

Destruction of Supplies, 96.
DeWitt, Henry A., 14.
Dickerson, Wm. A., 61.
Disabled Gun at Po River, 281.
Discharge of the Three Year Men, 316-322.
Dodge, Roland L., 158.
Donation from Hon. J. Y. Smith, 50
Donnelly, Thomas, 332.
Dorr's Battery, 302.
Doyle, John, 259, 265.
Douchy's 12th New York Battery, 327, 329, 331, 333.
Doubleday, Abner, Maj.-Gen., 168, 206.
Drugged Beer, 21.
Duane, J. C., Capt., 113.
Duffy, Michael, 140, 204.
Dwight, G. Lyman, Lieut., 52, 53, 57, 58, 97, 118, 127, 135, 177, 214, 263.
Dye, J. M., Corp., 210.
Dyer, William S., Q. M., 15, 48, 54, 86, 87, 88 135.

Early, J. C., Lieut.-Gen., (C.), 171, 307.
Eatock, John, 262.
Eaton, Martin V. B., 250.
Eckington Hospital, 14, 20, 27.
Edward's Ferry, 29, 30, 33, 196.
Embarking for the Peninsula, 67.
Evacuation of the Peninsula, 114.
Evacuation of Yorktown, 82.
Evacuation of Petersburg, 343.
Ewell, R. S., Lieut.-Gen., (C.), 214, 246, 254.

Fairchilds, R., Lieut., 329, 336, 337.
Fairfax Court House, 191.
Fair Oak Station, 89-92.
Falling Waters, 225.
Farmville, 344, 345.
Field Artillery, 176.
Field of Clover, 112.
Fifth Maine Battery, 274.
Fine for Profanity, 19.
First Field Drill, 2.
First Rations, 9.
First Pay Received, 23.
First Rhode Island Cavalry, 159, 239.
First Uniforms, 7.
Fishing at Falmouth, 184.
Flag of Truce, 36, 37, 123, 142, 298.
Fletcher, Calvin C., 262.
Flynn, Michael, 203, 213.
Flys on the Peninsula, 106.
Ford, Miss A. T., 159.
Ford, Patrick, 266.
Fortress Monroe, 69, 71, 117, 320.
Fort Stedman, 335-340.
Fowles, Ezra L., 278.
Fox, John, Corp., 317, 330.
Franklin, W. B., Maj.-Gen., 101, 102.
Frank's (J. D., Capt.), Battery, 100, 122.
Furloughs, 160, 261, 262.

Gales Farm, 14.
Gallup, Richard H., Sergt., 32, 53, 207, 241, 259, 317.
Gallup William H., 214
Gardner, Alfred G., 209, 213.
Gardner, Henry A., 141.
Gardiner, John T., 194, 250.
Gettysburg Gun, 209, 210, 379.
Gettysburg, Town, 217.
Gibbon, John, Maj.-Gen., 167, 171, 173, 200, 211, 278, 288, 290, 304, 311, 325, 341.
Glynn, John, 262, 332.
Goddard, H. B., Capt., 268.
Godori's field, 202, 204.
Goldsmith, Samuel J., Corp., 207, 332.
Gorman, W. A. Brig.-Gen., 28, 88, 90, 99.
Grant, U. S., Gen., 271, 284, 298, 299, 334, 340, 344.
Grape Vine Bridge, 88.
Gregg, D. M., Maj.-Gen., 242, 245, 323, 326.
Greene, Caleb H. H., 141.
Green, John, 101, 102.
Guard detail, 16, 18.
Gun left in road, 212, 216.

Halleck, H. W., Maj.-Gen., 108, 109.
Hamilton, William, 64.
Hampston, John, 332.
Hampton Roads, 69, 70, 114-117, 320.
Hancock, W. S., Maj.-Gen., 122, 123, 127, 133, 184, 187, 189, 192, 195, 198, 202, 207, 232, 283, 284, 288, 291, 299, 309, 323, 327, 337, 348.
Hanover Court House, 88, 105.
Hanson, John F., Sergt., 141, 207, 257, 298, 300, 317.
Hare House, 302.
Harnesses, 20.
Harrison's Island, 40, 41, 42, 43, 53.
Harrison's Landing, 103, 106-112, 320.
Harper's Ferry, 61, 62, 64, 126, 129, 227.
Hart, Bartholomew, 141.
Haskell, Solomon A., 265.
Hatcher's Run, 338-341.
Haymarket, 192, 194.
Hays, A., Brig.-Gen., 207.
Hays, W., Brig.-Gen., 244-247, 259.
Hazard, John G., Capt., 118, 126, 127, 128, 134, 136, 137, 139, 140-145, 148, 149, 150, 155, 157, 164, 167, 177, 183, 199, 202, 209, 211, 214, 221, 233, 234, 237, 250, 257, 258, 262, 263, 266, 268, 270, 272, 306, 324, 329, 333, 341, 345.
Heal, Morrison, 232.
Healy, John, 227, 262.
Heintzelman, S. P., Maj.-Gen., 81, 102.
Hendrick, Albert E., 141.
Heth, Henry, Maj.-Gen. (C.), 246, 252.
Herman, Frederic G., 332.
High Bridge, 344.

Hill, A. P., Maj.-Gen., 308.
Hoof disease of horses, 132.
Hooker, J., Maj.-Gen., 93, 110, 121, 152, 158, 160, 163, 166, 167, 168, 175, 176, 177, 186, 298.
Horton, Anthony, B., Sergt., 64, 135, 140, 207, 241, 257, 261, 265, 317, 334, 336, 338.
Howard, Edward, 317.
Howard, O. O. Maj.-Gen., 91, 123, 136, 167, 206.
Humphreys, A. A., Maj.-Gen., 271, 337, 340, 345, 317, 348.
Humphreys, L. L., 322.
Hunt, Chester F., 250.
Hunt, Henry J., Maj.-Gen., 137.
Hunting for Rebel gunboats, 235.
Huston, J. W., Lieut.-Col., 201.

Ide, Sylvester G., 32, 53, 61, 99.
Inspections, 52, 56, 108, 180, 181.
I promise to pay Orders, 193.

Jackson, T. J., Maj.-Gen. (C.), 98, 175.
Jenks, Hezekiah, 20.
Johnson, E., Maj.-Gen. (C.), 346.
Jones, William, 53, 209, 213.
Jordan, William T., 140.

Kelly, John, 262.
Kendrick, John, 317.
Kenyon, W. J., Sergt., 265, 316, 336, 338.
Keyes, E. D., Maj.-Gen., 81.
Killing a steere, 48.
Kimball, N., Brig -Gen., 104.
King, David B., 203, 213.
Knowles, Edwin H., 141.

Lacy House, 137, 138, 144, 169, 174.
Ladies of Baltimore, 10.
Laird, Robert A., 53, 317.
Last firing of the battery, 343, 344.
Laurel Hill, 286, 288.
Leach, John, 236, 259.
Lee, R. E., General (C.), 24, 119, 171, 186, 187, 206, 207, 217, 222, 260, 298, 299, 344, 345.
Lee, W. R., Col., 34.
Lewis, Jacob B., Sergt., 14, 15, 16, 53.
Libbey, Charles A., Sergt., 23, 29, 53, 135, 241, 270, 317, 319, 341.
Long Bridge, 67.
Loomis, Col., 5, 8.
Longstreet, J., Lieut.-Gen. (C.), 345.
Loudoun Heights, 61, 128.
Luther, Joseph, 140, 141.
Lutheran Theological Seminary, 217.

Macomber, Calvin L., Sergt., 213, 262, 266, 267, 288, 317, 330, 332.
Magruder, J. B., Maj. Gen. (C.), 73, 82.
Maine Nelson B., 317.
Manassas Gap., 228.

March to Culpeper, 238.
March to Falmouth, 134.
March to Harper's Ferry, 60.
March to Maryland, 119, 189.
March to Petersburg, 300.
March to Poolesville, 27.
March to the Rapidan, 256.
March to Virginia, 227.
March to Warrenton, 128.
March to Washington, 64.
March to Williamsport, 221.
March to Weverton, 225.
Marshall House, 68.
Marye's Heights, 170-175.
Maryland Rabbits, 31.
Mason Henry A., 317.
Massachusetts Regt. 15th, 29, 79, 97, 144, 368.
Mattapony River, 290.
Matteson Benj. F., 35.
Matteson George R., 35, 119, 317.
Matteson, William F., 34.
Maxey, William H., Corp., 204, 265, 317, 330-332.
McClellan, George B., Maj.-Gen., 22, 73, 80-83, 104, 108, 112, 126, 128, 131, 132.
McCombs, John, Sergt., 15, 29, 53.
McCullum, William, 262.
McCune, A. M., Capt., 299.
McGunnigle, George, 204.
McGunnigle, James, 266.
McKnight's (James Capt.) Battery, 12th N. Y., 304, 311.
McMeekin, Josiah, Corp., 287, 317.
McNamara, Thomas, 332.
Meade, George G., Maj.-Gen., 167, 199, 215, 271, 284, 288, 348, 350.
Meade's Station, 335, 338.
Meagher, Thomas F., Brig.-Gen., 97, 158, 163.
Merrill, Sumner, 232.
Merrimac, 70, 320.
Miles, N. A., Maj.-Gen., 281, 286, 296, 304, 325, 326.
Military Ball, 265, 266.
Military Execution, 233, 234, 240.
Miller's (D. R.) House, 122.
Milne, Joseph S., Lieut., 135, 137, 139, 140, 141, 184, 187, 199, 214.
Monitor, 69, 70, 320.
Monocacy, 30, 36, 47, 48, 77.
Monocacy Junction, 120, 196.
Morris, L. O., Col., 296.
Munroe, J. Albert, Col., 13, 257, 268.
Monument Dedication, 395.
Morgan, Chas. H., Col., 130, 142, 150, 156, 157, 177, 179, 245, 248, 253, 254.
Mott, Gershom, Maj.-Gen., 271, 311, 337.
Moulton, Lewis, 204.
Mount Vernon, 69, 321.
Mud, 73-75, 83, 103, 152, 156, 167, 175, 267, 346.

Munson's Hill, 347.
Muster in Roll, 5.
Muster out, 350.
Mutton Epidemic, 132.

National Military Cemetery, 25.
Negros, 92.
Negro Wedding, 55.
New Guidon, 237.
New Guns, 48, 49, 109, 232, 335.
New Stores, 345.
Newton, John, Brig.-Gen., 172, 174.
New York Regiments, 9th, 54; 6th, 93; 34th, 90; 42d, 33, 249; 69th, 97; 82d, 90, 249.
Niles, Robert A., 208, 216, 277, 309, 317.

Occoquan Creek, 191.
Old Church, 88.
Olney, Luther C., Corp., 34.
Orders, 136, 146 149, 159, 177, 180, 184, 186, 189, 195, 197, 215, 226, 232, 254, 262, 346.
Oysters, 114.

Padelford, Seth, Lieut.-Gov., 322.
Paine, Charles H., Corp., 204, 317.
Paine, W. W., Brig.-Gen., 322.
Painting Gun Carriages, 266.
Paris, 130.
Parkhurst, Wm. H., Capt., 3, 7, 8.
Parrott Guns, 48, 79, 311.
Patrick's Station, 338, 340.
Patterson, David B., Corp., 98.
Pay of Soldiers, 265.
Paymaster, 23, 49, 57, 80, 93, 126, 153, 165, 183, 231, 240, 267, 305, 314, 335, 339.
Pearce, Harvey, 99.
Pearce, Wm. W., Corp., 119.
Peckham, Edwin M., 20, 317.
Pennsylvania Regiments, 69th, 89, 202; 71st, 33, 89; 106th, 77, 202.
Perrin, William S., Lieut., 136, 137, 174, 189, 190, 193, 199, 204, 207, 211, 213, 214, 216, 221, 226, 231, 232, 234, 236, 237, 240, 242, 243, 250, 263, 265, 267, 268, 373, 274, 287, 288, 307, 324-330, 332, 347.
Perry, Nelson E., 262.
Perry, Raymond H., Lieut., 9, 10, 12, 15, 19, 30, 32, 33, 47, 49, 52, 53, 56, 57, 58, 61, 62, 64, 74, 76, 78, 79, 86, 89, 90-94, 112, 113, 114, 118, 127
Pettis' New York Battery, 166-168.
Phetteplace, David, 317.
Phetteplace, David H., 265.
Pickett's Charge, 211.
Picket Duty on the Potomac, 55.
Pierce, Willard B., Lieut., 232, 233, 239, 240, 257, 263, 266, 268.
Poague's Battery (C.), 246, 247, 249, 256.
Point of Rocks, 11, 196.
Poolesville Village, 28, 196.

Potter, J. N., Lieut., 162.
Pork and Beans, 32.
Porter, Fitz John, Maj.-Gen., 76.
Porter, James B., 250.
Place, Joseph B., 281.
Pleasanton, Alfred, Maj.-Gen., 188.
President Lincoln, 108, 109, 126, 148, 162, 163, 167, 199, 345, 346.
Priestly, Francis, 317.
Proficiency in Drill, 51.
Promotions, 32, 53, 56, 61, 64, 86, 135, 154, 178, 240, 257, 259, 298, 317.

Quaker Guns, 83.

Railroad Battery, 92, 97.
Railroad Mortar, 313, 314.
Rathbone, Calvin W., Corp., 101, 140.
Reckless Artilleryman, 54.
Recruits, 20, 32, 61, 65, 76, 118, 119, 144, 150, 232, 236, 256, 263, 267, 271, 324, 336, 340.
Red Letter Day, 81, 222.
Re-enlisted Men, 262, 265, 266.
Remington, William B., 317.
Reno, Jesse L., Maj.-Gen., 121.
Reports, 37-46, 141-144, 250-254.
Reviews, 109, 151, 157, 271, 340, 347.
Reynolds, J. F., Maj.-Gen., 200.
Reynolds, William F., 141.
Reynolds, William H., Capt., 9, 12, 13.
Richards, John H., 140.
Richardson, I. B., Maj.-Gen., 109, 122.
Richmond, 346.
Rickett's Battery F, 1st Pa., 243, 248, 249.
Rider, Charles J., Sergt., 262, 270, 317, 330-332.
Riley, Charles F., 332.
Rhodes, John H., Sergt., 70, 212, 213, 241, 259, 264, 266, 281, 285, 316, 317.
Roast Pig, 31.
Robinson, J. C., Brig.-Gen., 206.
Rockville, 27, 29, 49, 64, 119.
Roder's Battery K., 4th U. S., 306, 339, 349.
Rogers, Horatio, Col., 171.

Salem Church, 174.
Sanford, Colonel, 9.
Sanford, Herbert D., 204.
Sanitary Commission, 155, 306, 321.
Savage's Station, 93, 96.
Scott, George O., 15.
Scott, Lewis W., 140.
Second R. I. Regt., 15, 19, 171, 175, Sedgwick, J., Maj.-Gen., 72-74, 78, 80, 87, 109, 110, 123, 148, 154, 168, 171, 172, 174, 207, 271.
Shaler, Colonel, 172.
Sharpsburg, 125.
Shay's Tavern, 325.
Shelter Tents, 72.

Sheridan, P. H., Gen., 312.
Sherman, W. T., Gen., 346, 347.
Shevlin, Peter, 204, 205.
Ship Point, 74.
Sickles, Daniel E., Maj.-Gen., 200, 207.
Siege of Yorktown, 73-76.
Signal Station, 29.
Sisson, John J., 141.
Skirmish at Sniker's Gap, 129.
Slack, Isaac W., 56.
Slaigher, Francis, 262, 275, 297.
Sleeper's Battery, 10th Mass., 305, 327, 328, 329, 332.
Slocum, H. W., Maj.-Gen., 167, 206.
Smith, B. H., Capt., 127.
Smith, Francis A., Lieut., 15, 30, 33, 51.
Smith, James Y., Gov. of R. I., 50, 262, 322.
Snow and Ice, 57, 153, 158, 162, 267.
Soldiers' Rations, 17.
Soldiers' Rest or Retreat, 10, 64, 161.
South Mountain, 121.
Spaulding, Captain, 113.
Spear, Colonel, 172.
Spencer, Gideon, Lieut., 273, 277, 281, 288, 307, 316, 325-332, 345, 348.
Sprague, Charles G., 212, 265, 317.
Sprague, William, Gov. of R. I., 8, 12, 23, 51, 80, 266.
Stafford Court House, 190.
Staples, Ernest, Sergt., 20, 33.
Staples, Peleg, 204.
Stone, Chas. P., Brig.-Gen., 25, 28, 33, 42, 45.
Stoneman, Geo., Maj.-Gen., 84, 167.
Stone Wall, 140, 141, 171-173, 202, 207.
Straight, Albert, Sergt., 53, 203, 207, 209, 210, 213, 230, 231, 240, 241, 259.
Stuart, J. E. B., Maj.-Gen. (C.), 104, 158, 159, 194, 243, 244, 245.
Sugar Loaf Mountain, 29, 31, 60, 196.
Sumner, E. V., Maj.-Gen., 84, 109, 119, 120, 126, 131, 147, 148, 152.
Sweet, James A., 55, 56, 317.
Swiss Military Celebrity, 166.
Sword Presentation, 268-270.
Sykes, Geo., Maj.-Gen., 207, 246.

Tallman, Irving, 332.
Tanner, William H., Corp., 32, 34.
Taps, 16.
Taylor, Daniel C., 20.
Terry, Brig.-Gen., 11.
Testaments, 8.
Thanksgiving Day, 51, 135.
Thayer, Ziba C., 53.
The Awkward Man, 181.
The Capture of Two Guns, 286, 287.
The Coverted Gun, 80.
The Milk Peddler, 25.
The Soldiers' Home (regulars), 24.
The Soldier's Postage Stamp, 151.
The Volunteer Batteries, 166.

The Volunteer Helmsman, 67, 68.
Three Saucy Maidens, 130.
Thomas, G. H., Maj.-Gen., 339.
Thoroughfare Gap, 192-194.
Tidball, J. C., Col., 267, 268, 275, 306.
Tillinghast, Merritt, 85.
Talbot, George H., 119.
Tompkins, C. H., Col., 9, 13, 51, 56, 77, 78, 90, 96, 108, 147, 149, 266, 268.
Tucker House, 340.
Tucker, Silas G., Sergt., 15, 31, 34.
Turner's Gap, 121.
Twenty Minutes for Lunch, 9.
Tyler, Hon. John, 70.
Tyler, R. O., Brig.-Gen., 287, 290.

Vaughn, Thomas F., Capt., 20, 23, 27, 29, 30, 33, 35, 36, 37, 47, 48, 50, 51, 52.
Vegetables from R. I., 157.

Wadsworth, J. S., Brig.-Gen., 206.
Walker, Benj. W., 332.
Walker, Pardon S., Sergt., 32, 207, 241, 261, 266, 317.
Walker, William R., Lieut., 14.
Ward, Geo. H., Col., 201.
Wardlow, John E., Sergt., 53, 86, 114, 154, 178, 241, 257.
Warner's Battery, 3d New Jersey, 327.
Warren, G. K., Maj.-Gen., 232, 234, 245, 246, 250, 254, 271, 284.
Washington's Birthday, 155.
Washington, Mary, 170.
Washington Public Buildings, 24.
Watermelons, 115.
Watkins House, 340.
Webb, A. S., Brig.-Gen., 207, 245-250, 259.
Weeden, Wm. B., Capt., 12, 18, 19.
Welden Railroad, 303-308, 325, 339.
Wellman, Henry A., 332.
Wells, William P., Corp., 64, 115, 151.
Westcott, William B., Lieut., 337, 339-341, 344, 345.
West Point, 85.
Whipple, Albert J., 204, 317.
Whipple, Edward B., 317.
Whiskey Ration, 93.
White House Landing, 92.
Whiting, Leonard J., Sergt., 61.
Wilkinson, Robert, 265.
Williams, Alanson A., Sergt., 141, 154, 207, 231, 241, 257, 260, 262, 288, 298.
Williamsburg, 82, 84, 85, 114.
Wilson, J. H., Brig.-Gen., 326.
Winchester, 63.
Winsor, William W., 332.
Winter Quarters, 50, 146, 261.
Wood, Charles W., 262, 270, 285.
Woodmansee, Clark L., 140, 212, 213, 317.
Working a Mortar, 314.
Worthington, Clark B., Corp., 32, 204, 275, 317.

ERRATA.

The reader is requested to make the following corrections:

Page 99, for Harry read Harvey Pearce.

Page 221, for Lieut. A. Brown read Lieut. Charles A. Brown.

Page 336, for Lieutenant Clarke read Lieut. Robert Fairchilds of Clarke's Battery.

Page 337, for Lieutenant Clarke read Lieut. Robert Fairchilds.

www.ingramcontent.com/pod-product-compliance
Lightning Source LLC
Chambersburg PA
CBHW051855300426